NO GREATER SERVICE
A Peace Corps Photo Memoir
(Philippines 1969-1974)

ALVIN J. HOWER
and Prima Guipo Hower

LifeRich PUBLISHING

LifeRich Publishing is a registered trademark of The Reader's Digest Association, Inc.

LifeRich Publishing books may be ordered through booksellers or by contacting:

LifeRich Publishing
1663 Liberty Drive
Bloomington, IN 47403
www.liferichpublishing.com
1 (888) 238-8637

Because of the dynamic nature of the Internet, any web addresses or links contained in this book may have changed since publication and may no longer be valid. The views expressed in this work are solely those of the author and do not necessarily reflect the views of the publisher, and the publisher hereby disclaims any responsibility for them.

Any people depicted in stock imagery provided by Getty Images are models, and such images are being used for illustrative purposes only. Certain stock imagery © Getty Images.

J.B. Phillips New Testament (PHILLIPS)
The New Testament in Modern English by J.B Phillips copyright © 1960, 1972 J. B. Phillips. Administered by The Archbishops' Council of the Church of England. Used by Permission.

Cover concept by Prima Guipo Hower.

Foreword by P. David Searles Deputy PC Director 1975-76

Editors: Dottie Anderson and Chris Lee Gammon

ISBN: 978-1-4897-2755-8 (sc)
ISBN: 978-1-4897-2754-1 (hc)
ISBN: 978-1-4897-2756-5 (e)

Library of Congress Control Number: 2020907455

Print information available on the last page.

LifeRich Publishing rev. date: 06/30/2020

For my Mom and Dad
Siblings Joyce, Bud, and Dean
Children Linda and Lee
For being there

&

Grandchildren Zoe, Lexi, and Summer
Just so you'll remember that Grandpa is more
than just a baker of snickerdoodles!

CONTENTS

FOREWORD

Alvin Hower, with a strong assist from his wife Prima, has produced a fascinating account of his remarkable five and a half years of service as a Peace Corps volunteer in the Philippines. The story he tells is a very personal one, as are most Peace Corps memoirs. The challenges and rewards of Peace Corps service touch on every aspect of one's life. Whether it is one's job, eating habits, health, and hygiene, friendships, or the absence of a familiar support system, how one reacts to them is dependent on who one really is deep down. Al's account, supported as it is by letters, journal entries, and commentary actually written during his Peace Corps years, leads the reader directly into Al's inner self. Not many of us would be so willing to allow such an intrusion.

Yet, as other Peace Corps veterans will confirm, Al's account contains aspects that others will find familiar. To an outsider, the Peace Corps experience seems to be a uniquely personal one. But, for those involved, it is one with many commonalities. Put a group of former volunteers together, and the stories they exchange will have many similarities. One can best understand the Peace Corps experience by being there, but reading Al's story is a good alternative.

One of the least expected results of Peace Corps service is learning just how American one is. There is nothing like living in another's culture to cement in our minds our own version of how things should be done. In the Philippines, there were aspects of its culture that challenged American ways. We had to learn that nepotism was a highly valued and expected part of life. A simple 'yes' or 'no' was avoided because it might cause offense. There is no room for the simple declarative sentence beloved in America. One commentator described the Filipino way as 'to be nice, agreeable, and pleasant as the general ideal.' Perhaps the most troublesome aspect for us was the fatalism that led Filipinos to shrug their shoulders when a project went awry and say, 'well that's the way things are!' We wanted to take action, fix blame, get back on schedule, but not our Filipino coworkers. In time we adjusted, but not completely.

His years of service – 1969-1974 – were important years for the organization itself. During that time under the leadership of Peace Corps Director Joe Blatchford, the agency shifted its programming priorities from an earlier emphasis on education to one that emphasized aid in matters of health, nutrition, animal husbandry, social welfare, and anything agriculture. Often these new emphases were lumped together and called 'community development.' Al's three different Peace Corps jobs reflect the organization's old and new programming priorities.

His last assignment was at a remote, often ignored, village of a still primitive minority called the T'boli. It is hard to imagine that a group of people in the twentieth century could never have seen a movie, used a phone, had indoor plumbing, left the village, let alone fly on an airplane. Al and Prima worked tirelessly on community development projects in the area. The story makes for excellent reading.

Many have questioned the value of the Peace Corps to the United States as if its benefits are all exported. This is far from an accurate appraisal and, Al and Prima are fine examples of the contribution to the American life coming from returned Peace Corps volunteers. As have most of them, Al and Prima have continued to contribute to their community in ways both large and small. And, their community includes many schools in the Philippines, which are the recipients of thousands of books sent each year from Rhode Island. The Howers have also supported Filipino crafts by creating markets for them in the United States. Perhaps of even greater importance is their determination to create an awareness here of the fact that the United States is just one part of the world. The many other parts are to be accorded respect, friendship, and help when needed. There are about 50,000 former Peace Corps volunteers in the U.S. doing the same thing. And we all benefit from their efforts.

Which brings up another unexpected element. No Greater Service is also a love story! Prima was part of Al's work life from his earliest days in the Philippines. Gradually over the years, Al began to feel more than comradeship with her and finally expressed his true feelings by saying, 'the light is now shining on my part of the mountain.' The implication being 'is it also shining on your side.' Prima demurred. Months go by with Al hoping for the best but fearing the worst. Many pages later, we learn that Prima said to Al, 'the light is now shining on my side of the mountain.' When I read that sentence, I said aloud 'Finally.' I bet you will too.

Recently David Brooks, a well known NY Times columnist, wrote a book called The Second Mountain. In it, he suggests that we should all abandon the climb up the first mountain and concentrate on the second mountain. For Brooks, the first mountain is the one we all climb as we get an education, find a job, marry and have children, buy a house, and establish a social presence. It is ego-driven and very individualistic. Now it's time to move on and climb the second mountain, which is 'other' centered, community-oriented, and requires a genuine effort to make the world a better place. I think you will agree that Al and Prima are securely positioned atop that second mountain.

P. David Searles
PC Country Director Philippines 1971-74
Region PC Director 1974-75
Deputy PC Director 1975-76

INTRODUCTION

I had never written a journal. Nor had I been to a former nudist camp. Nor been assessed by a psychologist. I did all three when I flew to the west coast for the first time to start my Peace Corps (PC) Training. Almost daily, between the lined pages of a thirty-five cents Stenographer's Note Book, I faithfully recorded in detail the happenings from the day I left home in Bethlehem, Pennsylvania, until two weeks before my first day of teaching in a foreign land. I'm glad I did. It's the main reason you are holding this book in your hand.

Tuesday, March 11, 1969: An entirely new world opened up today! I am going to Escondido, California, to start my Peace Corps Training at a former nudist camp. I flew in an airplane for the first time. The flight stewardess served beverages for free, cocktails for $1. Dinner was thick steak, mashed potatoes, green beans, salad, roll, dessert, and tea or coffee. What a meal! This plane has earphones for private listening with 7 different channels…During the first day of orientation, I met with a psychologist, was referred to another psychologist who asked me to return for a second interview.

Thursday, June 24, 1969: At the moment, I am vacationing in Jolo, Sulu, since classes at the college don't start until July 7. Three weeks ago, Bill Kieselhorst and I flew to General Santos to visit the Notre Dame of Dadiangas College, where I will be teaching in the next two years… I finished getting my rented house ready for habitation. It is located a few blocks from my work site.

I flew back to Cotabato City to complete the three-month-long Peace Corps training. On June 11, Fr. Billman asked, "Well, how do you all feel tonight on the eve of becoming a bonafide Peace Corps

Volunteer?" That brought back memories for me. How do I feel? During the first week of training in Cotabato City, I was sick with diarrhea. There were only two bathrooms for the entire hotel at Castro's Place, where we were billeted for a month... I was profoundly depressed by the sight of children bathing in the polluted Rio Grande river, children playing near open sewers, abject poverty all around, bedbug-ridden mattresses, rats, the repulsive smell of fried dried fish. Five days in the Philippines, and I was ready to quit! Today, some of the very things that bothered me then, that made my stomach churn, have become so commonplace that I don't give a second thought to them ... I have even eaten fried dried fish. I won't say I liked it, but I tried."

Then the journal entries ceased. Perhaps, culture shock gave way to acceptance. Perhaps, the exotic became ordinary. Perhaps, life got in the way. I had to adjust to two instead of four seasons in a tropical island. I learned to eat exotic food groups, teach Economics I and II to more than 300 college students in seven individual classes, and listen to a babel of no less than six dialects being spoken around me wherever I went.

When and where my entries ended, my wife continued my story from her perspective after we were married. While I stopped writing in my journal, I continued to write newsletters regularly for mass mailing to family and friends in the U.S. A condensed version of these newsletters appeared in my hometown newspapers back in the States. And the copious letters that I wrote to my dad and siblings, which they preserved and returned to me when I came back to the U.S., became my personal diary and form much of the backbone of this book.

I served as a Peace Corps Volunteer for five and a half years in the Philippines. My first assignment (1969-1971) was to teach for four semesters, the second (1971-1973) was as a community development worker. Both appointments were completed in the coastal city called General Santos on the island of Mindanao. In the last twenty months of my term as a volunteer, I re-enrolled and moved to the hinterlands of Lake Sebu, Surallah, to work in a Catholic mission called Santa Cruz. It served the indigenous tribes of the province, particularly the T'boli people whose sad plight was featured in the August 1971 issue of National Geographic Magazine.[1]

I went back to the Philippines in 1998 after being away for twenty-five years. My host province had grown so much – its population swelled, and the region I used to know as Cotabato Province (North and South) underwent a complicated territorial realignment. As of the date of publication, the former North Cotabato, as I knew it in 1969, was split into a few provinces. Some of which are now a part of the autonomous region called BARMM (Bangsamoro Autonomous Region in Muslim Mindanao), and some joined the southern Region XII. The South Cotabato of 1969 is now a part of Region XII referred to by its acronym SOCCSKSARGEN comprised of four provinces - South Cotabato, Cotabato, Sultan Kudarat, Sarangani, - and the chartered city of General Santos. The total population of the area grew from half a million inhabitants in 1970 to 4,545,276 in 2015.[2]

General Santos City, my home for four years, became highly urbanized. Nothing was more prominently altered than the city's infrastructure now sprawling in every direction like the tentacles of a hungry octopus, fueled by the boom in the fishing industries. The small-time fishermen who used to donate fish to the community centers that I managed in the Barrios Bula (pronounced as Boo-la) and Silway (Seal-why) are now owners of huge fishing companies that boast of fishing vessels. Not just a few but fleets of them - plying the international waters as far south as Papua New Guinea, Indonesia, and neighboring countries.

So much had changed in my own life too. I was twenty-five and a bachelor when I joined the Peace Corps; I was thirty and married when I came home. During my first year as a Returned Peace Corps Volunteer (RPCV), I endured a very challenging readjustment process. There was a glut of teachers in the Lehigh Valley area where we lived in Pennsylvania, such that I could not find a teaching job. I jumped from one tedious sales job to another just so I could support a wife and child. Doubly frustrating was the sheer consumerism everywhere I turned, and the wastefulness of a throwaway society that I was sure was conspiring to gobble me up. The idealistic Peace Corps in me kept getting in the way of a quick recovery from the funk.

Exactly one year after I returned home, I accepted a teaching job at the Cheyenne Sioux Indian School and relocated my family to Eagle Butte, South Dakota.[3] The population ticked up to 303 as soon as the three of us crossed the border. Living on an Indian reservation plus the constant reminder from my wife that I should take up the raising of our daughter as my "cause" cured the do-good desire to change the world with my every move. After two years, we pulled up stakes again and went to Florida, where we lived for thirty-two years and raised a daughter and son to adulthood.

I retired in 2010, defied a retiree's typical urge to fly south, and moved north to Rhode Island to be close to my grandchildren. Much of my retirement years have been devoted to helping our daughter and son raise their three girls. We live in the same neighborhood, within half a mile of each other. If you remove the grandchildren from the picture, I would be a Peace Corps volunteer in some far-flung third world country by now.

In my tiny universe, I continue to try to make a difference whenever I can. I joined the Sierra Club, Friends of the Barrington Library (serving as a member of the board), and the Organization for Zero Population Growth. I had solar panels installed on our roof. I drive an electric car, manicure the grass with an electric mower, plant edible gardens at my children's yards, and my own. And I helped my wife to establish three children's libraries at Notre Dame Schools, where I was affiliated as a Peace Corps volunteer. In 2018 and 2019 alone, we shipped 25,000+ donated books to thirty libraries in the Philippines.

Recently unearthed from the basement ~ a journal, photos, newspaper clippings, and letters half a century old written in a foreign land 10,000 miles away ~ jogged my memory. Awash in nostalgia, I organized a reunion to celebrate the 50th anniversary of my joining the Peace Corps (March 11, 1969-2019). Through the magic of the Internet, I reached out to members of my NDEA Group 31. All septuagenarians now, we were twenty-something idealists with B.S. and M.A. degrees then. Our stated mission was to temporarily replace teachers at Notre Dame Schools in Mindanao so that our counterparts could pursue their master's degrees. This was a collaborative project between the Peace Corps and the Notre Dame Education Association, known as NDEA. Fourteen trainees in NDEA Group 31 made it to the Philippines and were inducted into the Peace Corps. Out of the fourteen, three had passed away, two I could not locate, two I found but did not respond, and two were not able to attend.

Five attended! A thirty-three percent success rate, an above-average number based on statistics that showed 20-30% on average, attend class reunions according to GroupTravel Org.[4] Tom Perardi from California, Marilyn Maze from Maryland, Patty Flakus Mosqueda from Washington State, Nancy Nicholson, and I from Rhode Island gathered together in Warren, Rhode Island, on June 14-16, 2019. Dottie Anderson, a member of Group 23 that arrived in 1968, also made it from Idaho. She was a volunteer staff secretary at the Mindanao Regional Office that oversaw our Group 31 and took care of all things administrative – our allowance remittances, banking and periodic communiqués from our regional director, etc.

For three days, we "rolled back fifty years and reminisced" as Marilyn Maze put it. She continued, "It seemed that the one thing we all had in common was a driving force to make the world a better place."[5] I totally agree, then and now. All five of us have changed: our gait a little slower, our hair grayer, yet at the same time, we stayed the same. We all shared an unbelievable experience that was and still is hard to fully explain to our family and friends who have never been in the Peace Corps. Reminiscing with the Returned Peace Corps Volunteers (RPCV) about those days brought to mind the words of President Kennedy, "no greater service" than our having served as Peace Corps volunteers. Some members of my NDEA Group 31 and RPCVs that I have forged friendships with agreed to share their Peace Corps story in Postscript: Fifty Years Later, namely David Delasanta, Marilyn Maze, Tom Perardi, Matthias and Andrea Reisen. Nancy Nicholson shared her letters to her parents and copies of the Peace Corps Handbook and Volunteer Magazine. If we could inspire just one to follow our footsteps, sharing our stories now would be worth it.

Reliving the Peace Corps experience and reuniting with NDEA Group 31 stirred a torrent of mixed emotions. Sadness for the demise of some of my RPCV friends, pure joy for the opportunity to reconnect with the other members still alive, nostalgia for people that populated the five and a half years of my life as a volunteer, and gratefulness for the chance to make a difference.

The Peace Corps Mission has not changed since its inception. It still offers future volunteers a singular opportunity to make a difference. To promote world peace and friendship by fulfilling three goals:[6]

1) To help the people of interested countries in meeting their need for trained men and women.
2) To help promote a better understanding of Americans on the part of the peoples served.
3) To help promote a better understanding of other peoples on the part of Americans.

As of June 25, 2019, more than 235,000 Peace Corps volunteers have served in 141 countries.[7] Peace Corps still has a strong presence in the Philippines, although, for the period of 1990 to 1992, PC/Philippines pulled out of the country due to concerns for the safety of volunteers. I recently met Marc Forte, who lives in Rhode Island, a volunteer who served in the 1980s. He narrated a terrifying incident during his training in the province of South Cotabato (where I had served six years before his arrival). A bomb was planted under the Toyota 4x4 while it was being readied to transport Marc and his fellow volunteers to a training center. According to Marc, "The vehicle was used mainly for training staff. Thankfully, a meticulous Filipino mechanic found the bomb while doing a routine check. The bomb was an anti-tank grenade, a big round thing the size of a coconut. The volunteer trainees were rushed out of the area by plane to Cebu for a few days. Some were transferred to other provinces." Marc served out his two-year term in Masbate.

President Kennedy, through the Peace Corps, exhorted us to go to far-flung third world nations to cultivate mutual understanding, and to teach a skill. During the years I spent in the Philippines, countless Filipinos shared with me their food, shelter, language, customs, traditions, and enduring friendships. The students at Notre Dame College, the members of the community I served at the Our Lady of Peace and Good Voyage Parish, and the indigenous T'boli people of Lake Sebu, thanked me for what little I imparted to them that they deemed to have improved their lives. Like the many Peace Corps Volunteers who came before and after me, I returned home to the United States with the humbling realization that I received more than I gave.

Most self-help books on memoirs advise neophyte authors like me to keep photos to a minimum, as they tend to distract the reader. I chose to buck the norm and decided to write a photo memoir. With my Bolsey 35mm later replaced with a

Minolta SLR 101 camera, my lens captured over two thousand colored slides and still photos in black and white of my personal experiences during my volunteer days. With modern gadgets, they are all in the digitized form now. On Wednesday, May 14, 1969, I wrote in my journal: *The Peace Corps so far has been a fascinating adventure and marvelous experience. Many of these experiences are recorded on film and will do an excellent job of jogging my memory.* These photos defeat their purpose and lose their meaning if they are not shared.

Many of the people who touched my life and whose lives I touched are dead now. They made my Peace Corps experience memorable and meaningful. My wife and I have kept in touch with many of their children, my former students, and colleagues. I shared photos with Francis Chiew (son of a fellow teacher at the college), Joey Odicta (son of the Parish Church secretary), and Elvin Oliveros (son of my first host family). They emailed back saying along a similar vein. "When my siblings and I saw the pictures, we cried. This is the only photo we have with our parents."

Craig Diamond,[8] a friend who is a committed connoisseur of indigenous artifacts, went a step further. He took the photos that we shared with him and had them reproduced and enlarged. Then, on many of his visits to Lake Sebu, Philippines, he painstakingly searched for the rightful owners of the "stolen" shots that I took of the T'boli people. Craig emailed: "I found Myrna Bebing Pula, most likely a student of yours. She speaks nearly perfect English. I gave her a photo of her and another of her father with his six wives." According to Craig, Myrna has no pictures of their father. She and her brother cried when they received the photo. She remembers the day these photos were taken but never received a copy. (The picture of Myrna's parents is included in Chapter 7).

As well, I have regaled my children, family, and friends with my Peace Corps story. They expressed how much they appreciated the slide presentations and anecdotes of those days as a volunteer. It is for all of them that I write this photo memoir.

The two years that I spent living and working with the T'boli people of Lake Sebu made the most stirring and unforgettable impression of my Peace Corps years. I decided to highlight that part of my life in Chapters 12, 14, and 15. On the cover, I featured Gumbay Sulan playing the s'ludoy (bamboo zither), three-year-old Siding, and our pupils at the Mission school, Floro Gandam, Sr. and his wife, Maria Loco Gandam. Floro is now the Mayor of Lake Sebu and Maria, the President of the Santa Cruz Mission, Inc. They represent the best of the T'boli people – in the visual arts, generosity of spirit, and the strong sense of service and leadership.

I have diligently secured permission from people whose stories are included in this book. However, I changed specific names and details of the description of others whose consent I was not able to obtain to respect their privacy. All quoted materials from my journal, newsletters, and personal letters are italicized to differentiate them from articles cited from other sources.

The Peace Corps Agency was enacted by an act of Congress in 1961. Eight years later, I became a volunteer. The Peace Corps will turn sixty on March 1, 2021. With all the divisions and discord in our world at present, there is no question in my mind of its mission's relevance yesterday, today, and tomorrow – to impart a skill and to promote mutual understanding and friendship around the world.

One of my favorite cartoons that I saw from a Peace Corps Newsletter when I was in the Philippines was this caricature of two U.S. Diplomats and a Peace Corps volunteer. Imagine a shiny black government issue, chauffeur-driven stretch limousine crawling down a dusty, narrow dirt road in any third-world country. Two rotund men in perfectly tailored suits sit in the back seat watching a tall and lanky Peace Corps volunteer in his blue jeans and t-shirt walking along the side of the road like a pied piper followed by a bunch of kids and some adults. In the conversation bubble, one of the diplomats said to the other, "Boy, these Peace Corps kids they sure make diplomacy look so easy."

On the afternoon of June 14, 1962, President John F. Kennedy pitched his pet project on TV to advertise the Peace Corps. His remarks were recorded at the White House in the Cabinet Room.[9]

> The Peace Corps gives us a chance to show a side of our country, which is too often submerged – our desire to live in peace, our desire to be of help. There can be no greater service to our country, and no source of pride more real than to be a member of the Peace Corps of the United States. I hope that you will join.

"There can be *no greater service* to our country, and no source of pride more real than to be a member of the Peace Corps of the United States. I hope that you will join."

I heeded JFK's words. I joined.

This tectonic shift in the direction my once placid life would take was one of the best and the most life-changing decisions I ever made.

It was also one of the most rewarding.

Alvin J. Hower
June 30, 2020

The Peace Corps Regional Office in Zamboanga City, June 1969.

My first of many visits to the Peace Corps Regional Office in Zamboanga City, June 1969. Unless otherwise noted, all photos are by the author.

A T'boli woman wearing the traditional distinctive style hairdo that was swept back in a ponytail and coiled in a bun with bangs parted in the middle framing both cheeks.

The T'boli women on market day at Santa Cruz Mission, Lake Sebu dressed in their traditional hand- embroidered blouses and skirts accented with anklets and traditional hats.

On My Way to the Land of the T'boli

I imagined a telegram that read: "PC VOLUNTEER FELL OFF MOVING BUS STOP DETAILS FOLLOW STOP." That would have sent shivers down the spine of any Peace Corps country director, or would have caused him nightmares, or worse.

The imagined telegram was never sent. The incident was kept secret within my circle of family and friends. Until now, that is. This happened in 1972 when P. David Searles was the country director for Peace Corps Philippines (PC/P). Twenty years after serving in PC/P from 1971 to 1974, David wrote a very comprehensive, extraordinarily candid and insightful book about his own Peace Corps experience, and what goes on in the inner PC/Washington sanctum and its bureaucratic workings. He discussed, among other things, the changes that needed to happen during the first decade of the Peace Corps that ensured its survival as a government agency for almost sixty years. And he addressed the challenges of the daily life that volunteers encountered, bus rides included. In his book ascribed to me on page 118 was my fourteen-word claim to fame, a description of a typical Philippine bus as "a wooden body over a truck frame, [with] wooden benches, a low ceiling and [glassless] windows."[1]

During this period in Peace Corps history, when speed was critical, a telegram transmitted through the wires was the highly recommended means of communication (no cell phone or email then). The Peace Corps, in fact, had a whole page dedicated to telegrams in the PC/Philippines Volunteer's Handbook of 1970. It included hints on cutting costs.[2]

"Composing telegrams can be fun, but try to economize on words, conjunctions are rarely used, punctuation marks are not used, STOP serves as the terminal punctuation signal; words are often combined, or initials of several words run together to form one word like REURTEL, ETA, ETD, ASAP." As with texting, there was telegram jargon.

In the first half of 1970, as I was just finishing my first year as a volunteer, eleven Peace Corps volunteers died worldwide, according to *Volunteer*,[3] a Peace Corps newsletter sent to all volunteers. A majority of deaths were caused by vehicular accidents. A tragic loss for the Peace Corps for sure, and a sobering statistic considering that in the first nine years of Peace Corps, a total of seventy-one volunteers were killed overseas. The Peace Corps took the safety of every volunteer very seriously.

When I was working at Our Lady of Peace and Good Voyage Parish (OLPGV) in General Santos, I was overseeing three community centers in three different locations. The parish had a motor pool of two vehicles. My supervisor believed it would help me tremendously if I could use one of the vehicles occasionally. I wrote to my brother, Bud, on May 10, 1971. *By now, you must have your new car. Getting a new car here sounds funny because most people don't own one. Fr. Albinus Lesch (the American head parish priest) sent a letter requesting permission for me to drive the parish jeep and motorcycle. The Peace Corps wrote back asking for P100,000.00 liability insurance from the parish and a letter relieving me of all liability for accidents. Fr. Albinus changed his mind about my driving because the jeep was in such bad shape. So meanwhile, I continue struggling along with my bicycle, walking a lot, or using public transportation.*

The article in *Volunteer* advised, "...wear a seat belt anytime you are traveling in a motor vehicle, wear helmets when riding a motorcycle, make sure that vehicles you use are properly maintained," etc. Excellent reminders though some were moot in many places. A Peace Corps physician named Dr. Roger

Clapp residing in a galaxy far far away called Washington, D.C., was assigned to review accident reports from overseas. He concluded, "The majority of those deaths have been needless, unnecessary, meaningless, foolish and senseless."[4]

True, perhaps. However, I would vehemently differ with Dr. Clapp's conclusion. When accidents occurred in my part of the world, it was not always foolish happenstance. To assume so implied that we, the volunteers, had control over said accidents all of the time. It was really an exercise of futility to argue with Dr. Clapp. I would hazard a guess that he had not ridden on a Philippine bus - if you could call them that - or been on the roads, that said bus, and I had traveled.

Growing up on the farm, kids like me learned to drive tractors at an early age. My older sister Joyce drove her first tractor when she was five years old. I had racked up a lot of practice-driving miles before I owned a car at age eighteen. When I became a volunteer at twenty-five, my driving skills were honed instead into chasing after buses and other means of public transport of all shapes and forms with foreign names – *jeepneys, tricycles, calesas, bangkas,* the Reo, etc.[5] Some were roofless, some windowless, some without doors; all have no seat belts and broke down often. Ask any volunteer who served in the Philippines, and they'd tell you a variation of one or all of the personal experiences I listed below.

I never left home without my TIME magazine in my back pocket.[6] You'd never know when the bus might burst a tire with no spare. Or a river swelled from flash floods would force the bus driver to wait until the river subsided. Or the road along the beach was under tidewater that one must wait hours for low tide before crossing. Striking up a conversation with fellow passengers or reading the TIME magazine was one of the best antidotes to boredom while waiting (no Facebook then).

Granted, I could have avoided what happened to me if I had stayed in bed that morning and steered away from riding on a bus "needlessly, foolishly and senselessly!" but I had no choice. It was time for me to relocate to Santa Cruz Mission (SCM) to live on the banks of Lake Seluton with my T'boli neighbors. It was midday just after Christmas, 1972. I was ten thousand miles from the iconic Star of Bethlehem festooned on top of the mountain that shone upon my hometown of Bethlehem, Pennsylvania. Away from family, baked turkey, apple pie topped with mounds of homemade ice cream, and dreaming of a White Christmas as crooned by Bing Crosby.

Here I was at the palengke (open-air market) in Surallah looking for a bus. I briskly walked along a narrow path lined with wooden stalls tended by men and women selling fish, meats, vegetables, and dry goods ~ Coke, San Miguel Beer, cigarettes, matches, flip-flops, Salonpas, Tiger Balm, Katol.

There were still colorful, handmade Christmas lanterns called *parol* hanging from the eaves. A Christmas tree stood doleful at the corner of a stall. It was fashioned from a broom made from a bunch of coconut midrib called tingting. The base of the broom was carefully positioned inside an empty large Dole Pineapple juice can; the three-foot-long tingting painted white was spread out like quills from giant porcupines and decorated with balls of cotton for snow. I skipped over puddles of runoff water from the fish stalls that had turned into murky, foul-smelling cesspools.

"Hey, Joe," someone hollered.

"Magandang hapon," I hollered back. (Good afternoon).

"Oy marunong ka ng Tagalog Sir?" (Wow, you speak Tagalog Sir?)

"Oo, hindi mo ako pweding ipagbili," was my canned reply in the colloquial term that elicited low chuckles from vendors and shoppers around me. In the local jargon, my response literally translated to, "Yes, you cannot sell me." In other words, "Watch out, I understand what you're saying."

My modus operandi to combat the "Hey, Joe" syndrome never failed. The mocking tone usually transformed into a smile, even a friendly chat. When I first arrived in the

Philippines, I bristled when someone called out "Hey, Joe," as many Filipinos habitually did, young and old alike, when they meet any foreigner or light-skinned person.

No matter how many times we were reminded by our language instructor or cross-cultural coach that there was no malice meant behind the greetings, hearing it for the first few times still rankled. Coming from the kids, it sounded innocent enough that I usually answered with playful banter. Coming from an adult Filipino, it felt derisive. I had never heard it from a decorous Filipina. During cross-cultural training, I was told that the greetings originated during World War II when the US Armed Forces were in the Philippines. They were referred to as "GI Joe."

Upon arrival at the V.I.P. Trading Hardware store, I inquired about a ride. V.I.P. Trading was the designated parking lot (albeit unofficial) for vehicles owned by Santa Cruz Mission (SCM). A few times in the past, the owners Pio and Cita Lagdamayo offered me a place to stay when I missed my ride. They told me that the massive twelve-wheeled military truck called the Reo bound for the mission had just left without me. It was not the first time. Only in this instance, I was in a bind. Santa Cruz Mission provided the only means of direct transport from Surallah to my destination.

In a few days, I was to start at my new Peace Corps assignment at SCM, a non-profit organization aimed to break the cycle of poverty, illness, and educational deprivation among the T'boli people. I had made numerous visits to this Catholic mission, but this time, I was moving in to stay for twelve months.

Home to a sizeable population of 18,000 T'boli, Lake Sebu at 3,500 feet was nestled atop the remote region of Surallah, South Cotabato. The T'boli people were one of the six indigenous peoples of the province. Not unlike the story of the Native American Indians, they were pushed to dwell in the mountainous area after World War II (WWII) when the

Philippine government opened southern Mindanao to landless settlers from the north.

Fr. George Nolan founded Santa Cruz Mission in 1961. He arrived in the Philippines in 1958 and was the first Passionist missionary priest assigned to Bolul Mission dedicated to the Blaans tribe. He lived with the Blaans for ten years. After Fr. Nolan established a school and a chapel, the nomadic Blaans settled around the Mission area. Fr. George, with the aid of Catholic Relief Services, helped to combat tuberculosis prevalent among 90% of the Blaans. As a Pastor, he had to face the issue of polygamy. Fr. George learned to speak Blaan and covered his territory by jeep.[7] He later spearheaded the establishment of the DXCP radio station in General Santos City.

In 1961, per the request of Datu Ma Fok, Fr. George opened the first school for the T'boli in Lake Sebu called the Santa Cruz Mission. Datu Ma Fok, the T'boli chieftain of Lem-ehek, had heard of Fr. George and the Bolul Mission School. The Datu contacted Fr. George and offered his territorial domain if the missionary priest would build a similar mission school, as long as the chieftain could continue to live in their ancestral land with his people.

In 1963, Fr. Rex Mansmann, took over as the director. Progress crawled like a slug in the remote mountains. Ten years later in 1973, a brochure published by SCM painted a dire picture of the T'boli people – "...until 1964, an average T'boli had not seen a truck, a safety pin was a wonder to him, he ate only one meal a day and fewer than five pounds of meat a year."[8]

Nomadic by nature, the T'boli subsisted on root crops, rice, corn, and small game, including snake, rat, wild boars, and fresh-river clams. An archaic system of dowry was still in place. A horse was the most cherished form of dowry. The average T'boli woman was married within a year after puberty, had a child before she was fifteen, shared a husband and household duties with other wives, and had only two blouses and two skirts in her wardrobe. It was not uncommon for a T'boli man to have two or more wives,[9] or for the wives to embrace arranged marriages with unalloyed resignation. (At present, the younger generation of T'boli is monogamous, according to Angeles Maghari. However, divorce, which is not legal in the country, is still being practiced).

My title as Management Consultant sounded a bit pompous for my taste. But I looked forward to working with managers, assisting the director in identifying the mission's needs as it related to Economic Development, Health, Agriculture, and Education and writing feasibility studies and project proposals to raise much-needed funds to support the projects. I was confident I could handle the technical aspect with relative ease. This was my third term as a Peace Corps Volunteer. I had fulfilled my teaching job and community development stint following the goals of the Peace Corps. I surmised my regional director Mr. Charles White thought so, or he would not have recommended me for re-enrollment. The primitive living conditions in one of the most remote areas of South Cotabato would be my biggest challenge.

THERE WERE other reasons for wanting to get to the mission. The horse fight! And the cow and pigs roasted whole on open fire pits to celebrate a special milestone. Fr. Rex was turning forty, and a big birthday bash was planned in his honor. The Bishop and many of the Passionist priests I worked with would be in attendance. The T'boli and other indigenous peoples served by the mission in Lake Sebu area were invited too. I had to be there or miss the opportunity for a veritable photographic extravaganza of men and women in their traditional garb.

On a good day, it took two to three hours to get from Surallah to the barrio of Lake Sebu, despite it being merely twenty-three kilometers (fourteen miles) distant. Past Barrio Buenavista, we had to cross the capricious Allah Valley River with no bridge because rain swelled the river dangerously, flooding its banks and shifting its course, making a fixed bridge useless. The road gradually wound around the foothills of rolling hills and towering mountains midway at Lemkemunig, and quite abruptly, it serpentined to the top. On a hard rainy day, the trip took four to six hours if one was lucky. At times, Canahay Road could only be tackled on foot, which then took ten to fourteen hours.

Having missed the Reo, I went looking for an alternative ride to Lake Sebu. I would have to walk another four miles and cross Lo El (the River) to reach my final destination. I raced to the other side of the palengke, hoping to catch the last transport of the day. The owner, Pops Weaver, was an American veteran who fought the Japanese Imperial army alongside the Filipinos during World War II. After the war, the U.S. Forces departed from the Philippines, leaving a massive naval and air presence in military bases at Subic and Clark. Pops Weaver opted to stay. He married a local lady, raised a family, opened a *sari-sari* (small corner) store, and settled in Bon Nowong near Lake Sebu.

Although I heard about Pops Weaver a lot, I only met him once. I now wished I sought him out more. He was an interesting fellow from Georgia. Pops Weaver told me that since WWII ended, he had not set foot on United States soil and intimated with a tinge of longing that he would have loved to visit his only sister whom he had not seen in twenty-seven years.

The personnel carrier owned by Pops Weaver was parked near a *turo-turo* carenderia literally translated to a point-point eatery. You point. They serve.

"Pwede pa isang pasahero going to Lake Sebu?" I asked in my Taglish - Tagalog peppered with English. (Is there room for one more for Lake Sebu?)

"Pwede pa Sir leaving two PM," confirmed the driver.

I decided to grab a late lunch at the *turo-turo*. I settled on one of the two tables, dusted the top with my hat, and set on the bench my sleeping bag and earthly belongings packed inside a woven basket called *tampipi* about the size of a small overnight bag. I had sent the rest of my stuff with Fr. Albinus, who was driving with the other priests to Lake Sebu. There was no seat for me in the Jeep, so I woke up early in the morning to catch a Yellow Bus to Surallah.

I went over to the lady standing behind the glass-covered counter. I pointed to the *siopao* (pork bun), still cooking inside a steamer positioned on the countertop, filled with pre-cooked Filipino dishes. I ordered two pieces of *siopao* and a cold bottle of Coca-Cola. The hot steaming *siopao* had been my safe go-to.

Amoebic dysentery, an intestinal infection caused by a protozoan parasite called Entamoeba histolytica, had ravaged my system since my arrival in the Philippines, so I was most careful with what I ate at public places. The Peace Corps warned us during training to ensure that what we ate had been washed and cooked thoroughly, and what we drank had been sterilized or boiled in places without a water treatment system. I had heard of the story about a Peace Corps Volunteer in the Philippines who died from liver complications that might have started as amoebic dysentery.

I went back to my table and started reading the TIME magazine that recently arrived in my Peace Corps mail while I ate my lunch. It was full of articles about the U.S. Election, the landslide win of incumbent President Nixon over Senator George McGovern of South Dakota. I participated with my absentee ballot but was not sure if it reached the U.S. in time for the count. A month-old TIME magazine and the letters from family and friends were my prized connection to home. Airmail letters usually took two to three weeks from my hometown to my post.

For the first two and a half years of my Peace Corps term, I never heard the voice of any member of my family. In my host town of General Santos, there was an operator-manned telephone system PLDT (Philippine Long Distance Telephone). One could make an overseas long-distance call by ringing up one of the operators who placed your request and called back when he reached the party at the other end. However, it was rather expensive relative to my meager allowance of $65 a month. The exchange rate was four pesos to a dollar. I saved my phone call money for emergency purposes.

Since my arrival in the Philippines, I considered bus rides as an extreme sport and a classroom for lessons on cross-culture. There was no rest area to relieve oneself along the way, so one must learn to take his whizzes in public. The men would stand against the tires when nature calls. Some women carried a *patadyong* (tube-like skirt) and went behind a bush if there was one nearby, then squat inside the *patadyong*. The top was hoisted above their heads with two extended arms to shield them from prying eyes. I surmised those without *patadyong* just did not go to the bathroom until the next stop. But what the bus lacked in bathrooms, more than made up for it by allowing traveling food vendors on the bus for free.

Every time the bus stopped for passengers along the way, these vendors boarded to sell their products and alighted at the next stop to board another bus going the other direction. The system assured them of a steady flow of new customers.

"True Orange. Coke, Coke. *Mani, mani, balut, itlog?*" they would peddle. The young boys and girls, men and women, sold American made products, peanuts, boiled eggs, etc. They competed for your gastronomical desires and the money in your pocket. I thought it was very entrepreneurial, practical, and convenient for all. The bus did not have to stop for everyone to get down to grab a bite.

And talk about those Filipino and Filipina bus conductors of my days in the Philippines! When you rode a bus, you did not have to pre-pay for your ticket, you just found a seat and waited for the conductor to collect the fare. Nobody lined up to ride a bus or anywhere for that matter during that time. Everyone just milled around the bus terminal. When a bus arrived marked with his or her destination, everyone just rushed to the door and literally fought for his seat. It would take decades and another generation for Filipinos to learn how to conduct their business in an orderly manner. (When I visited the Philippines in 1998, twenty-five years after I left my host country, everyone formed a line and took his turn in the majority of places. Littering was minimal too.)

Those conductors, what photographic memories! Fully loaded, a bus with a maximum capacity of thirty would hold anywhere from forty to fifty passengers. Five squeezed in benches for three, some stood in the middle aisle, some hanging outside, some sitting on the roof, plus some livestock scattered here and there. To this day, I still wonder how those conductors remembered every detail. First, he'd issue a ticket to every passenger, generally starting from the front of the bus making his way to the back. He'd ask for your destination and punched the information on his ticket stub. If you have the exact amount for your fare, he will take it. If the cost of your ticket is one peso and you only have a ten-peso note, the conductor will either give you the difference on the spot, or he will come back with your change later. I had never observed them forget to give the change. They seemed to remember everything.

In 1969, buses and jeepneys were always crowded. Once I went to the market to catch a ride. I saw two jeepneys going to the same destination. One appeared to be full and the other empty. I decided to ride in the empty jeepney rather than the full one where I would have to hang on the back for dear life or get squashed inside as the jeepney raced down the dirt road. The full jeepney soon sped away. I waited for another forty-five minutes until the empty jeepney was overloaded, and I was squashed in a seat with live chickens and a piglet at my feet. Lesson learned! Get on the first full jeepney or bus that you see, because at least it will leave sooner.

AFTER LUNCH, I found my way back to Pops Weaver's personnel carrier. Its roofless cab without a tailgate had two wooden benches facing each other. The backrests were adequate to support a Filipino (average height of 5'4" in 1972), but barely supported my 5'11" frame. The vehicle was already full. I positioned my lightweight custom-made travel pillow on the last seat at the extreme end of the right bench and sat down.

At this time, I weighed about 125 pounds, quite a bit less off my average weight of 140, having lost a lot from amoebic dysentery. Although I gained some of the lost weight during my month-long home leave a year before, it only took two weeks back in my adopted country to lose it all again. When amoebic dysentery hit, my digestive system became a virtual sieve.

The thin pillow that had become a permanent travel companion was to protect my backside (now skin and bone) as most transportation in the Philippines had hard wooden seats. There was hardly room to park my long legs. Cargo cases of Coca-Cola, San Miguel Beer, boxes made of cardboard filled with dry goods, a few five-gallon kerosene cans, live chickens, and numerous *bayong* (bags made of reed) full of foodstuffs, were piled helter-skelter in the middle of the truck bed.

The personnel carrier was overloaded. The cab barely cleared the fast-moving Allah Valley River. I got sprayed a little bit as the truck lurched from side to side when the tires skipped over rocks worn smooth by erosion.

It was a welcomed relief though, cooling me from the merciless midday sun. After crossing the river, the terrain leveled off. We drove on one of the smoother portions of the otherwise uneven and rocky Canahay road. The driver increased speed to make up for the lost time. My fellow travelers were all non-T'boli settlers that lived in the heart of the barrio called Lake Sebu, surrounded by a pristine lake that bears its name. The weapons carrier creaked, rattled, and jiggled as the diminutive driver deftly maneuvered it along the three-mile stretch of dirt road before it began its ascent on the most perilous portion of the journey.

We were enlightened during training that Filipinos admired light skin; some won't go to the beach because they'd turn darker. After almost four years in the country, being stared at for my fair skin became a common occurrence that I learned to ignore. But it took longer for me to get used to pregnant women ogling me in public, more so in buses, believing in the superstition that by doing so, her child would be born looking like the object of the stare or with the same color hair as mine. Sometimes, the more brazen (or perhaps determined was the better word), seated behind me would touch my red hair.

But there was something I had gotten accustomed to a fault: sleeping while a vehicle was in motion. And thanks to this uncanny ability to be able to sleep anywhere, under any circumstance, I had no trouble catching shuteye on buses, *jeepneys*, or even on a personnel carrier bouncing around while navigating the precipitous road to Lake Sebu.

Filipinos usually take *siestas* (naps) after lunch, the hottest time of the day. A hush descended on the passengers in the cab of Pops Weaver's personnel carrier. Only the monotonous sound of the engine dominated the lush green landscape. I was getting drowsy from boredom. The hillside along the road was uninterestingly bald, stripped of trees that were made into huts, or used for firewood. There were a few patches of farmland planted with rice or corn, created by employing the enormously destructive *kaingin* system, which according to the American cultural anthropologist A. L. Kroeber was "a technique of clearing land by slashing and burning underbrush and trees and plowing the ashes under for fertilizer...stripping the land of valuable timber."[10]

The stately bamboo clumps parading along the side of the road vied for my attention and tried unsuccessfully to hide the bareness and to keep me awake. A few solitary huts were close to the road, but most of the inhabitants lived on higher elevation barely discernable from the truck. There, just below the clouds, the mountains were clad in a verdant rain forest. I dozed off.

Suddenly, the tires hit a big rut on the road without warning. I flew out of my seat. Pops Weaver's personnel carrier continued moving. I didn't. I levitated momentarily. Then gravity took over. What goes up must come down.

"Paaara! Para! Nahulog ang 'Kano," someone screamed.

Stop! Stop! The American fell off!

My butt met the ground with a dull thud. I woke up pronto. I had to say this: Filipinos are a very respectful lot. No one laughed, although I could read amusement written all over the faces of my fellow travelers. The personnel carrier slowly backed up. I dusted off my dungarees, gathered my traveling pillow, and the TIME Magazine that had spilled out from my back pocket. I clambered back on to the truck and reclaimed my seat. It was a miracle that I did not break a bone. Only my pride suffered some bruising.

The day ushered in the inauspicious beginning to my stint as the incoming Management Consultant of Santa Cruz Mission. The personnel carrier deposited the passengers at Santiago Diaz *Sari-Sari* store, our terminal destination in Lake Sebu. I gathered my belongings and followed the four-kilometer footpath to Santa Cruz Mission. The trail passed through T'boli houses on stilts made of bamboo with cogon-thatched roofs. I could hear the distant drumbeat of *agongs* and the wail of dogs as I crossed the Lo El River without the benefit of a bridge.

I paused to put back on my socks and shoes and continued on my way. I arrived at the mission just before sundown. That night, I laid down on my sleeping bag inside my assigned room at the Men's Dormitory located on the banks of Lake Seluton. The haunting chant of a T'boli woman emanating from my neighbor's hut about 200 hundred feet away filled my room.

I contemplated how to turn my bare dormitory space into a home for the next twelve months. Visions of my childhood room came to mind inside a century-old farmhouse on Route 512 in Bethlehem, Pennsylvania, where my journey began.

Volunteers adapt to the *palengke* (open market) as their new supermarket.

The weapon's carrier driven by Fr. Rex during our first visit to the Mission. We had to winch for about three kilometers.

Life Before Peace Corps   2

JOHN F. KENNEDY made a singular impact on my life like no other. When I was sixteen, he ran for president of the United States. The Liberty High School Band of Bethlehem, Pennsylvania, performed at his campaign rally held at the Moravian College Johnson Hall in Bethlehem on October 28, 1960, ten days before the election. I was one of 9,000 who attended the rally; 6,000 of us got seats inside the hall, but 3,000 more were in the overflow area outside the Moravian gym.[1]

I played the flute and the piccolo in orchestra and band. Seated in the front row at the center of the room just in front of the podium, I could almost touch JFK. When he won the presidency against Richard Nixon, our band director, Dr. Joseph Recapito got in touch with our Congressman, Francis Eugene Walter, a personal friend of Mr. Kennedy. Dr. Recapito lobbied for our band to participate in JFK's inaugural parade. Although he was unsuccessful in getting our Liberty High School band to march during the parade, we were invited to go to Washington D.C. to watch the ceremony from the grandstand. Logistics prevented our one-hundred-member band from attending the inauguration. It turned out we did not have time to raise the much-needed funds anyway.

The blizzard of January 1961 blanketed the Washington D.C. area with snow. It covered the northeast all the way to New England. The U.S. Army Corps of Engineers was mobilized to clear the streets during the evening and morning before the inauguration. First Lieutenant Domenico Sciubba remembered the inauguration very well. He emailed: "I was with the 19th Engineer Battalion Company B out of Fort Meade, Maryland.

We were assigned to remove (not "blow") the snow for the parade. We used front loaders to pick up the snow and truck it to designated government parking lots where we dumped it. The government users of the lot were told not to leave their cars in the lots. My troops reveled in burying a lone VW in one of the lots! After the snow was removed, we employed the multiple racks of flamethrowers, which were mounted on the front of trucks to dry the street. Mission accomplished, we went back to Fort Meade and did not stay for the parade."[2] (Dom Sciubba is married to my maternal cousin Aletha Riegel).

Not having the Army Corps of Engineers to remove the snow in Bethlehem, our school district was closed for a week. After doing our farm chores, my family and I watched in our living room the inaugural ceremonies. We listened attentively to JFK's fourteen-minute speech on TV. For me, it was the best and most memorable elocution. It was also the first presidential speech viewed in color. Like many in my generation, I was utterly inspired.

> And so, my fellow Americans:
> ask not what your country can do for you,
> ask what you can do for your country.

Barely six weeks into his presidency, President Kennedy signed an executive order establishing the Peace Corps on March 1, 1961. Congress enacted the executive order into law (Peace Corps Act) in October that same year. Its first Director was Sargent Shriver, the brother-in-law of Kennedy, married to his sister Eunice (Maria Shriver is their daughter). Volunteers were rapidly deployed to five countries in 1961, including the Philippines. After five years under Director Shriver, Peace Corps volunteers were serving in fifty-five countries with more than 14,500 Volunteers.[3]

I WAS a senior at Liberty High School when the Peace Corps came to be. My classmate Ronnie Klayton and I were in the band room one day.

"Where are you going to college?" he asked after practice. Kids like Ronnie, very smart and son of a medical doctor, were predestined to go to college.

"Me, go to college? I have not thought about it. I don't think I'm smart enough," replied this son of a farmer.

I came from a long line of farmers. My Hower family's progenitor Hans Miehl Haüer from Neureut, Germany, sailed with his wife and six children of five boys and one girl on the ship *William*. They arrived at the bustling port of Philadelphia on October 31, 1737, to escape religious persecution. Family legend has it that Hans Miehl was the official hunter for the Palace of Karlsruhe turned farmer in eastern Pennsylvania.[4]

The name Haüer was Anglicized to Hower when the family bought land during the British regime. Howertown, next to Kreidersville, PA, was named after Hans Miehl's descendant. The Howers and my mother's German family, the Judds, were expected to take over the laborious work of eking a living out of the land and to inherit the rhythm of life of a Pennsylvania Dutch farmer keenly attuned to the cycle of the seasons. Education beyond high school was not something that was discussed at our house. At the dining table, we scarfed down Mom's delicious shoofly pie. And we talked instead of kids going to college like Ronnie Klayton, among many other things.

To earn extra spending money, I worked with my older siblings Joyce and Bud, at the Swirly Top, where Hanover Eatery now stands. It was a 24/7 diner frequented by truck drivers located along Route 512, also called Bath Pike, just a few hundred steps from the northern edge of our farm. My older siblings readily found jobs after high school without the benefit of a college education. There was no doubt that I was going to follow in their footsteps. But Ronnie Klayton believed

I was smart enough and encouraged me to look into applying to college anyway.

After band practice, that same afternoon, a recruiter from Rider College (now University) invited by our teacher Mr. Gilbert, came to speak to us in accounting class. That night at dinner inside our farmhouse, I talked to my mom and dad for the first time about going to college. Without a pause, they supported my decision, and they generously offered me a no-interest loan. A few months later, my dad accompanied me to the campus of Rider College in Lawrenceville, New Jersey.

Bookkeeping was my favorite subject in high school. I had long admired Henry, the son of my parents' best friends Ralph and Eleanor Shoemaker. Henry was a bookkeeper. He was the scorekeeper when we played cards or darts. I was fascinated by his ability to add a column of numbers in his head quickly and accurately. I thought business education would be the best fit for me because I was comfortable with numbers more than Shakespeare. And I had zero science credit to my name. I applied and was accepted at Rider College in the fall of 1961.

I finished my Bachelor of Arts in Business Education at Rider College in 1965. After graduation, I accepted a teaching position at the Henry Hudson Regional High School in Atlantic Highlands, New Jersey, and I taught at Fleetwood High School in Fleetwood, Pennsylvania, the following year. To drive from our house on Route 2, Bethlehem, PA, to Fleetwood, I took US 22. The route took me through Maxatawny, a little town noticeably dominated by one name. One day I came home and mentioned my observation to my dad.

"Maxatawny should have been named Fegelysville, Dad. It seemed like every other building along the main thoroughfare had Fegely emblazoned on it."

"Yes, it should have been," my dad replied. "And for a good reason too. The Fegely family is very altruistic and does a lot of good for their community. One of the sons was my favorite teacher at Northampton High School. He taught

Physics, Geometry, Trigonometry, but his passion is printing. He organized a Printing Club at our school.[5] I was in his math class, and I joined the Printing Club. Guess what his name is?"

My dad paused and revealed, "It's Alvin N. Fegely. Your mom and I named you after my favorite teacher."[6]

Later, my dad made sure that I got to meet my namesake. One Sunday afternoon, we took a drive to Maxatawny to meet Alvin N. Fegely. He was a skinny old man with round-rimmed glasses, vast forehead, and receding hairline. He was amiable, soft-spoken, so scholarly looking. His living room was kempt and lined with file cabinets filled with his students' tests and papers. That I became a teacher was pure coincidence, but it made Alvin Fegely proud to know one of his students named a son after him, and that son became a teacher.

At Rider College, I met Roger Knaus from the Parkland area of the Lehigh Valley. We car-pooled often. In my sophomore and junior years, Roger and I were roommates. I had followed the news about the Peace Corps all through my college years, the harrowing adventures as well as heartwarming anecdotes of the volunteers in foreign lands. One day Roger walked into our room and announced that a Peace Corps recruiter was on campus and asked if I'd want to check it out. We did. We took the Peace Corps six-hour admission test, passed, and were given application forms. I painstakingly filled out the twenty-page application that required forty references, mailed it, had my fingerprints taken, and waited for an FBI background check, which took several months to complete.

What made me do it? In the book written by P. David Searles in 1997, the author proffered a reason that still resonates with me. He wrote, "...The attraction depends on the congruence of Peace Corps purposes and personal motivation. Where the congruence is close, the attraction is high; where distant, the attraction is negligible."[7] That congruence for me could not have been any closer. To cobble a list of forty people who could vouch for my character was the most daunting part of the application process. I was twenty years old. Cars, beach parties, hootenannies, and girls took precedence over building my network of professional contacts. But I did manage to find forty. I don't remember any of my references except a neighbor, our pastor, and my employer Mrs. Ackerman at Swirly Top. Mrs. Ackerman related to me that suspicious strangers knocked on her door, asking questions about me.

It is of interest to note here that President Kennedy inspired to a great extent the path I chose that led me to the Peace Corps. Two others, Ronnie Klayton and Roger Knaus helped to pave the way. (Both surnames begin with K as in Kennedy with the same initials RK. Ronnie became a doctor. Roger did not send in his Peace Corps application, but became a teacher and taught for thirty years. We all still keep in touch).

Before college graduation in June 1965, at age twenty-one, I received an acceptance letter from Sargent Shriver to teach in Ethiopia. I deferred the Peace Corps offer and took a teaching job at Henry Hudson High School in Atlantic Highlands, New Jersey (1965-1966). After school was out, I moved back home to help care for my mother, Harriet, who was diagnosed with terminal breast cancer. I accepted a job teaching at Fleetwood High the following school year (1966-1967). On February 8, 1967, my mother died. Had I accepted the Peace Corps offer and served as a volunteer in Ethiopia, I would have been 6,000 miles away.

The school year 1967-68 was devoted to teaching at Churchman Business College (CBC) in Easton, PA. Starting in 1965, I pursued a master's degree in Business Education for three years, going part-time (attending the regular semester classes and summers) while teaching full-time. It meant a lot of long and arduous commutes from home, to work, to school, and back. But I appreciated the valuable lessons on commitment, patience, and perseverance that the exercise in driving long-distance instilled in me. After completing my master's degree in June 1968 from Rider, I reactivated my Peace Corps application while I continued to teach business courses at Churchman until the fall of 1968. It was during this period that I met Jane. We dated and got engaged before I left for Peace Corps Training.

My letter of acceptance into the Peace Corps/Philippines arrived while I was teaching at Churchman. I received it at the beginning of the fall semester of 1968 with a notification to report to training on March 11, 1969. I did not renew my contract at the college for the spring semester (January-June). In an ultimate act of benevolence, Churchman decided to retain me without having to teach because the college president appreciated my joining the Peace Corps.

The college kept me on the payroll for three months and found something for me to do – tutor students and help out in the library. My degrees were in business education, and nothing in my transcript showed any courses in Library Science. In short, I was clueless about the Dewey Decimal System of cataloging library books. I arranged the books according to size much to the amusement of our librarian and my dismay.

Before reporting for Orientation at Escondido, California, I voluntarily closed my budding camper rental business. I sold my two VW Campmobiles and my VW Bug in exchange for a $65-a-month Peace Corps allowance, adventure, and most important to me, the chance to make a difference. On balance, I believed it was a bargain tipped heavily in my favor.

I WANTED to be a Peace Corps Volunteer or die trying! But first, I must jump over the gigantic hurdle - the Peace Corps Selection Group – composed of highly trained psychologists, psychiatrists, and assessment officers. Plus, the minor obstacles of unheard-of-before-maladies called culture shock and amoebic dysentery. P. David Searles quoted the prolific author and JFK's campaign aide Harris Wofford in his book, "…it sometimes seemed like the selection officers expected that 'the ideal candidate for the Peace Corps must have the patience of Job, the forbearance of a saint, and the digestive system of an ostrich.'"[8]

For the first decade of the Peace Corps, intensive training took place in many universities and sites within the contiguous United States, Puerto Rico, U.S. Virgin Islands, and Hawaii. Since 1972, Peace Corps training was moved to the host countries. The combined three-month training for our Group 31 NDEA and Group 30 Elementary Math was conducted in California, Hawaii, and one month in the Philippines. Setting aside my growing trepidations of not making it into the Peace Corps, I resolved to savor the moments in training. It was not difficult to accomplish this while living in Hawaii for two months. I read through my Peace Corps memorabilia from fifty years ago. My experiences in Hawaii, grand and small, substantial and trivial, happy and sad, are palpable and still warm the heart. There is no better way for me to paint an accurate picture of the twelve-week training than using the words written in real time in my journal.

Escondido, California
March 11, 1969

An entirely new world opened up today… I am on my way to a tiny island country I know nothing about. Except that it is in the Pacific called the Philippines, and my paternal Uncle Aaron Harrison Hower was stationed there during World War II.

Taking off at Allentown-Bethlehem Airport on my first airplane ride sounded like flooring it with my old 1955 Desoto. Arriving at San Diego airport, lugging three suitcases, I took a local bus to the Greyhound Terminal in town. The next bus to Escondido was at 5:15 PM. With three hours to kill, I sauntered to the pier. An old sailing ship came into view, the nautical museum called Star of India. For seventy-five cents, I took the tour. Back at the Greyhound Terminal after the tour, staff and trainees boarded a bus to a former nudist camp, our Peace Corps Training Center. After a quick supper, we registered, filled out forms, and checked in to our rooms. Our group appeared to be racially, economically, and geographically diverse. The staging center was like a Boy Scout camp with an atmosphere akin to college orientation.

March 13, 1969

Yesterday, we were driven into town for dental and eye examinations. Peace Corps ensures that their trainees are in the best of health before they are deployed to their host countries. While in town, I found an art gallery but could not find anything that I like that was small enough to mail to Jane. On tap for today is polio vaccine, smallpox shot, two and a half hours of meeting this afternoon, and an all evening meeting plus one-hour assessment meeting with a psychologist.

March 14, 1969

After lunch, I had another assessment interview – this time with a different psychologist. He was not pleased with one of my recommendations to spell out to the trainees, precisely what they expected of us instead of keeping us guessing. From the beginning, I thought the assessment process was unfair, and I may have telegraphed across my true feelings. He wanted a second interview. It made me wonder if I'd make it. Later I had a chance to talk to Bob Currie (Philippine Operations Officer). He gave me a good deal of encouragement. I told him about my fiancée Jane. He said he would try to get Jane into the English program in the same or neighboring town where I'd be assigned if she is interested...Yellow fever shots were given today. We also had another meeting with Don Berman (the training director for the Philippines in Hawaii). He discussed the courtship and marriage customs in the Philippines. Very interesting. A going-away party completed our day.

Looking back on the psychological assessment sessions, the psychologist and the assessment officers could not spell out the Peace Corps' expectations of their trainees for a reason. Searles wrote, "The reason that volunteers did not know the standards on which selection decisions were based was that there were none...During the 1960s, it was common practice for a board of trainee assessment psychologists to rank all volunteers on a scale of one to five. Those ranked one were considered hopelessly unfit for volunteer duty, whereas, those ranked five were considered to be surefire candidates for attaining the status of 'super vol.'"[9]

In his memoir, *Those Were the Days*, James Beebe revealed that our scores from the "psychological evaluations for our suitability for the challenges of being a Peace Corps Volunteers were posted and discussed by our peers."[10] Two of the volunteers in my group with the best assessment, went home after one year; two of the volunteers, including me, with the worst assessments, extended beyond two years.

March 15, 1969

Early rising today. We packed our bags and boarded a bus to Los Angeles. We are moving to Hilo, Hawaii. I called Jane from the airport, and we talked for thirty minutes. It was so good to talk to Jane.

Onboard the plane, we were given complimentary champagne and dinner. After a five-hour flight from Los Angeles to Hilo (pronounced Hee-lo), the travel-weary trainees perked up when we arrived at the airport. The Peace Corps training staff dressed in Hawaiian outfits welcomed us warmly with leis that they placed around our necks. The smell of the delicate flowers was intoxicating, as was the sights and sounds of the tropics. An official photo of PC Group 30 and 31 was promptly taken compliments of Pan American Airlines.

The training center is located at the edge of Hilo in an abandoned county hospital building. We live in what used to be the nurse's quarters; classes and meals are held in what used to be the hospital itself. Tonight, we had supper at the dining hall (formerly the morgue!). The inside of the buildings has not had regular use or cleaning for a long time. Our rooms are filthy and minimally equipped. I cleaned up a bit before unpacking. There was still a lot of dirt, but we are getting accustomed to it for when we begin work in the Philippines.

March 16, 1969, Sunday

A day of rest and relaxation. After breakfast, we toured the buildings and the falls. Before lunch, we got rides into town. I bought a necklace with a pineapple pendant made of lava for Jane, a bathing suit for me, and some other supplies... After lunch, six of us guys played touch football and went swimming in the nearby creek. The creek was relatively large and swift, fed by the cascading waters of the 150-foot Rainbow Falls. After supper, I played a family favorite card game called pinochle with three other trainees.

March 17, 1969

Today the stuff hit the fan! Our Tagalog class started at 6:30 AM, taught by Filipina ladies. They used the aural (listening) and oral (speaking) method, which meant we learned mainly by verbal communication. The classes were conducted strictly in Tagalog, and it was rare to hear an English word. Sometimes it was difficult to understand what the teacher was trying to convey, but we have got to keep trying...

After breakfast, I had Tech – short for intensive study and preparation for a particular area of work. Today's session consisted of outlining my job. I will be teaching at Notre Dame of Dadiangas College and work directly under the Director. The college is located in General Santos, which is on the bay in southern Mindanao. I will replace two faculty members who are going for their master's degree sponsored by Ford Foundation. During the training here in Hawaii, I will do my practice teaching in a high school and a vocational-technical school. Although the Peace Corps had not heaped work on me directly, there was plenty I must do on my own.

Lunch: 12:00-1:00.
Hooray, the mail is here. I got three letters from Jane!
1:00-3:00. C.C.S. – Cross-Cultural Studies. An exciting course where we learn about the history of the Philippines and its culture. The one instructor, Fr. Gerry Rixhon, is a Catholic priest of Belgium descent who lived and worked in the Philippines for most of his life. The other instructor was Juan Faune (CCS Coordinator), an attorney from the Philippines.
3:00-5:30. Language class
6:00 PM Supper

7:00-9:00 PM Group assessment with a psychologist again!

Wow, am I beat! This has really been an exhausting day. The pace was fast, but most aspects of the training were fun and worthwhile. There is always a good conversation. Every time I talk to someone who is from the Philippines or has lived there, I learn something new. P.S. My roommate is Jerry Oberman from California.

March 18, 1969, Tuesday

Up at 5:15 this morning to shower and get to class early. It is my turn to make coffee for the trainees. Language class went better today, and I feel more comfortable about learning Tagalog. For Tech class, Muriel Cooke, two other language instructors, and I went into town. We hitchhiked. Volunteers do not have difficulty getting rides if there is a girl in the group. Muriel Cooke is sixty-seven years of age and a retired audio-visual coordinator. She is quite a person to volunteer her technical expertise to the Peace Corps during her retirement.

While in town, Muriel bought a portable typewriter (I carried it for her). I bought a dictionary and some stamps and started a banking and post office business. People come to me for change and postage all the time. Today, I signed up for volunteer library duty one night a week. We have only been here for three days, and it almost seems as though we are becoming part of the fixtures.

March 19, 1969

Classes were as intense as usual, but today we had an additional meeting with a selective service representative from the U.S. Military. We had to fill out a form and sign a letter for change of address. Uncle Sam wants to keep an eye on his boys in case he needed more soldiers. There were kids in my group who are vocal about their views of the Vietnam War. Some expressed openly that they joined the Peace Corps instead of being drafted to go to a war they did not believe in. I also had a one-on-one lesson with my Tagalog lady teacher. During this individual meeting, we reviewed the language and talked about the customs and culture of my host country.

At 7:30 tonight, we had our nightly meeting with the Assessment Officer (AO). The meetings consist of discussions with no topic, no purpose, no result, and no nothing. Why do we have such sessions? Is it because AO needs a job, and this is his way of justifying his salary? Is it because the Peace Corps is trying to show us how depressed and dissatisfied we may get in the next two years? If so, will this help predict how we are going to act? If so, what acts would they consider positive indicators of success? The only other theory I can think of is that AO is using us as an experimental group, perhaps for his doctoral dissertation?

March 20, 1969, Thursday

After classes today, I played volleyball with the trainees and the staff. It was a welcomed pressure release from the tension that can build up after several days of intense classes. Tonight we have a meeting with AO, the psychologist again. This is another waste of time. I'll use it to update my diary... At 7:30, we met with two staff members who are returned volunteers from the Philippines. An excellent meeting! We were given more insight into the way NDEA (Notre Dame Education Association) schools are run. There was a Q&A about the Philippines and Peace Corps in general. The feeling of despair and dissatisfaction with some aspects of the training lifted some. P.S. Letter from Jane today.

March 21, Friday

I received three letters from Jane today, including clippings of newspapers about the fire in Easton, where I used to teach. TGIF Day in Hawaii, also known as Aloha Day. The people dress extra special – especially the ladies – in long dresses made of beautiful color prints with flowers in their hair. The ladies' clothing from the Philippines is really something. Expensive looking gowns but made inexpensively, I was told. The men wear embroidered shirts made of pineapple fibers. I wish I did not bring so many clothes with me because I would really like to own some of the clothing Filipinos wear.

After supper, we sang some Filipino songs and performed some dances, including tinikling, using bamboo poles. A jogging club was organized, and I joined them for tonight's jog. I took my laundry along and stopped off at the Laundromat. When I got back, some kids were sitting on the porch singing the popular songs with their guitars – Leaving on a Jet Plane, Blowing in the Wind – this went on to almost 2 AM. I enjoyed the sing-alongs; it helped to ward off homesickness. I got into the habit of calling trainees as "kids" those who are younger than twenty-five-year-old me.

March 22, Saturday

Breakfast at 8:00 was followed by four hours of Saturday Tagalog class! It went fast. After lunch, I went downtown to order flowers for Jane, one for Palm Sunday and one for Easter. Later, several of us went to Rainbow Falls to go swimming. The swift currents made it difficult to swim upstream very far. The water is about twenty feet deep, with no place to walk in; we jump off the rock ledge. Later, about twenty of the trainees went to see the movie, "The Yellow Submarine" by the Beatles. I was so tired that I slept through half of the film.

March 23, Sunday

Five of us, including David Hsu (an NDEA trainee I have become close to), went to the Methodist Church in Hilo today. The people were amiable and welcoming. We wore dress shirts and ties as hinted on the Peace Corps Handbook. We were overdressed! Most men wore sport shirts.

March 24, Monday

A beer Co-Op! Doug Cannon (Elementary Math Group 30) and I are going to organize one. We got the ok to use the center's refrigerator to keep the beer cold. In Hawaii, the law controls the price. The regular price is $6.27 per case, which is more than twenty-five cents a bottle. P.S. Received two letters from Jane.

March 26, Wednesday

Prince Kohee Day – a holiday in Hawaii. Schools are closed. Instead of Vo-Tech, Keith Linder (PC Staff Tech Advisor) and I discussed the school and my job in the Philippines...The Peace Corps Training Center has a lot of trees, including coconut and bananas. Before class this morning, a coconut dropped out of a tree and almost hit Byron Lee (one of the trainees). Byron cracked it open, and we had it with our coffee before 6:30 AM class. Before supper, we found two more coconuts. One was very young and had lots of milk in it. We poured the coconut milk into a cup, and it really is tasty. The young coconut is good, also very tender. P.S. received letters and an Easter card from Jane.

March 27, Thursday

After breakfast, I ordered for our Co-op fifty cases of beer, the minimum cases required to get a discount. Now Doug and I must raise $300 to pay for the beer. We need the money by 5:30 this afternoon. I sure hope that we can drink 1200 bottles of beer before training is over. The remainder of the morning I spent at the Vo-Tech School. I set up a schedule for student teaching, which starts on April 6. I will be teaching Human Relations – which is really Psychology and Accounting IV. Mrs. Shaffer is the Human Relations Instructor. She invited me to her home for a picnic during the Easter weekend...

After lunch, Doug Cannon and I were worried about raising the $300. We made a special request for everyone to contribute and pitched the advantages of having a beer Co-Op. By 5:30, we raised $300 plus a reserve of promises in case we needed more. We filled the refrigerator and put a box on top for the trainees to leave their money (honor system).

As we sell the beer, we can repay our investors. We got a discount on our total bill. We can sell the beer at twenty-five cents a bottle and still have $ left for a party at the end of the training. The beer Co-Op functioned well on the first night of operation. P.S. received letters from Jane and Ed Spadt.

March 28, Friday

Aloha Day. The language teachers and the native Hawaiians at the Vo-Tech School dressed in Aloha tradition. The girls wear some stunning outfits called mu-mus. They are floor-length dresses with bright colors and striking patterns. P.S. After three weeks, I finally received letters from family Joyce, Earl, Wayne, and Karen

An important memo from yesterday, Joe left the program. He was a real social guy, tall, good looking, plays the guitar and sings, former radio time salesman and disc jockey. He graduated from a four-year business college in New Hampshire. Joe was in Group 30 Elementary Math program and was working very hard to fit into the Peace Corps mold. The PC Field Representative told Joe that he was too much of an individualist for this program. This discouraged Joe. He decided to leave. He said that he hopes to get into another Peace Corps Program somewhere else.

Mary is leaving too. She is a memorable trainee, bubbly, friendly, and accomplished. Two nights ago, at supper, Mary came and sat next to me. After most of the people left the table, she said she wanted to talk. We walked around outside. Mary is thinking about terminating her contract with the Peace Corps to return to Baltimore, Maryland, to marry someone she left behind. Mary has a master's in Biology from the University of Maryland, where she met her boyfriend. He has one more year to go to finish his Ph.D. They dated seriously for over a year. They were not engaged.

When they parted, they said goodbye, good luck, take care, and we may not see each other again. Mary called him tonight before supper and is now seriously considering leaving the Peace Corps. She really wants to serve in the PC but knows her boyfriend has no such interest. She is still going to continue training while making a final decision. I am the only one who knows, so I kept it to myself... Mary announced tonight that she is leaving tomorrow.

The 1968 Peace Corps Handbook explicitly did not encourage marriage under specific conditions while in service. It listed the impediments. "Any Trainee or Volunteer who wishes to marry and continue as a Trainee or Volunteer must obtain in advance the approval of the Peace Corps...Approval will not be granted if the future spouse has come to the host country from the U.S. expressly to marry a Volunteer. Nor may a Volunteer return to the United States to marry during his term of service."[11]

Simply put, if you want to get married, you have Peace Corps' blessings, but you must terminate as a trainee or volunteer. In my case, I understood it to say, "Take the girl or take the Peace Corps." In other words, serve your two-year term, be prepared, and willing to sustain a long-distance relationship and hope it survived the rigors of separation. Or break up the relationship. Take your pick. Even the psychologist alluded to it when I sought his guidance. I did not blame Mary. I believed then, as I do now, that she made the right decision. I hope life turned out well, according to her plans.

In retrospect, fifty years later, I totally get it. Looking through the prism of a Returned Peace Corps Volunteer, marriage as a trainee or volunteer while in service to a non-volunteer from the U.S. would have triggered a myriad of complications. Peace Corps must make their informed decision based on the merit of each case. The Peace Corps Handbook listed this complicated rule. A Volunteer must seek consultation in advance with his Regional Director if he wishes to marry and continue in service as a Volunteer.

The Regional Director must decide whether the marriage "will hamper the Volunteer's effectiveness...The Peace Corps will not continue in service a Volunteer who marries (within or outside the host country) a non-Volunteer U.S citizen unless the Country Director determines that the non-Volunteer spouse (1) has an adequate knowledge...of the local country's customs and language, (2) has demonstrated a capacity to live successfully in that or a similar overseas situation, (3) has a job that is compatible in all respects with the goals of the Peace Corps..."[12]

After Mary's revelation, I wrestled with my own state of affairs. Mary and I were in the same boat. I, too, left someone behind – my fiancée Jane. I clearly understood the repercussions. The hardship of sustaining a long-distance relationship for two years loomed largely. In my naiveté, I even posed to Jane various scenarios and avenues to mitigate the circumstances. Perhaps she could find a job at the U.S. Embassy in the Philippines. Or maybe she could join the Peace Corps and request for assignment in the Philippines, etc. I know of one person in my group who struggled with a similar situation. In the end, this person and I both diverged from the road that Mary chose.

March 29, Saturday

During language class, I began getting the chills and started to feel sick. I mentioned this to some of the other trainees, and they said it's maybe a reaction to the typhoid shot, and there were two other trainees affected. Apparently, the reaction to the shot is to be treated seriously. I went back to the dorm, took two aspirins, and went to bed. Later I went shopping downtown with Doug and Marty...I also paid for the orchids that the florist sent to Jane.

March 30, Sunday

Today fourteen of us trainees went on an excursion to some of Hawaii's famous volcanoes. In Kilauea, we hiked down the side of the mountains and across lava fields that resembled concrete that someone poured and forgot to smoothen. Big cracks in the surface and mounds of buckled lava continuously emit steam and sulfur... Certain areas had sparse ground vegetation. As we got to the other side, we looked down into the immense Halemaumau Volcano Crater, spouting forth steam and vapor. Smelling like a rotten egg, the sulfur was overpowering to the senses. It was a fantastic experience beyond description; one has to be there to appreciate its grandeur.

On the way in and out, we hitchhiked. Going home, the first few cars passed us by. Finally, one car stopped. We were only three in our group this time, Don, Nancy, and I. The young married couple that picked us up was from Minnesota. They were very friendly and drove us extra miles to see the recent eruption, the lava tube, and back to Hilo right to our door! They are not the typical indifferent tourists that are usually found on this island.

May 14, 1969, Wednesday, 12:30 AM

We are waiting in the lounge at the Honolulu airport for our flight to Manila. For a month and a half, I made no entries in my journal for a crucial personal reason. I broke off my relationship with Jane. In hindsight, with both of us knowing my plans to join the Peace Corps for two years, the whole thing should not have been started. It was, however, and now that I have broken my engagement with Jane, I have been honest with her, myself, and everyone else.

What happened between March 30 and today? During the eight weeks of training, I learned a lot from the Peace Corps from its unsung language instructors and staff. They are memorable – always kind, friendly, and helpful and, most of all, accepting of everyone. The latter is one valuable trait I will take away from training. I have changed in many ways too…I have learned to keep my mouth shut (sometimes).

I got to intimately experience Hawaii, its people, and its culture and the bountiful, diverse natural scenery. There is every type of climate. Snow-capped mountains, desert, tropical rain forest, volcanoes, striking skies, breathtaking sunsets, moon and stars, beaches of white, black, and green sands, and lava rocks, colorful waterfalls, lovely orchids and hundreds of other flowers and plants plus friendly, kind and welcoming locals who are willing to accept people no matter what race, color, creed or origin. Needless to say, I fell in love with Hawaii and hold a special place in my heart for this state and the people we met.

The Peace Corps so far has been a fascinating adventure and marvelous experience. Many of these experiences are recorded on film and will do an excellent job of jogging my memory. With leis around our necks, tears in our eyes, and burning enthusiasm in our hearts, we said goodbye to Hawaii. Peace Corps treated us to a one-day stopover in Honolulu. Everyone took advantage of the last day in the U.S. soil. I believed all fourteen volunteers did not sleep for twenty-four hours.

David Hsu had a friend who turned tourist guide and took us on top of a mountain where we enjoyed the spectacular panoramic view of the city below.

David Hsu and I met on the first day of training and became the best of friends.

En route to the Philippines, our airplane made a stop in Guam to drop off mail at the large military base. We landed in Manila and lived like kings at Mabuhay Hotel for three days. We slept in immaculate rooms with soft pillows and freshly laundered bed sheets, luxuriated in hot showers, our last perhaps for the longest time.

Outside the hotel, it was a different story. We were exposed to a hefty dose of unpleasant reality in Manila. In essence, the economic disparity between rich and poor was as stark as the darkest night and brightest day. The squalor in the slums without a sewage system and kids playing in the black water flowing through the neighborhood, made my stomach churn. The stench that assaulted the senses stayed with me for a long, long time. I wondered sadly how the poor survive in such filthy, dismal surroundings. How could these upper-class men and women in smart business suits and expensive high heels driving their fancy cars, witness this ugly underbelly of Manila daily and seemingly not be bothered by it?

...There were a lot of nightclubs in Manila. Some were wholesome, some with a lot of hostesses. A hostess we were told was a local descriptive term for women who entertain men for a fee. Two things on the upside: I had my first taste of Chinese food. David Hsu ordered for us, and it was delicious! One last comment about Manila: Maganda ang mga babae sa Manila. (The girls in Manila are beautiful).

THE FLIGHT to Cebu was quite comfortable. Then things went downhill from there. We changed planes in Cebu and continued our trip on a World War II vintage twin-engine turboprop aircraft. The hot cabin was stale and filled with sweaty but uncomplaining travelers. A majority were fair-skinned, blue and brown-eyed, brunette, blonde, brown, and redheaded Volunteers.

The turboprop made a quick stop at an unpaved runway in Ozamiz City. We were on our way to continue our PC training for one more month in Cotabato City. There were a lot of people at the airport when we landed on a paved airstrip in Cotabato City. My illusion that the throng came to welcome us evaporated instantly at the sight of countless men and boys with machine guns slung over their shoulders. I found out later that they were bodyguards for a political leader who arrived at the airport shortly before we landed. We all boarded a semblance of a bus, a wooden body over a truck frame, wooden benches, a low ceiling, and windows.

We checked in at Castro's Place, where we stayed for a month. The hotel had a few inconveniences - two bathrooms for the entire hotel, no running water most of the time, and it was located in a noisy main street on Sinsuat Avenue. Nancy Nicholson, one of the Peace Corps Trainees, wrote to her parents about our accommodations: "We're staying temporarily at Castro's Place - a local hotel-eating place. Mr. Castro doesn't have a beard or smoke cigars - he is a dentist. His dental office is off the main lobby of the hotel. The door is always open so that relatives and friends of the patient may observe what is going on. Yesterday must have been a particularly busy day for him because he had one person in his dentist's chair. As I walked by on my way to lunch, I saw him convince an old Muslim woman sitting in the lobby that he wouldn't hurt her by trying to look in her mouth with his instruments. He was holding a needle behind his back at the time, probably trying to find a chance to shoot her with it – she must have needed a tooth pulled or something. It was quite a sight – there in the hotel lobby – the old woman, her family, and the dentist."[13]

No sooner had we retired on our first night to get some much-needed sleep than seventeen gunshots were fired. I heard the next morning that it was a skirmish between two opposing political parties. As if that was not enough, a fire broke out at the open market three blocks away. It sent a mushroom of red flames ringed with orange, illuminating the sky before turning into billowing black smoke. One of the trainees, Tom Perardi, captured the image on film.

At four in the morning, the *jeepney* engines started revving, there were loud shouts on the street "*Pan de Sal, Pan de Sal*" (from street vendors selling salt bread roll) and a lot of people up and about. I thought there was a parade, but it took only a day or two to realize that it seemed like everyone in Cotabato City was up before dawn.

When we woke up in the morning, we smelled a dead rat. We looked for the source but to no avail. We sat down for breakfast. There on the platter in front of us was the thing that smelled like a dead rat. It was part of the breakfast menu called fried *daing* (salted, dried fish).

Our training continued for another month in Cotabato City, which included cross-cultural lectures, more language training, and practice teaching before a group of Filipino students. I struggled to get over the jet lag, was overwhelmed by open sewage on the streets, and suffered from diarrhea. On top of all this, our microteaching students rated our practice teaching sub-par. Then hearing (inadvertently) language instructors call us "*bobo*" (stupid in Tagalog); and staff who seemed indifferent about our struggles. I had enough and made this confession in my journal.

Cotabato City
May 19, 1969

    Since we arrived in the Philippines, I have had many thoughts about self-deselection (fancy Peace Corps term for quitting). More times than not, I am so depressed by the poverty, the environment, and being sick that I really wondered why I am here. Last Wednesday night through Friday, many of the trainees suffered from varying degrees of diarrhea. Even Kaolin with Pectin, did not help me. After several close runs, I was given a particular pill, after three of which I started to feel okay again. In the meantime, I spent almost all the time in bed, sleeping. I began to lose weight. Five days after arrival, I went to see our Peace Corps/Tech Representative, Keith Linder. He was a kindly man who took the time to listen, a man not much older than me. "Please get me out of here," I pleaded. "It's Friday," Keith reminded me. "Since there is not much that can be done, why don't you try to enjoy the picnic at Bongo Island this weekend. If you still feel the same on Monday, come see me, and we'll facilitate your departure."

For the weekend, we were taken to an island on a *Bangka*. The motorized canoe was about thirty-feet long and four-feet wide powered by a forty-horse-power Evinrude outboard motor. Going to the island, there were eighteen people plus all our food and gear. Coming home, we had twenty-four people plus the equipment. There certainly was not much room to move around during this one-hour-and-forty-five-minute ride each way along the Rio Grande River to the middle of the Moro Gulf.

Jimmy Rosales, the owner of a coconut plantation on the island, feted us. We stayed in his comfortable facilities. His people took care of everything. We did not lift a finger to cook, and the food was out of this world. They were served on an ingeniously designed plate made out of the miniature boat-like coconut spathe (the sheathing bract enclosing the coconut flowers about two feet long).

We went swimming in the ocean one moonlit night. The first quarter moon illumined the skies. The waves of the Moro Gulf were covered with fluorescent plankton turning the beautiful beach aglow with bioluminescence. It was such a sight to behold. It filled my senses. Something I probably will not see in my lifetime again. Something I will never forget.

On Saturday afternoon, a group of Muslims played for us their native music on gongs. About 150 of the local people gathered. They came partly to listen to the music but mostly to welcome and see the Americans. We were a novelty to them and they to us. They were all decked out in the very best that they had. Most or maybe all lived in the *nipa* huts on the island, but they walked out of their homes with spotless, clean, and pressed clothing.

The girls donned on fashionable western style dresses similar to the kids in the U.S. Most of the men came in white shirts. The older Muslim ladies wore their typical native dresses consisting of a see-through mesh blouse and a bra. They wore a skirt called *malong* made of one continuous piece of material sewn tube-like, about twice the size of the waist where it was tucked tightly in place. It was a really relaxing weekend, a welcome respite after a rough week.

Just before sunset one day lost in my thoughts, I walked alone on the white sandy beach staring at the waves lapping at my bare feet. I embarked on an earnest discussion and debate with myself – to leave or to stay. When that failed to affect an acceptable result, I resorted to talking to a supreme being to send me a sign. I looked up. There on the shores of Bongo Island, I saw an apparition: a little Muslim boy about five years old, with a tan the envy of us all fair-skinned volunteers; his bare chest showing a faint outline of three ribs protruding above his slightly bulging belly. The sun was behind him, making his face indiscernible through the lens of my camera.

He was holding a piece of wood. A string was tied to a piece of driftwood at the end of which a wooden tugboat bobbed with the gentle waves of the clear, serene, blue ocean waters of Moro Gulf. The toy boat was meticulously and intricately hand-carved to a precise scale. The omen I was hoping for.

This was my final entry in my journal about the training in Cotabato City.

Back at Castro's Place on Monday, I did not seek out Keith. I decided that if I terminated my contract with the Peace Corps now, I would only contribute to the dead inertia of the world. As Peace Corps Volunteers, we may not deliver solutions to the abject poverty, the open sewer, and the stark inequality of wealth distribution, but at least we could try. If for no one else, we could do it for the sake of the children.

Dr. Merritt Kimball of the Ford Foundation came to address the trainees.[33] He expects all of us to be perfectionists, and it is tough to accomplish that under the conditions we must work under. The living condition I have accepted. Now, if I can please Dr. Kimball, I will be all right.

The Hower Family on Mom and Dad's 25th Wedding Anniversary (1939-1964). L-R: Joyce, Mom Harriet, Dad Clarence, and Dean; Bud and I at the back.

Our old farm on the corner of Route 512 and Hanoverville Road, Bethlehem, Pennsylvania, where I lived until I joined the Peace Corps.[14]

Group 31 Arrival in Hilo Hawaii, March 15, 1969.

Departure May 14, 1969 after training was completed.

The photo above was a gift to all Peace Corps Volunteers from Pan American Airways. In 1991, the airlines went out of business. Delta Airlines purchased Pan Am's trans-Atlantic and Shuttle routes, and United Airlines purchased the trans-Pacific routes. Permission granted by Pan Am Airways, Inc. Records, Courtesy of Special Collections, University of Miami Libraries, Coral Gables, Florida.

In 1972, the Training Center was closed. (I revisited Hilo, Hawaii in 2003 with Prima and stopped at the training center site & see the Rainbow Falls).

BRO. SAM'S dramatic accounts about the labor union unrest and the turbulent political landscape at General Santos City piqued my sense of adventure. But I did not make too much of it. I was certain the Peace Corps would not send us to a hotspot where our safety could be compromised. Besides, Peace Corps volunteers were not supposed to get involved in the politics of their host country. Apolitical by nature, I would not be hard-pressed to keep my part of the bargain. I came to teach. However, I could not get our conversation out of my head to this day.

"Where did you say are you going to teach?" Bro. Sam Geveso asked. A member of the Marist Brothers religious order,[1] he and I met while he was visiting the campus of Notre Dame of Cotabato City during my Peace Corps Training.

"Notre Dame of Dadiangas College, Brother," I replied.

"Oh General Santos, the Wild, Wild South. Did you hear about that?" I shook my head.

In just a few minutes, I gathered from Bro. Sam, all I wanted to know about the dockside intrigues that were happening in my future host town. Notably, between one of the union leaders named Adan de las Marias, Adan's nemesis, and the dynamics of their relations with the local government. The power struggle for control of Makar Wharf and the labor unions had escalated since General Santos became a city eight months before my arrival. A murder occurred at the waterfront. Adan de las Marias was suspected of having masterminded the killing. Some believed him to be the local Robin Hood. His enemies likened him to a Mafia Boss.

Adan was arraigned, but he was freed on bail. Ultimately the case was dropped against him and his bodyguards.[2] Bro. Sam predicted that the opposing party might be gearing for a skirmish reminiscent of the "shootout at the O.K. Corral." (O.K. Corral was the Old Kindersley livery and horse corral in the late 1800s in Tombstone, Arizona). Bro. Sam speculated that Adan would exact revenge and that the constabulary might tighten its control over the city.

I met Fr. Albinus Lesch, the parish priest of Dadiangas, a few months after my conversation with Bro. Sam. From the pulpit, Fr. Albinus openly railed against Adan. The Parish church published a version of his sermon on an eight-page Sunday Bulletin.

"But, don't you worry," Bro. Sam assured me. "You are safe at Notre Dame. I'm assigned there too. In case you arrive before I do, look out for the tumbleweeds." His light-hearted parting words about the tumbleweeds were seared in my memory.

A week before our official induction to the Peace Corps, the Notre Dame Educational Association (NDEA)[3] trainees split up. We went to visit our respective sites for the first time. It couldn't have come any sooner for me. I know that as necessary and essential as the Peace Corps training was, everyone in Group 31 was itching to get it over with so we could begin the real action in the field. Bill Kieselhorst and I flew to General Santos City to visit the Notre Dame of Dadiangas College (NDDC). Bro. Paul Meuten met us at the Buayan Airport, one of the most picturesque landing sights I have seen. The blue waters of Sarangani Bay and the lush, green, dormant Mt. Matutum rising 7,500 feet above sea level welcomed us, as the airplane approached the well-constructed and tightly-packed dirt runway.

Bro. Paul informed us that the Japanese constructed the airport during World War II. He led us to the parking lot occupied by no more than a dozen vehicles. Bro. Paul introduced us to Mang[4] Carling ensconced in the driver's seat of the white VW Kombi, a combination pickup with a crew cab. It reminded me of the VW campers of my rental business. The two that I sold just before I joined the Peace Corps were full camper models, including table, sink, icebox, and cot bed. One had a pop-up top with a cot in the pop-up portion; the other had a built-in-cot installed over the front seats instead of a pop-up. I thought of how convenient it would be to have one of those VW campers to travel around the Philippines.

Mang Carling drove the VW Kombi through a stretch of a rural dirt road lined with coconuts. A *nipa* hut appeared under a group of coconuts every half mile or so. Occasionally, a *jeepney* or a privately owned vehicle going the opposite direction stirred the thick dust and sent it swirling our way. It was suffocating. Welcome to *Dustdiangas* Bro. Paul commented. Thirty minutes later, we arrived at the college. Bro. Henry Ruiz, the director of the college to whom I was going to report directly, was waiting inside his non-air-conditioned office. The room was of considerable size but minimally furnished.

Dominating the room was a large office table situated at the far end, close to a set of tall and wide windows. The windows were glass louvers. A vintage 1940s Royal typewriter sat in the middle of his table. The only other furniture in the room were three metal filing cabinets to his left, in front of which was a round table with four chairs by the door that adjoined the office. The door was marked "Office of the Dean of Men." His secretary's small desk with two drawers and a chair was by the door on the right as one entered.

Bro. Henry stood up when he saw us. He was wearing a white *polo barong,* an embroidered Filipino short-sleeved dress shirt. A kindly man in his fifties and no more than five feet four inches tall with a thick brow and kind eyes, Bro. Henry was born and raised in Spain. He spoke English with a slight accent. He seemed to wear a permanent smile and was very soft-spoken. At times it was difficult to hear him. After a brief discussion of our assignments, he led us to the spacious faculty room a few doors down the hallway. The meeting in progress stopped when we walked in. Bro. Henry briefly introduced Bill and me to our fellow instructors and sent us on our way.

Bro. Paul took us on a tour of General Santos for the remainder of the day. We stopped at the Makar Wharf. It reminded me of the intriguing story that Bro. Sam told me. But on this day, all was peaceful on the waterfront. The place was bustling with workers loading a ship docked along the pier. We saw stevedores - naked from the waist up - trudging in a long line like a row of leaf-cutter ants. The line of stevedores started from inside a *bodega* (warehouse). There were sacks of rice stacked from the floor nearly to the ceiling. The line led to planks on a cargo ship with "M/V Filipinas" emblazoned on its side. The stevedores loaded the sacks one by one and piled them inside the cargo hull. The cows mooed, and the pigs squealed, as they were picked up in huge nets fastened to a crane. They were deposited directly on the deck above the cargo hull. Most of the animals were on their way to Manila to feed the city folks. A few would be butchered to feed the passengers onboard.

Bro. Paul dropped us off at the forty-two-room Matutum Hotel built a few feet from the shores of Sarangani Bay later in the afternoon. (I am not so sure now, but I believe the other trainee, Bill Kieselhorst, went back to Cotabato City the following day. He eventually asked to be transferred to Notre Dame of Marbel, located thirty-six miles further inland).

I stayed in General Santos for a few days and cased the neighborhood, looking for a place to live, to do my banking, and to mail my letters. Walking up and down Pioneer Avenue, I counted at least six banks. There were two more hotels, many general merchandise stores, two colleges, bakeries, medical offices, and to my delight, a lot of snack bars and restaurants, including one called Cotton Bowl Grill, a hamburger and steak joint.

There were three cinemas along Pioneer Avenue - Capitol, State, and Pioneer Theatre. The latter was the only air-conditioned movie house showing "To Sir With Love," starring Sidney Poitier. I stopped and took pictures wherever I went, including the City Hall, located in the center of town. It was surrounded by the Catholic and *Iglesia ni Christo* (Philippine Church of Christ) churches, the provincial jail, the Philippine National bank, the PLDT telephone company, and the post office.

The following day, I went back to NDDC to meet with Bro. Henry. Bro. Sam was just leaving the director's office when I came in. Bro. Henry introduced me to the newly arrived Dean of Men.

"Did not see any tumbleweeds yet," I reported.

"Wait for a windy day by the shores of Sarangani, you'll see them," Bro. Sam replied. "Sorry, I have to run. Mang Carling is waiting outside for me. Welcome to Notre Dame. See you around."

General Santos City was definitely more cosmopolitan than Cotabato City. The town was cleaner, carefully planned, and built along the bay with several piers for large vessels. I did not see any open sewage downtown. There was even a wooden sidewalk like in western movies along Morrow Boulevard, one of the four main avenues. It was named after an American settler, leader, and local hero Albert Morrow.[5] The Japanese executed him during World War II. A civil engineer, Mr. Morrow, had a hand in the physical design of the settlement thirty years before General Santos became a city. The roads downtown were paved, and curbs had been put in place for future businesses and homes. There was a vast expanse between the curb and the rows of business buildings to allow for ample parking.

Six years before my arrival, Dole Philippines Inc. (DolePhil) relocated from Hawaii to the adjacent town of Polomolok at the base of Mt. Matutum. All the pineapple company's shipping and banking operations were conducted in General Santos City. As well as its sister company Stanfilco (Standard Fruit Philippines Company) that produced Cavendish bananas shipped to neighboring Asian countries and beyond. Other agri-businesses arrived between 1963-1967 like General Mills, with its subsidiary UDAGRI (Uytengsu-Dimaporo Agri, Inc), and Coca Cola Bottling Company.[6] The fishing industry was beginning to flourish. The economy was booming. New construction was evident everywhere. Later, the city was called *The Boomtown*.

Local public transport was limited to a few *jeepneys* (jeeps converted into taxis) and the ubiquitous *tricycles* (motorcycles with sidecars). However, I noticed a lot of private Jeeps with canvass tops, a Mercedes Benz, and at least six VW bugs parked along Pioneer Avenue. I saw one VW bug of the same shade of blue, like the one I owned before I joined the Peace Corps. Strangely, the VW bug made me feel at home. I flew back to Cotabato City after the visit to NDDC to attend our Peace Corps induction ceremony.

Three weeks before school started, I was back in General Santos again. I moved into my new home on Champaca Street, named for a tree logged for its valuable timber. My rented house was a two-room cinder block structure about twenty feet wide by thirty feet long. Located behind the residence of my landlord, Dr. Enrique Romero, Sr. I designated one room as my living area and kitchen, and the other as my bedroom.

The place was screened, but mosquitoes still found a way in, so I also slept under a mosquito net. My house had a single bed, running water, a flush toilet, and a shower (albeit cold water only). The furnishings were modest. With my Peace Corps settling-in allowance, I added two rattan chairs and a small writing table. The Peace Corps shipped our belongings by sea from the States inside a metal trunk. I used the metal trunk as a coffee table when it arrived three months later.

One of the first necessities I took care of was to buy a can of Raid insect spray at the local Carlos Hardware Store. On the first issue of my bi-annual Newsletter that I mass-mailed to friends and relatives in the U.S. in December 1969, I wrote: *By now, you must know that I am a Peace Corps Volunteer and a teacher in the Philippines for six months now...I live in a rented little house. At first, I had to kill off or chase out hundreds of ipis (cockroaches) and millions of langgam (ants), but now I have them pretty well under control. I drew the line at the doorstep and promised them that they could live outside without disturbance if I could live inside without disturbance. Occasionally, one crosses the line, but a quick shoe or some Raid discourages others from following.*

IN GENERAL SANTOS, the rich and the poor lived together in any given area. Dr. Romero and his family were well to do. They lived in a big house that stood next to a humble *nipa* hut. No zoning laws governed where people should live. However, there was a subtle class distinction. There were the professionals and the businessmen. There were the workers: their maids, their *Yaya* (nanny), their houseboys, and their driver if they have a car. Their workers usually get a minimal room and board and a little pay for working from sun-up until late at night. In a few cases, if the workers were married with children, the whole family received accommodations. Some younger unmarried workers were sent to school as part of their compensation in exchange for their services. Filipinos are very passionate about education. (The Philippines has one of the highest literary rates in Asia. In 2015, the adult literacy rate for age 15 and older was 98.2%...growing at an average rate of 0.81% since 1990).[7]

For meals, I went across the street and ate with the Oliveros, my adopted family. They also owned a big house surrounded by a solid concrete wall with a wide metal ornate gate. Flowering red and pink bougainvilleas spilled over the top of the fence to welcome visitors. Mr. Pedro Oliveros was the head cashier at the Philippine National Bank (PNB). Mrs. Oliveros, a stay at home mom, was an excellent cook. She acted like a mother hen to four of her boarders: Mr. Remberto Karaan, the Registrar at the Notre Dame College, two guys working at PNB bank, and me.

Dr. Romero was a licensed veterinarian but worked at DBP bank. He and his wife had three boys and a girl. Surrounded by so many children at the three households alone, there were plenty of opportunities to practice my Tagalog. The Romeros had a houseboy (a term commonly used for a helper).

My little house was relatively upscale from the average Peace Corps living standards but comparable to my colleagues at Notre Dame and befitted a college instructor. I was grateful that, Bro. Henry and his staff made all the living arrangements for me before I arrived. The only housework I did was to wash my own clothes by hand and to clean my house a little bit. I could even have had my clothes washed for fifteen pesos a month ($3.75), but I needed something to do, or I would be helpless when I got back to the States.

On my first night in General Santos, I committed my first *faux pas*. I was not sure if I was expected for supper at the Oliveros. To play it safe and not go hungry all night, I went to Sanny's Cotton Bowl Grill for a steak dinner. It was delicious, cooked with all the American fixings complete with French fries and green beans. I ordered a bottle of San Miguel beer (the national brew) and scoops of Magnolia ice cream for dessert. When I returned, Mrs. Oliveros was in the yard talking with the owners of my house. Mrs. Oliveros asked if I had eaten dinner. Mindful not to hurt Mrs. Olivero's feelings, I did some quick thinking and said yes, I went downtown for something and stopped to visit my friend Sanny. Of course, my friend Sanny insisted that I stay for dinner. It saved the day. My explanation was accepted, and everything was just fine. Soon my little house began to feel the semblance of home. I even got the ants and roaches trained to stay outside.

Roxas Avenue was only two blocks away. Made of concrete, the avenue ended at the National Highway to the north, led toward downtown to the south, and to the west of it was the NDDC campus. This main artery was lined with businesses. Development Bank of the Philippines, Betty Lou Bakery owned by the daughter-in-law of Gen. Paulino Santos, Lautengco snack bar called Elvie's Nook, and a few *Sari-Sari* stores (small corner stores carrying general merchandise).

I bought my toiletries at the *Sari-sari stores* in cases of emergency. Or I'd pick up my favorite snacks - home-cooked salted garlic peanut or fried-roasted corn kernels. The *Sari-Sari* stores also sold pre-cooked dried *pusit* (squid) pre-packaged in cellophane. It was my favorite *pulutan* (appetizer) that went well with a cold bottle of San Miguel beer. Walking to school took me about fifteen minutes.

There was no government-sponsored running water or sewer system in town during this period. The middle-class residents owned old-fashioned pumps that had a lever or a handle. A person pushes the lever up and down. The Filipinos called this pump *bomba*. The rich, like my landlord, had running water that worked by gravity.

The water was pumped electronically from the well into a tank with a five hundred-gallon capacity. The tank sat atop an A-frame scaffolding fifteen to twenty feet off the ground. Dr. Romero's pump had to be turned on and shut off manually. One day, everyone was out. I was home with only the Romero houseboy. I could hear water gushing down from the overflowing tank. I ran outside and looked for the shut-off valve. Finding none, I screamed, "Help! Help! Busog na ang tanke, busog na ang tanke!"

The houseboy came running, barely able to suppress a grin. He shut off the valve and said, "Sir Alvin, when the tank is full, we say, puno na ang tanke." I learned that although *busog* also means full, the word itself is used explicitly for when a person had enough to eat.

THE PEACE CORPS encouraged volunteers in the Education Program to immerse themselves in a project outside of their schools that offered direct and personal interaction with the members of the community. I met Fr. Albinus during one of the fund-raising projects to finish the construction of the parish center. He was the local head priest of the Our Lady of Peace & Good Voyage Catholic Church. Through Fr. Albinus, I started working in the community development programs of the parish during my free time. One of the programs was a nutrition center in the poor section of town called Silway, started by the assistant parish priest named Fr. James. Just a few years older than me, we hit it off right from the start.

I settled in very well in General Santos City. I bought a bicycle and rode my bike around town: to school, the post office, downtown just like the Mormon boys I had befriended. Sometimes, I'd go home late at night without concern about my safety. I felt safe in General Santos City as Bro. Sam had predicted. The locals had grown accustomed to the disruptions caused by Adan de las Marias and the simmering clashes between him and the opposing union leadership along the Makar Wharf.

Working with Fr. Albinus afforded me a closer look at the Adan de las Marias story. Fr. Albinus told me in confidence that one of his biggest benefactors and close friend received a neatly wrapped gift box, inside of which was a *barong Tagalog*. He was a wealthy owner of a local rice and corn mill. There was a note to extort a large sum of money tucked inside the folds of the traditional Filipino shirt. It was a not-too-veiled warning to the businessman to pay up or be buried in the *barong Tagalog*.

Fearing for his safety, but unwilling to pay the money, the businessman chose to uproot his family to Manila where he and his wife originally came from. His plan was to wait it out until the conflict was under control then return to General Santos City with his family. But shortly upon arrival in Manila, he died untimely of cardiac arrest. For the first time, I was a bit concerned. Not so much for my safety, but the implications for the city and its residents. For sure, the peace and order forecast looked bleak for the year 1970.

In his book, *The Awakening of Milbuk,* a missionary priest Arthur E. Amaral recalled in detail the events of that period and the involvement of Fr. Albinus in the Adan de las Marias saga. Amaral wrote: "Albinus became somewhat of a hero and celebrity when he challenged a certain Adan de las Marias and his gang of cutthroats from the pulpit. Adan led an armed gang of hoodlums that threatened and intimidated the business owners in town. He ran a protection racket and controlled the docks in style reminiscent of the "American Mafia" ...Fr. Albinus made such a disturbance with his sermon that journalists from Manila came down to General Santos to cover the story..."[8]

On the surface, it was peaceful and calm. Life in General Santos went on as usual. Bro. Sam invited me to join the Marist Brother's picnic in Tambler one Sunday after Mass. Even Bro. Henry, who seldom went out to socialize, came along. There were Bros. Michael O'Keefe, Pius Tajo, Vic Braza, Roger Bagares, Manuel Javier, and Herbert Daniel.

Driving through the winding road over the arid plains along Sarangani Bay, the high winds from the sea whipped the landscape. I observed the mature plants torn from their roots one by one. The clumps formed into large round balls and rolled across the highway.

Bro. Sam nudged me on the ribs. "There you go, Al. Tumbleweeds!"

I dispelled any doubts about my concern. I know life would go on. As sure as the tumbleweeds were rolling away from the seashores to rest in the valley below. And the bangkas were skimming across the blue waters of Sarangani Bay.

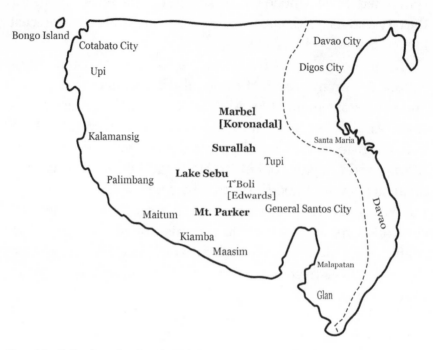

Map of South Cotabato showing General Santos City and Lake Sebu where I lived.

This was how the live cargoes were loaded in 1969. Today farm products, fish, chicken, and pigs are processed in many processing plants in General Santos and transported outside the city by refrigerated containers on cargo trucks and internationally, by container ships, freight transports on Boeing 747 aircraft, etc.

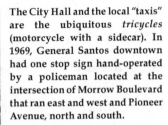

The City Hall and the local "taxis" are the ubiquitous *tricycles* (motorcycle with a sidecar). In 1969, General Santos downtown had one stop sign hand-operated by a policeman located at the intersection of Morrow Boulevard that ran east and west and Pioneer Avenue, north and south.

Below: The Peace Corps teacher at the door of his rented home in General Santos City and Bro. Henry Ruiz, Director of Notre Dame of Dadiangas College. Bro. Henry and I were wearing the short-sleeved polo barong that was a bit more casual. In the tropics, it was a useful and practical piece of clothing, very comfortable, and one never had to worry about neckties.

A Host of Settlers at the Melting Pot

4

I was not the first Peace Corps Volunteer to be assigned in General Santos. Four years before my arrival, Mary Ellen Reid and Louise J. Stapleton taught at the Public Schools and lived in General Santos for two years. They were members of the Peace Corps Group VII who came to the Philippines as teachers in 1963-1965. Another volunteer named JoAnne Thomsen came in 1968, but she only stayed in General Santos for three months. She was a part of the Rice Production Program, a joint venture of the Peace Corps and the Passionist Priests under Fr. James McHugh. Mary Ellen and Louise lived in a little house in Barrio Bula built for them by the Public Schools. JoAnne stayed with the Guipo Family in Barrio Lagao.

My friends remember them fondly. Fel Akol Pedrena, who now resides in San Diego, narrated that Ms. Mary Ellen Reid taught English at Barrio Buayan Elementary School when Fel was a pupil there. There were no reliable means of daily transportation. Ms. Reid came on horseback from Bula to Buayan, traveling about five kilometers. My students at the college who were pupils at the public schools during that time recall helping Ms. Reid and Ms. Stapleton beautify the yard of their *Bahay Kubo* with stones painted white. The volunteers actively participated in the local Girl Scouts activities. I benefited from the goodwill that they had spread.

The Peace Corps assigned me to the Philippines. A country I hardly knew except that it was located in the Pacific and that my paternal Uncle Aaron Harrison Hower, was stationed there during World War II. A first lieutenant in the Army Corps of

Engineers, Uncle Aaron, was one of the men in an amphibious craft LVT (Landing Vehicle, Tracked) that paved the way for General Douglas MacArthur's famous "I Shall Return" arrival in Leyte.

Aside from Uncle Aaron, my dad had three other brothers who served simultaneously in the Military during WWII. Uncle Allen was in the army and served in the European Theatre. He was in Italy when Mt. Vesuvius last erupted on March 17-23, 1944. Uncle Paul was wounded at the Battle of the Bulge. He was rescued, hidden from the Germans, and cared for by a Belgian farmer until the U.S. Army brought him to a military hospital. After he recovered, he went back to the battlefield. He received a Purple Heart. Uncle Warren served in the navy in the Pacific. He was on the battleship USS Missouri when the Japanese signed their surrender. My brother Bud also served in the military (Army Reserve) as well as my mom's brother Uncle Ernie Judd and my cousin David Laubach (both Army) and my cousin James Riegel (Air Force).

I initially was schooled about the Philippines and General Santos City during the Peace Corps Training. The Philippines was a colony of Spain for more than 300 years. Ferdinand Magellan, a Portuguese explorer who had a falling out with the King of Portugal, set out to sail around the world in search of spices under the Spanish flag. He discovered the Philippines in 1521 and claimed the islands for the King of Spain.

"On April 27, 1521, Magellan was killed by a poison arrow during a skirmish on the island of Mactan..."[1] Mactan is a city of Cebu in the Visayan Islands that commemorates the bravery of the local ruler named Lapu-Lapu, the chieftain who killed Magellan. He is regarded as the first Filipino hero for his valiant resistance to the Imperial Spanish Colonization. (Whenever her American peers tease my daughter, she impishly warns them, "Remember folks, my people, killed Magellan!").

Spain and the United States signed the Treaty of Paris in 1898, officially ending the Spanish-American War. Spain ceded

Puerto Rico and Guam to the United States of America. The U.S. bought the Philippines for $20 million, and the Philippines became an American protectorate.

The Philippines is an archipelago of more than 7,000 islands. Over eighty languages were spoken, but there was no official language. The Spanish Missionaries from Spain started parochial schools in 1565. Spanish was taught in school. It was not until 1863 when a free public school system was opened. The University of Santo Tomas is the oldest university in Asia, founded on April 28, 1611. It is twenty-five years older than Harvard. According to K12 Academics: "The Educational Decree of 1863 provided a free public education system in the Philippines...The schools were under the responsibility of the municipal government. The establishment of a Normal School for male teachers was under the supervision of the Jesuits. Primary education was also declared free and available to every Filipino, regardless of race or social class..."[2]

After the Spanish-American War, the public schools were closed briefly. In 1901, the United States reopened the Public Schools, and English became the medium of instruction. The army servicemen were the first teachers. The U.S. Government legislated Act No. 74, which installed an experimental public school system that exposed the severe shortage of teachers.

The U.S. sent American teachers to the Philippines; the batch of 600 was called the Thomasites, after the transport ship USS Thomas that brought them to Philippine shores.[3] American teachers arriving on subsequent ships up to WWII were also called Thomasites. After the Philippines gained its independence from the United States in 1946, the fledgling democratic government established a national language. *Tagalog* became known as the Pilipino language in 1959.[4] According to Bro. Willy Lubrico, President of Notre Dame of Marbel University, the Philippine Constitution was amended in 1973 and again in 1987, naming Pilipino (Filipino) and English as the official languages of the country.

We had immersive language instruction during our Peace Corps training. There were six major dialects taught at the training center. We were matched to a specific language predominantly used by the locals at our site. Language lessons sometimes lasted four hours at a sitting plus almost daily one-on-one tutoring with a language instructor. During these language classes, we also learned the Filipino customs and traditions.

To those language instructors, I hold *"utang na loob"*,[5] to be able to speak Tagalog and teach my *apos* (grandkids) to count and sing *Maliit na Gagamba* fifty years later. Fellow RPCV Nancy Nicholson's letter to her parents painted this evocative picture of an endearing Filipino trait and of language instructors going the extra mile. She wrote: "Philippine hospitality is something wonderful, indeed. One of our language staff at Hilo lives near Manila. She let her sister know when we were arriving in Manila because she wanted to welcome us. Well, the sister was waiting for us at the airport (our plane was about an hour late). She waited there for us while we went through customs, etc. Then she waited while we came into Manila, checked in at the hotel, etc. When we finally had some free time, several of us went with her to her brother's house in the city and had lunch. Wow, did they feed us! And it was a little embarrassing too. Many Filipinos serve their guests first, and then they eat. This is what happened to us – we PC Trainees sat down at the table, ate, were hovered over, and catered to by our hosts, and then we went back into the living room while they ate (in shifts, so as not to leave us all by ourselves at any time). And, they didn't even know us – they merely wanted us to feel welcome."[6]

Angelita Altea, one of the former Peace Corps language instructors and staff for sixteen years who now resides in Boston added, "Hospitality…it's just something we do for friends. My family hosted three Peace Corps Volunteers."

THE PHILIPPINES is divided into three major island groups: Luzon, Visayas, and Mindanao. In 1969, there were eighty-three known different tribes, eighty-three different languages, and eighty-three different sets of customs.[7]

General Santos City is located at the southern tip of Mindanao about a thousand miles by land from Manila. The city is named for Major General Paulino Santos, former chief of staff of General Douglas MacArthur before WWII. Dwight Eisenhower, aide de camp for Gen. MacArthur in the Philippines wrote in his diary on December 27, 1935: "Soon after our arrival, Gen. MacArthur announced his intention to secure the appointment of Colonel Paulino Santos as the chief of staff and of Brigadier General Valdez as deputy... Jimmy (Maj. James B. Ord) and I have worked a great deal with General Valdez and Colonel Santos. With the possible exception of the President (Manuel L. Quezon), they are the two most able executives we have met here."[8]

In 1939, Major General Paulino Santos was appointed by President Manuel L. Quezon as the Manager of the National Land Settlement Administration (NLSA) created by the Commonwealth Act of 551. This socio-economic program was designed to stem the rising discontent of landless people from Luzon and the Visayas. It created the Monkayo-Compostela Project in Davao Province and the Koronadal Valley Project in South Cotabato.

In the same year, Major General Paulino Santos led sixty-two settlers under the NLSA "land for the landless" program to what was known then as Buayan (later named General Santos) in the Koronadal Valley. It was called the Lagao Settlement. Not unlike the story of America's west, settlers from Luzon and Visayas were encouraged to go south as homesteaders. They populated the land of *cogon* grass and forests in a "lifestyle of self-sufficiency, characterized by subsistence agriculture, and production of food for household use or sale."[9]

And not unlike the story of the Native American Indians, the indigenous people called Blaans were displaced from their ancestral homes, forced to move inland toward the mountainous and less desirable part of the settlement. General Santos City became a veritable melting pot. Filipinos from numerous northern provinces of the Philippines migrated to the Lagao Settlement.

Thirty years after the settlers landed, I arrived in General Santos. The town was populated by a high number of young adults, their parents having moved to the area as settlers. At least six predominant dialects were spoken. By air, General Santos was accessible from major cities by flying the country's flag bearer, Philippine Air Lines, or Air Manila (now defunct).

When an aircraft landed on the dirt runway, it sometimes required grounds people to shoo away goats, pigs, chickens, and cows promenading on the landing strip. When it rained, no airplane could land! (According to retired pilot James Reamon who was born and raised in General Santos City, there were no landing instruments at the Buayan Airport during that time. The cancellation of flights was more a problem of visibility than an issue with the runway contrary to common belief. The airport runway at that time, he said, was made of macadam, compacted gravel, sand, and soil.)

I marveled at the view that welcomed me every time my flight arrived in Gen. Santos City. Breaking through the low-lying clouds revealed two of General Santos City's magnificent landmarks – Mt. Matutum and Sarangani Bay. Looking out the window, Mt. Matutum provided a panoramic backdrop. It gently slopes down into a city that hugs the shoreline of Sarangani Bay. Between the sea and the mountain was a carpet of lush green forest, meadows, farmlands, a splash of colorful tropical flowers, and the city of General Santos. The confluence of the fertile land around Mt. Matutum and the rich fishing ground of Sarangani Bay played a vital role in the rapid

urbanization of the town. The waters of the Moro Gulf and the
Celebes Sea feed into Sarangani Bay.

TO BETTER understand the story of my host town, it is
necessary to tell the story of the settlers. There is no narrative
that I could use to illustrate the plight of the immigrants
more than the story of Mr. & Mrs. Guipo. I met them not
too long after I arrived in General Santos. They came from
barrio Tacdangan, Iloilo province, on the island of Panay in the
Visayas. They were students of the Thomasites. Mr. Doroteo
Guipo was an alumnus of the Iloilo School of Arts & Trades
(ISAT) established in 1905, and his wife, Trinidad, graduated
from a Normal School (now Western Visayas University)
founded in 1902. The U.S. government established both schools
after the Spanish-American war.

Mr. Guipo and his older brother Jose started their own
construction company after the brothers graduated from ISAT,
both valedictorians of their class. They were awarded their
most significant contract when they won the bid to renovate
the Cabatuan Municipal Hall in 1939. They also helped
their father Mateo, the Tacdangan barrio captain for eight
consecutive years, to establish and build the first Primary
school in their barrio. Mrs. Guipo (nee Trinidad Grana, also
a valedictorian) was a third-grade teacher at her alma mater
Cabatuan Elementary School. Doroteo and Trinidad met, fell
in love, built a house, got married, had two daughters, and
lived a relatively comfortable life, both earning and enjoying
a steady income.

Then the Japanese bombed Pearl Harbor on December 7,
1941. Everyone in Tacdangan, where the Guipos lived, had to
evacuate to the mountains to evade the atrocities meted out
by the enemy. Mr. & Mrs. Guipo worked in the underground
Guerilla Movement throughout the war. When the war was
over, they struggled to find work to feed their growing family.
By this time, they had four children. Mr. Guipo's paternal uncle

Segundo Diaz had become an NLSA settler in 1939, and two of Mr. Guipo's siblings (Jose and Caridad Guipo Villa) followed the uncle to General Santos City before the war broke out.

The recruitment process for the NLSA settlers was stringent. Gen. Paulino Santos' report stated, "...a settler must be an American or Filipino citizen, not over forty years old and preferably married with children, so he has the incentive to stay, healthy, trade school graduate or have experience in the farm and must have recommendations from leaders or prominent persons in town to vouch for his character."[10]

Mr. and Mrs. Guipo were in their early thirties. They decided to migrate south. They raised funds by cobbling contributions from Mrs. Guipo's siblings, who sold what little piece of property they owned to help defray the cost. The couple and their four children – Josie (seven), Nena (five), Susan (three), and Angelo (ten months) - arrived on the shores of Sarangani Bay on June 30, 1947, on board SS Virgin del Mar with twelve pesos left inside of Mrs. Guipo's gold-plated coin bank, a part of her wedding gift.[11] (Four more children were born in the settlement).

Mr. Guipo was at the post office one day and saw an advertisement for interested parties to sign up for a lottery to own twelve-hectares (roughly thirty acres) of deserted farmland. Awarded to settlers who arrived before the war, many farms were abandoned by the original owners who went home to Visayas and Luzon due to homesickness, ill health, or inability to withstand the rigorous and lonely life of a settler. Mr. Guipo was awarded twelve hectares near the base of Mt. Matutum, twenty-five kilometers from General Santos City, where he would build a hydraulic rice and corn mill with his two brothers.

In 1949, the couple received some money from the war reparation program. They used the money to buy a home lot in Lagao three kilometers from Dadiangas. Five years after their arrival, the couple sent for Mrs. Guipo's siblings, who contributed to their moving funds to migrate to General Santos. The couple helped the newcomers buy land in the settlement. Five of the eight siblings of Trinidad and three of the six siblings of Doroteo became settlers in General Santos.

Mr. & Mrs. Guipo taught at the Public Schools, retiring after thirty-five and forty years of service, respectively. While he was teaching full-time, Mr. Guipo went back to school part-time during summer sessions starting in 1952 and finished his college degree from Southern Island College in 1969 at age fifty-four. He would become the Industrial Arts Supervisor of the city. Together with the Superintendent of Public Schools, Mr. Agustin R. Ferrariz, Mr. Guipo lobbied and established the School of Arts & Trades in General Santos. This settler story is just one of thousands who built from the ground up the highly urbanized city of General Santos today, ranked as one of the twenty largest cities in the Philippines populated by 594,446 people.[12]

Mr. & Mrs. Guipo likened the Peace Corps program to the *Thomasites,* some of whom were their teachers. In 1968, Mr. & Mrs. Guipo hosted one volunteer for three months, and their home was always open to transient volunteers. When Melvin Beetle, the Peace Corps Training Director/Philippines, was in town, the family offered their spacious porch as a meeting place for the trainees in the Rice Production Program. The Rice Production Program's experimental rice paddies were located a few hundred feet from the Guipo's house.

The Stories of my Host Families

I lived with host families during the four years that I stayed in General Santos City. They provided me with shelter, food, friendship, and a sense of belonging, just like a real family would do for its members. Their presence in my life was vital during those times when I felt the need for a healthy support system to combat the isolation. My wife and I have kept in touch with my hosts' children and grandchildren, who happily shared their compelling stories through emails and Facebook Messenger. Many of them are now living in Canada, Australia, the United States, and all over the Philippines.

The Romero Family on Champaca Street
(May 1969-May 1970)

Dr. Enrique Romero Sr. was my first landlord. He is from Kalibo, Aklan, a province on the island of Panay. His wife, Marcela Ang Romero, came from Alegria, Cebu. Of my hosts, Dr. Romero and his wife are the only ones who are still alive. He is enjoying his retirement years. Now in their eighties, Enrique and Marcela are still living in the same house.

The Oliveros Family on Champaca Street

The Oliveros was a poster family for diversity. Mr. Oliveros, who came from Mangaldan, Pangasinan in Luzon, was working as an employee of the Philippine National Bank (PNB) in Jolo, Sulu, southernmost province of the country. He met a local beauty, Rahma Taib, a Muslim lady. Mrs. Oliveros was a descendant of Hadji Abdul Buto, the first Tausog Senator of the Philippines sent to the United States to represent the Moros.

The *Philippine Government Senators Profile* reported, "... General Francis Burton Harrison, U.S. Governor of the Philippines, appointed Hadji Abdul Butu as a senator in December 1915. Senator Butu represented the 121st Senatorial District (Mindanao and Sulu). He was thus the first Muslim to sit in the Philippine Senate. He proved to be an able parliamentarian so that he was re-appointed senator by Governor-General Henry L. Stimson in 1928."[13]

The Oliveros family moved to Cagayan de Oro City almost a year to the day after I met them. It was a devastating period for me as it was like losing a real family. Through the years, I had kept in touch with their children and met up with them in Florida when the oldest Elvin visited his brother Pedro Jr. who now practices medicine there. In my second newsletter in May 1970, I wrote: *Saying goodbye to my present home and the Oliveros family was difficult to do. The past year had been good to me. As I looked around and saw the many souvenirs hanging on the walls and the memories associated with them, packing up and moving was almost unbearable.*

Elvin emailed recently: "If my mother were alive, she would be happy to share our family story. She held Sir Alvin close to her heart. My mother loved to cook. That's why she ran a boarding house. She loved to talk to Alvin. She spoke English fluently. She also admired the Americans for their generosity. When the American soldiers liberated Jolo from the Japanese occupation after WWII, the GIs gave her and other children chocolates, but most importantly, education for her tribe, the Tausugs."

Mr. Oliveros met Mrs. Oliveros at a fundraising event held in Jolo for visiting Philippine Military Cadets (PMA). Elvin shared, "...my father requested someone to ask my mom for a dance. It was taboo for Christian boys to seek acquaintance with a Muslim girl and worst if he courted her." Mr. Oliveros persisted, won the love of the young Rahma, but because of the strong family opposition, the young lovers eloped. With the intervention of the governor related to Mrs. Oliveros, Elvin shared, "...my dad had to convert to Islam and renounce his Christian belief. My dad took the bitter pill so he could marry my mom and be saved from death. So the story ended happily ever after!"

When Mr. Oliveros was reassigned to Naga City in southern Luzon, far away from Jolo, he had all his boys baptized in the Christian faith and changed their names. Elvin's name was Kemal, Renato, (the Jesuit priest) was Ombra, Joseph was Yusop, Pedro was Abdul, and Rey was Reysoni. Elvin continued, "My mom, because of her love for my father, had to learn how to cook the Christian way. Imagine a Muslim girl frying pork belly to a crisp with hot cooking oil spurting all over her. I can say it was not only tolerance, but she almost embraced our Christian faith. I asked her once why she won't convert and become a Christian. She answered, 'Your God is Allah to us. When we die, we will go to heaven just like the Christians as long as we all love God with our whole heart and obey His commandments.'"

Elvin is now retired from the Development Bank of the Philippines, residing in Cagayan de Oro City. Rey is an agriculturist working as a consultant for three corporations in Davao City. Pedro Jr. is a doctor in rehab medicine residing in Orlando, Florida. Rene, a former Jesuit priest, is still connected with the Ateneo de Manila University. The youngest, Joseph, is a businessman residing in Cagayan de Oro City.

The Santos Family on Roxas Avenue
(June 1970-December 1970)

Before Mrs. Oliveros left for Cagayan de Oro City, she arranged for all four of her boarders to eat our meals at Mrs. Florence Santos' house on Roxas Avenue. It was somewhat inconvenient to walk three blocks from my home for three meals daily. So I successfully negotiated with Mrs. Santos to rent me a room. With the board, lodging, and laundry service, the amount was less than what I had been paying. The laundry service I appreciated very much because it freed me from washing my clothes by hand. I saw for the first time how some Filipinos washed their laundry by the river behind the Pasonanca Park in Zamboanga. The ladies folded a piece of clothing, laid them on a rock, and pounded them with a paddle. They rinsed the garments in the river, wrung out as much of the water, and hung them on the branches of bushes and trees to dry. I also watched our *labandera* (laundry lady) at the Santos home laboriously wash the cumbersome bed sheets by hand. She'd take a portion of the bed sheet in both hands and rub them together with water and soap, working from one part to the next until she had rubbed the sheet all over, thus "agitating" the cloth to get the dirt out.

There had to be an easier way to replicate the process of "agitation" that a washing machine performed, I thought. I don't recall now, but it may have been on one of the issues of our Volunteer newsletters where I saw design to make a simple washing machine without the use of electricity.

I went to the local tinsmith and had him make a 20" wide by 30" deep metal tub. I demonstrated the process to the *labandera*. We placed the bed sheet inside the tubful of water and added powdered Tide laundry soap. Using a plunger handmade by the tinsmith, I "agitated" the bed sheet for a few minutes turning the bed sheet around every now and then. We set aside the sheet inside a separate laundry basin and filled the "washing machine" with smaller pieces of clothing and repeated the process. When the water turned cloudy from dirt, we emptied it and filled it with fresh water to rinse the wash.

The Santos family came to Gen. Santos in 1939 when Lagao settlement was all cogon grass and forests. Mr. and Mrs. Ofreceno "OT" Santos were among the sixty-two original settlers. Their early pioneering days mirrored the lives of Americans from the east coast who ventured out west. While there was upheaval when Japan occupied South Cotabato province, it was short-lived. General Paulino Santos decided to cooperate with the Japanese to save his followers from harm. The area was one of the last Japanese strongholds during the war. Aside from the airport, the Japanese built tunnels and bunkers (one not far from the Santos' farm in Conel). The Japanese also raised cotton and established a school. According to Dr. Anastacio Hoyumpa of Texas, he and his Filipino first grade classmates learned how to sing and how to count in Japanese.

The Santos family owned a farm in Conel with coconuts as the main crop. They also owned fishponds where they grew fish commercially. I was invited to their farm on weekends. I was part of a three-generation family living under one roof. Two of the Santos children lived in the same house, son Carlos with children and an unmarried daughter Marilyn working at a bank. There were little children ten and under around the house all the time. I practiced my Tagalog with them, and they practiced their English with me. I remember playing outdoors with the Santos children a lot.

"Our Yaya said we have to go in now for our *siesta*. Or the White Lady will come and take us away," the oldest said to me one day.

"But we are not finished playing our game yet. And what White Lady?" I teased.

"The one who lives in that *baliti*," pointing his nose and tightly pursed lips toward the strangler fig tree in front of the house.

The *Yaya* appeared at the door, and the little kids promptly scampered back indoors. I never got to meet the White Lady. Local legend had it that a lady dressed all in white had been seen around town walking about in the middle of the night. Some opined that it was all a mirage, an apparition, or perhaps someone saw a Marist Brother or a Passionist priest attired in their all-white cassock.

Margareth Rose, the daughter of my host's oldest son, sent a message through Facebook. Margareth Rose, whose family used to live nearby, was a frequent visitor at her Lolo and Lola's house. She recalled the Christmas of 1969 when she was about ten. She emailed: "The grandkids have vivid memories at the Big House and of Lola's borders...I remember Sir Alvin very well. One Christmas, he gifted us with wooden puzzles for children that he hand made himself. I think it was a part of the puzzle project he tried to jumpstart for the inmates at the Provincial Jail."

Margareth Rose recently finished her term as a city councilwoman. Her grandmother Mrs. Florence Santos (nee Maxey), was the daughter of an American married to a Filipina. I met Mrs. Santos' brother Frank Maxey on one of the trips on M/V Filipinas mentioned later in Chapter 7.

The Gavilan Family on Claro M. Recto Street
(January 1971-October 1971)

One of the Gavilan daughters, Belinda, remembers the time I grew mushrooms under the jackfruit tree in their backyard for the fun of it. She also recalled a little brown monkey that I bought. I took a long bamboo pole, tied one end on a branch of the jackfruit tree, and the other on an avocado branch. The little monkey was on a leash so it could run back and forth on the bamboo pole. "My father used to watch the monkey from the terrace with such great amusement," Belinda emailed.

Belinda now lives in Canada. She shared her family story in a recent email: "My father, Manuel Fernandez Gavilan, was from Guimaras Island, Iloilo. My mother, Lydia Alvior Bona, was from Dancalan, Negros Occidental. They met when they were both eighteen in Negros, where Manuel owned a transportation business. He used to leave money in an envelope for my mother to spend every time he passed by her town. Then the war came. They got married during wartime. The whole family went to my grandparents' farm in the mountains where they were safe from the Japanese atrocities."

After the war, the Gavilan couple decided to move to Lagao Settlement in 1950. They sold their businesses and embarked on a boat to the unknown island of Mindanao. They settled in Banga, South Cotabato, where they started the Blackhawk Trucking Company. They moved to Dadiangas, General Santos, in 1953.

Belinda recalled, "Sir Al might remember the time when Mother baked a turkey, especially for him, as he missed turkey a lot. He ended up in the hospital. It concerned Mother very much. Unbeknownst to us, Sir Al was already suffering from a recurring bout of amoebic dysentery. My mother was so relieved that it was not her turkey that made him sick. He always looked forward to *merienda* time in the afternoon when mother cooked Filipino delicacies as *biko, palitaw, suman served with mango*. His favorite merienda was chocolate cake. I also remember going on beach picnics. My sister Alla and I used to climb the guava tree to our rooftop and gather some young coconuts from that height. Sir Al joined us on this adventure too. He was like a big brother to us."

Drs. Jorge and Aida Calderon Family on Quirino Avenue (January 1972-December 1972)

After my one-month home leave (November-December 1971) in the United States, I came back to General Santos as a homeless volunteer. I told Fr. Albinus, I was looking for a place to stay. He made a phone call, and on the same day, I moved in with the Calderon family.

Jorge Calderon and Aida Calderon were medical doctors. When the newly built Doctors Hospital opened, the Calderons closed their inpatient clinic and continued to see outpatients in the front rooms of their house. I occupied a room in the back, which was once a part of the Calderon Clinic for inpatients. I had my own private bathroom with a shower, a luxury for a volunteer during that time.

Dr. Jorge Calderon Sr. was from Nueva Ecija, and his wife, Dr. Aida Uychutin Calderon, was from Laguna. Jorge and Aida met in Medical School. They got married in 1953. Dr. Jorge Calderon decided to go to Chicago for five years to train in Pathology after their three children were born. In 1964, the Calderon family moved to General Santos City. The couple had both passed away. Their oldest daughter Cynthia now practices at her parents' clinic on Quirino Street. She is in active practice in the field of pediatrics in General Santos City. Jorge Calderon Jr. is an obstetrician, and the youngest, Lorna, works in the Beauty Box and Laser Center owned by Dina, wife of Jorge, who is a dermatologist.

General Santos was a melting pot, indeed. Not only was it inhabited by Filipino settlers from different provinces of the Philippines, but also by expatriates from different parts of the world. The majority of the business sector was owned and managed by the Chinese. But there were also numerous families from other countries like Jethanand Balani from India who was the proprietor of Ram's Bombay Bazaar. Tracing their roots to Tunisia and Yemen, the Bajunaid family owned the Bajunaid Department Store. One of the biggest cattle ranches belonged to the Cesario Palacios family from Spain. Mr. Antonio Zolina, Sr. married a lady named Christina Balendo from British Columbia, Canada, and settled in Barrio Lagao, just to name a few.

MY LIFE became a pleasant routine of teaching at Notre Dame College full-time and working at the Community Centers in Bula and Silway part-time. My free time was spent on local travel and picnics on the beach. Sarangani Bay offered twenty-three miles of pristine beaches teeming with sea life. Snorkeling was like being on an undersea escapade with Jacques Cousteau. It was quite an experience to observe the ubiquitous lionfish, clownfish, and seahorses, sea stars in many shapes and colors, and a variety of corals along Sarangani Bay. I had Fr. James, to thank for teaching me how to snorkel, another first that I learned as a Peace Corps volunteer.

I frequented Calumpang, Tambler, Bawing, Cabo, and Dupalco beaches with fellow Peace Corps volunteers, students, and host families, as these locations could be reached easily by land. My favorite, however, was Tinoto, accessible only by *Bangka*. I'd go to the Fish Port early in the morning and find a fisherman who had sold his catch from the previous night, and on their way home, I'd get a ride out to Tinoto.

After snorkeling and eating lunch, I'd hike up the steep hill to the highway and hitch a ride with delivery trucks like Coca-Cola, ESSO, or Shell cargo trucks or whatever vehicle passing by that would give me a ride. There was little traffic on that road in those days. Sometimes I waited two to three hours for a ride, but I always got home on the same day!

Beach picnics were definitely my favorite weekend getaway. The contents of our picnic basket depended on who came with me. With my American friends, a loaf of bread, a bottle of peanut butter, and a knife with which to spread it, a hand of banana, a few bottles of Coke, and some garlic salted peanuts usually sufficed. With my Filipino friends, we brought everything except the kitchen sink.

One weekend, a group of us – Notre Dame students, staff, and faculty members – picnicked at the Tambler Beach. At lunchtime, my all-Filipino companions unfolded a tablecloth on the beach and displayed a culinary spread as though it was a *fiesta*.

Around this time, I pretty much got my Tagalog language down pat. But in General Santos, the Cebuano and Ilongo dialects were spoken predominantly. One word in one dialect could have a wholly different meaning in another, sounds the same, or takes on an entirely different spelling. When we sat down to eat, one of the staff apologized.

"Oh, Sir Al, we forgot to make you a sandwich," said Rosela Datoy. "I hope you will eat our Filipino food."

"Don't worry. I eat anything," said I, proudly. "I even eat *bulati*."

They all gave me a quizzical look with a grin on their faces.

"But Sir Al, you just said that you eat tapeworm or earthworm. Really?" Rosela said incredulously.

Realizing my gaffe, I quickly corrected, "Oh, I mean *bulad*."

Bulad is salted dried fish in Cebuano and Ilonggo.

In Tagalog, the word is *daing*.

Philippines Group VII PCV teachers Louise J. Stapleton & Mary Ellen Reid at their school cottage in Bula, General Santos, South Cotabato, Mindanao, 1965. Mt. Matutum can be seen in the background. Photo courtesy of Phil B. Olsen, former Regional Peace Corps director in Mindanao 1965-1967 and posted online by journalist Edwin Espejo.[14]

Major General Paulino Santos. Oil painting by acclaimed Filipino artist Bueno Silva, a high school alumnus of Notre Dame of Dadiangas. Buenosilva.com

The Settlers: On June 23, 1947 the Guipo family gathered in Tacdangan, Iloilo for a going away party for the young couple Doroteo and Trinidad (seated holding baby Angelo and Susan) and their two girls Nena (seated front left) and Josie (seated front right) before they migrated to southern Mindanao.

All of the three Guipo boys – Jose, Doroteo, & Paulino – migrated to Mindanao. In 1952, five years after Doroteo arrived in the settlement, he and his brothers harnessed the Silway River and built a hydraulic rice and corn mill a few kilometers from the base of Mt. Matutum. A very entrepreneurial person, Mr. Guipo added a Popsicle factory later. The hydraulic mill was converted to gasoline in the 1970s when the river changed its course due to constant flash floods caused by erosion after Dole developed the area.

The photo of Dr. Romero was taken during his 80th birthday in 2018 (photo courtesy of Ricky Romero). Mrs. Romero and her kids in 1969.

The Oliveros Family.
PNB Christmas Party 1969

The Ofreceno Santos Family
Courtesy of Margareth Rose Santos

The Gavilan Family.
Photo courtesy of Belinda Gavilan Colon.

The Jorge Calderon Family
Courtesy of Leslie Savina

The Peace Corps volunteers got together as frequently as our schedules allowed. I often organized a beach picnic for volunteers. At this picnic, PCVs from Notre Dame of Marbel attended: Bob Reeves (striped shirt), Bev Reeves (hidden with hat), unknown, Tom Perardi, Catherine, and Fred Bedford, and my community center staff. Vilma Bordamonte (next to me) was a working student living with Tom & Marilyn Perardi. Her story is in Postscript: Fifty Years Later.

Visiting volunteers Janet and Diane hitch-hiking with me after a wonderful day at Tinoto Beach.

Janet, Diane and I found a bangka early in the morning and the fishermen dropped us off at my favorite Tinoto Beach. There was not a soul on the stretch of white sand - we had the beach to ourselves. Note the lamp above the ladies' head; the only source of light when the fishermen went fishing while it was still dark.

My favorite rock formations below. This beach is very close to Cesma Cliff

The Notre Dame Spirit 5

I AM not a fan of spectator sports, but I happened to enjoy watching the bands. On weekends during football season in America, it was hard to miss the century-old rivalry between the University of Michigan and the Notre Dame University Football teams. At half time I always enjoyed watching the precise choreography of the band and color guard. They marched in a variety of exquisite formations, all while performing flawlessly. It reminded me of my Liberty High School band at Bethlehem, PA. The Notre Dame band always played the distinctive and notable Victory March, commonly known as the Irish Fight Song, instantly recognizable at the sound of the first ten notes.

The first time I heard the same catchy Irish Fight Song being played at a tropical isle ten thousand miles away from the campus of Notre Dame University, South Bend, Indiana was quite a pleasant surprise. It happened on my second month of teaching at Notre Dame of Dadiangas College.

It was on a day that strained a teacher's patience to the limit. I was trying to make sense of the Fundamental Laws of Economics before my students in Economics I class. All fifty-five of them - mostly sixteen-year-old freshmen - were without textbooks, were used to learning by rote, and were a bit intimidated. Not by the fact that I was a twenty-five-year-old Peace Corps volunteer, but because they needed to speak English in front of the only American on the faculty who was not a Marist Brother.

Teaching the concept of supply and demand any time of the day would not have mattered; on the *siesta* period, it was tough. I left my classroom on the third floor, a bit exhausted, and followed the flow of students toward the wide staircase. We descended down the steps four to six abreast. At least six dialects were being spoken simultaneously.

At the bottom of the stairs, I turned left toward the spacious lobby. I heard the familiar sound of instruments being tuned. The high school band was rehearsing. Having just finished my last class for the day, I decided to follow the music. I walked out of the decorative metal door leading to the quad. I sat on one of the benches next to a sapling pine tree and watched the Marching Band practice near the high school building.

Then it happened. The band played the familiar, unmistakable Irish Fight song vigorously and full of pep. The band marched toward the entrance of the campus. I followed. They continued their rehearsal on the grassy expanse in front of the college. A piece of land that belonged to the City, it was also used by the college for ROTC pass and review pageantry. The Irish Fight song looped inside my head incessantly for the remainder of the afternoon. It made my day.

It seemed to me that all of the Notre Dame students in Dadiangas, from age six and above, including their siblings and their parents, could sing by heart the Notre Dame Victory March and the *Notre Dame, Our Mother.* They seemed convinced that the songs were composed solely for their alma mater. They belted out the former with gusto and crooned the latter in three-part harmony with a fervor that would make U.S. Notre Dame alumni Joe Montana and Regis Philbin proud.

According to the U.S. Notre Dame University Alumni Association website, "The Alma Mater song *Notre Dame, Our Mother* was composed as a response to the tragedy of Rockne's death. Since then, it has been used to accompany the fight song to end all football games and other University events."[1]

Knute Rockne was a coaching legend at Notre Dame. He died when his wooden Fokker plane crashed in a wheat field near Bazaar, Kansas in 1931. Eighty-eight years later, Rockne still remains the coach with the most number of wins in Notre Dame football history. A statue honoring him stands in front of the Notre Dame Stadium in Indiana. He is best remembered for helping the poor immigrant students and shaping them into a team that could compete against America's elite universities. He was an immigrant himself from Norway.[2]

When I found out during Peace Corps training that I would be teaching at a Notre Dame College in barrio Dadiangas, I wondered how the school got its name. Notre Dame translates as *Our Lady*, referring to Mary, the mother of Jesus. The Oblate Fathers,[3] who started the Notre Dame Schools in Mindanao in 1939, celebrated its Silver Jubilee in the Philippines in 1964. An article was submitted to the Canadian Catholic Conference Information Service titled, *It's All in the Name.* It read: "Canadian-born Fr. Gerard Mongeau discussed the question of a name for the school in Cotabato City with his fellow Oblates, all of whom were Americans. They decided promptly and unanimously to call it Notre Dame after the famed University in South Bend,

Indiana. A tremendous spirit of unity developed among all Notre Dame padres, students, and their parents."[4]

General Paulino Santos had died while in Japanese captivity toward the end of the WWII. The settlers in Lagao Settlement regrouped after the war and carried on the rebuilding without their leader. A steady stream of immigrants arrived on the shores of Sarangani to populate the whole Koronadal Valley from General Santos to the northern inland towns. There was a Public Elementary School in General Santos, but the residents clamored for secondary education. Fr. Joseph McSorley, an Oblates of Mary Immaculate Order priest who later became the Bishop of Jolo, Sulu, founded the first Notre Dame High School in General Santos in 1947. The newly established co-educational high school was called Notre Dame of Lagao (NDL).

Its first Director was Fr. Joseph Milford. In 1952, the Oblates invited the Marist Brothers to take over the school so the priests could concentrate on ministering to the ever-growing influx of settlers. The Marist Brothers were known as a teaching order. The two most prestigious schools run by the Marists are the Archbishop Molloy High School in Queens and the Marist College in Poughkeepsie, New York.

In 1954, the school leadership segregated NDL high school into boys and girls departments. The Marist Brothers invited the Dominican Sisters to take over the NDL Girls Department. Students from all over the Lagao Settlement attended these high schools. Bro. Joseph Damian Teston, its first Marist Director, raised donations from benefactors in the U.S. to buy a cattle truck to transport the kids to school.

From 1952-54, the students were picked up from a central point in Dadiangas in the morning and were taken to Lagao three kilometers away. The process reversed in the afternoon. When the number of students increased, instead of buying another bus, Bro. Joseph Damian founded the co-ed Notre Dame High School in Dadiangas (NDD) in 1954. It relieved the students from the arduous daily commute. (As of this writing,

Bro. Joseph Damian Teston is 99 years old and living in Bronx, New York after almost forty years of missionary work in the Philippines).

In 1956, the Notre Dame of Dadiangas co-ed high school was segregated into boys and girls departments as well. The NDD Boys High School moved to a new location one kilometer away. When I arrived, there were four Notre Dame campuses in General Santos City.

WEEKS BEFORE my first day of teaching, I prepared my lesson plans, visited the college a few times to familiarize myself with the lay of the land, and to pick up my mail. A stop at the Registrar's Office to get a list of my prospective students brought home an unforeseen inadequacy. Although I had gained more confidence speaking Tagalog, nothing prepared me for the challenge of a roll call. We were supposed to take attendance at the beginning of each class. A majority of the 300 names on my roster were Greek to me.

While some of the first names had a familiar ring to it (like Elizabeth Cruz), the surnames coupled with the first names in Spanish, Chinese, Arabic, Indian, Japanese, and Filipino were tongue twisters. As best I could, I practiced how to pronounce them before classes started: Haron Marohombsar, Zenaida Kinjiyo, Bienvenido Cajigas, Luzviminda Agoncillo, Zoraida Mamalumpong, Liwayway Ronquillo, etc.

July 7, 1969, marked my first day to teach in a foreign land. Bro. Henry Ruiz introduced me to the student body at the opening of the first semester. It was low-key compared to the welcome party for other volunteers. I heard stories circulated among volunteers of elaborate receptions that included a parade complete with a band, a welcome speech from the Mayor, Philippine folk dances, vocal renditions, etc. My reception at Notre Dame during assembly was without fanfare but heartfelt; the applause from the students was welcoming. At every assembly, my red hair stood out in a sea of black-haired people. Being almost a foot taller than most Filipinos, I could also see over their heads. I usually stayed at the back to avoid blocking their view.

Notre Dame of Dadiangas College specialized in Commerce and Business while the neighboring Notre Dame of Marbel College concentrated on education and the sciences during that time. As a temporary replacement for Mr. Leonardo Yu and Miss Vitaliana Cabatingan, who were pursuing their master's degrees, I taught Economics I and II for the first two semesters. My job also comprised planning a business curriculum, including some courses not offered.

Along with suggesting the coursework, I outlined what was to be covered in each class and prepared to teach said sessions. Curriculum planning was in two areas: 1) accounting and business administration, and 2) business education, including student teaching. The Peace Corps and NDEA had no prepared materials for me. It was my job to get the materials I needed and work on my own. In the third semester, I taught five new courses in six classes.

Economic Problems (50 students)	Economic Problems (48 students)
Economic Geography (28 students)	Business Organization (28 students)
Introduction to Business (28 students)	Audio-Visual Aids (11 students)

The college offered four-year degrees in Bachelor of Science in Education, Commerce, Elementary Education, and Liberal Arts as well as a couple of two-year associate degrees and a one-year Certificate of Secretarial Science. The college population was about 700 and was projected to double in a year or two. The campus had stand-alone buildings for the elementary and high school departments that were built in 1959.

Ten years before my arrival, the high school and the college departments shared the same building. Most college courses were offered in the evenings after the high school classes ended. Saturday classes were also held for college courses. Bro. Henry was transferred from Notre Dame Marbel to Dadiangas to oversee the construction of the new college building in 1967. It was completed in 1968 one year before I arrived.

Made of solid concrete, the new structure was strategically located on a campus of five acres covered with green grass and dotted with *camatchili* and pine trees. To the north stood the imposing Mt. Matutum. To the south, one could enjoy the sight of the often peaceful, sometimes-choppy blue waters of Sarangani Bay. The roofless fourth floor had two concrete cisterns designed to catch the rainwater to supply the college. Between the water tanks was a wide-open space for events where many Acquaintance Balls, Valentine's Day parties, Prom dances, and Christmas celebrations were held.

Before classes started, I cased the classrooms and found the one that I would be using for my first Economics I class on the third floor. A series of five glass louver windows roughly two feet wide by six feet tall allowed for natural lighting during the day and superb cross-ventilation. The windows afforded me an unobstructed view of the Sarangani Bay from the platform where I stood, a well-planned space conducive to learning and teaching. It reminded me of my first teaching post at Henry Hudson Regional High School in Atlantic Highlands, New Jersey. From the window of that school, I could see the ocean at Sandy Hook State Park nearby. I used to take my students there for beach picnics. We'd build human pyramids and sandcastles and play tug of war.

During my stay in the Philippines, I was never without my Bolsey 35mm brought from the USA, and later my Minolta SRT 101 camera bought in Hong Kong after my home leave. They were like a trusted friend sharing the joys that came from encounters with new experiences in exotic places and its inhabitants. As soon as the films were developed, a few choice images were dispatched to loved ones back in the States who eagerly looked forward to my regular reports from the developing country.

Some recipients submitted to the local newspapers a copy of the newsletter that I sent bi-annually. Friends and relatives who wrote back enclosed the clippings from the papers: "Local Teacher Is A Peace Corps Volunteer Abroad," "Brother of Northampton Man Serving in Peace Corps," "A Volunteer in Foreign Land," etc. It called to mind the time I was a college student religiously following the news about the novel and sometimes unsettling adventures of Peace Corps Volunteers. My newsletters effectively served their intended purpose, to share with folks back home a glimpse of the life of a Peace Corps Volunteer. P. David Searles noted in his book, "Letters home were avidly awaited by family and friends and taken to schools for 'show and tell' by younger siblings."[5]

In the Philippines, the medium of instruction starting from the first grade onward is English. I found that most Filipinos spoke English fluently. Or when they spoke Tagalog, each sentence is peppered with English from which, one with a rudimentary understanding of the language could easily discern the meaning. *"Punta tayo sa beach sa Saturday."* (Let's go to the beach on Saturday) or *"Mag snack na tayo"* (Let's have a snack). Taglish it was called.

During the semesters that I taught at Notre Dame College, I could have muddled through without learning Tagalog. The students from elementary to college were so eager to practice their English with a 'Kano (as in *Amerikano*). My being able to speak Tagalog became invaluable when I interacted with the folks in my community, at the post office, or the bakery, or when I traveled. I realized that more than just the ability to communicate with the locals in the market for *isda* (fish) or a hardware store for plywood, being able to speak Tagalog afforded me instant acceptance and smiles. They didn't have to verbalize it; I felt their appreciation. "Yes, you're one of us, thank you." Knowing how to speak Tagalog also came in handy when taxi drivers in Manila realized they could not take advantage of this foreigner.

THE FIRST two weeks at Notre Dame went like a flash. I felt good that I had not made a significant blunder with my roll call. When I mispronounced a name, the person usually waited until class was over to come to the rostrum to bring it to my attention. My Filipino students were very respectful, a bit timid, but receptive. Disciplinary issues were unheard of, unlike my first year of teaching at Henry Hudson Regional High School in New Jersey.

I believe every teacher has had his own Sidney Poitier moment at least once in his teaching career. In the movie *To Sir With Love*, Sidney Poitier, an Oscar award-winning American actor from Jamaica, played the role of Mark Thackery. He portrayed an immigrant, "...out-of-work engineer who takes a job teaching a group of undisciplined white students in the slums of London's East End."[6] His students tested his mettle at every turn. With patience and calm demeanor, he treated his students as adults and expected them to act like adults. In time, he gained their respect and love. They afforded him the highest title a teacher could appreciate. His students called him *Sir*, something they never bestowed upon any of their previous teachers.

I had my Sidney Poitier moment at Henry Hudson when I was twenty-one, the new teacher on the block fresh out of college. Henry Hudson Regional School district had upper-income students from Atlantic Highlands, whose parents were professionals, many commuting to New York City for work. Other students came from Highlands, whose parents were fishermen, laborers, etc. A few of them lagged behind in their studies; they were almost as old as I was.

One kid in my class, a husky six-foot-four senior and a member of the football team, was causing trouble. One day he challenged me to pick up my VW bug. We went to the parking lot where my VW was parked. I told him to go first. He lifted the back of the car (where the engine was located) a foot off the ground as though it was nothing. I watched how he did it. I put my back against the bumper, and using my legs, I lifted the car. After that incident, he stopped acting up in my class.

My goal for the first semester at Notre Dame College was to encourage everyone to speak up in class, participate in discussions, and to stay engaged. My students were at least two years younger than my college students at Churchman Business College at Easton, Pennsylvania, where I taught before joining the Peace Corps. In 1969, kindergarten classes were not mandatory in the Philippines, and pupils entered First Grade at age seven on average. Filipinos attend elementary school for six years, Primary Grades 1-4 and Elementary Grades 5-6. There were no 7th or 8th grades.

Instead, Filipino students entered four years of high school after sixth grade, placing a majority of my freshman students at sixteen years old. (The Enhanced Basic Education Act of 2013, also known as K-12 Law was signed into law by President Benigno Aquino III, son of Cory and the slain Benigno "Ninoy"

Aquino Jr., mandating the addition of 7th and 8th grades in all private and public schools in the Philippines).[7]

One afternoon, I noticed a slip of paper on the podium, listing four additional students. After the roll call, I called out their names: Norberto Caberoy, Carmen de los Reyes, Nicolas Galas, and Prima Guipo. The latter I pronounced as Prima (as in primary) and Gweepo. I knew I botched it the moment I noticed the suppressed but knowing smiles from the students in the front row.

After class, the person in question came to the rostrum and said politely, "Sir, my name is pronounced Preema, and the G-u-i-p-o is pronounced as in Gui-tar."

"Thank you. But I am rather confused. Are all four of you additional enrollees in my class?"

"No, Sir. Bro. Henry sent us to audit your class. Just to see if the students are connecting with you and vice versa. Mr. Caberoy, Ms. Delos Reyes, Sir Galas, and I, all of us agreed, so far so good," she assured me.

Teaching only Economics I and II for the first two semesters made preparation easy. However, having 300 students, roughly half the population of the whole school, was challenging to put it mildly. Soon afterward, I started to feel overwhelmed by teaching seven courses, with an average of forty-five students per class. I was putting in eight to ten hours of schoolwork a day.

Some days I left my classroom as late as 9:30 in the evening to accommodate the working students. Their school day did not begin until after 5:00 PM when they were let out from their respective workplaces. The college offered one-hour classes for them from 5:30 to 9:30 PM. Their areas of employment included banks, agri-businesses, the city hall, etc. I also taught on Saturday mornings and came in a few hours on Sunday. How was I going to deal with checking quizzes and exams, grading homework, reading up on my lesson plans, and still continue to teach effectively?

Although the college had an excellent library, it had a glaring handicap. There were no textbooks. All exams must be typewritten and sent to the Registrar's Office to be mimeographed. A semester had three grading periods, and report cards must be distributed to the students after each grading period. Before I went to the Philippines, I taught a maximum of four courses per semester, with no more than twenty students in each class.

In the second week, I decided something had to be done. I explained my predicament to Bro. Henry. He listened and assured me that he would look into finding me a teaching assistant (TA). He had just the right person in mind. I told him that I needed help for at least five hours or so a week. I was willing to pay a weekly sum in pesos out of my pocket equivalent to minimum wage. Two days later, Bro. Henry formally introduced me to Prima Guipo. She was the same person who audited my class, the same person who had been handing me my mail since the day I arrived, the same person who occupied the secretary's desk by the door of the director's office. Prima was not only an excellent teacher's assistant; she also straightened any remaining misconceptions I had about the local customs and traditions and helped me with my roll call.

Prima was a junior in college pursuing Economics as a major and English as a minor. An associate editor then editor of the college paper and yearbook since her freshman year, she finished a one-year Certificate of Secretarial Science with highest honors.

Bro. Henry promptly "hired" her as his secretary on a work-study program. Accorded the pedestrian title "Working Students," these industrious ladies and gentlemen functioned as a vital academic support team. (Most of them would later become hugely successful. They held influential positions in government as well as the business sectors, attended and worked for Ivy League Schools in the U.S., are professors at top-notch universities in Manila, and excel in their careers domestically and abroad).

Their presence in all of the administrative offices was highly visible - the Registrar and Bursar's Office, the Offices of the Deans, the library, the Book Room, etc. The Book Room was an exciting place; among its functions was to rehabilitate old books that were falling apart. Books were treasured commodities. Notre Dame College probably had the best library in the city, but we had no textbooks available. As well, the library was in short supply of books for children and beginner readers.

Whatever administrative help we need as faculty members, we could depend on the working students to assist us or find someone who could. They worked unpaid, but they received free tuition. Prima's case was unique because she was one of the fifteen students on a merit scholarship. Bro. Henry gave her an allowance as extra compensation, which, according to Prima, he took out of his petty cash. I doubt if Mrs. Loretta Sevilla, the Bursar, was any the wiser.

Prima's three older siblings, one cousin, an aunt, and two uncles, also taught at the college. On Prima's nineteenth birthday, I was invited to a party at the Guipo's house in Lagao. It was about three miles from my home. In the Philippines, it was customary for the celebrant to throw a party on his or her birthday. It was my first birthday invitation in the Philippines.

There were only two *jeepneys* that serviced the route going to the Guipo's house during that time. But it was a close-knit town where everybody still knew everybody. The *jeepney* drivers delivered the passenger at his doorstep, and on occasion, would pick up and wait for a tardy passenger while she bathed, got dressed, or put on her make-up. I gave the name of my destination to the jeepney driver. He deposited me right in front of the main gate. As it turned out, Prima invited a few of my students, some faculty members at the college, and most of the working students. After dinner, a sing-along ensued of the popular songs of the time. Accompanied by guitar, *bandoria* (twelve-stringed guitar), and harmonica, everyone harmonized my favorite songs by the Kingston Trio, The Brothers Four, Peter, Paul & Mary, and Joan Baez, etc.

I gave Prima a pink piggy bank from Ram's Bombay Bazaar for her ceramic collection. It was in honor of Frisian, a remarkably toilet trained pet pig that slept inside the Guipo's house or the porch but relieved itself in the yard. Named Frisian after a brand of milk it loved to drink, "she" identified with the pet dogs and cats and romped with them. Filipinos inherited from the Chinese culture the belief that a pig was a symbol of wealth, and brought good luck.

MY ADOPTED hometown celebrated its first year of cityhood on September 5, 1969, four months after I arrived. All government offices were closed as well as the schools. All of the four Notre Dame Schools in the city participated in the event as well as a few other private schools. The students, the faculty, and the bands marched in the parade. There were floats sponsored by local businesses, civic organizations, and schools. They were mostly decorated with live flowers and plants. I watched the Notre Dame Band in their full marching regalia of khaki pants striped with green on both sides and matching polo shirts. They played John Phillip Sousa's Military Marches, the Stars and Stripes, and the Notre Dame Fight Song.

Three days later, on September 8, the college celebrated Notre Dame Day, the feast of Mary. Three hundred years of Spanish rule converted the Philippines into a predominantly Roman Catholic country. Every hamlet, barrio, town, or city had a patron saint. Every patron saint's birthday was celebrated with a *fiesta* (religious festival). The Filipinos loved their *fiestas* and would save their money to lavishly celebrate the occasion. Notre Dame Day stretched into a weeklong celebration dubbed, *The College Week*. It was marked with inter-departmental competitions – debates, scrabble and chess tournaments, essay writing and cheerleading contests, basketball, baseball, volleyball and track competitions, and a beauty contest with a twist. Not only was the beauty contestant chosen for her poise, good looks, and pleasing personality, she must also be able to raise the most amount of money to win.

The Dadiangas parish church, Our Lady of Peace and Good Voyage, was building one of the first and biggest civic centers in the city. It was a dream project of Fr. Albinus Lesch. Even before the construction was completed, the center hosted basketball tournaments, college graduations, fiestas, social and cultural events, and weddings. The Student Council of Notre Dame College voted to earmark the profit from the beauty contest fund-raising project to finish the Parish Center. Usually, the beauty contestants were picked from affluent families who used their own money to bankroll the competition.

The Commerce Department chose Miss Emie dela Cerna as our contestant. The daughter of the owner of the Dela Cerna Music Store, Emie, was pretty, smart, amiable, and a stylish dresser who could sing also. To raise money, the students and teachers from each department sold raffle tickets to prominent people in the city, to local businesses, family, and friends. Mrs. Kaiser, an accountant who was an advisor in the Commerce Department to which I belonged, deputized me to be her assistant chair for fund-raising. We went door to door to ask her clients and friends in the city to donate toward our cause. My involvement in this project led me to Fr. Albinus' circle. I also met the assistant parish priest Fr. James.

During the feast of the Our Lady of Peace and Good Voyage patron saint, another beauty contest was held. Emie won as the First Princess.

SURROUNDED by mountains, General Santos was protected from typhoons. In the morning, the breeze from Mt. Matutum fanned the city, and in the afternoon, the Sarangani Bay provided natural ventilation. Seldom did it get oppressively hot in General Santos, while it was a regular occurrence at other towns like Marbel. Located inland, Marbel sat in a valley trapping the heat within the walls of the mountains that surrounded it. My fellow volunteers who were teaching at Notre Dame of Marbel College often complained about the humidity and the heat. We experienced the same in General Santos City, but not as often.

One hot and humid evening, a swarm of stinkbugs came out of hibernation. A thick mass of them invaded all the classrooms, including my night class, buzzing and flying about in circles. I was afraid to open my mouth for fear they'd fill the cavity. I turned the lights off. But we could still hear the whir of their wings and feel them creepily hit every exposed portion of our bodies from every direction. When I turned the lights back on, we saw many of them lay dead or dying on the floor. But as many as there were dead bugs, many more flew in through the unscreened windows and doors. I told my students to gather their belongings and leave the classroom. As we exited, we heard the crunch, crunch of dead bugs beneath our feet. It was gross and messy. Classes were suspended that night.

There were two other occasions I could remember when classes were closed prematurely and unscheduled. One night, the building built of solid concrete creaked and trembled.

"*Lindol!*" Someone screamed. (Earthquake!)

My whole classroom emptied, as did the other classes. Everyone rushed out of the building. We stood outside for a while, waiting for the earthquake to abate. We could feel the earth's tremor. We did not go back inside the building. Along with the other professors, I sent my students home. Bro. Henry noted to me the following morning that the building was designed with a wide staircase to allow students to evacuate as fast as they possibly could for just such an emergency.

Another time, Notre Dame College closed because some students staged a strike. A few years before President Ferdinand Marcos declared Martial Law on September 23, 1972, student unrest was brewing in the capital city of Manila and other

large cities. It later erupted into violence during the Battle of
Mendiola Street in Manila, a clash between the military and the
student protestors that left four students dead. The Mendiola
incident was the beginning of the student demonstrations
that escalated and was used as one of the justifications for the
Declaration of Martial Law.

Student protests were unheard of in the small towns like
General Santos. However, Notre Dame of Dadiangas College
experienced student activism on campus, led by a charismatic
student leader Ely Manalo. He was expelled from Notre Dame
for committing an infraction listed in the Student's Handbook.
About fifty students marched from downtown to the front gate
of Notre Dame, shouting "Down with America" and displayed
their protests on placards they carried with them. Although
there were some of our students in the group, most of the
demonstrators were friends and admirers of Mr. Manalo from
two other local colleges. They disrupted classes. Bro. Henry
relayed messages to every classroom advising the teachers to
keep their students inside the college campus until after the
demonstrators had left. The noise was so loud we could not
resume classes. Bro. Henry declared the closing of the school
for the day.

Bro. Sam invited Mr. Manalo inside his office and listened to
his grievances. Bro. Sam was a slight, soft-spoken math genius
and the very empathetic Dean of Men. The demonstrators
dispersed after Bro. Sam promised Mr. Manalo that an
arbitration committee would be assembled to hear the side of
the aggrieved party and to discuss their demands. Some of
their demands were rather trivial. Others were quite serious.
"No Classes on College Week," "Reinstate Ely Manalo As
President of Student Council," one of the placards they carried
read, "Embrace Communism," etc.

I took quite a few slides to chronicle the aberration. Mr.
Manalo, a brilliant kid, handsome, and taller than the average
Filipino, was in one of my Economics classes. Bro. Sam asked

me to be a member of the arbitration panel. At an appointed date, we met with Mr. Manalo and the members of the arbitration panel at the City Hall. Mr. Manalo was allowed to re-enroll after he signed an agreement not to cause any more disturbances at the college. But he never came back. He went to school somewhere else.

THANKSGIVING soon came, a special holiday for Americans but just another ordinary day in the Philippines. I taught classes the entire day. I am not one to succumb to loneliness easily, priding myself at being able to enjoy my own company and find my way out of the doldrums with relative ease. Put me on a solo canoe to paddle for hours down a river or tent camping in the wilderness with just the critters, the sun, the moon, and stars, and I'd be content. But the first Thanksgiving away from home really hit me hard. On my way home from class the Wednesday before the holiday, I saw Mang Carling, the man Friday for the Marist Brothers, carrying a live turkey.

I was sure there was soon to be a table laden with a Thanksgiving dinner somewhere, but I wouldn't be one of the guests. I was home alone. It was one of the most depressing days of my Peace Corps stint, made even worse when I later found out that all my Peace Corps friends in Marbel spent Thanksgiving with the Wycliffe Ladies in Sinolon and enjoyed an oven-roasted turkey with all the fixings.

One of the Guipo sisters, Susan, loved to bake. She invited me to bake cookies and pretzels at their house after Thanksgiving just before my birthday. The wood-fired oven that their father hand-made had a broken thermostat. We had to guess at the temperature and burned a lot of the cookies that we baked! Our pretzel was not perfect but edible. It was a special birthday treat.

Some of my fellow teachers and students got wind of my twenty-sixth birthday. I received store-bought cards and many handmade ones. I came home from class feeling rather low, missing home, and the usual cake and ice cream that my mom or sister usually prepared for the occasion.

I had just removed my tie when I heard the bark of my landlord's dog. There was shuffling of feet outside my door, followed by a tentative, soft strum of guitars. Then a chorus of voices in two-part harmony sang one of my favorite songs in Tagalog, "*Dahil sa Iyo, nais kong mabuhay...*" (Because of you, there is joy in living). I opened the glass-louvered window and saw a dozen or so of my students serenading me. Prima and her two brothers Tito and Felipe, were among them.

In the Philippines, *Mañanita* is a custom of serenading a birthday celebrant as a surprise present. It is usually conducted at early dawn (derived from the Spanish word *"mañanita,"* meaning early morning). But since most of my serenaders did not live nearby or had to attend classes, they did it during their afternoon break.

Adapting the Philippine custom for the birthday celebrant to throw a "blowout" (Filipino term for to treat friends to a party), I invited everyone to Talion's Refreshment Parlor located downtown, a few blocks from my house. Appreciative and feeling benevolent, I spent half of my month's allowance on ice cream, cookies, and soft drinks. We walked back toward my home, singing the popular songs of the time.

At the corner of Roxas and Marist Drive, my students headed toward the college. I retraced my steps home to Champaca Street. Although I spent the evening alone, it was one of the happiest and most memorable birthdays I could remember.

CHRISTMAS 1969 was my first away from home. I had high hopes of spending my two-week Christmas vacation in Manila. David Hsu and I looked forward to playing tourist in the biggest city in the Philippines. I had planned to meet up with David at the airport in Manila to celebrate our first traditional Filipino Christmas holiday in our host country with our language instructor and her friends. But it rained all week in General Santos before and until Christmas. It did not let up. The Buayan airport was closed, and all the flights were canceled. David made it from his host town Cotabato City to Manila without me and spent his holiday as we had arranged.

Having no contingency plans, I spent my first Christmas in the Philippines on Champaca Street. Always thoughtful and maternal, Mrs. Oliveros sent someone to knock on my door at midnight to join them for *Noche Buena*, a holiday custom in the Philippines. It is a very festive dinner served after midnight mass on Christmas Eve. I was feeling so low; I didn't want to dampen the mood of the other guests. I did not answer the door. It was my first Christmas away from Bethlehem, Pennsylvania, and family, and I was alone.

On New Year's Eve, with the airport still closed, nowhere to go, and still feeling miserable about missing a proper Thanksgiving and a Christmas in Manila, I took a *jeepney* and arrived at the Guipo's six-bedroom house. The family of ten plus an elderly aunt Eyay Eya was getting ready to sit down for supper. There was a case of San Miguel beer on the floor next to the dining table. Nena and Angelo had just come home from the U.S. and Ireland, respectively, so the family was complete for the first time in years. The New Year was a cause for a family celebration.

Mrs. Guipo raised turkeys and fattened them up for the holidays. Nena prepared an American dinner of roasted turkey, mashed potatoes, steamed green beans, and all the fixings plus the exceptional Filipino food traditionally served on holidays. It was topped with San Miguel beer. Mr. Guipo gave all his children, five girls, and three boys, the license to drink beer as long as they drank at home. For some of the girls, it was their first time to taste the beer. Prima got tipsy. Nena also showed slides of her U.S. trip as a 4-H Club International Exchange Scholar, followed by a sing-along. The merrymaking, including the firing up a homemade bamboo cannon (a good substitute for firecrackers), lasted till late at night. There was no more transportation to go back to Dadiangas. The family accommodated me overnight. My letter to my family described a novel Christmas experience, one that was so different from what I was used to:

Let me share a little about Christmas in the Philippines. Here Christmas starts very early. By the end of November, kids are making and testing out their bamboo cannons. They hollow out a bamboo tube about six-feet long and four inches in circumference, place a hole on one end, erect it on a stand, and there is the cannon. The kids pour kerosene in the hole and then light it with a stick. When the kerosene lights inside the tube, it causes combustion, and the result is a big bang and a blue flame out of the front end. Some little boys will spend their last ten centavos for kerosene.

Before the middle of December, folks will come "serenading" with Christmas Carols. Traditionally, a group of adults does it to raise money for a cause. But groups of five-year-old kids and teenagers do it to earn extra money. Caroling may last until the first week of January (Filipinos celebrate the holidays until the Feast of the Three Kings). It makes me smile when I hear little kids sing at the top of their voices, "Dashing through the snow..." in eighty-degree heat.

Everybody spends most of his or her money for the holiday season. Kids get gifts and money from their godparents, mostly. Santa Claus exists in pictures but not in legend. There is no telling a kid to be good, so Santa will come. Gifts are given at any time before or after December 25. There is no big surprise on Christmas morning. In school, the students partake in Kris Kringle's custom of exchanging gifts.

"Simbang Gabi," also called Misa de Gallo in Spanish term, is a Filipino tradition of attending mass at the break of dawn from December 16 until December 25. The Notre Dame High School band is transported in a cattle truck around town at 3 AM to awaken the parishioners with Christmas carols, so they attend these masses at 4 AM. Usually, a merienda (snack) is served after mass. Some meriendas are simple with pan de sal and coffee. Still, some are elaborate serving Arroz Caldo (hot rice soup) and other Filipino rice

delicacies such as suman, puto, bibingka, etc. On Christmas Eve, everyone attends midnight mass at the Catholic Church. After mass, the family gets together for as big a party as they could afford.

For the wealthy, there's always the lechon (roasted whole pig). On Christmas Day, the serving of special foods continues. People usually visit friends, neighbors, and relatives, giving gifts if due and eating something at each home. There are not the traditional Christmas cookies, but they do have special native delicacies for holidays that are served to all. The Christmas decorations are many and varied. If the house has electricity, there is sure to be a set of colored lights. Some have Christmas trees, although seldom a pine tree, they are limited only by one's imagination. Some use mangrove branches decorated with imitation snow using cotton balls or soap sods that were beaten till the sods hardened. At the college, students exchange Christmas cards. I received quite a lot, mostly hand made from creatively repurposed old cards.

In the middle of December, the kids have perfected their bamboo cannons. They continue shooting until the first weekend of January. By now, the store-bought firecrackers are joining the bamboo cannons. By six o'clock New Year's Eve, the noise becomes unbearable. At midnight, it sounds like the world is ending. Of course, firecrackers would not keep until next year, so the next day or two, the noise continues at a mild rumble. Peace, Alvin

AT THE College, my students often asked me for the stamps on my correspondence from the U.S. Many of them had pen pals. On my behest, they organized a Stamp Collecting Club and bartered stamps among them. Every time I wrote to my family and friends abroad, I'd send out a plea for them to cut the postage off their envelopes and enclose them in their letters. My dad was a collector and the biggest supplier. He'd cut the stamps from the envelope, making sure he allowed a fraction of an inch around the postage keeping the perforations intact. Thus increasing the value of the stamp. I wrote to my sister: *I would like to make one more request if it is not too much trouble. Next time you go to the post office, please ask for commemorative stamps and stamps of different values totaling 25 cents. Then, use them for the letters you send me. I give the stamps to friends, teachers, and students, and they really are happy to get stamps that are different.*

In my first newsletter, I sent another request. *Many of my students here have requested pen pals. If you have any friends or students interested in corresponding with a pen pal from the Philippines, please send me their name, address, age, desire for a pen pal – boy or girl – and I will find someone to write them.*

The ladies were not allowed to wear their uniforms above the knee while on campus during the height of the miniskirt fad. The previous Dean of Women took out the hem of the skirts of those who broke the rule against exposing their knees. The new Dean, Sr. Antonia Falgui, was not quite as severe.

During the college parties, however, the girls wore the fad of the moment, long flowing black hair, bell-bottomed pants, miniskirts, etc. I was quite amazed that the teenagers in the Philippines were just as conversant with western fashion, musical bands, rock groups, and movies from Hollywood as the teenagers in the United States.

The students in the Philippines addressed their teachers as "Ma'am" (pronounced like mum), and "Sir" all the time. When I came home to the U.S. after my Peace Corps service, my brother Dean offered for me to live in his house. I stayed for a whole year.

One day, I told my brother that my former students at Notre Dame still kept in touch with me, and when they wrote, they continued to address me as "Sir Al."

My brother said quite amused, "What's this about the Sir Al thing. Did they bestow knighthood in the Philippines?"

No, they didn't, but they did one better. Sir Al in the Philippines almost had a ring of endearment to it. To this day, my former students at Notre Dame still call me Sir Al.

Old habits die hard like the Notre Dame spirit.

Prima's birthday (behind me with guitar). The first birthday party I attended in the Philippines. To my right is Eyay Eya, a remarkable aunt not quite four feet tall who was a *Yaya* (nanny) to most of the eight Guipo children.

It was quite extraordinary that three of the Guipo siblings were my co-teachers as well as cousin Victorio, and uncles and aunt (not in the picture), Raymundo Asencio, and Atty. Johnny Asencio and his wife, Mercy.
Courtesy of VOX Notre Dame Yearbook 1970 & Ruben Tugari, Alumni Coordinator

Bro. Sam Geveso, Dean of Men, holds a sign after the students' strike .

Princess Emie and the Jorge dela Cerna family with Fr. Albinus, Mrs. Kaiser, and Author.

The student leaders requested me to help organize an International Night event. The guests dressed up in costumes from around the world. We had international representation from our students and faculty whose families came from India, Japan, Saudi Arabia, China, the U.S., and Australia. My student Roberto Borromeo is next to me (front), his story is in Postscript: Fifty Years Later at the end of the book.

When It Rains It Floods 6

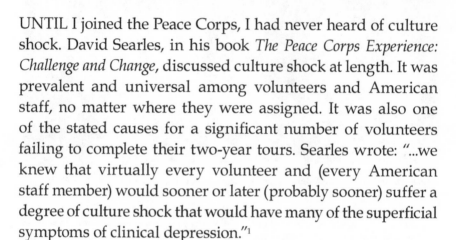

UNTIL I joined the Peace Corps, I had never heard of culture shock. David Searles, in his book *The Peace Corps Experience: Challenge and Change*, discussed culture shock at length. It was prevalent and universal among volunteers and American staff, no matter where they were assigned. It was also one of the stated causes for a significant number of volunteers failing to complete their two-year tours. Searles wrote: "...we knew that virtually every volunteer and (every American staff member) would sooner or later (probably sooner) suffer a degree of culture shock that would have many of the superficial symptoms of clinical depression."[1]

It was a culture shock that I experienced in Cotabato City that almost caused me to quit the Peace Corps and go home only five days after arriving in the Philippines. Searles continued, "The difference between the two is that clinical depression requires chemical or psychiatric treatment, whereas culture shock can be 'cured' simply by having a good day."[2] Case in point, I recovered quickly from that particular culture shock after spending a weekend on Bongo Island and finding the inspiration to stay – a little Muslim boy with his tugboat. Searles further pointed out that culture shock can recur many times. "The intensity of the affliction varied depending on such factors as age, previous experiences, job quality, and how one dealt with loneliness and making new friends."[3]

The year 1970 put me through an emotional wringer, the likes of which I hope never to see again. When I look back now, I realize that I survived the year only after I had learned valuable lessons on how to deal with loneliness. Keeping myself busy, knowing my limitations, and recognizing the trigger points and to avoid them when I could. Talking to friends and leaving my post for a few days of vacation worked effectively for me.

Mike Tidwell, the author of the acclaimed Peace Corps memoir *The Ponds of Kalambayi*, shared his experience in Zaire, formerly the Belgian Congo in Africa. Tidwell narrated the instance his Peace Corps boss asked him to extend for a third year. The boss wanted him to continue his success in providing protein-rich tilapia to a malnourished population by building fishponds on the ponds of Kalambayi. He was torn between staying and leaving. In the end, he decided to go home after two years. He wrote, "I was afraid of what living in Kalambayi was doing to me. I was afraid I was drinking too much."[4] Tidwell was referring to the local village-brewed moonshine called *tshitshampa*.

George Packard, a Peace Corps Volunteer in Togo, West Africa, wrote about the despondency, isolation, and the constant exposure to his villagers dying in *The Village of Waiting*.[5] He went home just short of completing his two-year contract.

Writing for me was a panacea. During one of the lowest points in my life, I wrote, *"When the whole world seems to cop-out, you can always sit down and write to somebody, even if that somebody has to be yourself."* Thankfully, I had an incredible support system in my dad, my sister Joyce, and brothers Bud and Dean; I only wrote to myself once. I don't know what I would have done if I didn't have them to unburden myself, albeit through letters. I could only wish we had email or cell phones back then.

It was a somber Notre Dame campus I walked into when the school opened shortly after New Year's Day in 1970. Terrible news rocked the college. One of our students, Diana Lin Salazar, died in a car accident. She was a beautiful and charming nineteen-year-old senior, a popular student leader, and a friendly scholar. I found out from club members that Diana Lin had expressed interest in joining the Stamp Collecting Club that the students and I organized. The college held the annual Valentine's Day celebration and honored her memory as the Valentine's Queen the year before. Filipinos are very resilient. Classes resumed as usual, following a period of mourning.

After the holidays, I picked up where we left off at the Provincial Jail. I revived interest among the prisoners, an enterprise we started in September - handcrafting wooden puzzles for children. Using my own Peace Corps allowance, I bought the tools and the materials to get us started. I made some prototypes and gave them as Christmas gifts to test the product. The Santos kids (grandchildren of my host) enjoyed playing with them, which was encouraging. I suspended the project at the jail in November because the inmates were busy making *parols* (Christmas lanterns). With the holidays over, I hoped that the prisoners would take more interest in learning a skill and earn some money in the process. *Parol* making was a lucrative venture at the jail. If we could be half as successful with the puzzle project, I'd consider it an accomplishment.

My weekends were occupied with helping Mr. & Mrs. Kaiser prepare the chicken coops for the arrival of the chicks ordered from Davao City. We were running a month behind schedule with Mrs. Kaiser having been ill off and on since the New Year. I met Mrs. Kaiser at the opening of classes at Notre Dame College the previous July, and we became great friends. She was like an older sister to me.

There were four departments in the college at that time, namely Liberal Arts, Education, Elementary Education, and Commerce. Mrs. Kaiser and I belonged to the latter. She was the advisor for Commerce 2-3-4 (Women); I was the advisor for Commerce 1 (Men). Mrs. Kaiser married her pen pal from Germany. They had been married for two years and decided to live in the Philippines.

Mrs. Kaiser's husband had invested his money in a taxi business in Manila when he came to the Philippines. Then he opened a branch in Cebu. When the company was turned over to Mrs. Kaiser's father, the couple moved to General Santos City. Mrs. Kaiser found a teaching job at Notre Dame College, and her husband worked for Dole Philippines as a mechanical engineer. Mrs. Kaiser was an accountant. She was also a partner of a CPA firm with two other faculty members at the college, Mr. Fortunato de la Cruz and Mr. Rodolfo Maulino. Her partners belonged to the Commerce Department also. On weekends they invited me on their trips to see their clients as far away as Malapatan and Glan, where I explored the neighboring countryside and barrios.

One day Mrs. Kaiser and I were in the faculty room, along with a few other instructors waiting for our classes. Someone asked where I came from. I mentioned that I grew up on a farm in Bethlehem, Pennsylvania.

"My father started as a dairy farmer but later switched to poultry," I said.

"You are just the person I should be talking to," Mrs. Kaiser said. "My husband and I would like to start a poultry business. We own a piece of land in Apopong just outside the city. Would you help us?"

I was happy to oblige. At our eighty-two acre farm in Pennsylvania, we raised chickens for eggs. At the height of my father's poultry business, we had more than 6,000 laying hens. The eggs, gathered twice daily, were sold mainly at our farmhouse. Small grocers, bakers, restaurant owners, and other customers would pick up at our farmhouse, and whatever remained was taken to the Lehigh Valley Egg Co-op. My dad was the Co-op president for many years. One of our notable customers was the Four Chefs Restaurant in Allentown, Pennsylvania. The original owner was an uncle of Lee Iacocca, the CEO of Ford Motors, who transferred to GM and brought

Chrysler back to life and fame. My brother Bud worked at the Four Chefs Restaurant.

The Kaisers decided to raise fryers for meat and a few for eggs for family consumption. Going to the farm was a welcomed respite from my hectic schedule at the college. The land was readied. The chicken coops were built. The formulas and feeding schedules were planned and discussed with the relatives who were living on the farm. Everyone was on the same page. By the beginning of March, 400 chicks were delivered to the Kaiser's Farm.

In the U.S., it took about seven to nine weeks to grow fryers ready to butcher. Ideally, they would weigh three to five pounds or approximately two and a half kilos. We calculated that in two months or so, the fryers would be suitable to sell. Mrs. Kaiser's partners at the CPA firm, Mr. Maulino, Mr. de la Cruz, and I went to the farm to welcome Mrs. Kaiser's chicks.

Soon after the 400 chicks were delivered at the Kaiser farm, another disheartening news spread on campus. Mr. Nicolas Galas was hospitalized. A very amiable man in his early fifties, Mr. Galas, the English, and Sociology professor, was distinguished for his wisdom and experience. He had been teaching at the college for many years before I arrived. Often, the younger instructors sought his advice on the professional as well as personal level. Sometimes garrulous but often philosophical, he enjoyed a good conversation. Learning of my penchant for collecting Filipiniana handicrafts, he gave me animal horns to add to my collection – horns from deer, wild pig, and *carabao* (water buffalo). Some came from his farm in Banga, South Cotabato. I displayed them on my wall.

A fascinating man, Mr. Nicolas Galas, was born in Currimao, Ilocos Norte, on the island of Luzon.[6] He spent all his childhood in Currimao along the South China Sea. His family belonged to the landed gentry. His uncles, cousins, and relatives were the first recruits of the Americans who were sent to Hawaii to work in the sugar and pineapple plantations. Nicolas' father, however, "refused the allure of leaving", wrote his son George, and focused on his tobacco and garlic plantation instead.

Nicolas was sent to the best schools and studied Law at the University of Sto. Tomas. However, World War II interrupted his studies. He joined the USAFFE (United States Army Forces in the Far East). He fought side by side with the Americans in the mountains of Northern Luzon. "During the lull in the battle, my father Nicolas found time to marry his girlfriend, Maria Estanislao, a nursing student then at the Manila Central University," George added. Nicolas finished his law degree in 1947 but failed the bar exams. He migrated to Mindanao as one of the pioneering officers of the LASEDECO (Land Settlement Development Corporation). LASEDECO was tasked to distribute land for the landless settlers in Cotabato.

The week before he was taken to the hospital, Mr. Galas and I were in the faculty room waiting for our classes to start. He proudly informed me about the prolific blooms of his red bougainvillea shrubs, overgrown, and in need of a trim. Mr. Galas went to class one day. I observed that he had difficulty moving his jaw. His students noticed he was slurring his speech in the classroom. He was taken to the hospital, but it was too late. On March 4, 1970, he died of tetanus, leaving a wife and ten children. The doctors suspected that he might have contracted the fatal disease while working in his yard.

A MONTH later, Mrs. Kaiser summoned me to take her to the doctor. A wave of apprehension instantly engulfed me. I knew that she would only go to the doctor when she was in intense pain. I stepped inside the door of the apartment she shared with her husband and her fourteen-month-old baby. I saw her, and I was deeply concerned. During that period of my life, my dad lived in Tampa, Florida. My sister and two brothers stayed in Pennsylvania. They were my faithful sounding boards and the regular recipients of my dear diary kind of correspondence. They passed my letters around, so I didn't have to worry about duplicating the subject matter. The series of letters I wrote to them helped me to unburden the emotionally concerning events of the year 1970.

April 30, 1970
Dear Joyce, Earl and all,
There is so much to write about I do not know where to begin. Maybe it would be best to say that I am doing fine and as usual very busy. School for the second semester in the Philippines is over. I can't believe I have completed a whole year of teaching.

I am in Manila on vacation now. I'll tell you more about my vacation later, but I want to tell you about Mrs. Kaiser. I wrote about the deaths of our student in January and our fellow teacher Mr. Galas in March. I also wrote about Mrs. Kaiser before when I first met her. She was so thoughtful she even sent a Christmas card to Dad and received one from Dad in return.

Early in our meeting, she told me that she and her husband were planning to start a poultry business. Mrs. Kaiser wanted to provide a means of livelihood for her poor distant relatives in the barrio. One of them is a polio survivor without education and will be hard-pressed to find a job. Our friendship started as advisors at the Commerce Department. It deepened when I offered to help her and her husband start a poultry business. We worked together at their farm on weekends. I got to know her husband too, who is from Germany.

Mrs. Kaiser has been sick off and on since the beginning of the year. Sometimes she goes to the doctor for medicine, but she told me that she usually does not follow the doctor's orders. Several times the doctor told her to get a shot every day for three days straight. However, she would only go when sickness was so bad that she could not stand the pain. This is somewhat typical of Filipinos. Even those with excellent insurance coverage from their workplaces will forego an annual executive check-up provided free by their companies. They would wait until they are really sick to see a doctor.

On Sunday morning, April 19, Mrs. Kaiser sent for me. I took her to the doctor while her husband took care of the baby. After examining her, the doctor asked Mrs. Kaiser to stay in the waiting room. He then asked me to step into his office and said there was nothing he could do for Mrs. Kaiser. She was suffering from uremia.

I was shocked to hear that and began asking questions. The doctor described her condition as follows: two years ago, Mrs. Kaiser had a kidney infection. At that time, the doctor told her to come every day for treatment. She saw her doctor then stopped coming. In the meantime, her kidneys got worse. Gradually the kidneys stopped functioning. The poison normally filtered by the kidneys remained in her blood. This caused additional complications of anemia and high blood pressure. The doctor said it would be only a matter of time before the poison in the blood killed her. After more questioning, I learned about some possibilities of help available in Manila: 1) dialysis (filtering the blood) with a machine or 2) a kidney transplant.

Armed with this information, I went first to Mr. Kaiser and told him of the seriousness of Mrs. Kaiser's condition. Then I told Mrs. Kaiser that the doctor recommended she see a specialist in Manila. She decided to go first to Cebu City to take her fourteen-month-old baby to her parents so her husband can continue working at Dole. Since I was going to Manila for my much-needed vacation anyway, I offered to accompany Mrs. Kaiser to Cebu. I was already packed. In an hour, we were on the way to the airport and got her ticket there. The trip was rather exhausting for Mrs. Kaiser. She had very little sleep and very little to eat for nearly a week because she was so sick. Combining that with her weakened condition from the disease made it so that she practically had to be carried most of the way.

Going to Cebu City, it is necessary to change planes in Davao City. There was one young American man sitting in the General Santos airport with a Filipina girl. This couple boarded the same flight too. I saw them while waiting for our plane in Davao. Since Mrs. Kaiser could barely walk by this time, I needed to find someone to carry the baby. I found out that the couple was also going to Cebu. I asked if they could help. They were glad to take care of the baby. Mrs. Kaiser's family met us at the airport in Cebu, and she was taken straight to the hospital.

David Hsu (Peace Corps friend in Cotabato City) and I were initially scheduled to go to Manila on April 22. I was in Cebu with Mrs. Kaiser's family. I did not leave until April 23. By coincidence, David also arrived in Manila on the same day. Our language instructor from our training in Hawaii met us at the airport. David was with her and her friends last Christmas when my flight was canceled, and I had to spend the holiday alone in my little house. Our hosts here in Manila are all Filipinos teaching at the University of the East. It is a group of men and ladies that are still single who travel around together. We had a good time in Manila. Most of the time, we stuck around the city and explored. Our language instructor had graduate classes to attend every day, so we could not take long excursions.

While in Manila, David and I stayed at a boarding house near the University of the East. The group we traveled around with is a fun-loving bunch of "kids" ages twenty-five to thirty-two. We had three parties and one night we went to a nightclub. It's not my thing, but it was a novel experience for me. I live a quiet life in General Santos - to experience something new in the big city was a welcomed change of pace. Another night we strolled around Fort Santiago and Luneta Park as a group. During the day we went to a couple of movies and did some shopping. It is sweltering in Manila. The air-conditioned stores and theatres are welcomed respite. We also went on an excursion to the Province of Laguna, about forty miles south of Manila. We hiked to an area overlooking Laguna Lake. The lake was really pretty from a distance. The water was sparkling green as the lake was nestled in the mountains.

May 2, 1970, Saturday

I am back in Cebu City again. I had to cut my vacation short. Yesterday morning I received a telegram that Mrs. Kaiser was in serious condition. Last night I got a night mercury flight back to Cebu from Manila. The latest word is that Mrs. Kaiser had peritoneal dialysis on Tuesday of this week. On Thursday, she was unconscious, and her heart stopped beating for a while. Mrs. Kaiser has regained consciousness, but her body is filling up with fluids and not passing very much urine. She knows I am here. We are still able to communicate. She asked for pancit canton (noodles dish with meat and vegetables sautéed together). She didn't eat much. It appears that the end of Mrs. Kaiser's life is near in sight. There is nothing left for us to do except to pray.

According to the doctors here, there is no use going to Manila. The dialysis using a machine is no better than the one performed here without the device. Filtering the blood does not cure the disease. It is a very temporary measure that cleans the poisons out but only lasts a few days or weeks until the toxins fill up in the blood again. The kidney transplant is a risky operation and still experimental in nature. It would mean a brother or sister would have to give up one of their kidneys to Mrs. Kaiser or find a donor of a perfect match. The operation would have to be executed in Manila by specialists.

If the surgery were performed, it would endanger the donor's life. If Mrs. Kaiser were to get a new kidney, her chances of living are very slim. Even if she does live, it would only be for a couple of years. Considering all the things plus the high cost, the family decided to leave Mrs. Kaiser here in Cebu in the hospital. At least here in Cebu, the family can visit Mrs. Kaiser. Her husband also arrived last night from General Santos. He was sleeping, so I have not talked to him yet. We are both staying at the house of Mrs. Kaiser's parents.

An important cultural note: In the Philippines, medical treatment is not as sophisticated or technically advanced as in the U.S. It is a lot more concerned with the human aspect. The doctors have taken the time to explain everything to the family. They do what the family considers best for the situation. The family also spends a lot of time with the patient in the hospital. In fact, for most hospitalized patients, a member of the family is always with them. For example, last night, four members of the family stayed in the room with Mrs. Kaiser in addition to a private nurse. Even in the wards, someone will sleep with the patient.

The hospital here in Cebu is excellent. The rooms are spotless, well furnished, and well maintained. Mrs. Kaiser is in a private room, costing P15 per day ($2.50). She has two private-duty nurses, each *working 12 hours per day. The nurses receive P32 ($5.33) for the day shift and P36 ($6) for the night shift. Even though these prices are low compared to the U.S., it is going to be a significant burden on the family since their earning capacity is not as high.*

The doctors here have all had some training and practices in the U.S. They do seem to know what they are doing. Dr. Berry (a doctor working for the Peace Corps) took a look at Mrs. Kaiser at my request and has made the same diagnosis. Dr. Berry happened to be a specialist in the treatment of kidney diseases.

May 4, 1970, Monday

Last night at about 8:40 PM, Mrs. Kaiser died. She's only thirty years old.

May 12, 1970, Tuesday

Eight days later…finally, I have time to get back to my letter to you. The funeral for Mrs. Kaiser was last Wednesday, May 6. On Saturday, May 9, Mr. Kaiser, the baby, and I returned to General Santos. Mr. Kaiser does not feel comfortable leaving the baby with Mrs. Kaiser's parents in Cebu, as they are elderly. Saturday and Sunday, he took care of his baby at home by himself. I babysat for a short time, and I helped him do the laundry.

Monday morning, I convinced Mr. Kaiser to take the baby to Doctor Mosquera. She is a lady pediatrician who had worked in the United States. In fact, she had treated patients at our community centers pro bono. The doctor will keep the baby in her home for the time being until Mr. Kaiser decides what he wants to do. At least the baby will get the proper food, medical care, and the attention he now severely needs.

Mr. Kaiser is staying in the same apartment that he was in before with Mrs. Kaiser. He has been going through some things to look for any valuable papers that may be needed. I have spent most of my time also following up on stuff for Mrs. Kaiser. Right now I have something to do, but it is raining, so I am at home…Mr. Kaiser has a lot of issues to attend to right now. I know many of them will be challenging to settle. I don't really know what he has in mind to do. But I intend to help him wherever I can. Later I will be doing things for the school but no teaching load this summer. Take care, Alvin

P.S. If you have some patterns for stuffed toys, maybe you could make a copy and send some to me for our Community Center Sewing Class.

Saturday, May 16, 1970
Dear Dean,

Everything is fine with me here, and I hope my little brother is doing fine too. If you read my last letter to Joyce, you know about the Kaiser family. The most recent report I can give you is that Mr. Kaiser has not gone back to work and does not plan to return at this point. He is more seriously considering going back to Germany. In times like this, I really appreciate that I have my family to share these experiences, someone to unburden.

I would like to tell you about funerals here in the Philippines. First of all, when a person dies, the body is taken to the funeral home and embalmed. Members of the family accompany the dead and make the arrangements. The body is placed in the coffin made of wood. The coffin is covered, but half can be opened with a glass window for viewing.

From the time the person dies until the burial, friends and relatives keep a twenty-four-hour vigil with the body in the funeral home. On Monday morning, when we arrived at the funeral home, two big candles were burning. Catholics (95% of the country) burn candles for the dead all the time.

Mrs. Kaiser's sister was serving coffee and refreshment to the visitors. Later in the day, they began bringing out games and cards to play. I guess it will give people something to do to stay awake for the vigil. By evening time, a lot of people had come to the funeral home. They were all talking loudly, laughing, singing, playing mahjong, and card games. By Tuesday night, many of the guests were drinking, to the point of being drunk, including family members. It made me uncomfortable to witness such a different custom from when Mom died, so I left the place. I am not saying one tradition is correct over the other, just different.

The next day Wednesday was the funeral. At one in the afternoon, the coffin is placed in a car and driven to church. The family and friends follow the car walking to the church. The casket was put into the car after the mass. The mourners walked behind the vehicle to the cemetery for about two miles. I took pictures of the cemetery. The cemetery is like most in the Philippines – already overcrowded and not well cared for. Mrs. Kaiser was buried in one of the boxes on the wall made of concrete (kind of an above-ground crypt). To save space, they have built hollow block walls four layers high, and the coffin is inserted and then sealed shut. There was no service at the cemetery. The crypt where Mrs. Kaiser is buried is actually rented for five years. After that, the family either renews the lease or removes the remains.

It is not like in the U.S. where people may be buried for centuries in the same place, and there is perpetual care. Mr. Kaiser tells me that in Germany, things are also crowded. A person may only be buried for fifteen years, and another person is buried in his place. According to him, cremation (burning of the body) is becoming a prevalent practice. The ashes are either thrown in the sea or kept in a small urn by the family, or buried.

The people of India have been using cremation for centuries. Cremation makes a lot of sense. It will certainly kill any germs or diseases that may have caused death, thereby preventing the spread of disease. It also eliminated the big problem of overcrowded cemeteries where there is not enough land space. Anyway, when we die, it is the spiritual being that remains not the physical. I think I would prefer cremation if I had a choice.

Tuesday, May 19

I'll bring you up to date on some of the local news here. When I arrived in General Santos from Cebu, Mrs. Oliveros and her family had already left for Cagayan de Oro City. They moved there because the Philippine National Bank transferred Mr. Oliveros as assistant manager. That meant that I would start taking meals somewhere else.

Mrs. Oliveros had kindly made arrangements for all four of her boarders to eat at the Santos' home. At the end of this month, I will transfer to the home of Mrs. Santos. It will be very convenient and more economical. I will get my room, meals, and laundry done all at the same place, and the total price will be less than what I am paying now. The food at Mrs. Santos is delicious. I'm glad for that because I lost about ten pounds in Cebu from amoebic dysentery.

Since returning here from Cebu, I have spent most of my vacation time helping Mr. Kaiser follow up papers. Yesterday, we finished off the social security and workman's compensation forms. Mr. Kaiser also straightened out his wife's business affairs with the C.P.A. firm, of which Mrs. Kaiser was a partner. Basically, there are only four significant things left for him to attend to. 1) Two home lots that they put down payment on, 2) savings account of Mrs. Kaiser, 3) the two taxis in Cebu, 4) the poultry farm with 400 chickens. I will probably end up in charge of selling 400 chickens! Want to buy some?

It is tough to follow-up on things in this country. You always have to see the individual in person to transact business, as telephones are not common. Frequently when you go to see someone, they are not in. If they are in, they may be busy. If in and not busy usually you must eat merienda (snack) that they serve first or at least sit and visit a long time before you can leave.

Starting this afternoon, I will be doing some work for the college. Bro. Henry assigned me to compile statistics on the testing process of entering students and also a study of where our students come from geographically. Next semester, we are planning a community survey and a follow-up review of our alumni. All of this information can be used in making plans for future course work.

Last week, there was an auditor for FNCB (First National City Bank of New York) here in General Santos to check on their financing company branch. Prima Guipo works for FNCB as a cashier/secretary. When she told me an American was coming from New York, I told her I would like to meet him. I was expecting some executive type auditor wearing a dark suit and tie, etc. When he arrived, I asked Prima how old he was. She said he's maybe in his early 40s. Well, this fits my *picture. I went to the bank to meet him last Wednesday, and to my surprise, there was a young man of twenty-nine wearing a sport shirt and very casual.*

He is one of the Vice-Presidents of the bank with a home office in the posh Makati Business District in Metro Manila. I invited him to dinner that evening, and he accepted. After dinner with the Santos family, we went to my tiny two-room house, talked, and drank San Miguel beer (famous local brand) until late that night. Bob Wilcox (that's his name) was in the Naval Air for five years and then applied for a job at the FNCB International Office. He has been in the Philippines for more than a year and is married to a Filipina. Currently, he lives in one of the upscale and exclusive housing developments in Manila. I hope to visit him when I get to Manila again.

Talking of Americans, I might as well tell you of some others I met. I don't usually have a chance to socialize with expatriates here except the missionary priests and brothers. The majority of expatriates, like the employees of Dole, live in a gated community at the base of Mt. Matutum thirty or so miles from where I live. The Kalsangi Housing has an eighteen-hole golf course, swimming pool, a restaurant with guest rooms, and upscale houses surrounded by manicured lawns, lush gardens, and avenues lined with spruce trees. In short, a little slice of America with all the modern amenities of the good life tucked in the middle of a tropical paradise.

At times, when I really am feeling low and needed to socialize with a fellow American to recharge, I visit my Peace Corps friends in Marbel. There are five volunteers there; I am the only one in General Santos. There are a couple of Mormon Missionaries in town about my age. They can be frequently seen going around town wearing dress shirts and ties carrying a briefcase or bibles. When I was in Manila, five young men got on the bus, my friends and I were riding on. I told my companions they were Mormon Missionaries. My friends didn't believe me until I started talking to one of them. How did I know? I said because you all dress up and carry briefcases like my friends in Gen. Santos. The Mormon boys are expected to serve two years of missionary service.

Another notable American I met was Carl Gordon. On our way to Cebu, I needed help with the baby when Mrs. Kaiser could barely walk anymore. I had to carry her. I saw a young man with a Filipina Girl on the same flight. We made our introductions. They took care of the baby. Carl Gordon is, of course, from Lake Ariel, Pennsylvania, graduated from Bloomsburg State College and did his student teaching at your alma mater Freedom High School in Bethlehem. What a small world, huh! He spent three years in the army as a Chaplain's assistant in Vietnam. While he was in college, the Filipina girl was studying at Marywood College in Scranton, Pennsylvania. Through mutual friends they met... He came to the Philippines to get married to her. They are on their way to the States. The girl was teaching at Notre Dame College of Marbel, where Peace Corps Volunteers teach. Carl, his wife, and I know many of the same people.

And there's an American that bears comment - Allen Rothenburg, the deputy director for Peace Corps/Philippines. I know him from before, but while in Manila I had a chance to visit his home. While vacationing in Manila, I got a telegram saying to return to Cebu because Mrs. Kaiser was in critical condition. My language instructor from Hawaii has a car. She took me to the airport to get a plane reservation. At the airport, we met Don Beaudreault, a volunteer from Jolo, who was in the same training program with me in Hilo, Hawaii. Don just came from Jolo and was carrying a huge bamboo mat and a big suitcase. We offered him a ride. He put his suitcase in the trunk and the mat across the back seat. We took him to Allen Rothenburg's place. They live in a beautiful huge apartment with all kinds of furniture and decorations made in the Philippines.[7] The bamboo mat was for the Rothenburgs.

After we delivered the mat, Don decided to wait for his friend, a Swiss guy, who was picking him up. My language instructor went to open the trunk so we could retrieve Don's suitcase, but she broke the key while it was half inside the keyhole. Just like an American always ready to help, Mr. Rothenburg quickly came to the rescue. Armed with hammer and screwdriver and in no time at all, he had the lock destroyed beyond repair. And the trunk still locked. When Don's friend arrived, he suggested we go to a locksmith. The locksmith had to drill the lock out of the hole because it was all banged up.

Well, we got the trunk open, but now the lock is destroyed, and it will require a new one. Moral of the story: don't let Americans help you. They are too impatient, and they think first of banging and destroying things with the attitude that it can later be replaced! A Filipino will patiently try to fix it first. Now you have your cultural lessons for the day. And I have fulfilled my Peace Corps Goal#2 to spread mutual understanding of two different cultures. Take care, for now, Alvin

CLASSES for the school year 1970-71 started on July 6, but the first week was orientation and testing. Things really did not get started until July 13. Four days before, I went to Cotabato City to see my fellow volunteer, Muriel Cooke, the Audio-Visual Coordinator at the Notre Dame of Cotabato City. She gave me some materials for the Audio-Visual course I was teaching. It was so good to meet up with my fellow volunteers to exchange news and updates. The airport was closed because of a bad storm. I had to take a bus back to General Santos early on a Monday morning. At the end of the trip, my rear was hurting. I went to school to teach on Tuesday. I found out that Bro. Roger Bagares had died of leukemia. He was just ten months older than me. Bro. Roger taught math at the college the previous year, and we had gotten to know each other well. I visited him when he was in the hospital in Davao City a month before he died. His burial was in Tamontaka Marist Monastery in Cotabato City the following day. So at two in the morning on a Wednesday, I joined the Marist Brothers, faculty, and students on a chartered Dulawan bus back to Cotabato City. We went home the same day, another sixteen-hour round trip ride. By the time I got home, my butt was really, really sore! Buses in Mindanao had wooden seats, no air-conditioning, and the roads were unpaved!

Three co-teachers I considered my friends, and a student dying all within six months proved to be draining, throwing me into an emotional roller coaster. Thanksgiving triggered another bout of loneliness. I wrote a letter to my sister. By December, things were back to normal again. I wrote to my dad.

November 26, 1970, Thursday
Dear Joyce and all,
I arrived here in General Santos yesterday afternoon. I attended a seminar in Manila. While I was there, I went to see a person at USAID (United States Agency for International Development) about a donation of books for the college. Upon my return, I found a stack of mail waiting for me. I read all the personal letters and business letters but not yet the magazines and newspapers. There has been a big typhoon in the Manila area, and so mail services are disrupted.

When you get a chance, please take a look around over at the farmhouse for the book titled Up The Down Staircase. It is a paperback book and is probably with my stuff somewhere. If you find it try to send it to me. Mark it "used book donated to the school library." Thanks.

I have no classes to teach at Notre Dame College this semester. Charlie White, my Regional Representative in Zamboanga, okayed my request to work in community development under Fr. Albinus. However, I will be here at the college every Tuesday and Thursday morning, working with Miss Pat de Leon. She is in charge of the testing office, a new addition to the College. We are still drifting around in terms of what to do. Miss de Leon has many good ideas and is prepared to develop a useful testing program. I am writing this letter here at Notre Dame College.

Starting next week, I will be spending most of my time working with Fr. James in Community Development. This morning I went with him on his motorcycle to Bula and Silway – two of the sections of town where mostly poor people live. Kindergarten in the Philippines is not mandatory. The Bula Community Center has a kindergarten sponsored by the Parish Church. Silway has a Nutrition Clinic, a

study center, and is trying to start an adult education project. Fr.
James would like Bula to do some of the same things. He has entrusted
that responsibility to me.

Another thing I am working on is trying to find a new place to stay
closer to the community centers, so I don't have to commute. My bicycle
is okay for getting around. However, on rainy days and on the dark of
night, I have to take the tricycle. It can prove costly after a while.

Moving to another place creates several problems, though. First of
all, I need to find a new place to live. Second I need an excuse to give
my host family to move out. In the U.S. we just inform our landlord
we are moving on such a date. And they'd say goodbye and wish you
well. Here, I might offend my host if I just said I was leaving. I have
to find some kind of reason. I am also not sure where I want to live.
There are specific problems I am confronted with:

1) I would like a location near my work. But in Bula and Silway,
   there is sub-par housing, conditions are not very sanitary, and
   I run the risk of illness.
2) Living in poor conditions depresses me so, and I don't think I
   could take it for too long.
3) In some ways living with a family has its advantages but I
   want to try another kind of accommodation

I guess I am suffering somewhat from culture fatigue. Some signs
are the profound dismay I still get at seeing poverty, idleness, and the
prevalent "bahala na" attitude (indifference). Another sign is the food.
When I was in Manila for over a month, I ate rice only once or twice
my whole stay. Most of the time, we ate American style food.

Today is Thanksgiving in the U.S. (not celebrated here). Fr. James
told me that the priests from the area are having a big turkey dinner
tonight in their R&R Monastery in Calumpang. At Notre Dame
College today, I saw turkey feathers in the trash pile at the Marist
Brothers Convento (where I parked my bicycle). I know they are going
to have turkey also. Thanksgiving without a turkey and all the fixing

is just not the same. This will be my second Thanksgiving alone. Well, somehow, I'll get over this too.

Miss Josie Guipo was just here and invited me to their house for Sunday to make pretzels and cookies. The thermostat in their oven had been fixed. We baked last year, and her sister Susan wants to try making pretzels again. Well, that's a little consolation. I'll have pretzels and cookies for my birthday.

Next week or sometime after December 1, Charlie White (my regional representative) and Phil Waddington (the director of Peace Corps/Philippines) will be traveling through this part of the country. Charlie mentioned that they plan to stop in General Santos sometime. This will probably be the first time in Peace Corps History that a country director will be in General Santos. That gives you an idea of how far my assignment is from the main flow of things.

It is almost like the Pope coming to the Philippines. Schools and offices are closed for the next two days for the Pope's arrival.[8] All kinds of archways, statues, and banners were erected in Manila. Many were destroyed by the recent typhoons, though. A lot of people from my town are going to Manila to see the Pope. Actually, I do not think we will go that far for Phil's trip to General Santos, but it is a very rare occasion indeed!

Well, that is about all the important news. Take care for now and tell Wayne to keep up the excellent work in school and Karen to keep practicing her dancing. Alvin

January 8, 1971, Friday
Dear Dad and Gladys,

I hope this letter finds you all well and happy. I hope you enjoyed the holiday season. Needless to say, things have been busy here. Before the Christmas vacation, I made a tape recording to send to Joyce. It did not turn out very well - I did not mail the tape. I will redo and post it later. This way, at least you'll hear my voice.

The last letter I got from home was from Joyce, dated Dec. 1. So far, only three Christmas cards have arrived from the states. I usually get a lot. The mail system here is kind of messed up right now. First, the three typhoons and flooding have slowed things down. Then the pilots of the major Philippine airline went on strike. After a court order to return to work, they refused and instead filed their resignations. The company is hiring new pilots as they can find them, but that is a slow process. A few of the major airports have planes in operation now. The company hopes to reopen our airport by January 15. If the weather stays as it is, there will not be any planes because it rains every day. Water seems to sit almost everywhere around here. If you dig one or two feet deep, water fills the hole. Typically, this is the dry season, and this part of the country is very dry. This year, however, we are having an overabundance of rainfall.

Briefly, I will just say that I had a delightful Christmas vacation spending most of the time with three Filipino families:

December 22-25
The Ang family in Marbel invited me to their family Christmas party. Pattie Flakus stays with them (another volunteer). I stayed at Perardi's house. The Ang family served lechon (roast pig) for Christmas dinner.

Dec 25-28 - I was with the Lim family in Cotabato City, where David Hsu is staying. David was married to Becky Carag on December 27. I was the best man at their wedding… I also shook hands with President Ferdinand Marcos while waiting for my flight back to General Santos. He made a brief stop at the Cotabato City airport.

Dec 28 – traveled back to General Santos City. Fr. James and I met with the governor and prison officials concerning the recent riot.

Dec 29-Jan 3 – stayed with the Falgui family while helping with the weeklong Notre Dame Student Leadership Seminar in Kiamba.

That's all for now. You'll get full details when the tape recording arrives.
Take care, Alvin

A carabao (water buffalo) is an important work animal for farmers in the Philippines and a handy prop for a photo opportunity for volunteers.

Mrs. Kaiser and I welcomed the 400 chicks delivered at the Kaiser farm

Once there was M/V Filipinas

"PERHAPS I should say something about tourism since this is becoming an important income producer in the Philippines." This was the serendipitous opening line on page three of a newsletter that I sent to everyone in my address book in December 1970.

Fifty years later, the tourism industry indeed became one of the biggest income producers of my host country. In the first half of 2019 alone, the Philippine Department of Tourism recorded, "an all-time high of 4,133,050 international tourists", according to the Secretary of the Department of Tourism Bernadette Romulo-Puyat. She continued, "The country has also reached an estimated 245 billion pesos in visitor receipts over the period, a huge spike of 17.57 percent from the half-year gross revenues in 2018. The tourism industry remains the third engine of economic growth, contributing 12.7 percent to the country's gross domestic product."[1]

The tourists that flocked to the Philippines in the first six months came from many countries. South Korea comprises the highest number of tourists at 946,025, which makes up 22.89% of the total market share. China comes in second at 866,561, and the United States with 569,204. Japan and Taiwan rounded off the top five countries. Four days before 2019 ended, the Philippine Department of Tourism celebrated the arrival of its eight millionth guest.

Map of the Philippines

In my bi-annual newsletters and letters to home, I pitched to my family and friends in the United States the natural beauty and the rich culture of my host country to entice them to visit. But there were no takers. Many wrote back that they were content to live vicariously through the adventures of this Peace Corps Volunteer.

For five years, I dispatched letters that read like a cross between a travelogue and a Peace Corps periodic report, the bulk of which was sent to my dad and siblings. They kept the pile of correspondence with great care and returned them to me. The stories of fifty years ago committed to paper became the heart of this book. My escapades were shared on four to six pages of paper, mostly handwritten on translucent onionskin to save on postage.

The farthest south I ventured into was the Muslim territory of Jolo, the capital of the Sulu Archipelago, an island chain located just southwest of Mindanao. The most distant north was Baguio City in Luzon. I regret that I was not able to make it to the Benguet Province, where the famous thousand-year-old rice terraces of the Philippines are located. It was another eight-hour bus ride from Baguio City.

The newsletter dated December 1970 continued: *"There are many ways to travel here. You can go first-class tourist and stay in a hotel that costs $25 or more per night, or ordinary hotels for $5-20 for an air-conditioned double. Or you can travel Peace Corps style and stay in a boarding house without air-conditioning for $2 or less or on someone's floor for free...Anyone interested in an inexpensive vacation should try this part of the world. The fare to get here is expensive, so plan on staying several weeks or months to immerse in the rich culture.*

Actually, I did not have to go far to enjoy such beauty and adventures. My host province of South Cotabato is blessed with natural resources. The tourist or the photographer's eyes could feast on mountains, beaches, waterfalls, the Blaan, Kalagan, Ubo, T'boli, and other indigenous tribes endowed with a vibrant culture.

I could ride my bicycle or walk to the scenic Alunan Beach. Every June 24, the feast of St. John the Baptist, Filipinos from as far as Surallah flocked to Alunan Beach to celebrate the *San Juan Fiesta*. They came in busloads to bathe in the waters of Sarangani Bay. Immersion in a body of water was supposed to remind a Catholic faithful about his baptism. On this day, people also splashed water on anybody and everybody, including people riding on *jeepneys* or tricycles going about their daily business. I had never been doused with water in this manner, but I heard horror stories where dirty water from mud puddles was used to drench an unfortunate traveler on his way to work. The bizarre festivities could quickly degenerate into free-for-all water fights.

Unfortunately, some portions of the Alunan beach became one of the most enormous "flush" toilets. Near Barrio Tinago (*tinago* means hidden where the poorest lived) human excrement came and went with the waves, polluting Sarangani Bay. Sewage treatment was non-existent at that time. Outhouses were common in my host town, and septic tanks were available for indoor bathrooms for those who could afford them; a majority could not. Needless to say, it was not one of my swimming holes. However, some of my favorite photos were taken along the Alunan beach.

Fr. James took me to the Passionist Monastery in Calumpang, a thirty-minute drive from my house. Built on a promontory just a few hundred feet from Sarangani Bay, the beach on the property was an ideal spot for my first lesson in snorkeling. The sport opened my eyes to a whole new world under the waves. It was like swimming in a natural aquarium teeming with lionfish, turtles, parrotfish, angelfish, wrasses, clownfish, seahorses, sea stars of different colors and shapes, conch, and much more. Since the Peace Corps years, I snorkeled in Hawaii, Belize, Florida, and Bitter End Yacht Club in the British Virgin Islands. Also, I have been to St. John, U.S. Virgin Islands ten times, just to go snorkeling. But nothing could surpass the memory of that first snorkeling trip in the Philippines in 1969.

Nicknamed the Amazon of the Sea, my host country has large species of marine and coastal resources. The archipelago is "… a part of the coral triangle and area with more species of fish and corals than any other marine environment on earth. Tropical reefs are the richest marine ecosystems on earth, and those found in the Philippines boast a diversity of life and color that is unparalleled."[2] The country offers one of the best scuba diving and snorkeling experiences. World Atlas rated the Philippines as having the sixth longest coastline in the world.[3]

I COULD travel to a large part of the 7000+ islands of the Philippines in three ways from my host town. The fastest method was by air. Or when my budget was limited, I would go by bus. Or by sea when I had the time and the yearning to savor the island flavor. My first trip on board M/V Filipinas happened a month after I arrived in the Philippines. M/V Filipinas was the largest and fastest inter-island vessel at that time. The leading shipping company in domestic routes was Compania Maritima. It introduced the two fastest cruisers - M/V Filipinas in 1968 and M/V Mindanao in 1970.[4] Both were capable of eighteen knots, the referenced speed in that era to be considered fast. M/V Filipinas and M/V Mindanao were promptly dispatched to the Manila-Cebu-Zamboanga-Davao-Cotabato-General Santos City seven-day route. It was my first taste of long-distance travel in the country by sea. I was hooked. The novel experience was noted in my journal.

June 24, 1969

At the moment, I am vacationing in Jolo, Sulu... We just completed our Peace Corps training in Cotabato City. A few of us newly-inducted Peace Corps members took advantage of our free time one week before classes started. Pattie, Pauline, Gerry, and I took the M/V Filipinas ship from Cotabato City to Zamboanga City. The facilities were excellent. We had meals, and the bathrooms had showers with hot and cold water.

Zamboanga is a lovely place, aptly called "the city of flowers." The recreational parks (Pasonanca was the best), and the beaches were enticing. The open-air market was a shopper's paradise. Our Peace Corps Regional Office and the Ayala Training Center are located in this city. The Ayala Center, built at the edge of the ocean, is used for in-country training. It is the most massive bamboo and nipa structure in Mindanao. Excellent accommodations. For twelve pesos a night, one can get room and board at the Center. There were also hotels for lodging in the city for three pesos a night.

While in Zamboanga, I met Fr. Crump from Notre Dame of Jolo College. He invited me to go south. I mentioned to him my financial resources were low but will consider. I did not tell him that on one of our shopping trips to the open market, I tucked three $20 bills inside my sock for safekeeping. When I went back to the Ayala Center, I removed my socks. To my dismay, the $60 was gone - a whole month's allowance!

He said to come anyway; he'd take care of me. I boarded the vessel Sulu Queen. Accommodations were adequate, but I was not able to secure a bed for overnight travel. The captain gave up his peacock chair inside the bridge for the 'Kano, where I stayed for the duration of the trip. The view, of course, was much better from that vantage point. To be able to visit with the crew was quite an experience. The captain peed in a can and threw the contents out to sea.

Don, one of the volunteers in my group, was assigned to Notre Dame of Jolo College. I offered to carry his book locker from Zamboanga to Jolo on the boat. Peace Corps provided us with a collection of sixty or so paperback books for reading entertainment as well as our choice of subscription to magazines and newspapers. When I arrived at the college Fr. Crump promptly escorted me to my room at the gym. The place was dirty and smelled of a dead rat. There was also evidence of live rats scurrying along the beam overhead. Well, anyway, beggars cannot be choosers.

After cleaning up a bit, I was taken on a guided tour of some tourist spots of Jolo. This is one Muslim territory inhabited by the Tausugs that Spain was not able to subjugate in its 300 years of control over the country. Everything looks exotic. My tour guide took me to a beautiful mosque; he said it was one of the smaller around.

Along the wharf, there were houses built on stilts over the ocean made of bamboo with a thatched roof. Bamboos were also used as footbridge from one home to the next. Dotting the waters nearby are vintas, which are traditional outrigger boats with the colorful sail of vertical patterns that reflect the Muslim culture.

At lunchtime, my guide took me to the La Jota Hotel and arranged for my meals there. At that time, I didn't know what was going on, but I later learned that Fr. Crump picked up the bill. I dropped Don's book locker at La Jota Hotel, where he was staying and crashed on his floor. I went back to General Santos, well-rested, and ready to face my first semester of teaching.

After teaching for one year, I was able to travel by M/V Filipinas again. My travelogue-cum-Peace Corps periodic report thus began:

June 5, 1970
Dear Dad,

How are things going with you in Florida? I am doing well but on the move as usual. At the moment, I am on a ship from Zamboanga to Manila. In Manila, I will be going to our Peace Corps office for personal business. I plan to visit the USAID office to see about getting more much-needed books for our school library.

Last Saturday, May 30, I moved my things to the home of Mrs. Florence Santos. I will be living there when I return to General Santos City next month. After the move, I was going to take the plane to Cotabato City to do some work and have a little vacation. Unfortunately, the runway was not usable (again) because of a bad storm. I wanted to get to Cotabato City by Sunday morning. I took the bus to Marbel and stayed overnight at the Perardi's house (Peace Corps couple). Going to Marbel the day before and then getting on the early bus cuts down at least 3-4 hours of non-stop bus travel. At 2:30 on Sunday morning, I got on a Dulawan Bus. At 6:30, I arrived at my destination.

Last year, I wrote to you that I promised myself I would never ever again ride the bus between Cotabato and General Santos. It is such a long, crowded, and rough eight hours ride one way. But a guy can change his mind, can't he? Also, I readily accept things now that I would not accept before.

In Cotabato, I visited David Hsu and his host family. We went to a Lutheran Church. The Pastor, Rev. Shaser, is an American from the Missouri Synod, and he gives communion every Sunday. That is the reason I wanted to get here on a Sunday. There is no Lutheran Church in General Santos. I once went to the Philippine Church of Christ, but the services were conducted in the Cebuano dialect, not Tagalog.

After Church, David's host family, Mr. and Mrs. Lim, took us to a Fiesta in the Chinese section of town. Both David and the Lims are Chinese. We stopped at three houses and had to eat dinner at each. Filipinos love to throw a party, and they serve good food, a ton of it during fiestas. There was a lechon (roasted whole pig) at all three residences. If you don't eat, you can offend your host. So the secret is to eat just a little at each house. You can then spread your goodwill by eating their food. You know how I love good food. I was really stuffed!

Monday, Tuesday, and Wednesday were spent with Mr. Leonardo Yu and Miss Vitaliana Cabatingan (teachers in my school whom I replaced). We selected some textbooks for next semester's courses, discussed our goals, and I updated them about my teaching experiences at the college.

Later this month, I will order the books when I get to Manila. I also spent some time talking to Dr. Lovell of the Ford Foundation. I am trying to lay some groundwork with Ford Foundation to sponsor a graduate program at our school. Of course, while in Cotabato, I visited most of the volunteers in my group. As I am the lone volunteer in Gen. Santos, it feels so good to talk to Americans to exchange ideas and stories. We only see each other during conferences once or twice a year.

On Thursday morning, I caught a flight to Zamboanga City, where our Regional Office is located to straighten out my checking account. The bank charged me with a P100 peso check that belonged to someone else's account. After accomplishing that, Dottie Anderson (PC Secretary) and I took Kay White shopping (wife of our regional director Charlie). The Whites are going back to the U.S. for a vacation. It will be their first trip home in more than three years. We helped Kay select gifts about P4000 worth of goods. That is only about $66, but Kay had four big boxes of gifts to take back to the U.S. Zamboanga is an excellent place for shopping because there are a lot of quality native crafts plus intricately woven cloth and other smuggled goods from Borneo.

Now I am onboard M/V Filipinas. Most of the afternoon, I stood by the deck watching the cargoes being loaded and the Badjao people in boats on the ocean side of the ship. There were a lot of ladies and children on those boats that looked like dugout canoes. They wait for passengers to throw coins, and they dive to retrieve them. The Badjaos are an indigenous Muslim tribe that lives practically in boats. Although I was told that the Badjaos are slowly making the transition of living in houses built on the water.

On the ship, I ordered a first-class ticket. Typically, this is the accommodation on the top deck outside. Since the boat is crowded, Compania Maritima turned the air-conditioned lounge into sleeping quarters for first-class passengers. This is where I stay and sleep. It is quite comfortable although you sleep in rows of cots without privacy. I got used to it and actually enjoy visiting with fellow passengers. Please keep the enclosed letter because I will send a copy to Joyce and Bud. I already wrote to Dean two weeks ago. Love, Alvin

June 7, 1970, Sunday
Dear Joyce and Earl,

By now, you must have returned from your vacation and visiting Dad in Florida! I, too, am on vacation, combined with some personal and official business. I am going for my annual physical and buy books for our college. I am now on a ship going to Manila. If you have read the letter I sent to Bud, Daddy, and Dean, you are updated. This system seems to work very well, circulating my letters among you. I don't have to repeat myself. Saves postage for me too! Once in a while, I make copies by hand when I have extra time, like while traveling for three days during this trip.

M/V Filipinas is one of the biggest and fastest vessels capable of traveling eighteen knots per hour. At the moment, I am sitting on my cot. It is after breakfast, and this place is a bit noisy now, but it is a nice kind of noise. There are a group of young high school age kids sitting at the foot of my cot playing card games (mostly girls). Two elementary girls are playing hand-clapping games while their parents are carrying on a conversation. Farther away, someone is singing while playing his guitar. Many others are reading or sleeping this morning.

Others are eating. It is a pleasant atmosphere for traveling except for the person nearby eating durian (a fruit that smells like the garbage dump, really stinks!). I had been told they are the most delicious fruit around. However, I am not about to check the veracity of that claim. As one of my friends put it, "it smells like hell but tastes like heaven."

The boat ride is smooth, accommodations quite different, but fun and kind of interesting. Not the typical boat cruises we know in the U.S. The air-conditioned lounge is filled with cots wall to wall with a small aisle in between cots to walk. It is probably hard for you to picture rows upon rows of cot beds about one hundred or more very close to each other. It's like a big slumber party at a summer camp with everyone housed inside a building without any walls. I met so many fascinating people traveling on the boat with me.

Early this morning, I met Mr. Frank Maxey. He is also from General Santos. In fact, his sister, Mrs. Florence Maxey Santos, is my future landlady, where I am going to be staying when I return from this trip. He told me that their father was an American who came to the Philippines as a teacher in the early 1900s and later was a government official under the American regime. He married a Filipina. Mr. Maxey (the son) is a farmer. He makes a good living, but he told me he is not wealthy. He is going to Manila to visit his daughter and family. On this boat, I have my share of spreading the Peace Corps brand of goodwill to a community of travelers. I also had a chance to practice my Tagalog much to the delight of my fellow passengers. They are just as eager to practice their English with me.

Yesterday we arrived in Cebu. The boat docked for twenty-four hours to unload and load cargos. M/V Filipinas is actually 50% cargo ship and 50% passenger. In Cebu, I visited the Peace Corps Office in the morning to take care of business and to leave my belongings. For lunch, Neal (a volunteer) working at the Eversley Leprosarium,[5] the Peace Corps Secretary, and I went to a restaurant. After lunch, we went to the Leprosarium. We met with other volunteers working there.

Remember learning about lepers in biblical times during our Sunday school? Seeing them in person is kind of sad and makes one wonder why the disease has not been eliminated by now. We visited their arts and crafts exhibit on the premises and the experimental laboratory. The lab is the best equipped for leprosy for the entire world. They are trying to find the cause and cure for the disease.

On my way back from the Leprosarium to the Peace Corps office, I stopped to pay for the stone that Mr. Kaiser ordered for Mrs. Kaiser's grave. The stone was already finished. I made a P100 payment. From there, I walked around the city alone to meditate about life here and death, and the personal losses. Then I had an extra big snack of pancit Canton, two glasses of ice tea, and a dish of Magnolia ice cream.

After walking around some more, I went to the Peace Corps Office to get my things to return to the boat. But at the office, I met Brian Furby (Peace Corps Regional representative in Cebu) and his wife Cely (a Filipina). They invited me to join them to attend an event back at the Leprosarium... After the program, the volunteers at the Leprosarium, Brian and Cely, and I went to a restaurant. We shared a couple of hours of eating, drinking San Miguel beer, and talking, and then we all went our own ways. I feel totally recharged! Before we split up, one of the volunteers asked me to join him in working at the Leprosarium next summer.

I picked up my things at the Peace Corps Office and went back to the ship. It was after midnight. Most of the passengers were asleep. In the hallway, I met Mrs. Cajigas from General Santos. Her husband, Bienvenido, was one of my students last semester. Traveling in this manner, you strike up meaningful conversations even with total strangers.

I spent many hours out on the deck earlier today. It is so exhilarating to be out in the fresh air and watch the boat glide through the blue water. The Philippines is a chain of 7,000 plus islands. From the deck, the land is almost always in sight. Occasionally a pod of dolphins playfully swim along with the ship. Sometimes we pass small fishing boats and cargo ships bigger than M/V Filipinas. We seem to be about the fastest moving vessel at sea, though.

This afternoon, I was taking pictures of the sunset from the deck. While taking pictures, I saw some people all the way up the top. They shouted an invitation to join them. I followed their directions, which took me through a door that said: "Navigators Only." The captain's quarters are on the top along with his crew that steers the ship.

I will try to finish this letter before they turn the lights down. Most people will go to sleep. Then maybe I can sneak down for a leisure hot shower (a luxury for volunteers here). Tomorrow morning, we will be arriving in Manila. Bud and Daddy have a copy of this letter (duplicated by hand). You can keep this copy. Take care now. Alvin

July 9, 1970
Dear Bud and Enid,

How are you all? I don't remember to whom I wrote last. There was a time when I kept a meticulous record of all the letters I wrote, but lately, I just write when the mood hits me and time allows. At the moment, I am back in General Santos for the first time since May 30.

June 5, I took a three-day trip on M/V Filipinas from Zamboanga to Manila. Monday morning arrived too soon. The stewards turned on all the lights and came around, ringing their bells to wake everyone as the sun lazily peeked over the horizon. The ship was soon bustling with noisy people getting ready for the last leg of their journey. Meanwhile, we were served coffee and breakfast. By the time the ship docked in Manila, all the beddings and cots were piled together waiting to be stored until the next batch of passengers came on board.

At the port in Manila, we crowded our way off the boat and finally got through. I went to my language instructor's house. After lunch, she took me to Manny's house (co-teacher of hers), where I stayed for the duration of my visit to Manila.

While in Manila, I helped Mrs. White shop for woodcrafts... Dottie Anderson and I went shopping with her in Zamboanga, but she needed more. Also, I took care of some personal business at the Peace Corps Office headquarters, bought some textbooks and supplies for the college, and obtained books from the Asian Foundation for our college library.

One day I was running short of cash. I was near the Makati section of town, the new Commercial Center of Metro Manila. I knew Bob Wilcox was working for FNCB Bank at the center. Prima introduced him to me when he visited General Santos. I decided to take a chance that he could help me cash a check. Well, his bank could not do it, but there was a Philippine National Bank not too far away (the same bank where I do business in General Santos). It was almost closing time, so I took a taxi until the meter read thirty-five centavos. I got out and walked the rest of the way because I had no more money. Just as I entered the door, they locked the bank behind me. I just made it!

That same day, I visited Josie Guipo in the same area; she was staying with her cousin, Atty. Marcelo Villanueva, a corporate lawyer for Toyota. He owns a beautiful six-bedroom two-levels concrete house enclosed in a twelve-foot tall concrete fence with broken glass lining the top to deter intruders. The outside walls of the house were finished with marble. As you enter a metal gate, you step into his spick and span garage open on two sides under the second floor. No clutter, just a white, shiny Toyota Corolla parked inside. One side of the garage has a wall decorated with live flowering orchids hanging from custom made pockets of metal pots arranged here and there. The interior of his house is paneled with narra (Philippine mahogany). The roof was made of Spanish tile that he bought and transported back to the Philippines on one of his European trips.

Dilapidated houses made of wood surrounded this posh house along both sides of narrow streets. Nipa palm leaves are not used in the city. Instead, houses had a tin or galvanized iron roof. One house in a state of disrepair had walls made of metal recycled from a Coca-Cola billboard. The stark contrast between the rich and the poor is evident everywhere in Manila.

I needed to get from Josie the burned-out bulb of the family's slide projector. I was hoping to find one exactly like it here in Manila. She was getting ready to leave for Japan to study at a special seminar sponsored by NSDB (National Science Development Board).

Her sister Nena and their parents were also in Manila. Nena was in the U.S. for the International 4-H Convention last year. If you remember, Joyce sent her some dollars from my bank account so she could buy a slide projector made in America. The family paid me in pesos. Nena works for PRRM[6] (Philippine Rural Reconstruction Movement, like a local Peace Corps) in Nueva Ecija province north of Manila.

Three days after I arrived in Manila, June 12, is Independence Day in the Philippines, and all the stores and offices are closed. I went with Nena and Mr. & Mrs. Guipo to a small village in Pampanga – one of her assigned territories - where Nena has organized a farmer's cooperative and a youth group. We visited a family there.

You would never believe this. But you do remember my intense dislike for rats, right? Well, for dinner, we were served broiled rats! Surprisingly, it was tasty enough. The rats were caught in the rice fields. They ate wholesome foods, unlike the city rats that feed on garbage. We stayed overnight at this house, and the next day proceeded farther north to Nueva Ecija to the PRRM Training center.

After the day visiting the PRRM center, we returned to Manila by bus. Traveling through that area of the country was very entertaining. It is known as the Central Plain of Luzon. The region is flat land and planted mostly to rice. I saw a lot of people working in the rice paddies. It was the rainy season. The fields are all flooded with water. Even though it was raining, the farmers were out plowing with their carabaos (water buffalo) with the water knee to waist-deep. The people can catch fish and shrimps under their houses. Most dwellings were elevated with stilts. During the rainy season, the rivers overflow the banks, and everything turns into one big, lazy river!

I stayed overnight in Manila. The next day, I took the bus to Baguio for HILT (High-Intensity Language Training). Although my Tagalog has improved, I don't get to use it much at the college. But when I work in community development with Fr. James, Tagalog becomes a vital form of communication with the poor people we serve.

I treated myself to a first-class bus – that means padded seats instead of a wooden bench. A young Filipina girl sat next to me. She was dressed in a bright pink pantsuit, loaded with jewelry, and wore thick makeup. She asked if I was from Clark U.S. Air Base in Angeles City. She was kind of disappointed that I was not. She then proceeded to tell me all about her U.S. Air Force boyfriend in Vietnam. She just came back from a year's stay with him. He is still in Vietnam. She did not say anything about her future, but as best I could figure, he gave her some money and sent her home to the Philippines never to be seen again. Now she is looking for another 'Kano (Amerikano) to live with.

I learned to read the signs. Some of the barbershops here have massage parlors where a man can get a complete treatment from a girl. I had my haircut done in a barbershop in General Santos once. It was recommended by an acquaintance and frequented by businessmen that I knew around town. You wait for hours for your turn. Girls were hanging around with lots of makeup and dressed in tight mini-skirts, asking if you want a massage. I quickly learned to cut my own hair with a Trim Jim,[7] a manual haircutter that I bought from Maricel Store.

Anyway, this is my first trip to Baguio. It is located in the province of Benguet 150 miles north of Manila, about eight hours by bus. The road is paved all the way. It was reasonably comfortable. The scenery was nothing special until we got to the mountains and started the climb up to Baguio City, 5000 feet above sea level.

It is unbelievable how the road was carved on the side of the mountains; it zigzags along the mountainsides for about thirty kilometers (eighteen miles). There are so many rivers and waterfalls along the way. When we reached the top and looked down, we saw the road aptly named ZigZag Road. The view was absolutely breathtaking. The closer we got to the heart of the city, it progressively got colder, and the homes tended to be more substantial. There were no more homes made of nipa or bamboo owned by poor people. Those that can afford, use wood or stone or concrete which are more expensive.

I read somewhere that the ZigZag Road was built by the U.S. Corps of Engineers in 1903 and was opened in 1905. It was called

Benguet Road but later named after the Corps of Engineer Col. Lyman Kennon. Called the City of Pines, Baguio is the summer capital of the Philippines. There is a U.S. Military R&R place here called Camp John Hay.

The entire city is built on the mountaintops. The streets are very steep. Many of the houses have concrete or wood posts twenty to thirty feet long, holding up the back of the house with the front door at street level. Because of the cold climate, Baguio is the most attractive vacation spot for tourists, both local and foreign. The city is the cleanest I have ever seen in the Philippines. It also appears to be one of the most prosperous.

There is an avenue called the Mansion Row, with huge houses owned by the wealthy people of the Philippines. There are also first-class colleges. The market is a paradise for people who love to shop. There are all kinds of hand made products and at reasonable prices.

I could spend days just looking at the piles of fresh strawberries, large peppers, all sorts of vegetables and fruits all grown locally. I bought a bunch of carrots for my snack and a lot of woodcrafts to send home. Four pages and I ran out of space. I'll tell you more about Baguio in the next letter.
Take care, Alvin

August 9, 1970, Sunday
Dear Joyce and Earl,
It sounds like you are going camping all the time this summer. No wonder though with that new camper and a big station wagon, it must be easy to enjoy the great outdoors. That's the way to live, but I think I would prefer to rough it. To me, setting up the tent or cooking on an open fire is half the fun of camping.

Here is an idea for you. Try taking rice along. For breakfast, cook it, drain the water, add chocolates, and serve hot with milk and sugar. It is my version of what is called "champorado" here. I eat rice three times a day every day I don't get tired of it. Champorado is usually served with fried dried fish for breakfast. I can't get used to the dried fish, but I do like to eat fried dried pusit (squid) with my San Miguel beer.

You asked about my new room here at the Santos family – today I cleaned, rearranged the furniture, and decorated. I used some mats to cover two walls. I hung decorations using my collection of native hats, deer and carabao horns, woodcarvings, and brassware on the mats. The place really looks homey now.

The biggest problem is "lamok" (mosquitoes). The house is screened, but with the kids coming in and out holding the door open all the time, it is always full of lamok. I use my mosquito net for sleeping, but I have bites all the time. Mrs. Santos is an avid gardener. There are a lot of plants in jars of water all around the house. Mosquitoes hatch the eggs in the water. Maybe when I put color film in my camera, I'll take photos of the room. Speaking of photos – I have about 400-500 slides. I have not had the time to caption them and get them ready to send home. That will be my next big project.

Last Sunday, we made pretzels at the Guipos using Aunt Sadie's recipe. Somewhere we did the wrong thing because they did not come out perfect. They tasted good, though. I hope we can try the recipe again soon. I also want to try the recipe of Aletha and Dom for soft pretzels. At present, we are not prepared to try Bud and Enid's recipe, as it is a bit more complicated.

School started here on July 6. The first week was orientation and testing. Things really did not get started until July 13. My original schedule was five courses with all different subjects. I still have five different preparations, but now I have six courses. It really keeps me busy always preparing lesson plans, etc. I am pleased to have four small classes, with thirty students average. That means grading papers and preparing grades will not be so difficult compared to the past two semesters. It is also better for teaching because I can get to know more of my students personally. This week marks the end of the third semester. Examinations are given three times each semester. At the end of this week, we have exams with grades due the next week. It means a lot of work coming up again. Prima still helps me with checking papers, typing exams, and letters...

It is more interesting this semester because of a variety of subjects. I have also improved my teaching methods a bit from talking and listening to other teachers. I set a personal goal of meeting my requirements and work for students each semester. This, in my opinion, is a way of upgrading the quality of our graduates. Most students accept the challenge willingly. Apparently, other teachers are raising their standards too. The library is continuously crowded with students, and many teachers have ordered new reference books for the library.

Time to go now. Take care and let me know if your packages arrive. Alvin

November 17, 1970
Dear Dean and everybody,

Lots of new things have happened lately. I'll start by going back to the last letters I received. When I was in General Santos last, no planes were flying, so the previous letters I got were from Dad, Oct 11, Bud and Enid Sept 25, and Joyce and Earl Sept 21. You can see that I am quite a bit behind in responding to my mail from the States.

I finished my teaching job at Notre Dame College. Mr. Yu and Ms. Cabatingan completed their Masters in Teaching Economics, and they are back at the college. It is the semester break now. In January, I will transition to my new job in Community Development. On Nov. 1, I left General Santos, stopping to visit volunteers in Marbel and Cotabato City before proceeding to Manila and Los Banos, Laguna.

On Nov 3, in the evening, I checked in at Makiling Lodge in Los Banos. Nov 4-9, we attended a seminar in Family Planning and Community Development on the campus of the University of the Philippines, College of Agriculture (UPCA).

This extensive seminar will prepare me for my new job. The volunteers attending were mostly a group of married couples working in nutrition and agriculture programs of the Peace Corps. There were also a few odd volunteers like me working in family planning or getting ready to transfer from education program to family planning and community development. Our training was beneficial and very interesting. It was not wholly comprehensive, and perhaps further training for me will be needed later.

The training site was really something to write home about. UPCA is a massive campus with all beautiful new buildings and excellent lab equipment. The college has about 2,000 undergraduate students with nearly 1,000 faculty members, research assistants, and graduate researchers. The money for the buildings and lab pieces of equipment come from Ford Foundation and others plus the government loans from the World Bank. It is just amazing to see such excellent facilities and equipment here in the Philippines. There are so few of them and few places that they exist.

Another fantastic place is the IRRI (International Rice Research Institute). It has been built and financed by the Ford Foundation. There are people from all parts of the world working and studying there to learn how to grow better rice in larger quantities in the shortest period possible. As you know, rice is the staple food of the Philippines and countless other Asian countries. The laboratories and research projects are fantastic. They grow rice coming from all over the world and under all kinds of conditions. Not all rice is created equal; some varieties are preferred by some, but not by all.

Makiling Lodge, where we stayed, is located on Laguna de Bai, which means the "lake of the town of Bai." It is a vast lake and very polluted like most freshwater bodies in the Philippines. Part of the lodge is built out over the lake. All the trash and sewage is dumped directly into the lake (thus polluting the water).

They also have hot mineral springs at the lodge and a swimming pool. The pool is filled with lukewarm water. They use hot mineral springs to fill small pools in individual shower rooms. It was really relaxing to take a bath in the hot mineral springs. The hot water relaxes the body and cleanses the pores.

Sunday, November 8, was our day off. We went to Pagsanjan Falls. We rented a Bangka at a hotel down river complete with two men to do the paddling. As we went up the river, we traversed rocks and rapids. The two boatmen jumped in and out of the canoe frequently to guide it around and over big boulders. At some points, they actually lifted the canoe over the rocks to the next level of the rapids. The two passengers included.

When we finally reached the falls, there were nearly a hundred canoes and all the passengers plus boatmen. Under the falls is a gorge. Several canoe operators were willing to take people inside the gorge for an added novel adventure. Going under the falls is like being in four heavy rainstorms all at once. We got soaked! It was a bit frightening because the water was rough and the boat nearly capsized.

Going back down the river, we went shooting along except where the boatmen had to carry us over the boulders. The scenery along the river is quite awe-inspiring. The riverbanks slope up the hillsides filled with lush green foliage and coconut trees. At other places, the river flows through rock canyons rising high to the sky.

The people who attended the seminar were the most congenial Peace Corps Volunteers I have ever met. They were the epitome of what I had imagined volunteers to be like before I joined PC. They represent our country very well, indeed. We did many things together, went to many places as a group, and sat around singing and talking and playing games in the evening. All in all, it was a wholesome experience that I will remember for a long time.

On Tuesday, Nov 10, we came back to Manila in preparation for our return to our sites. Since that time, I have been running around Manila. Tomorrow I will be leaving for Iligan City... I will stop in Cagayan de Oro City first to visit the Oliveros family. From there, I will go to Marawai City to meet Dr. Hoyt of the Ford Foundation to see about book donations and tour Marawi City, predominantly Muslim population. I am short on time now so I will enclose a list of things sent home in the next letter. Take care now, Alvin

Jan. 9, 1971 Sat Night
Dear Enid, Bud and all,
    Here's hoping all of you had a Merry Christmas and Happy New Year. I had a hectic Christmas break and enjoyed myself very much spending the holidays with Filipino families and travel. Finally, I am getting around to sending my annual Christmas newsletters. This

morning I recorded a tape, which is going to Joyce and Earl...Just imagine when you listen to the tape that you are talking to me on the phone.

The graduation ceremony for the Notre Dame Student Leadership Seminar in Kiamba was enjoyable even though it was long. It ended with fireworks shooting off until two AM, and everybody dancing around like we did New Year's Eve.

Then we all got our things, had a snack, and headed for the seafront where a boat was waiting to take us back to General Santos City. The pier in Kiamba has broken down. We had to be ferried out to a large, rather old boat by a small one-oar dinghy rowed from the back. The sea was quite rough, and we had a hard time climbing aboard. The vessel looked like a yacht with an extra deck built on top in front and in back. The size is about as big as a small tugboat. The little dinghy had to make about ten trips to get all the people and baggage aboard.

I was on the second trip. While waiting for the dinghy to return eight more times, we ate on the boat as it rocked and tossed in the waves. Lots of the kids were getting sick and vomiting over the side. I kept myself busy helping passengers and bringing up baggage.

They put plywood on the floor for sleeping. When the last dinghy load came aboard, Sister Maria Theresa (Dean of Women from Notre Dame College) was with them. She gets very sick from travel, and I knew she would get sick here. As soon as she stood on board, she said, "I feel fine," and then she fainted. We carried her to the top deck.

Finally, at 3:30 AM, we were on our way. I was on a bench shared by four others. Every few minutes, someone leaned over the side to vomit. While it was still dark, we passed three ships heavily loaded with hogs bound for Japan, I was told. We watched the sunrise on the deck as the sun slowly came out. The morning mist lifted and dark changed to total daylight.

Mt. Matutum came into view. Being on a smaller vessel, more than a tenth of the size of M/V Filipinas, offered a brand new perspective. Mt. Matutum seemed more massive, and the beach stretching from Bula to Silway seemed longer. The scenery as we came into the Sarangani Bay was astounding.

Then the morning breakfast bell sounded. We were served rice, fried dried fish (a breakfast staple here), fried pork, and paksiw fish. Paksiw means the fish was steamed in water, vinegar, salt, and pepper until all the water evaporates. Breakfast was eaten off a community platter, using our hand, no forks, or spoons, and served with hot tea.

At eleven AM, we pulled up to a barge docked in General Santos. Wearily we carried our baggage ashore and went home to rest. All in all, it was a memorable, fun-filled trip. Take care now and write when you get time, Al

OF ALL the places I had visited in the Philippines, the most memorable for me was the trip to the land of the T'boli people in November 1969 during my first-semester break. The Peace Corps volunteers living in Marbel had told me about the Wycliffe Ladies living in Sinolon, Surallah, translating the bible to the T'boli language.

I invited Prima and her younger brother Felipe. We traveled on the Yellow Bus for three hours until there was no more bus service. Then we took a *jeepney* to the end of the line. We stopped at the open-air market at Barrio Edwards to buy some groceries and a block of ice to make ice cream. The volunteers had mentioned that the Wycliffe ladies had an ice cream maker. Since homemade ice cream was a staple dessert at our farm and my favorite, I had memorized my mom's ice cream recipe.

We encountered many T'boli men and women, young and old, at the market. The women were absolutely striking in their T'boli outfits. They wore intricately embroidered blouses, brightly patterned *malong* skirts, and layers of colorful beaded necklaces down their necks. Some had anklets from ankle to mid-calf that jingled with every step. My camera worked overtime, as each visual image that paraded before my eyes were just as fascinating as the last.

From the market, we hiked at mid-afternoon for two more miles uphill and downhill to the house of the Wycliffe Ladies. It was built on a gully surrounded by mountains. The three

Ladies - Vivian, Lillian, and Marge - were gracious enough to host us for the weekend in their beautiful nipa house. We met Gadu Ogal,[8] a T'boli kid who lived with the Wycliffe Ladies with three other boys. Gadu was a few years younger than Prima (nineteen) and Felipe (seventeen). Gadu assisted the Ladies in their translation project. He also did household chores for them. That night, we helped cook dinner. Making ice cream for dessert was fun, a new experience for Prima and Felipe.

It was the eve of the full moon. Felipe, Prima, and I joined Gadu and the three boys in the back yard after dessert. The moonlight was unusually bright. It illumined the otherwise very dark deep, narrow valley like it was just another cloudy day. The light of the moon was streaming through the branches of a lone tree behind the nipa hut. It created dappled patterns on the ground where newly hatched ducklings huddled under their mother's wings.

We could hear the sound of a musical instrument – a high pitch melody accompanied by a drone. "That's a T'boli two-string guitar called *hegelong*," Gadu told us. We stayed outdoors until the breeze turned chilly. I watched the moon from the window inside the *nipa* hut and listened to the T'boli guitar well into the night. It was magical.

At breakfast the following morning, the Wycliffe Ladies related the story of Datu Mai Tuan, the local leader of the settlement called PANAMIN (Presidential Assistance on National Minorities).[9] Led and mainly funded by Manuel Elizalde, Jr., (a Harvard graduate and the wealthy son of businessman Manuel Elizalde Sr.), PANAMIN was established in 1968.

Datu Mai Tuan, the PANAMIN Manager, was a protégé of the Wycliffe Ladies. His command of the English language was impeccable. He could speak in five native dialects. He left the Wycliffe Bible Translator's house to accept the offer from PANAMIN. Intrigued, I decided to explore the area, including a visit to the PANAMIN settlement. Prima and Felipe were interested too.

All morning we observed the Wycliffe Ladies attend to a sick child and dispense medication to an ailing man. A group of T'boli women in their colorful attire sat waiting on a porch bench. Some men were standing in the front yard chewing betel nut next to red bougainvilleas in full bloom. Flowers also surrounded the outhouse behind the nipa hut. Prima and Felipe were so fascinated watching one of the Wycliffe ladies do the laundry using a gas-powered washing machine.

When it was time to leave for the PANAMIN Settlement, Felipe was nowhere to be found. One of the boys who was getting ready to go home to his family's house for the weekend told us that Felipe went with Gadu to gather firewood. We waited for Felipe's return, but at ten o'clock we decided to leave without him. The hike to the PANAMIN settlement took an hour one way. We followed a footpath up and down the hills. We saw for the first time the singular T'boli houses on top of the mountain that resembled nothing like the *nipa* huts in the lowland or the home of the Wycliffe Ladies.

Sometimes we had to make our way through a series of bamboo clumps. We crossed the same stream a few times as it meandered along the footpaths less traveled. In some parts, there was thick forest to traverse where we had to part native brambles like curtains to pass through. Prima identified some of the vines twining around trees overhead as rattan. At one point, the stream was knee-deep. We found a natural stepping-stone to cross it to keep our shoes from getting wet.

At the crest of a hill, we looked down. Below was the PANAMIN settlement in front of us. It was built near a small lake. The houses did not resemble any T'boli house; they looked more like houses in a Polynesian village.

We met a T'boli man along the footpath. Neither of us spoke the T'boli dialect. He understood Ilongo, however, which was Prima's native tongue. He directed us to the house of Datu

Mai Tuan, who received us warmly. In the true spirit of Filipino hospitality, Datu Mai invited us, unexpected guests, to join him for lunch of broiled tilapia, rice, sautéed *kangkong* greens, and bananas. He told us about the PANAMIN operation. Before we left, he offered us jobs. Datu Mai Tuan arranged for Manuel and Finning to take us on a tour of the settlement. The newlywed couple, barely out of their teens, led us to the highest point in the area. From there, I took a lot of good pictures of the scenery below.

On the top of the hill, Manuel said in Ilonggo, "My father told us that when we die, our body would be taken on the top of this hill. From here, it is only ten-centavos fare for the soul to travel to heaven!"

After Manuel and Fining went back to the PANAMIN settlement, Prima and I lingered on top of the hill. We sat on the grassy edge of the cliff, dangled our feet over the ledge, and watched the pebbles roll down the hillsides.

We swapped stories about our childhood, raising goats, ducks, chickens, and turkeys for pets, family consumption, and to sell. Prima's family owned a thirty-acre farm in Silway 7, a remote barrio near Dole Pineapple Plantation just outside of the city. Before Mrs. Guipo's brothers came as settlers and took over the work at the farm, Prima's family maintained the farm themselves on weekends. They planted mainly rice, corn, mung beans, and cassava to augment the family's income, which supported eight kids through college.

Prima and I discussed our aspirations, our hopes of finding meaningful careers. We discovered our shared inherited family values that nurtured us.

"By the way, I've been curious. How did you get your name?" I asked.

"My parents coined it from the first syllables of the name of my paternal grandparents, Primitiva and Mateo," Prima responded.

"That's rather creative. Any preference in music?"

"I love all kinds of music, but if I have to pick my top three, it would be the songs of the Lettermen, the Beatles, and Peter, Paul & Mary," she enumerated.

"Except for the Beatles, I brought from the U.S. long-playing records of the groups you just mentioned and more," I informed her. "In fact, I saw the Lettermen perform on our college campus."

"Wow, lucky you. That must have been something!" Prima exclaimed. "Someone gave me a Lettermen record for my last birthday. We should swap records sometime."

"Yes, let's do that. I have the Up, Up with People record too. Have you heard of them?"

"Of course, Up with People. But I think my favorite is the Lettermen. Someday I hope to see them live when they come to the Philippines," she said. "Do you know that the Beatles came to the Philippines three years ago? But they had to leave fearing for their lives after they turned down the breakfast invitation from Imelda Marcos. The fans turned against them, threw rotten tomatoes at them."

"I did not know that. By the way, what do you intend to do after you graduate?"

"Not to work in a bank for sure after working four months there. It's a job for now but not a career for me," Prima said. "I think something in the line of what my sister Nena does at the PRRM. I tagged along with her all over Luzon for one summer. I believe social work would suit me fine."

"Well, maybe you'll find a job right here with the T'boli someday."

I shared my encounter with John F. Kennedy while I was in the high school band. Prima recalled precisely where she was on November 23, 1963 (November 22, 1963, U.S. time). She was thirteen. She was with her sisters on their porch, eating their *merienda* after trimming by hand-held cutters their Bermuda grass in the yard. They were listening to music on the radio. The announcer broke through the airwaves. "President Kennedy had been assassinated."

That weekend under the Kematu skies left an indelible mark on me. Six months later, Prima showed me a copy of the VOX, the Notre Dame College paper. Unbeknownst to me, she wrote about our Kematu visit. It was published in the college paper and the national teen magazine, *Homelife*, a Catholic church-sponsored publication. I included her essay in my bi-annual newsletter of May 1970: *"You may be interested in hearing about some of my little travel excursions around this area. Several times I have had the opportunity of visiting four American ladies (Wycliffe Bible Translators) that are translating the Bible into T'boli.*

On one visit, two students were my companions, Prima and Felipe. The T'boli people are one of the many minority indigenous groups found in the Philippines and particularly on the island of Mindanao. Most of them have little or no schooling. They live primarily in the mountains making their living by burning off a piece of forest and planting upland rice, corn, and a few vegetables. They also hunt and gather things that nature provides without human labor. I'll stop now and let Prima finish the story. She is a much better writer than me.

T'boli Hear Me Come!

You have come, and you have gone. I have seen you arrayed in nature's majestic vest. I've trodden your footpaths, combed your auburn sands, kicked your multi-colored pebbles, braved your streams, and I've come in time to see your pristine soul clad in all your moods...

T'boli, your memories will always cling to my heart, my mind. You will always remind me of your intriguing tribe, your tinkling anklets and booming brass agongs, your melodious ringlets and exquisite beadwork, your fascinating hair-do, and embroidered costume, and of Fining and Manuel's ten-cents-fare to heaven!

You will always want me to stay with you where I can strum my guitar and gaze endlessly at your crescent moon tucked against your fleecy clouds. Where I can forever watch your breath-taking twilight turning itself into a somnolent eve...

When alone I stand amidst the chaos, I'll think of you once more. One of these days, T'boli listen attentively to my footsteps. I'll race toward your encircling arms as Felipe, Al, and I have done one somber November.

When my world stops spinning, T'boli hear me come!

~prima guipo, 11.1969~

Prima is not only a junior student at Notre Dame. She is also my secretary that typed this letter and the secretary-cashier at the FNCB finance company in town. Prima is a young lady with a lot of talents and a bright future.

Here's hoping you enjoyed this letter enough to drop me a little note. Best wishes to all and remember God's nearby wherever you are. Very sincerely yours, Alvin Hower

Our tour guides, Manuel and Fining, took us to the highest
point to see the sprawling PANAMIN settlement.

Datu Bebing Siob was the chieftain of Lambisol, a village of Lake Sebu. A T'boli man can marry as many wives as he can afford. Datu Bebing is the father of Myrna Bebing Pula. Myrna received a copy of this photo recently and wrote, "This is the only photo I had of my father and mother Gumbay Tawal. Thank you for preserving memories".

The Wycliffe Ladies' house in Edwards, Surallah. The author of the *Lady of the T'boli*, Doris Fell, wrote fondly about *"this house in the gulley."* This is a typical *nipa* and bamboo hut erected by most lowland dwellers.

The Ayala Center in Zamboanga City was the original training center in the Philippines. It was closed in 1972 due to budget constraints. Courtesy of Phil B. Olsen, P/C Regional Director 1965-67.

A Badjao Community: about this time, the Badjao people were transitioning from living mainly on their boats to houses on stilts built at the edge of the ocean with a bamboo footbridge connecting the houses.

The Badjao women and children dived for coins thrown by passengers on M/V Filipinas. Because they live practically on their boat, the toddlers learn to swim at a very young age.

My New Directions   8

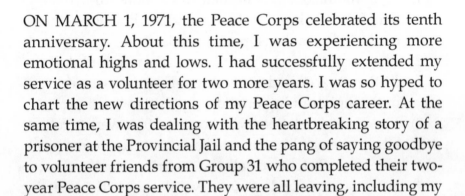

ON MARCH 1, 1971, the Peace Corps celebrated its tenth anniversary. About this time, I was experiencing more emotional highs and lows. I had successfully extended my service as a volunteer for two more years. I was so hyped to chart the new directions of my Peace Corps career. At the same time, I was dealing with the heartbreaking story of a prisoner at the Provincial Jail and the pang of saying goodbye to volunteer friends from Group 31 who completed their two-year Peace Corps service. They were all leaving, including my best friend, David Hsu.

The Peace Corps was only eight years old when I joined in 1969. At ten years, it almost met its demise until the New Directions revived and revitalized the ailing agency. Searles wrote, "By the end of the sixties, the Peace Corps had reached the point where it needed to change in some important respects or to accept the likelihood that it would disappear...In late 1969, President Richard Nixon's first Peace Corps director Joseph Blatchford announced a set of policies, which he labeled New Directions, that changed its nature and ensured its survival."[1]

Blatchford sent Phil Waddington to the Philippines in 1969 to become its country director, and to launch New Directions in my host country. However, before it was fully implemented, Waddington was recalled to Washington.

An interim country director Charlie White took over who was eventually replaced by David Searles in December 1971. Searles served as an officer in the United States Marine Corps and later as an executive in both government and business. Under his watch, the Peace Corps Philippines successfully implemented New Directions in the country. He would later become P/C Washington Deputy Director of Peace Corps, served as a deputy chairman of the National Endowment for the Arts, and authored several books. Searles reduced New Directions to five broad yet simple ideas.[2]

1) That volunteers jobs needed to be more immediately beneficial to host countries and in line with those countries' own development needs.
2) That volunteers needed to possess the required skills to do the job, acquired either through previous experience or through training provided by the Peace Corps.
3) The agency's relations with host countries were to reflect a true partnership, not one based on a donor-recipient mentality. Blatchford called it a spirit of *binationalism.*
4) Peace Corps volunteers were to participate in multinational volunteer efforts, whether under United Nations sponsorship or under one of the many nongovernmental international agencies.
5) New Directions encouraged greater use of volunteers upon their return home to address the nation's internal needs.

As I understood it, the main thrust of New Directions was to shift the involvement of the Peace Corps from education to agricultural and socio-economic development programs. New Directions also required a commitment from the host country to decide on the basic direction of their social and economic development program and, within that framework, bring the volunteers into equal participation.

In 1963, there were 630 volunteers working in the Philippines, the largest group in any country,[3] 500 of whom were in education. All of the volunteers in my NDEA Group 31 and Elementary Math Group 30 were in the Education program. All had either left the Philippines or were getting ready to exit. As they were leaving the country, the New Directions volunteers started to arrive. I was one of the few who served under the old Peace Corps philosophy and the New Directions. For me, the transition was seamless.

Teaching at Notre Dame College was an experience I will always treasure, but my job left me a bit wanting. After one semester, it felt like I never left a U.S. classroom. It seems like teaching Economics in the Philippines was no different than teaching the course in the U.S. except for having all-Filipino students instead of American kids in my classroom.

In my newsletter of May 1971, I wrote: *"It seems hard to believe that I have been away from home for more than two years. As I look back over what I have done since being here, it appears there is no measurable achievement. The several hundred students I have taught could have learned as much from a Filipino teacher. The changes at the college would have gone on without me.*

Although I taught Economics for three semesters, it seems the economy is going down instead of up. So now you are asking yourself, what is this guy doing wasting taxpayer's hard-earned money having a vacation in the Philippines?

Actually, Peace Corps volunteers are supposed to provide more than technical aid. The Peace Corps Program is also designed to encourage cultural exchange and better understanding between nations. I have, of course, learned a great deal about Philippine life, customs, and culture by being here. At the same time, the many students, teachers, community leaders, and everyday people I have come in contact with have had a glimpse of Americanism in me. Finally, Americans learn about other countries and their people through the Volunteers."

The walls of academia insulated me from seeing dire poverty that many Peace Corps Volunteers endured. In that regard, Moritz Thomsen's memoir *Living Poor* is considered a classic.[4] He experienced daily extreme poverty in a small fishing village on the coast of Ecuador. As a teacher, I had limited personal contact with my 300 plus students outside of the school. The optics of poverty was not readily visible in the college campus setting.

On the surface, there was no way for me to know if a student ate three meals a day. Or how many kilometers they had to walk to school. Or the condition under which they slept the night before. Prima had mentioned that during the rainy season, some students who could not afford umbrellas or raincoats used banana leaves to protect themselves on the way to school. Many owned just one pair of shoes. To squeeze extra mileage out of their footwear, on a rainy day, they wore their flip-flops on the way to school, carrying their good shoes in a bag, and changing once they entered the campus.

Unlike the Santa Cruz Mission School for T'boli in Lake Sebu, where teachers were required to do home visitation once a month, Notre Dame College did not have such a policy. My students all wore uniforms, the ultimate and convenient equalizer. The only time I had an inkling as to a student's financial strait was before exams. The first time I witnessed the long line that snaked from the Bursar's Office to Bro. Henry's office, I wondered what was going on. So I asked Prima.

"It's exam time," she said. "Students in line are carrying a statement of accounts from the bursar listing what they owe in terms of tuition. Unless the balance is paid, they are not allowed to take any exams. Those who couldn't pay fall in line to get Bro. Henry to sign a promissory note."

"What happens if he does not sign the note?" I asked.

Prima broke into a knowing smile and said, "With Bro. Henry, that never happens."

"Do they eventually pay?"

"A majority do pay in part or in full by the promised date. Remember, a good number of our students are children of fishermen or laborers or farmers. Usually, they pay after the harvest," Prima explained. "You'll find in that line the children of middle-class professionals too. Rarely does a student graduate and leave without paying. Bro. Henry moves such unpaid accounts to the bad debt column of the ledger for those who do. Although I must add, a majority do repay on installment after they get a job."

QUITE BY accident, the Peace Corps' New Directions program played well into my own plan to transition from education to community development. Concurrent to educating the students, I was already doing community services in my free time. It was more demanding but a vastly more fulfilling line of work. Unlike teaching, feeding malnourished kids had an immediate, measurable impact.

With New Directions in place, I also felt vindicated and validated all at once. The Peace Corps at long last did away with the psychological assessment process. For me, one of the best things that New Directions did for the Peace Corps is summed up in this statement by Searles, "Finally, and perhaps most dramatically, PC/P eliminated the traditional qualifying process for trainees with its formal assessments, psychologists, and review boards."[5]

The incoming New Direction trainees were officially sworn in as Peace Corps Volunteers a few days after arriving at their training sites. Under the old Peace Corps policy, we were inducted on the eve of our training's end. Harking back to the disquiet that the assessment board wrought on my peace of mind during my training days, I was happy for the New Directions volunteers. They did not have to endure three months of the ostensibly scientific method of evaluation. I thought these were irrelevant at best and inhumane at worst. From the first day I reported for training, the psychological assessment was like a sword of Damocles over my head.

The day the Peace Corps removed the psychological assessment from the vetting process, I wrote to my brother Bud: *"Last weekend, I went to Cotabato City to see David Hsu off and to say goodbye to him and Muriel Cooke, another volunteer. Having finished his Peace Corps tour of duty, David and his Filipina wife Becky Carag are going home to the States. He will be pursuing a Ph.D. in Chemistry at Harvard University. Most of the volunteers in my group have already left. Out of our group of fourteen volunteers, three went home within a year, one within one-and-a-half years, four finished slightly less than two years, four will complete two years, and two will extend (Pauline and me).*

Pauline is a volunteer we commonly call the phantom. None of the volunteers ever see her. I saw her once in two years since our training ended and it is not likely that I'll see her again in the next year. Her first two years were spent teaching English at the Notre Dame of Kidapawan near Cotabato City – a small isolated inland town. I heard that next year she would be teaching English in a college in Manila – the largest city in the Philippines.

It seems a bit ironic that all the people that I trained with are going back to the States. Pauline and I were both picked by the Peace Corps psychologists to be likely candidates for dropout during our training. We were given the lowest evaluation scores for everyone in my group to see. I keep thinking about how nice it is to know those psychologists were wrong. I faithfully filled out every periodic Peace Corps evaluation to tell PC to get rid of the "Head Shrinkers" (psychologists).

My fellow volunteers shared my views, and now Peace Corps finally agreed. When I submitted my request form to re-enroll for two more years, I was required to include a certain number of recommendations from my supervisor and host. It is truly heartwarming when I think of all the endorsements from Notre Dame administrators and Fr. Albinus. People around here treat me so kindly and tell me they are so glad that I am staying."

MY NEW position bearing the official title of Parish Coordinator of Social Action ushered in a very busy 1971 for me. I was to work with Fr. James in community services provided by the Passionist Fathers at the Our Lady of Peace and Good Voyage parish in Dadiangas. Fr. James was a hard-working young

American Priest concerned with more than just church masses. He was adventurous too, and fun-loving.

In Barrio Silway, an underserved section of the city, Fr. James gathered people together to build and operate a nutrition center for children. The Nutrition Center accepted a group of seventy pre-school kids and fed them two meals a day for three months. As soon as a batch graduated, a new group enrolled. The children were served lintels and other cost-effective protein sources other than meat because beef, pork, and chicken were beyond the means of some of these kids' families. We also got an ample supply of CSM (corn, soy, and milk) from the United States Assistance for International Development (USAID).

In January, we started the initial process of the weigh-in and deworming for the new batch. A chart was assigned to each child to monitor his or her weight gain. The mothers took turns preparing food under the guidance of a trained and salaried nutritionist working under our Manager Ligaya Saavedra. At the same time, the mothers were instructed on the basics of feeding their children a balanced diet. They learned about the five food groups and about affordable meat protein substitutes that are more healthful, like beans, nuts, peanut butter, etc.

We cobbled donors for tools and supplies needed for the Center from local, national, and international charitable organizations. Fr. James laid the groundwork in raising funds for our projects. I helped write feasibility studies and submitted project proposals to various not-for-profit organizations. CARE (Cooperative for Assistance Relief Everywhere) supplied us with electric frying pans and sewing machines. We received grants from CRS (Catholic Relief Services) that paid the salary of two nutritionists, and USAID donated the high-protein food, flour, oatmeal, corn, soymilk, etc.

Local merchants supplied us with whatever we asked of them – bananas from Stanfilco, fresh pineapples, and canned pineapple products from Dole Philippines, fish from local fishermen, etc. Coca-Cola Company was one of our biggest sponsors. All of our community centers acknowledged the company's vital donations with signs reading "*Courtesy of Gen. Santos Coca-Cola Plant*" on our buildings.

Other projects in Silway included adult education, a youth study center open in the evenings, and a children's medical clinic. We received medication donations from pharmaceutical companies. The medical professionals in the city were specialists and surgeons more than willing to help out *pro bono*.

My job was to coordinate and manage the operation of the Center in Silway. As well as to initiate and replicate the projects of this nature in Bula. As soon as I started working in the community, speaking Tagalog became a handy tool, especially dealing with the mothers and fathers who dropped out of school and might only have finished sixth grade. These parents hold education so high on their list of priorities that they worked as hard as they could to send their children to school.

Seeing the need for early childhood education, we added a nursery school. Other potential projects within our framework were a sewing center with training classes, training in carpentry and other trades, general cleanup campaigns, gardening, recreational facilities and most important, health and sanitary education, and anything that might come up.

And in Social Action, something always did come up. Some could be anticipated, others just hit you right smack in the face when you least expected, like this story from the jailhouse, one of the most tragic events in my service as a Peace Corps volunteer.

March 4, 1971
Dear Joyce, Earl & Everybody,
It has been a while since you heard from me. Things have been so busy, and life has been so active that I never have time to sit down and write... But there is something urgent that I must record while the

picture is still clear in my mind. Everything is fine with me here. My work is going exceptionally well at the moment, and I am in excellent health. So you do not need to worry about me.

Remember how, in the past, I kind of complained that teaching was becoming humdrum? Well, I should be more careful what I wish for. Brace yourself because the story is disturbing, but one I want to record in print so that I will not forget. I want to get it out of my system and be rid of the smell that lingers in my nose.

Back in October, when I first visited the Provincial Jail located here in General Santos to see about a puzzle project for the inmates, a man was sitting on the stairs in front of the prison. He was very skinny and had scaly skin and was very unhealthy looking. He just sat there for hours. Sometimes his eyes were closed; other times, he just stared straight ahead. It was pitiful to look at. Then in November, when we started the puzzle making with some of the prisoners, I would see this man every day. He was always just sitting there, never moving. Inquiry disclosed that he was brought in at night and placed outside during the day to get some sunlight because he was ill.

I knew there must be more to the man's case. Fr. James, who is the Chaplain of Prisons and Hospitals, informed me that the man was suffering from T.B., berry-berry, and malnutrition on the physical side. On the mental side, he was entranced in a catatonic state. The only other thing that I know about the man is that his wife lives in Kiamba about four hours of rough jeepney ride from here. No one can tell me his name.

In December, the prisoners rioted and went on strike. One of their chief complaints is unhealthy quarters and living conditions. I wrote to Dad that I was the best man at David Hsu and Becky Carag's wedding. On December 27, I was at their wedding but had to leave early the following day. I had to travel back to Gen. Santos City (thank God the airport was open) to attend the December 28 meeting at the prison. The prison officials, Fr. James, and I met with the Governor concerning the riot. The Governor promised better attention for the prisoners, including bringing this man to the provincial hospital. This man by December was really wasting away. He had become even thinner. And his health physically and mentally continued to decline. They continued to put the man inside at night and out in the sun during the daytime.

I witnessed the following once. A trustee prisoner named Adorio gave out some military orders, "March one, two, three, four!" This man got to his feet and marched outside. This continued on because the Governor, like most politicians, makes promises to garner votes, but they don't keep their promises.

The man, if we can call him that, had the physical features of a human male, but he had no more power to think or reason. His treatment was kind for a prisoner, I suppose, but still, far from being the treatment, a human being deserves. The food he tried to consume was far from being nearly fit for humans, but he sometimes ate some from his rusty tin can. Sometimes the food just sat next to him for hours with the flies eating at it.

Today was kind of an ordinary day. I got up early in the morning and was off to the Convento to meet Fr. James to start our usual rounds. I back rode on the motorcycle down to Silway and checked on the work at the Nutrition Center and the new medical office being built. No major problems. We moved on to Bula Nutrition Center. Progress on the construction of the Center seemed slow but OK. I am just glad that we got it going finally. I stayed to work on the chalkboards that we needed. The materials were all there, but some tools were lacking. One of the carpenters said the things I needed were at his house. We tried looking for a substitute. No substitute available – all right, send him home for it.

Before lunch Fr. James came back for me. He was having some problems. Nothing seemed to be going right for him today. Since I do not take a siesta after lunch, I went to Notre Dame College. I managed to squeeze in some phone calls for Fr. James and to see a teacher before she got to her class.

I also talked to Bro. Henry, which accomplished some business but also delayed me and caused me to get back to Bula later than expected. Some more talking with people and getting things organized like the Crocheting and Handicrafts Cooperative. Finished making *the chalkboards, took apart the gas stove that the Service Center man installed the wrong way. I reinstalled it. Pumped some water in the tank only to find that there is dirt in the pipes. All in a day's work.*

Fr. James came back and told me more of his troubles as other things continued to go wrong for him. Just an ordinary day except that the good-natured Fr. James is now upset. He usually manages to solve problems and overcome difficulties with a smile. This is the first time I have seen him become this agitated. I guess he has good reasons. He has so many good projects started, and now he is getting ready to leave for the states for his furlough.

Add to that, the Bishop got all upset about some of the nuns crying rumors that we are pushing the pill as an acceptable method of birth control. Fr. James never said pills were acceptable. Instead, we place the responsibilities onto the parents and make them decide in their conscience what is correct. The poor have eight children they are not able to feed!

This evening I went to the college to talk to Prima for an hour or so about a potential fund-raising project for the Bula Community Center. She will help us with the production of our souvenir program for the Opening Ceremonies of the Bula Center. The practice here is to "sell" a page to a donor to advertise their businesses. Individuals can donate a certain amount, and their names will be listed on the program. Prima's sister Josie will be teaching embroidery in our sewing class. Their Aunt Mercy Asencio and her husband Johnny offered to teach music and provide legal services, respectively.

When I got home at 8:20, I called Fr. James at the Convento. He just came from jail and asked me to meet him there to take a sick prisoner to the hospital. I got on my bike and rushed over to the prison. On arrival, someone shouted across to the guard, "He's dead!" I went inside to find the man I described above, lifeless on his filthy mat.

Do you recall seeing pictures of India or South Vietnam or Biafra of a starving man? This was the picture I saw. His ribs sticking out, the stomach flattened against the spine, with the pelvic bones sticking out like mountains protruding from flat land. A man in a fetal position lying on his side with his arms crossed over his chest and hands holding his shoulders. His eyes were still open as though he died zapped of the strength to close them.

He didn't have much care in the end. He was just lying on a mat and hadn't been taken out for going to the toilet. He was just lying in his own crap. He had no pants and only a dirty rag for a shirt. The smell was terrible, and the sight even worse. When Fr. James arrived, he took a look, felt for the pulse beat, and said to take him to be buried.

We left and made our nightly rounds on the motorcycle. We stopped at the Doctors Hospital, in Silway to see Mr. Aparente and to check on the Nutrition Center. On to Bula to drink a cup of tea and check on the progress of construction for the Community Center, and St. Elizabeth Hospital to find out what medicines the doctor needs for a bleeding ulcer patient we brought in last Saturday. All in a day's work!

I arrived at home at 10:10 PM and knew I couldn't sleep until I wrote to you. Oh, one more thing. On our way back to the convent (a few hundred steps away from the prison), we passed by the jail after our last stop. There was a big fire out front. I guess they were burning the mat and any belongings of the man. I do not know what they did with the body. I think it would be best to cremate it instead of just burying it and allowing all kinds of diseases and germs to contaminate someone's water supply.

Well, that's all for now on that story. I am ready to fall asleep. I'll try to write a few more lines tomorrow and put this in the mail.

March 5, 1971

I have a few free minutes in the afternoon because Fr. James is saying mass. It is Lent, and there are extra masses during the week, so I get a little free time.

Your letter with my income tax form arrived. There was a big fire in the International Post Office in Manila. The top of the envelope was burned off. Only the tax booklet was inside. Was there anything else when you sent it? Glad that you received the tape. I was getting worried it may have been destroyed in the fire. At least, now you can hear my voice.

I wrote to Bud that I requested an extension to serve as a volunteer for another two years. It was approved. Technically, I am entitled to a month's vacation all-expense-paid by the Peace Corps. But I decided to wait and go home during Thanksgiving in November and December to celebrate the holidays in the U.S. in a big way. With lots of food!

I hate to say it, but you wasted $1.75 in postage for my income tax. Peace Corps office sends me all the forms I need. Last year, I had to file a tax return because I had income in the U.S., which put me in the high total income bracket. This year, my total annual income was less than $1,700 – so I don't have to file or pay income taxes.

By the way, thanks for the pictures you sent at Christmas with your new puppy. I showed it to Fr. James, it brought a smile to his face. He is really big on animals. One time he got two baby puppies, and they would cry all night, so he took them to bed with him. Like most dogs here in the Philippines, they had lice and worms. He put up with the scratching for two nights. On the third night, one of the puppies urinated on his pillow. That was enough for him. The first thing the next morning, he took those puppies back to their mother.

Now someone gave him a German shepherd puppy. Yesterday morning, the puppy was pushing his way through a door with a spring on it. As he got his body out the door, his tail was still halfway in the doorway when it slammed shut and cut his tail. He was running around yelping with his tail half-hanging on.

I suggested to Fr. James we should operate on it. He said ok, so I went to the kitchen for a knife. The cook got a small cleaver and a piece of wood. I held the dog on one side of the door while the cook chopped off his tail on the other side. Then Fr. James and I put Merthiolate and gauze on it. He really looks funny with a short tail. Especially when he runs in circles chasing it or when he goes through a door rushing to avoid the slam...

In one of your letters, you asked me about cookie cutters. I have never seen them here. We usually make cookies that are dropped on a sheet or a full pan and cut after finishing. That reminds me. We

received twenty-seven tons of rolled oats (oatmeal), bulgur wheat,
CSM (corn, soy, milk) to be distributed to men working on the roads
from Catholic Relief Services. They are now stored under the bleachers
of the parish center. We are experimenting to find ways for people to
use it... Please try to find some recipes for us if you can. Maybe you'll
find some on the oatmeal boxes or request the company for some. One
last thing, try to find the address of cousin Kenny Wohlbach. Aunt
Mabel Lindenmoyer said he is in the Philippines, maybe she knows
the address. Take care now. Alvin

THE GRADUATION ceremony for the school year 1970-1971
at Notre Dame College was scheduled for April 1971. Since
I taught the previous semester and had been assisting Ms.
Pat de Leon at the Testing Office, I was expected to march
with the graduates along with the rest of the members of the
faculty. Prima and her older brother Tito were candidates for
graduation; Bachelor of Arts major in Economics for her (*Summa
Cum Laude*) and Bachelor of Science in Commerce major in
Accounting for Tito (*Magna Cum Laude*). Bro. Henry convinced
Prima to pursue a Bachelor of Science in Education and to
apply for a Ford Scholarship after she completed her degree.
She resigned from the bank and returned to Bro. Henry's office
so she could enroll in summer courses to be able to finish in
one year. It made it easier for me to collaborate with Prima
regarding our Bula Center Projects.

As soon as I started working at the Parish Center, Father
James introduced me to the leaders of Barrio Bula. Fr. James had
not been as successful in moving the people into action to build
a center. Bula, a coastal barrio like Silway, was a sleepy little
village back then. The most significant industry was fishing.
Marine fishing was more than just a trade in the Philippines;
it was (and still is) a way of life.

A majority of the population of Bula engaged in subsistence
fishing carried out primarily to feed the family and relatives.
But there was a family, the Congsons who owned the majority

of the fishing boats. Dominico "Doming" and Florentina "Flor" Congson were benevolent. Fr. James and the Passionist priests consider them special friends. When I took over the management of the Bula Community Center, they included me in their circle.

Significant donors of the Bula Community Center employing countless men and women in town, the Congsons also built *bangkas* and sold them to the local fishermen. While the entrepreneurial small-time fishermen mainly bring in their haul to sell at the local market, the Congsons looked beyond the boundaries of General Santos City. They delivered a significant supply of fish to the landlocked places like Marbel, Surallah, Davao, and beyond.

Doming Congson and his wife Flor, residents of Bula, pioneered the advanced fishing technology during my Peace Corps service. Ms. Andrea Villano-Campado wrote extensively about the couple's vital contribution to the fishing industry of the city. Ms. Campado, in her thesis, stated: "Using motorized *Bangka* in the 1960s resulted in the increased catch of 150-300 kilograms per fishing trip. This further improved with the use of bigger boats that could carry a load of 800 to 1,000 kilograms (NDDC Business Resource Center, 1994)."[6] In the 1990s, the fishing industry in General Santos was revolutionized by the use of a super seiner. A super seiner is a large, highly sophisticated fishing vessel with communications equipment, built-in cold storage, and brining facilities onboard.

Mrs. Flor Congson, who was elected Vice Mayor, said in an interview with Ms. Campado that, "the use of a super seiner enabled big fishermen of General Santos City to construct large carriers with at least 300 metric tons capacities." At the same period, the Japanese demand for "sashimi" graded tuna in the mid-seventies contributed to the increased rate of growth in the fishing industry. It was reflected in the General Santos City export book. Ms. Campado's wrote in her thesis: "An amount of $7.2 million worth of frozen, chilled tuna in its business transaction with foreign buyers, particularly the Japanese. In 1992, General Santos City was the second port in the Philippines next to Navotas in terms of fish landings but the leading port for high valued fish such as tuna. Complementary to this is the five fish canning plants which exported 19, 332 metric tons of canned tuna valued at the U.S. $ 30.8 million in 1992."

Daily every morning, one can watch the small-operation fishermen in Bula, as they get ready for their fishing trips. They load large blocks of ice in the makeshift icebox. The *bangkas* were outfitted with inboard engines, outriggers for balance, and a wooden icebox to hold the fisherman's daily haul. The Veneracion family owned a thriving ice plant in town that supplied the enormous blocks of ice vital to the refrigeration and transport of the fish.

THE BULA Community Center, the first project that I organized and established as a Social Action Coordinator, started slowly. With the help of potential leaders that Fr. James identified I called a meeting in early January 1971. The initial attendance was encouraging; a majority of the attendees were fishermen and their families. The Bula Community Center association was formed. By February, officers were elected. By March, the construction of the Center was almost finished. To accomplish this, I relied heavily on the cooperation of the barrio folks. Five months after I started my new job, the Bula Community Center was ready to open.

It was an old Parish *Convento* building that was repaired and repurposed to hold all the programs we planned to implement. While the carpenters were still busy finishing the other half of the Center, the other half was made ready to start a Nutrition Program, Nursery School, and Sewing Center. The staff led by Manager and Nutritionist Teodora "Dula" Pacomo did an excellent job with organizing and enrolling our first cohort of pre-school children.

The Commencement Exercise of our first Nutrition class was held to coincide with the Blessing of the Bula Community Center on May 31, 1971, at 3 PM. Thirty-one mothers in the Sewing Class and sixty small children from the Nutrition Program graduated. The Most Reverend Bishop Reginald Arliss was the guest speaker, and the Honorable Mayor Antonio Acharon delivered a very moving inspirational talk. My former Peace Corps Regional Director (interim Country Director during this time), Mr. Charlie White, came to cut the ribbon with the well-known local patron and supporter Mrs. Florentina Congson. More than a hundred businesses, schools, and individuals sponsored the event through our souvenir program. We raised a considerable amount of money from the souvenir program project.

The event was a festive affair. The mothers and the children performed dances, sang, and presented a children's fashion show featuring outfits the mothers created in their Sewing Class. Local restaurants and bakeries donated food for the occasion. Fr. Albinus was pleased and Fr. James was happy.

The mothers made voluntary contributions, a token amount of money when they enrolled their children at the Nutrition Center/ Nursery School. While the mothers attend the sewing classes, their children were in Nursery School. Following the successful opening, the Center expanded its services. It offered a Nutrition Clinic, Medical and Dental Clinic, Legal Services, Embroidery, and Sewing Class, and the Rhythm method of birth control.

A man named Arturo came to the Bula Community Center one month after the opening. He was the self-appointed leader and ambassador from a small village located near the open-air Public Market, and the cluster of oil depots owned by Shell, Caltex, and Esso. He asked to speak to me. Since we capped the number of children at sixty per quarter, he was disappointed that some of the kids in his community were turned away for lack of space.

He presented his idea to open a Nutrition Center in his community. He was willing to organize the effort and find the carpenters to help build the Center, mothers to do the cooking, and someone to manage the project, all for free. He had everything planned to the last detail except the funds for the building.

One day, I ran into the deliveryman for Coca-Cola. I had seen some old Coca-Cola cargo truck bodies sitting empty at the bottling company's lot. I asked him what they did with the truck bodies. He said, "just leave them sitting in the lot."

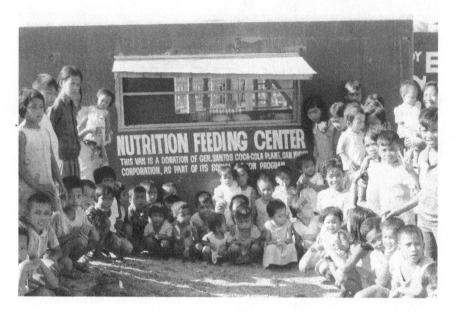

I went to the Coca-Cola Plant and convinced the person in charge to donate an old body of a truck. It would be an effective advertising tool for them, I reasoned. The company's logo and the red and white colors were highly visible. A few days later, a Coca-Cola truck body found its way to Arturo's front yard.

I found a very skilled carpenter to add screened windows, counters, and shelves inside the big red box. The carpenter also built picnic tables with benches to put outside for the feeding. When the Center opened, we had over forty children receiving two full meals daily. It was the most recognizable and my favorite of all three centers. It demonstrated the *Bayanihan* core value that Filipinos are famous for, a spirit of communal unity and effort to achieve a particular objective. I was able to procure funding from Catholic Relief Services to pay the salary for a Manager and Nutritionist. We hired Liberty Caderao to do both.

TEACHING SEVEN classes of Economics I & II to 300 students proved to be a cakewalk compared to the community development job. While teaching was satisfying, it pales in contrast to helping the little children get a fighting chance in life through proper nutrition, mending broken bones, and other disorders.

One day, a little boy, about seven years old, came to the Silway Nutrition Center with his mother. He held his right arm tightly across his belly just below his chest like it was glued on to his tattered shirt. He sat at the table with the other kids, and when his bowl of oatmeal arrived, he clumsily picked up his spoon and slowly scooped his food to his mouth with his left hand.

I could tell he was right-handed and quite hungry. I tried to talk to the boy's mother to find out what was wrong with his right arm. But she could not quite understand my Tagalog as she spoke the Cebuano dialect. Our nutritionist asked questions. She found out that the boy had a broken arm. However, the family did not have the financial means to pay for a doctor's visit. I conferred with the nutritionist. She explained to the mother that we would find a doctor to examine the boy for free. The mother agreed to take her son to a doctor. Examination revealed that the boy had broken his arm by his elbow a few months prior. His bone was sticking out of his skin. The doctor pulled the broken and detached bone from his arm, declaring the bone dead and useless. Typically, all the dental and health issues in our community centers were handled professionally in General Santos by local doctors, many of whom had training or had previously worked in hospitals in the United States. But this little boy's case was beyond the available local surgical expertise and equipment. We sent him to an orthopedic surgeon in Davao City who promptly repaired his arm. All in a day's work.

Another time, a little girl with cleft palate (harelip) about age six was brought to the Nutrition Center by her mother. A cleft palate can occur without a cleft on the lip. These are not noticeable as a cleft lip. But even if the parents noticed the defect at their baby's birth, without financial resources, they were left untreated. Cleft palate poses immediate feeding concerns at birth, like difficulty with breastfeeding because of the baby's inability to get proper suction.[7] Also, the afflicted kids face a variety of challenges depending on the severity of the cleft. They are highly at risk of developing hearing loss, dental issues, speech, and eating difficulties. Not to mention the social and emotional problems stemming from the way they look.

We recruited local doctors willing to do the surgery to repair the disorder *pro bono*. Once the word spread of our Community Centers' offerings, we found other children with similar disorders. By the end of my Peace Corps stint at the Our Lady and Peace of Good Voyage, we restored the smiles on the faces of eight boys and girls suffering from the disorder. All in a day's work.

After the successful opening and inauguration of our Bula Community Center, the staff and I organized a picnic at Bawing beach to celebrate. We invited all the Bula Center volunteers, including Prima and her friend Rosela, who were also friends with the staff at the community centers. There was a *jeepney*-full of us. As usual, we gathered shells along the beach for me to send to family and friends in the States, some waded in the low tide, some went swimming. I got ready to snorkel. Suddenly, I heard a scream. We all rushed to the source.

"Sir Al, Sir Al," Rosela ran to meet us. "Prima stepped on a sea urchin. She is in terrible pain. The spine of the urchin is stuck at the most sensitive bottom of her foot. It will break if we try to pull it out. My father told me that urine is the best medicine."

I quickly searched for an empty coconut shell that usually littered the beach and found one. I had never taken a whiz by the tire of a bus. I was too embarrassed to do it. But when push comes to shove, a Peace Corps volunteer has to do what he's got to do. I went behind a bush and brought back the coconut shell containing Rose's prescribed medicine.[8]

Rose poured the urine over the sharp thorn-like spine. I did not see the barb work itself out of the punctured wound, but Prima assured us she was quite ok. All in a day's work!

We resumed our beach picnic. We gathered driftwood scattered along the beach and built our bonfire for cooking. While preparing our meal, Rose got her guitar out, and we sang songs.

For lunch, everyone enjoyed a scrumptious spread of *sugba-sugba* ~ broiled squid, octopus, red snapper, pompano, and a variety of unknown fish that we bought from the spearfishermen of Tambler.

Using only their goggles, these spear fishermen's catch was an assortment of squid, octopus, pompano, red snapper, etc. They willingly sold their catch to beachgoers so they could buy hankered-for canned goods like sardines, Hormel corned beef, or Spam for a change of menu.

The Silway Nutrition Center was the first that Fr. James established. The programs in Silway were replicated at two other centers.

Feeding the children at one of our Nutrition Centers. It was always a full house when one of the doctors in town came to the Nutrition Clinics.

Dra. Teresita Catapang provided dental services to the children and some parents. Pharmaceutical companies supplied toothbrushes and toothpaste.

The Guipo family: Front (l-r): Nelly Grana (cousin), Mr. & Mrs. Guipo, Diana. Back (l-r): Josie, Tito, Prima, Nena, PCV, Susan, Angelo, Felipe. Like their parents, all the Guipo children except Felipe taught at private and public schools.

Prima and Leonardo M. Yu, the instructor I temporarily replaced so he could attain his Masters in Teaching Economics.

Mr. Charlie White, Interim Director of the Peace Corps/Philippines and Mrs. Florentina Congson cut the ribbon during the Opening Ceremonies at the Bula Community Center on May 31, 1971.

Left: The mothers who graduated from the sewing class performed Filipino dances. Peace Corps trainee Allan Spencer and his wife Annie (former Peace Corps language instructor), my Mormon friends, the Marist, and Oblates Nuns were among the 100 plus guests who attended.

Bottom left: His Excellency Bishop Reginald Arliss and Fr. Gabriel Baldostamon at the Blessing ceremony.

Below: The children graduating from nutrition class wearing outfits their mothers sewed for them. They sang and danced too.

Home Leave   9

THE NEW DIRECTION of my Peace Corps career kicked into high gear in March 1971. Fr. James slowly relinquished his managerial role at the community centers to embark on numerous other projects while preparing for his three-month furlough in Pittsburgh, Pennsylvania. I was busier than usual, which suited me very well. The new position expanded my network of friends and associates. I was invited to more birthday parties, fiestas, as a speaker at a Rotary Club event, as godfather at baptisms, and at weddings as a guest and as a sponsor.

In the Philippines, sponsors are an essential part of the traditional wedding. There are Primary Sponsors called "Ninang" and "Ninong" (godmother and godfather). They are listed in the invitation along with the Secondary Sponsors, which include the wedding entourage plus the coin, candle, veil, and cord sponsors.

Although I no longer taught courses at the college, I continued to assist Bro. Henry. He assigned me to gather alumni statistics. Tuesdays and Thursdays, I worked at the Testing Office with Miss Pat de Leon. Through her, I found a new place to live with the Gavilan Family.

I was content with my life in General Santos. I felt comfortable with being romantically unattached. Still finding wanderlust irresistible at twenty-seven, settling down was not something I considered seriously. But at times, when I snorkeled by my lonesome at Tinoto beach or witnessed a spectacular sunset, I thought how nice it would be if I had someone special with whom I could share such cherished moments. I began to contemplate on the new direction for my own personal life.

I dated a Filipina girl and promptly confided my secret to Prima. Our friendship was such that I felt comfortable doing so. Ingrained with the Pennsylvania Dutch values of my forefathers, I determined to observe the traditional customs of courtship in the Philippines, which was totally compatible with my own deep-seated beliefs and sensibilities. I put into good use everything I learned from Peace Corps Training about the customs of courtship in the Philippines, like going out in a group setting. I even invited Prima to come along as a chaperon a few times. Dating the Filipina girl, however, lasted only a few months.

The Peace Corps encouraged volunteers to extend their service after completing their term or to re-enroll. I opted to re-enroll for another two years. I notified my Country Director three months before my projected departure. My request was approved. By re-enrolling, a volunteer was awarded a special leave. "A volunteer who extends for a year or more may take up to 30 days of special leave in the United States, Western Europe, or any other part of the world outside the Communist-controlled countries."[1]

Some volunteers I knew traveled around Asia, the Middle East, or Europe, but I decided to go home to the States. Technically, I was entitled to take my special leave in March 1971. We were in the middle of the construction of the Bula Community Center, and Fr. James was preparing for his three-month vacation in the U.S. It just did not make sense for both of us to be gone at the most critical time of our projects. Besides, I really wanted to be home for Thanksgiving and Christmas holidays.

A few weeks before departing for my home leave in November 1971, I left the Gavilan house to live closer to my workplace. Fr. James was being transferred to Marbel, so I would be without the use of his motorcycle for transportation.

I decided to move to the Bula Community Center. There was a spacious second floor that I converted into my bedroom and living area. There were two closets with ample space to store my belongings for when I was away on my home leave. In fact, one of the closets was used regularly to store bananas donated by Stanfilco until they ripened.

I intended to make the Center my permanent place to live when I came back from vacation. But the Center was mice-infested. I bought sticky flypapers and spread numerous sheets around my living area. When I heard the squeaks in the middle of the night, I checked the flypapers. I thwacked the mice on the head and disposed of the sheets full of trapped and dead mice the following morning.

Before my departure, we held a few staff meetings at the three centers to ascertain everyone was on the same page. The managers had their instructions to ensure that the three Community Centers functioned, as they should while I was away. The nutritionists received their approval to attend a seminar to keep them updated. The staff also knew that Fr. James or Fr. Albinus would always be there should they need any guidance.

I went to the college to request Prima to hold onto whatever mail arrived in the next month. She said she'd place them in an envelope for me to retrieve when I came back from home leave, wished me a pleasant trip home, and reminded me to take pictures of the snow. Before I left the office of Bro. Henry, she handed me a brown manila envelope that just came in the mail that day bulging with correspondence and magazines. When I arrived back at the Bula Community Center, I sorted through my mail. There was a familiar airmail letter from Vassar College, New York. It was from Anne. Yes, she will be home for Christmas, she wrote.

The message brought a flood of memories. But there was no time to respond. There was *pasalubongs*[2] (gifts) to pack, last-minute reports to submit, and a suitcase to get ready. After being away for almost three years, I was eager to go home. The Peace Corps provided us with a travel voucher giving us the freedom to arrange our itinerary. I had specific places and persons I wanted to visit. I meticulously mapped out my schedule to maximize my one-month time in the United States. I noted on my itinerary to see Anne.

A week before Thanksgiving, I flew to Jaro, Leyte. I had accepted an invitation from Sister Andrea Solar, a nun of the Oblates of Notre Dame I had befriended at Notre Dame College. The province was famous for the Battle of Leyte Gulf that happened during WWII, where General Douglas McArthur's "I Shall Return" promise was fulfilled on the beachhead of Leyte on October 20, 1944. I was curious too, to see the place where my Uncle Aaron had set foot only twenty-five years before.

The nuns managed the Parish School named Notre Dame of Jaro. One day Sister Andrea took me around Jaro in the parish jeep. Aside from growing coconuts for copra, the province was also noted for rice. A trip along the countryside yielded a series of photos of the pastoral scenery. I was able to record the rice fields and the complete process of the harvest on film, depicting the typical rural life in the Philippines. It became an essential part of my slide presentations that I shared with family and friends during home leave.

One of the notable photos was of a farmer "threshing" rice. The rice was dried right on the surface of the concrete national highway. Vehicles had to go around the piles of rice being dried under the sun. The farmer used his feet as threshers. (On November 8, 2013, almost 42 years to the day I visited Leyte, the strongest typhoon to ever hit Asia named Haiyan, also called Yolanda in the Philippines, devastated the province and demolished the Notre Dame of Jaro campus. The Washington Post reported the wind speed of Typhoon Haiyan at 195 miles per hour. The minimum wind speed of a Category 5 hurricane is clocked at 157 miles per hour. Before Haiyan, the highest measured wind speed of any hurricane or typhoon was 190 miles per hour in 1969's Hurricane Camille. Haiyan broke that record.)[3]

From Leyte, I flew to Manila. Traveling light, I packed only one Samsonite hardcover suitcase filled with *pasalubong*. I saved enough space on one side for a small *tampipi* (valise woven out of bamboo) for my clothing and shaving kit. From Manila, Pan American Airlines made a stopover in Japan. I bought a Pentax SLR camera. My first destination was Tampa, Florida, to visit my dad and stepmother, Gladys Shoemaker. My mom had died in February 1967. My dad remarried in September 1968, six months before I left for the Peace Corps.

Gladys and her family moved to Florida in the mid-1950s and had lived there since. Her first husband died of a heart attack shortly after they moved into their new house in Tampa. They had five boys – Larry, Glen, Ken, Nelson, and Terry, and one girl Tina. Gladys was a foster child adopted by my dad's Aunt Stella, married to Lloyd Lerch. My dad and Gladys knew each other from their childhood. In fact, Gladys married Allen Shoemaker, the younger brother of my dad's best friend, Ralph.

Gladys and Allen raised turkeys on their farm in Pennsylvania but lost it all when a hurricane hit the Lehigh

Valley in 1957 and leveled their turkey pens. They could not even sell any of the birds that survived because they had wooden splinters embedded in their bodies. They moved to Florida soon after.

I MISSED my connecting flight from San Francisco to Tampa due to long lines clearing customs. I called my dad from the airline desk to inform him. The airport was packed with holiday travelers. The PA system was blaring holiday announcements in between Christmas carols. The next leg of my journey took me to Chicago. The plane from Chicago to Tampa had mechanical problems and had to return to the terminal. While waiting for a replacement plane, the airline desk arranged for another call to my dad and reassured me I would be home for the turkey dinner.

Landing at the brand new Tampa International Airport (TIA), I underwent a reversed culture shock. There appeared to be hundreds of airplanes at the airport. We had one flight a day at Gen. Santos airport and none when it rained hard. Getting off the plane, I searched for and found a payphone, put my dime in the slot, but there was no rotary dial! What was I to do? Hmm – push the buttons. It calls the number. Wow! Next, I heard voices coming from the wall saying, "Get on the people mover to go to baggage claim." Inside the driverless car, voices again gave instructions on where to find the baggage.

Navigating the new driverless people mover called an automated guide way transit (AGT) blew my mind. The system at TIA was a pioneering state-of-the-art concept, opened on April 15, 1971, just seven months before I came home. My dad told me that over 50,000 people attended the two-day TIA open house. The *Landside/Airside* design looked to me like something that came out of a science fiction movie.[4] The central terminal termed "landside" was connected by mass transits called "people movers" to four satellite air terminals and gates termed "airside."

Arriving at 2 AM, I was awed by the illuminated, sprawling city of Tampa as my dad drove me home to their house on Renfrew Place, a block away from the entrance of Busch Gardens. (Ten years hence, I would move my family right next door to Dad and Gladys).

Gladys was an excellent cook. She baked turkey for Thanksgiving, of course. Since it was a potluck dinner, the dining table was loaded with traditional holiday dishes I had not seen for almost three years. For the next three weeks, she fed me the good-old American dishes that I was hankering for. My stepfamily came to the Thanksgiving feast. The houseful of guests – family and friends - was a far cry from the past two Thanksgiving holidays I spent in the Philippines alone.

Disneyworld Orlando had just opened on October 1, 1971, a month before my arrival. My dad made sure that was our first stop. The amusement park was bedecked with Christmas lights of all sizes imaginable, holiday wreaths, and decorated Christmas trees all over the park. At the entrance to the Magic Kingdom stood the biggest tree, at least thirty feet or more, decorated with red and white ornaments.

The park was not as crowded as I had expected. The Disney characters were welcoming guests at every corner, it seemed. I had my photo taken with Mickey, Minnie, and Goofy without having to wait. A ride on the "It's a Small World" boat tour for ten minutes kept me whistling the theme song all day. Described by Disneyworld as *The Happiest Cruise that Ever Sailed*, it encouraged the tourist to "Sing along to the classic anthem of world peace during a delightful musical boat tour."[5]

Coming from General Santos, a city without any traffic lights and but one stop sign, the ostentatious Christmas lights display at Mickey's park was almost too much for this volunteer to absorb. Nevertheless, the novel experience that it offered was much appreciated. I was in a holiday mood after all.

The natural setting at Cypress and Busch Gardens and the scientific wonders of Kennedy Space Center was more aligned with my taste. During that time, entrance to Busch Gardens was free. (The 2019 Entrance fee is $109.99). The amusement park then owned by the Anheuser-Busch Brewing Company was just being developed as an African Safari-themed garden; it was mainly a brewery where visitors were served beer, entertained with a bird show and a rose garden.

We went on a weeklong tour of Florida starting from Cape Canaveral on the east, down to Miami, the Everglades National Park and worked our way up along the West Coast. We stayed in hotels during the trip and ate out every day. I ordered all kinds of food that I had missed.

I spent three weeks with Dad and Gladys in Florida. The tropical weather, similar to the Philippines, was an excellent place for me to start my R&R. I flew to Pittsburgh to spend two days with Fr. James' parents. That day, I woke up to summerlike temperatures in Tampa in the morning and landed at the wintry chill of Pennsylvania in the afternoon. Mrs. James pampered me like I was her son. To this day, I still remember the donuts that she prepared for me using the Pillsbury breakfast biscuit dough.

The next stop was Bethlehem, Pennsylvania, covered with snow. I arrived the day my sister Joyce, her family, and my younger brother Dean drove south to Florida to visit our dad. I never met up with them during that month-long vacation in the States. As a result, we did not see each other for five and a half years.

Looking back now, my siblings and I tried to figure out how and why our travel plans went awry. We could not imagine it happening after having planned my home leave for eight months. We had arranged a family reunion with Dad in Florida months in advance. The only plausible reason we could surmise is that I may have been forced to change my flight route at the last minute while I was still in the Philippines. It was too late to inform them by mail, or if I did, their plans had been set into motion and were irreversible, considering Joyce, her husband Earl, and Dean all worked full-time.

My brother Bud was not able to travel to Florida for some reason. He drove me around the Allentown-Bethlehem area. We both recalled the slide presentation at the house of our stepbrother, Glenn Shoemaker. Bud remembered the slide show very well because being a dog lover, he couldn't help but notice that most of the dogs he saw on my slides were so skinny. The audience was quite shocked when I mentioned that in some parts of the world, dogs were a food delicacy, including the Philippines.

WE DROVE by the old farm. Dad sold the farm sometime before my home leave, but the new owner had not taken over the property yet. My younger brother Dean, who had been living in the farmhouse since I left in 1969, had just transferred to a new place. He emailed: "When you came home in 1971, I just moved to Coplay. I remember I didn't have a phone yet. I went to Joyce to see if you had arrived. It was snowing badly. My car spun around and scraped the guardrail. I headed back home, and I think you didn't make it to Joyce that night anyway. I do remember going to Florida with Joyce and Earl and family..."

Seeing the old farmhouse and the barn made me nostalgic for the family picnics, hayrides with my siblings and friends, hiking with Dad around the iron ore mine nearby, and Mom's shoofly pie.

Oh, so many memories. Among them was this strange dream I had one night before I left for the Peace Corps Training in California. I dreamt of a girl with long, black hair wearing a toga. But images of another girl I met at church named Anne appeared unbidden. Anne, the girl I courted seriously but only eighteen at that time, getting ready to go to college and told me she was too young to get serious with anyone, including her other suitor Peter. I decided to bide my time and resolved to wait until she finished college.

When I arrived in General Santos City in 1969, Anne and I established contact again and continued to correspond until I left for home leave. Anne was twenty-one at this time, finishing third-year college plus real-life rewarding summer jobs and interim study projects in the ghetto, with Native Americans, and emotionally disturbed children. I was twenty-seven, a master's degree finished, five-and-a-half years teaching high school and college, and more than two years with the Peace Corps. The correspondence we kept during the first two-and-a-half years of Peace Corps was not frequent but intense and highly intellectual. Not a single letter from Anne ever mentioned Peter.

Before leaving for home leave, I hopefully entertained the idea of a possible romance with Anne. The letter I received from her the day before I left for Pennsylvania said she would be home for Christmas. Meeting Anne was going to be the high point in the vacation. Where should we first meet after so long? In church. Anne just stared when we met. I had been through so much of life already that it was easy to keep calm. She invited me to visit her that night. Well, no sign of Peter.

Gee, what will it be like after so many years? I still didn't know about Peter, though. Or, could there be someone else? Finally, the time came. We were sitting in the living room. Her younger brother was watching television in the family room, out of sight and sound. Everyone else was out. It was just small talk at first how's this and that. Then I managed to slip Peter into the conversation without making it noticeable. Yes, Peter still comes around, she said. That's about as far as that went. I quickly slid on to another topic. Perhaps the years with Peace Corps had done it. I managed to hold my feelings inside. Deep down, though, my heart dropped, and I felt a big defeat at that moment. Anne never noticed, and neither did her parents sense anything when they came home later. One night during that home leave, I sat down and wrote:

When the whole world seems to cop-out, you can always sit down and write to somebody, even if that somebody has to be yourself.

That was a long time ago, but the memory is still clear... One day, the Pastor asked me to be our church's youth advisor. Why not? I've been teaching high school for two years. Dean was in the Youth Fellowship. We have become very close since mother died. Dean's my little brother. Well, anyway, he used to be. He is bigger and taller than me now, but he is still seven years my junior.

It was springtime. Youth activities did not begin to pick up until summer vacation... Anne was in the youth group, but that didn't mean much. She often brought Peter to church or youth activities. I was between petty romances that sometimes lasted a few weeks and a few months. Anne's presence did not faze me then.

Things were going along great that summer. I owned a little Volkswagen Campmobile rental business. I just accepted a teaching position at Churchman Business College and was working on a master's degree with three-quarters under my belt.

The Youth Fellowship was really active when summer vacation began; our activities allowed Dean and me to spend a lot of time together. Hootenannies, informal gatherings with folk music and sometimes dancing, were still around and Sing-out! was really gaining popularity.[6] We often got together just to sit around singing folk songs, especially. The Volkswagen Campmobile was a useful bus too. There was always room for a big pile of kids. When there was not enough room in one, we used the second Campmobile. That was my style. I always enjoyed a group of fun-loving kids.

I subscribe to this philosophy about kids and parents; the parents like to know what their children are doing. They also prefer to see them have parties at home or be able to go with their kids. On the other side, kids can get to know each other better if they visit each other in their homes. They can learn the ways of other families, etc.

That summer, we went from house to house having parties and hootenannies. I took the group horseback riding, and we went hiking in the mountains around Lehigh Valley. Whenever we went someplace else, we tried to invite at least one member's parents. It did miracles. Parents trusted their children. When the Volkswagen Campmobile pulled up, the parents let the kids go without any hesitation. They had such confidence in our group...

Time has a way of passing and so with petty romances. Seeing Anne so often began to wear on me. At eighteen, she was poised and becoming of womanhood. What do they say about "true love never dies?" But there was Peter; and our age difference, six-and-a-half years.

What is this Peter's real standing anyway? I know he is a star football player in high school, and nobody has to tell me he is a good looking six-foot blonde with blue eyes and built like an all-American football star. I really want to know about his relationship with Anne. She says only a friend, but why is he always hanging around?

Anne is a really beautiful girl, but that's not what attracted me so this time. Getting to know Anne's parents and brother left a significant impression. It was such good family life. Then there were the many talents of Anne, cooking, sewing, honors in school, arts and crafts, the collections of little but important things, singing, remembering, love of people, ability to look beyond a small world so much rolled into one girl. Wow, what more could any man want?

Football training camp started in the middle of the summer, and Peter was awfully busy. He didn't come to see Anne much anymore, Anne began feeling she wasn't wanted. I guess my presence became more common then. At first, it was just with the youth group. But then I began coming to her house alone. I told Anne, I think I'm in love with you. Her first reaction was a thoughtful silence. Then we began writing letters exchanging the thoughts of our hearts.

We never got to be alone again that summer. Anne's mother began getting suspicious of our doings. Once, she caught one of Anne's letters. She had a long talk with Anne and asked the Pastor to talk with me. The Pastor never mentioned it to me. But I guess that guilty feeling showed all over when near the Pastor or Anne's parents. We still spent a lot of time together but only with the group. Our letters tinged with emotion as we continued our secret and forbidden correspondence.

Youth activities started to slow down that fall as school began. Anne was a senior in high school, and here I was a teacher in college. That was our big problem. Anne was too young, or I too old. At least that's how her mother saw things.

Then Peter began coming around again. I was really jealous. Didn't those things we said and wrote to each other mean anything? I know her mother likes Peter better. But I'll wait till Anne finishes college. Now I can look back and admit that I was jealous because I had so much to lose. There are lots of girls around, but it is rare to find one with qualities like Anne's. That's a pretty good reason to be jealous.

Well, knowing the mother's position, then Peter's coach asking Anne to go back to Peter so his sports performance would improve, and Anne agreeing that she was much too young to be serious about anyone all added up to a strike-out for me. There should be no malice after so long, but I still sometimes think of the significant loss to me. Anyway, Anne got somebody good. We still saw each other at church, but I decided to move on...

When I started my Peace Corps service, somehow, Anne and I started writing to each other again after I arrived in the Philippines.

Just before my home leave, our letters began to lend a little rhyme of possible love. But a possible love was not meant to be.

A WEEK till Christmas day and already, I wanted to be on my way back to the Philippines. Anne and I didn't see each other again while I was in the States. Admittedly, I was happy that my mom's sister, Aunt Valeria Laubach, who lived in Hellertown adjacent to Bethlehem, invited me for Christmas. At least I could go to a different church and wouldn't have to be reminded. With a heavy heart, I continued with my travel schedule as I worked my way back to the Philippines.

The day after Christmas, I landed in Boston. Becky and Dave Hsu greeted me at the airport. It was like being almost home in the Philippines, spending time with them. Their love made me feel so good, and all the more anxious to want to get back to the Philippines. The year before, Becky, Dave, and I were all in Cotabato City, celebrating their marriage. There was dancing and toasting of the newlyweds. As the best man at their wedding, I was so glad to be present at their first wedding anniversary celebration with a bunch of their friends from Harvard.

Needing some physical activity, I shoveled the snow on their sidewalk. Together we drove to New Hampshire to spend New Year's Day with Muriel Cooke, a Returned Peace Corps Volunteer from our Group 31. Muriel's cousin took us snowmobiling. I had no heavy winter coat except a sweater and a lined trench coat that I had brought to the Philippines in 1969. I layered a lot to stay warm.

After the New Year, I left for the Philippines. I stayed in Manila for a few days attending to some personal business at the Peace Corps office, visited some friends on my way back, and arrived in General Santos a few days later. The first thing I did upon my return to General Santos was to visit Notre Dame College to collect my accumulated mail.

It was after lunch. Prima was not at her familiar corner when I entered the office of Bro. Henry. I retrieved from her desk two manila envelopes that she had marked with my name. Bro. Henry must have read what was on my mind. Before I could ask, he said, "Prima's out somewhere on campus with our photographer Mr. Tony Cascaro supervising the photo-taking of the high school kids for the yearbook."

Bro. Henry and I chatted a while about my visit with my family and friends in the States. Then I went looking for Prima. She was sitting on one of the concrete benches under the pine trees at the quad, engrossed in a book. She had her back to me, her long black hair flowing freely, almost touching the bench. She didn't even look up until I tapped her shoulder with the rolled-up copy of TIME Magazine.

"That wasn't nice," she chided. "I almost jumped out of my skin. How was your trip?"

"Had a great time and gained twenty pounds in a month."

"You look it, but you could still use some fattening up. Are you glad to be back?"

"Yes, I am, just not sure if I'm ready to tackle the year ahead at the community centers. The vacation spoiled me," I said as nonchalantly as I could muster. Deep down inside, for a reason, I was not ready to admit to myself at that moment, I could hardly hide the excitement in my voice upon seeing Prima.

"I hope you did not forget to take pictures of the snow," she said making sure to remind me of my promise.

"As a matter of fact, I didn't. Let's do a slide show soon so I can show you how to shovel snow," I said.

Bro. Sam Geveso came along and joined us. He offered to take Prima home in the Marist VW Kombi. I tagged along. Prima was so excited for us to taste the tomato jam she had prepared using the recipe from the Good Housekeeping Magazine that her friend Mrs. Nena Yorro had given her. The jam was quite good spread over SkyFlakes crackers, a local favorite.

As we were leaving, I handed Prima a plastic shopping bag with my *pasalubong* inside. She opened it and took out a stuffed red lamb and a bunch of postcards of tourist spots in Allentown and Bethlehem, Pennsylvania, to add to her collection. On the back of the postcard showing the iconic Bethlehem Hotel, I wrote, "If you ever find yourself in this part of the world someday, do stop by for a visit."

Talk about *pasalubong*. During my home leave, I emptied my suitcase full of *pasalubong* for family and friends in the U.S. to make room for *pasalubong* for friends in General Santos. As I cited in Chapter 7, *pasalubong* is a common word for a "gift," but not just any gift. It comes from the Tagalog root word, "salubong" meaning to *welcome* or *to meet*, and the "pa" is a prefix. *Pasalubong* roughly translated means a gift to a relative or a friend from a traveler returning from a trip. Or from someone who had been living away from home. It is an ingrained Filipino value system, relished by some and viewed by others, as a necessary encumbrance because the possible alternative course of action or inaction could be worse.

A few months back in the Philippines, and everything seemed normal again. Then an unexpected but familiar airmail envelope from Vassar College, New York, arrived. Anne wrote a letter that baffled me at first. In fact, she admitted being confused in writing. She said, "When we met in the States, I wanted to throw my arms around you and hug and kiss you." Then she went on to explain her plans for marriage to Peter after her college graduation. Anne was very confused and still not sure she made the right decision about Peter. Partly, Anne expressed that she also felt a sense of guilt or debt to me.

Here I was 10,000 miles away and experiencing the same kind of confusion. This was what I wrote on a slip of paper tucked in my journal: *I reviewed my past while I spent a week with David and Becky and upon returning to the Philippines. I decided to pursue an emotion I once had in T'boli land a few years ago. I made up my mind to look seriously into a girl that had most of the same* qualities that I admired so in Anne and more. The same close-knit family ties, the same endearing ways, the same age. I remembered the things I wrote about Anne and the same could be said about this girl. It is hard to believe two people could possess so many of the same endearing attributes yet be so unique and special in their own way, of a different race, nurtured under two different cultures, and brought up ten thousand miles apart.

This girl has long black hair, which she wears in many styles, my favorite being in her girlish pigtails or just flowing freely. Her round cheeks surround her usually smiling, sometimes serious, concerned mouth. Top those with a pair of ever-loving brown eyes that melts the heart, and there's Prima. Even the name is unique.

After the letter from Anne, I had to examine my life and retake stock of the situation. Then a talk with God, and I wrote back. Peter is the man for Anne. Anyway, I have my love here in the Philippines. All was well, and Anne wrote back no longer confused. I was satisfied now and ready to pursue the possibilities of romance with Prima.

Well, maybe I'm slow, or maybe I want to be sure, or maybe I have too much or too little confidence. Anyway, I took my time courting Prima. Now I hear that a former boyfriend is after Prima.

Where does that put me?

Unnamed high school student, Annie Garcia, Bula Kindergarten teacher & Dula Pacomo, Manager & Nutritionist of Bula Center.

The rest of the photos (below) depict our activities: Sewing & Feeding program, the PC volunteer picking up a whole tuna donated by the Congson family, and Nutrition Class with the mothers

Social Action: Adventures, Pitfalls, & Rewards

10

THE DECEMBER 1971 massacre in Milbuk was obviously absent from my mind when I was savoring every morsel of my favorite foods in the States during the Thanksgiving and Christmas holidays. But it was definitely front and center, the day I reported to work twenty-four hours after returning from vacation on January 12, 1972. And quite unexpectedly, the tragic incident placed the parish of Our Lady of Peace and Good Voyage and me in the middle of humanitarian efforts that followed in the wake of the massacre.

During my debriefing on the "good news and bad news" that had occurred at the three community centers while I was away, Fr. Albinus dispensed with the bad news first.

"Fr. Hyacinth is arriving from Milbuk in a few days," Fr. Albinus declared. "There was a horrific massacre at his parish last month. The parish center is overrun by evacuees, and there is a short supply of food."

"What happened?"

"Oh, the usual age-old Muslim-Christian conflict about land issues," Fr. Albinus, said. "We may have to help out with the delivery of food. The other Parishes are pitching in what they could. You know of course that Milbuk could only be reached by sea. So, it would be a challenge. And by the way, it's official. Fr. James is now permanently transferred to Marbel."

I listened to Fr. Albinus' Christian-Muslim story. Mindful of my responsibility as a Peace Corps Volunteer not to get involved in the politics of my host country, I kept my opinions to myself. It was a very complicated matter that I only began to understand after reading Arthur Amaral's 2015 book, *The Awakening of Milbuk, Diary of a Missionary Priest.* He wrote in detail about the December massacre at Fr. Hyacinth's parish and explained succinctly in layman's terms the root cause of this particular local conflict; land grabbing and revenge. Perhaps Amaral's explanation was too simplistic, but it was applicable at the micro-level. Amaral was a missionary priest who took over the Milbuk parish in 1974 after Fr. Hyacinth Welka was transferred elsewhere.

The unprovoked attack happened early one morning at a farming village about twelve kilometers from Milbuk. A dozen Christian families were living in the village. Seven died horribly, their bodies mutilated. Fr. Hy drove up in his jeep hours after the massacre, and he was sickened by what he saw. Body parts strewn all over the people's yard. Several others were wounded. Amaral wrote, "…These settlers had friends and family living in Surallah, South Cotabato, who belonged to the vigilante group who called themselves *ilaga* or rats in Hiligaynon. The *ilaga* were successful in combating terrorist-like efforts of some Muslims in their area who attempted to drive them from their lands…Land grabbing and revenge is what this conflict was all about. The settlers had purchased the land from its Muslim 'owners' only to be told that the 'real owners' would also need to be paid for the land."[1]

I filed the Milbuk tragedy at the back of my mind while I attended to my troubles at hand. On top of the list, I was homeless! Immediately after my return from home leave, I realized that my initial idea of living at the Bula Community Center was crazy considering my aversion to mice. The large population of rodents at the Community Center seemed to have exploded while I was away. And the cuter mice had by this time metamorphosed into ugly rats. I was just glad they did not gnaw at my belongings. After one night, I decided I could not bear to sleep in the same house with these varmints anymore.

Secondly, I was without my dependable sounding board in Fr. James. I missed our stimulating conversations and our daily interactions as partners in our social action endeavors and adventures. But more than that, I missed his friendship and his contagious and seemingly inexhaustible zest for life. I recalled our motorcycle rides and our hunting jaunt. We went home empty-handed, but it was nice to be outdoors gallivanting with him, unhampered by work duties. Having shot at cans and small games on our farm growing up using only a single shot .22 Caliber rifle or a single barrel shotgun, I was rather impressed by his marksmanship. Especially for a priest!

About this time, I needed a dose of his sunny disposition. He was always an optimist. To compound matters, I was becoming disappointed with some of the staff at the Community Centers, and I was suffering from amoebic dysentery, all adding to my perplexing state of confusion. This letter to my dad reflected my frame of mind.

January 13, 1972
Dear Dad and all,

Yesterday morning I arrived in General Santos City. All is well with me. I hope everything is fine with everybody there. Just in case someone finds my sunglasses, please wrap them well and mark them prescription glasses and send them to me.

I have had really mixed emotions since returning to the Philippines. Much of the time, I think only of how nice and clean it is in the States (even Tokyo and Hong Kong were clean) compared to here. People just throw their garbage everywhere. Then I think how poorly things are managed here, everybody just seems to do things the hard way or for no reason at all, including here at the Convento and at the centers. The bahala na [fatalistic] attitude is prevalent.[2]

I think I brought too much of the German Pennsylvania Dutch work ethic with me that witnessing the fatalism, indifference, and indolence drives me nuts. Then I rationalize how much people need help. Then I wonder if trying to improve these physical aspects makes any difference. Maybe we should be doing more things to improve the moral and spiritual life of people. And then, I look at what other things I could be doing–well, I just don't know what it is I should be doing. Meanwhile, I guess I'll keep on trying, that's all.

Backtracking a bit - January 3, I left Boston, arriving in Tokyo on the evening of January 4 (Tokyo time). Our plane arrived too late to make the connection to Hong Kong, so Pan American Airlines put us up overnight at the Tokyo Hilton Hotel at their expense. Most of the Americans missing their airline connection were complaining and screaming at the Japanese clerks at the airport.

I sat back smiling because I had the good fortune of getting a free overnight stay. We were shuttled from the airport to the posh Hilton. And yes, that includes a free return trip to the airport and dinner at the hotel's restaurant. But one has to wear a coat and tie to be served. This Peace Corps volunteer did not bring a suit! The uniformed maître d' took me aside and guided me to a closet full of dinner jackets and ties. I enjoyed my scrumptious dinner in borrowed clothes.

We were booked for a morning flight to Hong Kong, which meant I could do my shopping without spending overnight in the city. I walked the streets of Hong Kong all afternoon, trying to find the best buy in camera. I ended up buying a single-lens reflex Minolta SRT 101 with flash, and a Japanese made slide projector.

When I got back to Manila, someone told me there was an American government-owned store with lower prices for U.S. government employees. Oh well, next time na lang as we say here in the Philippines. The camera is not for underwater use as I planned. It just seemed foolish to spend so much money on an underwater camera and not to have a good camera for general use. The Minolta costs $125 and is similar to the Pentax I bought in Japan on my way home last month. I gave my Pentax to David Hsu when I visited them in Boston.

When I arrived in Manila, it was about ten PM. As we walked out of the plane, the heat struck me. Note that I went snowmobiling in New Hampshire with Becky and Dave. I shoveled snow in Boston just *a few days before that. Going through customs, the officer confiscated the slide projector I bought in Hong Kong. Then the taxi driver tried to take me for a ride- after I told him my destination, he started taking the longer route. I was fortunate that I knew my way in Manila, and I could speak Tagalog. The heat, the smell of garbage, and the sight of abject poverty made me want to forget about coming back to the Philippines.*

The next day, the Peace Corps Director refused to help me get my slide projector. He got really huffy about it.[3] Well, that got me off to a good start with our new country director. I ended up paying P51 pesos ($8.50) to get it back from customs.

I tramped the streets of Manila for almost a whole day looking for the things people in Pennsylvania ordered and ended up not buying anything because the prices have gone up, and the selection is poor. This is the off-season for tourists. Please tell anyone who ordered Philippine products to wait a while. I'll try again next time I'm in Manila.

On January 8, at 4:20 AM, I took the plane from Manila to Zamboanga. The night before, I went to a classical piano concert at the Philippine Cultural Center in Manila with a friend. Afterward, we stopped for a snack and then sat around to talk until one in the morning. From there, I went directly to the airport and checked-in without any sleep. My body was in U.S. time zone, its precisely twelve hours difference.

In Zamboanga, I visited Charlie White (our regional director) and his family. Zamboanga was cleaner and cooler after Manila. After a day there visiting friends, I flew to Cotabato City and Surallah to visit friends in Marbel. As you may have noticed, I love to travel not only to see a place, but I like to visit friends in the process. The trip becomes more meaningful...

Back in General Santos, the first thing I did was to talk to Fr. Albinus to find out what happened while I was gone. I also asked him to help me look for a family to stay with. Being the Parish priest here since 1964, he has built a fantastic network. He made a phone call in the morning. In the afternoon, I moved to the home of Dr. Jorge

Calderon's family. His wife, Aida, is also a doctor. They are Tagalog speaking, although all are very fluent in English. We use English at home. Dr. Calderon lived and worked in Chicago for five years as a doctor. The food has been excellent, and the accommodations are more upscale than Peace Corps standards.

Yes, I really enjoyed my vacation in the States. I never thought I'd miss Pennsylvania pretzels so much! Everybody seems happy to see me.

Saturday all day is the Fiesta in Bula celebrating the Feast of Santo Nino (or Black Nazarene). One of the three community centers that I manage is located there. The Fiesta, a real big deal here, started on January 6 and will end on January 15.

Most notable was the fluvial (water) parade. Fishermen with their families join in the boat procession. They held induction of officers, crowning of a beauty contest queen, athletic tournaments, boat races, parade on land, and oh, I almost forgot, religious ceremonies for baptism, confirmation, and mass.

Everybody serves all the food he can afford during the Fiesta. I try to avoid an overdose of celebrating, but I'll be sure to attend at least some of the celebrations. One of the things they have lots of is gambling and drinking. I guess for people who are starved for entertainment, cultural events, and things of that nature, an annual fiesta is the next big thing. It is a huge party that attracts hundreds of revelers.

If you can get me a pack of those small squash seeds that they grow in Florida, please include them in your next letter. I ended up throwing away those we got down at the Everglades – they got moldy. The mothers want to start a garden at the backyard of our community centers with their kids.

That's all for now, Dad. Just wanted to let you all know I was back and alive! Alvin

The beginning of 1972 was the busiest and packed with adventures I could only dream of. The social "action" was not limited to my job at the community center alone. The interactions with a widening circle of friends definitely increased my presence on the social scene.

Soon I was back in the groove at work again. I started collaborating with the Office of Mayor Antonio Acharon at the Family Planning & Community Development sector, working closely with Dra. Pancho and her nurse assistant Ms. Grafilo. (Filipinos call a male doctor "Doctor" abbreviated "Dr." They call a female doctor "Doctora" abbreviated "Dra."). The training seminar that I attended for Family Planning and Community Development provided by the Peace Corps was more than adequate for my job. Mindful of the position of the Catholic Church on birth control, I had to tread lightly. My involvement at the Family Planning office was limited to administrative work at the office, arranging meetings, and the like.

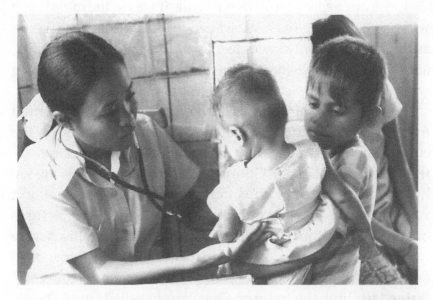

Natural Family Planning (NFP) was the only method that was allowed by the Catholic Church. NFP was an umbrella term for birth controls such as the rhythm method, the basal body temperature charting, and the Standard Days Method. These are forms of birth control that do not involve any hormones or physical barriers to prevent pregnancy but instead rely on periods of abstinence. At the Parish community centers, we concentrated mainly on nutrition, early childhood education and feeding, and adult education, teaching skills like sewing. As far as birth control was concerned, our role was limited to handing out information about the rhythm method.

However, at the Protestant Churches, the mayor's office found receptive and enthusiastic partners who understood and appreciated the fact that without some kind of intervention, the population explosion among the poorest of the poor would continue, and malnutrition among the children would worsen. Often I went with the team from the Office of the Mayor to the *sitios* (hamlets) outside of the city to hold meetings to discuss family planning at different non-Catholic churches. The sessions were well attended.

Once our *jeepney* broke down while it was in the middle of a wide, slow-moving river. We waded toward the opposite bank, as the water was only knee-deep. We sat around the riverbank, ate our *baon* (provisions), talked, and joined in a sing-along while waiting for parts to fix the jeepney.

One other instance, after a very successful and spirited meeting with church members and their friends in the community, a farmer from a local Mission sponsored by the Philippine United Church of Christ invited us to see his garden planted with different varieties of squash and vegetables. His garden could have been one of those pictures out of a horticulture magazine. Latticework and trellises were incorporated into the design. Instead of letting the squash crawl on the ground, they were planted neatly in rows and trained to climb the trellises. One variety called "upo" (bottle gourd), with edible fruits three to five feet long was hanging from structures made of bamboo latticework. Even the coconut seedlings were meticulously arranged under the lattice.

While roaming around the garden and taking pictures, I heard a commotion. The farmer caught a large *bayawak* (Tagalog word for monitor lizard) about five pounds or more. They roasted it and served it to us for lunch. It tasted like chicken!

As part of my job as Social Action Coordinator at the Dadiangas Parish, I was tasked to secure the support of the local government to help fund our successful Nutrition Programs. Before we presented our proposal to the City Council, I lobbied each individual Councilor to help our cause. The mission of our Community Centers fit right under Mayor Antonio Acharon's policy of *"Una sa lahat ay tao"* or People first. Mayor Acharon understood the plight of the poor people, and he embraced the improvement of their lot as his priority. Our partnership yielded financial aid for our centers.

The city was peaceful during this time. The intimidation and extortion era of Adan de Las Marias and his gang ended in his violent death at Continental Night Club in December 1969, seven months after my arrival. He was killed assassination-style (unlike the "shootout at the O.K. Corral" that Brother Sam had predicted).

When Adan died, it was the talk of the city. In March 1970, a dramatic movie about his life titled *Octopus* was showing in the local theaters.[4] Unfortunately, I was not able to see the movie that was filmed in General Santos City. The people of General Santos braced themselves for another turbulent period, but his demise actually brought relative peace and order to the city. The son of a prominent family and his bodyguard were suspected of the murder and were jailed, but they were later released.

A year later, Mayor Antonio Acharon was implicated in the murder and was arrested. He ran for re-election in November 1971 and had to campaign from inside the jail. In her Ph.D. thesis, Andrea Villano-Campado wrote of the period: "His [Mayor Antonio Acharon] political strength was dramatically proven by his re-election in 1971 while in jail charged with a double murder case (that of Adan de las Marias, the leader of the Octopus gang, and one Piding) filed against him by a powerful congressman whose wife ran for the position of mayor."[5] A staunch supporter of President Ferdinand Marcos, the mayor was later pardoned by the president and released from jail. Mayor Acharon was assassinated a few years later. He was the first to serve as mayor of General Santos when it became a city. He held the longest tenure of eighteen years.

Fr. Albinus was the source of all the information to which I was privy about the life and the death of Mr. de las Marias. The specific circumstances behind Adan's death are described in Arthur Amaral's book. One night, Fr. Albinus answered a phone call. A dying man was taken to Dr. Yap's clinic in Dadiangas. Since it was his turn to be available for such emergencies, Fr. Albinus went and returned at one in the morning. Amaral recalled asking Fr. Albinus about the incident and that Fr. Albinus answered in a matter of fact manner, "Adan de las Marias was shot... Adan was still alive when I arrived at the hospital. He seemed glad to see me. I ministered to him, and he died shortly after."[6]

WHILE THE Adan de las Marias saga ended, the Christian-Muslim conflict was beginning to escalate in neighboring towns outside of General Santos City. In December 1971, the massacre that Fr. Albinus described to me when I first arrived from home leave, took place in Milbuk. The biggest employer in Milbuk was the Weyerhaeuser Timber Company that employed around 700 Christian settlers. According to Amaral, "There were about 5,000 people living in and around the logging camp, 90% of whom were Catholic. Milbuk was a part of the town of Palimbang. Most of the population throughout the municipality was Muslim."[7]

When a Christian was killed, their family and friends retaliated and raided a Muslim *sitio* (hamlet) to exact revenge and vice versa. The vicious cycle of killings continued inexorably. Although murders that resulted from the Muslim-Christian conflict never occurred in the city, our Parish Center hosted countless evacuees while I was working at the Centers.

My association with Fr. Albinus and my being the Coordinator of the Social Action at the Parish Church embroiled me in the Milbuk tale a few weeks after I came back from home leave. I reported the terrifying incident to my family.

Thursday, January 27, 1972
Dear Enid, Bud and all,
    Your letter was the only mail I received since returning from home leave. It was so good to see you, Enid, and the kids. When I am home again, we can spend more time together doing fun things.
    Life has been hectic since I came back. There are plenty of required forms to fill out and records to be brought up to date. I am caught up now and have started to try to do some new work. Currently, in the fire are two main things. The first is a radio program about nutrition. If I can coordinate things properly, we will have a fifteen-minute broadcast every day. The duration of the program will depend on how it comes across and how our listener ratings are.
    The other thing I am working on is trying to get government support for some of the nutrition projects and to expand the existing programs. But before approaching the Council as a body, I am lobbying each Councilor individually, some of whom I knew personally. That way, when the proposal comes before the body, I hope they will feel obligated to the Peace Corps Volunteer and possibly get the support we need. Here in the Philippines, there is a custom called "utang na loob" (debt of gratitude). I am trying to make it work in favor of the malnourished children...
    Actually, the daily routine work goes on, and these are things added to the job. It does not mean I am doing more work, though. Since returning from home leave, I have decided that I should start acting like a supervisor and not a laborer. I refuse to continue doing some of the menial tasks; mainly carrying heavy loads of donated stuff like bunches of bananas, whole tuna fish, and cases of Coca-Cola as I used to do. Those were the things that wore me down. Which in Dr. Yap's opinion caused me then to be susceptible to amoebic dysentery when my resistance is low. Dr. Yap is my doctor here.
    There's little appreciation for it anyway. If the people in the community cannot do these jobs to pitch in, then they just will not

get done. I discussed my decision with the president of the Bula Community Center association and my all-women staff. The president instructed me to send word to him whenever we need to pick-up or unload donated items that are heavy, and he will send members to help. So far his suggested solution is working.

Last Sunday morning, I was up at 4:00 AM to take a little trip with Fr. Hyacinth to Milbuk. His parish is a small coastal town about seven hours by pump boat (motorized bangka) from here. It's the only way to get there; no road leads to Milbuk from General Santos. There has been a lot of trouble surrounding Milbuk since December. Most of the people have evacuated from the mountains into the towns to live. The Muslims have all gone to Palimbang a few miles north. The Christians have come south to Milbuk. Many people had been killed and wounded in the fighting; their houses and fields of rice and corn burned.

Fr. Hyacinth is supposed to be on the list of the ten most-wanted by the Muslims. Some priests and some of his parishioners warned him not to return to Milbuk. I knew one of Weyerhaeuser's former employees, Juanito Asencio, my co-teacher at Notre Dame and Prima's uncle, who was a lawyer at Weyerhaeuser. He and his wife, Mercy, and children moved to General Santos City before the killings began.

When Fr. Hy invited me to go with him to visit Milbuk, I felt it was safe because there is an American lumbering company there with two American families. Surely a big company like Weyerhaeuser would not allow its American employees to stay in a place where they are in imminent danger. It is a massive operation, and their facilities are built along the shores. There is an airstrip on the property, and the company also owns two Cessna airplanes. Like most of the people, we stayed within the camp and the town while I was there.

During this visit to Milbuk, I stayed overnight at the parish Convento. Fr. Hyacinth took me to the Weyerhaeuser Company to see their logging operation. I witnessed how plywood was made and was enlightened by one of the employees on the process. They fell these huge trees mostly six feet or more in diameter from the virgin forests where they are cut to the desired length. They are brought into the sawmill on big logging trucks, sprayed with water, and debarked.

Using a huge rotary lathe machine, the log is peeled into a thin veneer. After the pieces of veneer were adequately dried and trimmed, they are composed into the standard plywood 4x8 sheets or 3x7 sheets. At this point, the face (surface to be seen) and back (the part hidden) are determined. Then the bonding is done using adhesives such as urea-formaldehyde resins typically used for ordinary plywood. Marine plywood, on the other hand, uses melamine or phenol-based adhesives.

February 1, Tuesday evening
Dear Bud, Enid and all

Time waits for no one. Anyway, last Saturday morning, six days ago, I was on board one of the two large bangka full of food supplies to deliver to Fr. Hyacinth for the evacuees in Milbuk. At three in the morning, it was still pitch dark, and there was a chill in the air. The only source of light on the bangka was a small kerosene camping lantern fastened to a bamboo pole in the middle of the bangka. Surprisingly, the lamp provided adequate lighting.

This trip is not for the uninitiated. I had taken these trips before with professional fishermen who knew the sea. I'd catch a ride at the Fish Landing (sort of a fish port where fishermen unload and sell their catch of the day). They'd drop me at the Tinoto beach on their way to their fishing grounds. Daily, they start out very early in the morning to fish for a living. Although the sea was so calm at that time of day, it took us more than seven hours to get to Milbuk as we were a bit overloaded. The "killer" was not being able to move around with three people onboard. The Bangka is about four feet wide and forty feet long.

The owner of the boat whom I know from Bula and one of his men accompanied me. The second boat left ahead of us. We brought sacks of rice, oatmeal, sugar, fresh and salted dried fish, and other staples. When we arrived at our destination, we were told that the Christians called the Ilagas (meaning rats) shot and killed three Muslims that morning. While our cargoes were being unloaded, we ate lunch at the Convento with Fr. Hyacinth. We heard gunfire. After lunch, the convent staff reported that another Muslim was killed, and the Ilagas brought his ear to Milbuk to prove it.

We got out of Milbuk as fast as we could. On leaving Milbuk, our boat went far out to sea to avoid the area where the shooting was going on. We were almost halfway home when the propeller on the pump-boat broke! With one paddle, we got to shore. Thank God we were passing the friendly village of Maasim. The boat owner had a friend in Maasim, so we borrowed his propeller.

Meanwhile, Fr. George comes by with his jeep. He offered me a ride to Dadiangas. Rather than wait for the boat to be fixed, I took Fr. George's offer. Fr. George runs the new radio station DXCP here in town. It is where I'll be broadcasting from when we get going on that Nutrition project. Anyway, Fr. George was in a hurry because it was getting close to nightfall. After a forty-five-minute drive, we reached the barrio of Tinoto, a Muslim village. Just beyond Tinoto, the road ends. A vehicle must travel a few hundred meters along the sandy shore before the road resumes again. Well, when we got to the spot, the tidewater was high. Fr. George tried to cross. The jeep got flooded out. We pushed it to dry land and dried it off. We got it started, but it seemed to be running only on two or three cylinders.

After dark, we gave up and decided to spend the night. We bought some bottles of Coca-Cola and cookies from a local sari-sari store for our supper. The three girls with us were scared. Fr. George was a bit worried too. But the two boys and I were not concerned at all. I frequent Tinoto by myself to go swimming and snorkeling. I have never encountered any trouble in the three years that I had been swimming at my favorite beach.

Four of the Muslims from the village came down to talk to us and tried to help. These particular Muslims are Tausugs from Jolo and are not involved in the battle between the Christians and Muslims from the province of Lanao and North/South Cotabato. The three girls slept in the back of the jeep, the boys on the beach. Fr. George and I took turns on the front seat and walking around.

The next morning, the first thing coming by was a private jeep with two men. The girls and I hitched a ride to Dadiangas about an hour drive away. In Dadiangas, one of the girls got hold of a mechanic. They started back to Tinoto with his service truck.

Meanwhile, Fr. George sent one of the boys to Dadiangas to get a mechanic. A little bit later, Fr. George stopped a passing cargo truck and got a tow back to Maasim (the barrio where we met the day before). When the boy got to Dadiangas and found the mechanic had already left to look for Fr. George, he caught a ride with someone else going back to Tinoto.

Meanwhile, the girl and the mechanic in the service truck were having trouble. His clutch was slipping, and he could not make it up the big hills. They turned around and came back to Dadiangas. Returning, the girl and the boy met on the road. The girl joined the boy, and they went on to Tinoto to find Fr. George, who was already in Maasim. They continued on the road and found Fr. George, with the jeep, all repaired and ready to return back to Dadiangas. And so all three plus the other boy that stayed with Fr. George came back to Dadiangas safe and sound, and everyone was happy.

If you think that the story was confusing, well, I left out the part about Fr. George having to borrow money to pay for the repairs and had to return the money. That made the trip even worse. I also left out the part about my telling the boatmen that I would notify their families; that they were okay and on their way home. They made it back before I did. Everyone worried all night about what had happened to Fr. George, the rest of his group, and the Peace Corps Volunteer. Well, I won't confuse you anymore except to say that Maasim is the same place that Fr. James and I went on that exciting motorcycle ride about a year ago when we were caught in a flash flood and had to spend the night on the riverbank!

Life is always full of surprises and very exciting around here. There has been one big Fiesta that lasted for fifteen days at Bula. I attended several parties since I have been back, and that is only three weeks ago. Last Sunday afternoon (after our harrowing trip to Milbuk, etc.), I was at the birthday party of Mr. Guipo.

In the evening, I went to see a Sing-out program of the Notre Dame of Dadiangas High School for Girls. I loaned them the Sing-out record that I brought from the States. The music director Mr. Raymundo Asencio (Prima's uncle), is also a teacher at Notre Dame

College. He really liked it, and they used two of the numbers from the record for the program, "Up with People" was one of them. These kids are not professionals, but they do an outstanding job for the little bit of time they spend practicing. I enjoy singing programs more than the dance programs they always have.

Next Sunday, we planned a picnic to the beach with Prima, her siblings, and friends. Sunday night, I'll be visiting a co-teacher who was married before I went on home leave. Prima and I were the candle sponsors at her wedding. While in Boston, I bought two furry rugs for them, one shaped like a human foot three feet long, and the other a smiley face. That kind of thing goes over big here and is not available in the local market.

I have not given any slide shows since I am back yet, but I hope to try one soon to see how people like them. The Guipo family has a slide projector that we often used for slide shows at their house. I plan to keep the presentation short, that way it will hold their attention, and also, I'll have lots more to show if they want to see more. There are a lot of things I would like to do during my spare time, the problem is there just is not much spare time left in one day.

Well, I guess I'll close for now. It is almost bedtime. Take care now, Alvin

P.S. I forgot to tell you that the Manila International Airport was burned down to the ground by arsonists a week ago Sunday. I hope none of your mail or my mail was there when it happened. Peace Corps usually patronize Pan American Airlines - now their office is gone. I haven't had any international airmail since the fire.[8]

I never dreamed I'd be hosting a radio show in my lifetime, much less pitching Good Nutrition – the title of our show. It was another unique experience that I credited to being a Peace Corps. Fr. George Nolan, the DXCP staff, and I launched our radio program around March 1972. After the program was established with a respectable rating, a certain Mrs. Rivera took over as the announcer.

One of the most memorable events I witnessed while working at Our Lady of Peace and Good Voyage was a wedding held at the Parish Center. I had seen nothing like it so I took a lot of photos. During that time, the multi-purpose center was the largest in South Cotabato and was built to accommodate three thousand people. The Center hosted many social and cultural happenings, and sports events, etc. before it was finished. In fact, the Parish Center was still under construction when the grandest event took place on September 26, 1971, the wedding of Monera Bajunaid.

With live orchids and fresh flowers, Maguindanao fabrics, and colorful banners, the Center's massive and pedestrian open space was magically transformed into a beautiful, fairy-tale wedding reception hall. In the middle of the stage, a century-old tapestry hung from the wall. A bed covered with red fabric woven with gold threads was ensconced on the side next to it. The wedding cake was multi-layered, standing at five feet from base to top. A cage full of white doves hung overhead, just waiting to be released at the end of the ceremonies.

Monera was resplendent in her wedding gown. According to Moner, the dress was designed and created by the famous Filipino couturier Pitoy Moreno. Jose "Pitoy" Moreno, Jr. was regarded as the *Czar of Asia Fashion*, a personal designer of former First Lady Imelda Marcos, other First Ladies in Asia, and countless famous movie stars in the Philippines. He even designed gowns for the U.S. First Ladies Nancy Reagan, Betty Ford, and Pat Nixon. The groom, Magsaysay Biruar, wore the traditional Western white coat and tie. There were sixteen wedding attendants (eight ladies and eight gentlemen) and over 500 hundred invited guests, including the congressman, governor, mayor, and other government dignitaries.

Monera was an alumna of Notre Dame Dadiangas Class of 1971. The wedding was the talk of the town for years, and even to this day, many people in Gen. Santos City still remember.

The grandest event held at the Catholic Parish Center was a Muslim wedding.

Goodbye Sarangani 11
Hello Lake Seluton

IN AUGUST 1971, National Geographic Magazine highlighted the T'boli people in an article *Help for Philippine Tribes in Trouble* written by Kenneth MacLeish, editor, and writer for the National Geographic Magazine. Mr. MacLeish, who was the son of the poet, Archibald MacLeish, graduated from Harvard in 1938 with a master's degree in Anthropology.[1] The article about the T'boli also featured the Ubo, the Higaonon, and the Mansaka tribes.

I had wondered what kind of a fifty-four-year-old man would brave the untamed jungles of Surallah like Mr. MacLeish just to see the T'boli and the other indigenous peoples of the Philippines. Then I found out that he was not only a writer, he was also an anthropologist. He came to Surallah, South Cotabato, to write a moving article because he was interested in the study of human societies and cultures and their development. The report, including photographs by Dean Conger, tugged at the heart; it sounded like a "come on" ad for Santa Cruz Mission.

The T'boli people enamored me so during my first visit to Surallah, where the majority of them lived. Long before I submitted my request to extend my Peace Corps contract for a third term, I started asking around about the possibility of working with the T'boli people. It was the beginning of a long process of securing a position at Santa Cruz Mission (SCM), a non-profit organization dedicated to helping the T'boli and four other indigenous tribes.

I will never forget the moment when I took my first picture of a T'boli woman during our first face-to-face encounter at the *palengke* in Edwards, Surallah, on November 21, 1969, almost two years before the National Geographic article was published. As mentioned in Chapter 7, Prima and her brother Felipe accompanied me on a weekend visit of the Wycliffe Bible Translators in Sinolon, Surallah.

We stopped at the open-air market to buy some groceries at Barrio Edwards. As we wandered from stall to stall looking for ingredients, I saw a T'boli woman walking toward us. She held a child inside a *luwek* (T'boli skirt) slung across her shoulders to form a cradle. Instead of carrying the child on her back, she, like all T'boli women, positioned the baby in front so she could gaze upon her child at all times. A little boy about five years old clung to her skirt next to a precocious girl about twelve dressed in full T'boli accoutrements ~ bangles, beaded necklace, head cover, and all ~ her lips painted bright red. It was my first picture of a T'boli. In an instant, I was intrigued, awed, and fascinated.

"Kodak?" I asked, holding my Bosley 35 mm camera in front of my chest, its lens aimed at the group. I did not speak their language; they did not understand my Tagalog. They understood the Ilongo dialect, so Prima asked if I could take their photo. The mother and the little girl smiled and nodded. Soon a few more T'boli women came closer. They, too, said "Kodak, kodak" and posed for pictures. Others shied away.

There is no word for the act of taking photographs in the dialect. Kodak was the best substitute. In the Ilongo dialect, Kodak was even conjugated in its odd quaint forms: "kodaki ako" (you take my picture), "gin kodakan ko siya" (I took her photo), and so on.

After I visited T'boli land, I decided to check into the possibility of a summer project working with the T'boli. I happened to mention my idea to Fr. Albinus. He told me about Fr. Rex Mansmann, the director of the Santa Cruz Mission in the barrio of Surallah, called Lake Sebu. However, Fr. Albinus told me that Fr. Rex was not too keen about adding more *puti* (white folks) to his growing staff. Dottie Anderson and I went to see him anyway and visited Santa Cruz Mission for the first time around March 1971.

I first met Dottie Anderson during the last month of my Peace Corps training in Cotabato City. She was a volunteer staff designated as the secretary to the Regional Director of the PC Southern Region office based in Davao City from July 1968 to August 1969. When the regional office relocated to Zamboanga City, Dottie moved too, and she worked there from August 1969 to August 31, 1971. The office oversaw my PCV Group 31 and all the Peace Corps volunteers assigned to southern Mindanao.

During training, Dottie spoke before our group and enlightened us about the remittance of our allowances, banking and mail services, plus other administrative support functions that were provided by the regional office. As soon as I started working at Notre Dame College, I received regularly, a brown manila envelope mail pouch from Dottie.

Whenever I was in Zamboanga City, we got together. Our friendship steadily developed and grew. My dad and my siblings wondered if she was my girlfriend, as my letters mentioned Dottie a lot. In her spare time, she worked with the Yakan tribe of Basilan to help market their weaving and other handicrafts. Our shared interest in the T'boli people brought us to Surallah. (We had kept in touch regularly and remain friends to this day).

The road that led to SCM started in Surallah. An SCM Fact Sheet brochure mentioned, "Santa Cruz Mission builds and maintains farm-to-market roads. Government help is conspicuously absent, despite repeated requests."[2] During this period, Canahay Road was the only way to reach Lake Sebu from Surallah. Dottie flew in from Zamboanga City to Surallah to meet up with me. In Sinolon, we made a stop at the house of the Wycliffe ladies. I had visited the Wycliffe ladies before and had developed a cordial relationship with them.

We went back to Surallah, still not sure how we'd find our way to Lake Sebu. Enter Fr. Hilarion, a Passionist priest I befriended through my work in Dadiangas Parish. He was the Parish Priest of Our Lady of Lourdes in Surallah. On the day we knocked on the door of his *Convento*, Fr. Hilarion told us that Fr. Rex was in town and was stopping by for lunch before he returned to Lake Sebu.

Dottie and I grabbed lunch at the nearby *turo-turo* at the Surallah Public Market, came back to the *Convento*, and were promptly introduced to Fr. Rex. He was driving a vintage weapons carrier, a remnant of World War II judging from the "US ARMY FRANCE" emblazoned on its front bumper. The vehicle was covered with mud. We stopped for gasoline and were soon on our way. We crossed the Allah Valley River and started our way up the winding roads carved on the sides of the mountain.

Fr. Rex, of course, drove as though we were on a leisure Sunday afternoon joyride along a paved city highway. Dottie and I were on the edge of our seats. Intermittently we saw houses close to the road, but the majority of the inhabitants lived on the sides of the steep mountains. Just before we reached Canahay, the dirt road turned muddy. I mean, it was really, really muddy. When I jumped out to take pictures, my footwear sank at least a foot into the mud. We used the weapons carrier's winch to get the vehicle out of the muddy road for a kilometer or so.

Then the real adventure began. Fr. Rex maneuvered the weapons carrier up, up the steep S portion of Lemkemunig Road. At some point, the ravine on one side of the road dropped off a few hundred feet. There were no guardrails!

I breathed a sigh of relief when the weapons carrier reached the crest of Lemkemunig hill. From this point to Santa Cruz Mission, the roads leveled. I saw the smallest Lake Lahit first, and then I saw the beautiful Lake Sebu, its serene waters mirrored the blue skies above. The jitters slowly dissipated.

Three hours after our journey started, we crossed the *Lo El* River. Santa Cruz Mission soon came into view. The old section of SCM was built around 1961. Constructed on the side of the hill, the main administrative office sat at the lowest point. The woodworking shop and clinic were built on slightly higher ground.

Ten feet above are the classrooms; a library turned classroom, the office of the education manager and the SCM director, and the chapel. On the fourth level were the twin dormitories for the T'boli children and the teachers, and the little wooden house for administration staff painted white (aptly referred to as the White House). All the living quarters were situated on the top of the hill, including Fr. Rex's *Convento*.

We had to climb a steep hill to get to it. Dottie shared her experience of our first visit: "I also remember that when Al and I arrived in the weapons carrier, it stopped at the bottom of the hill (below the kitchen). My legs were so wobbly from the scary trip that I didn't think I could walk up the hill in front of me."

The rest of that trip has blurred from my fading memory, but I will always remember the view when we entered Fr. Rex's *Convento*. Perched on the side of the mountain, the *Convento* made of bamboo and *nipa* was built such that when you stepped out of the front door, you were level with the summit of a hill, 2600 feet above sea level. Two identical sliding windows about five feet tall and eight feet wide made of wood and capiz shell opened to a spectacular view of the valley below. In 1977, Marcus Brooke, a writer from the UK, described what he saw when he entered the *Convento* in his essay *The T'boli of Mindanao*. He wrote this about the house, "...the views were truly enchanting. The little house was modest enough, made of bamboo and *nipa*-palm, but it had one touch of luxury which, Fr. Rex ruefully admitted, accounted for about half the total construction cost of US$200: sliding windows of capis-shell [sic]- on two sides of the living room. It was money well spent. To the south, through the open windows, I looked out across a lush valley nearly two kilometers wide in which rice fields were occasionally interrupted by stands of coconut palms..."[3]

Looking southward, gaze down, and you'd see that half of the *Convento* sat on stilts surrounded by neat rows of vegetable garden below that the students cared for during their Gardening Class. The school children planted and maintained the plots of tomatoes, eggplants, and *camote* (sweet potato). The harvest was shared with Fr. Rex and the rest of the vegetables the children cooked at their kitchen.

Marcus Brooke continued, "Each day, toward noon, fluffy grey clouds would gradually cover the sparkling blue sky, drifting across and then, amoeba-like, engulfing the top of the forest. Then there would be torrential rains, thunder, and lightning...To the west, through the other capis-shell [sic] windows, I could glimpse Lake Sebu, the largest, more than five kilometers long, of a chain of three lakes – Sebu, Lahit, and Seluton."[4]

During this initial trip to Lake Sebu, Dottie stayed at the lady teachers' dormitory where the T'boli girls lodged during school days. I was supposed to stay at the dormitory for the T'boli boys and the male teachers. But the bed was infested with bed bugs; I was being eaten alive. I went back to Fr. Rex's *Convento*. He graciously accommodated me in the bedroom of Bro. Louis Bouchard, who was away on vacation in the U.S.

Peter Carado, one of the high school students at the mission, was our tour guide during our stay. A very personable and ambitious kid who spoke English very well, Peter hoped to be a lawyer he told us so he could help his people take back their ancestral land. He took us around the mission grounds and to the town called Lake Sebu that bears the name of the biggest of the three lakes.

Lake Sebu was the embodiment of beauty and romance that captures the heart at first glance. It did mine. Against the backdrop of its rolling verdant hills and three lakes cascading into a series of seven waterfalls, it was like an enchantress luring the unsuspecting lovers of nature.

For those of us who lived there almost fifty years ago, the images of Lake Sebu as a tourist destination, with its obtrusively showy welcome signs and a slew of brightly painted resorts that we now see on TripAdvisor® online, seems so incongruous with the unpretentious haven that we remember. Marcus Brooke had only high praise for the place, the T'boli people, and its culture. He wrote: "I have thrilled to the lochs of Scotland, enthused over the lakes of Switzerland and northern Italy, rhapsodized over the waters of Kashmir, but none can surpass the beauty of Lake Sebu."

It is in this setting where Santa Cruz Mission (SCM) nestled among the hills of Lem-ehek along the banks of the second largest lake called Seluton. It was just a few kilometers from Lake Sebu. The place was simply breathtaking. Alo was the first of the seven falls fed by the waters from Lake Seluton located just below our men's dormitory. The Alo falls about thirty-feet high was the frequent destination for our weekend excursions. On my second visit to Santa Cruz Mission in April 1972, the T'boli pupils at the school led me to Alo Falls to gather *keting*. We traversed rice paddies on our way from the mission to Lem-alo; the hamlet where the Alo falls was located.

The river from Lake Seluton was swift and deep in some areas as it followed the contours of the land downstream. We crossed the river using a handmade rickety and unstable bridge made of two bamboo poles complete with makeshift wobbly handrails. We'd approach the falls from the top and follow a slippery footpath down the slope to the swimming hole at the bottom.

Surrounding the campus of the Santa Cruz Mission were clusters of T'boli huts. Dottie wrote, "I remember visiting a

T'boli house and getting the weaving that we shared."[5] About those T'boli huts, the first time Dottie and I were invited to go inside, two things jumped out at me: the ingenuity of design and its utilitarian aspect. Some huts were bigger than others, but they all look alike. The roofs were made of thatched cogon grass, and the rest of the structure was bamboo. Supported by dozens of bamboo stilts measuring anywhere from five to ten feet in length depending on location (they tended to be longer when it stood alone on a remote mountain top), they were unlike any *nipa* hut that I had seen in the lowlands.

The two or three windows along the side of the hut swung open from the bottom and extended out held in place by a stick of bamboo. Or the windows were just a hole on the wall. A bigger window that usually ran the whole width of the front of the hut facing east opened from the top and folded down to create a platform upon which the woven *t'nalak* cloth was hung to dry.

There were no doors. Instead, a guest had to climb a ladder made of a single bamboo pole with a few triangular rungs carved upon one side of it. The rung was big enough for an adult to insert his toes to gain a foothold. The ladder led to a hole in the floor barely enough for a 'Kano to squeeze through. The guest entered headfirst. In the evening, the ladder was pulled up and stored inside the house, and a trap-like door was lowered to cover the entrance preventing uninvited guests from entering.

The house was one open-space living area, no dividers, and no walled sections for a room. A corner was designated for cooking. A square box bordered with bamboo on four sides approximately three feet wide and three inches deep was filled with dirt. Stones were used as "burners." It always amazed me that I never heard of a house burning down from this type of a "stove."

I observed with fascination, the T'boli men wore mostly westernized clothing, a few in their traditional pants made of *t'nalak*, (a very stiff fabric woven from abaca) and wearing T'boli hats. The hats were woven from reed, some ordinary, some decorated with a glass drawer knob adornment at the apex. They sat around in small circles of four or more chewing betel nut, tobacco, and powdered lime. They chewed and chewed while they visited with each other until their mouths filled with scarlet saliva before they spat on the ground. I had heard that for some chewing betel nut and ingesting some of the saliva staved off hunger.

The best place to photograph the T'boli women I found out was at the *palengke*. The women I saw at Kematu, Edwards and during succeeding visits to Lake Sebu, were attractive and impressive in their intricately hand-woven blouses and colorful beaded necklaces. Their bracelets and anklets made of brass jingled as they moved. They were all barefoot. Many wore the traditional hats, made of bamboo, and reed. It was covered with an appliqued swath of red cloth, a foot or longer fringe down the sides of their heads, ornate and practical. It fully shaded them from the punishing sun. Instead of a hat, some of the ladies wrapped towels fashionably around their heads.

In Edwards, Surallah, most of the T'boli ladies were shoppers or out for a stroll. Others were vendors who sold beaded necklaces, embroidered T'boli blouses, and all sizes of *t'nalak* on display from the rafters of the stalls. Wearing a distinctive style hairdo that was swept back in a ponytail and coiled in a bun with bangs parted in the middle framing both cheeks, they shopped at crowded stalls. They haggled with folks selling beaded jewelry displayed next to freshwater clams, bananas, and chickens flapping their wings trying to break loose from the rope tied around both legs.

Any T'boli woman in full regalia can engrave an indelible imprint on one's mind. Even in her everyday soiled and tattered clothes, a T'boli woman was just as memorable. I had seen them along footpaths walking to a spring to gather water or watched them as they gathered *keting* from the lake to be sold at the markets or weeding the cornfield. But a T'boli woman won't be caught dead without her adornment – beaded necklaces or earrings or anklets or all of the above.

My first visit to Santa Cruz Mission with Dottie in early 1971, impressed upon me a workplace so remote, so primitive yet so magnetic I could not resist; I wanted to be a part of it. Fr. Rex did not indicate one way or the other if he'd find a use for our skills, but I came away hopeful that I'd get invited for a summer project at the very least. Dottie and I were glad we visited despite my knowledge that Fr. Rex was not really planning on adding more Americans to his growing staff. Still, it was time well spent because by 1972, Fr. Rex had a change of heart. The mission was engaged in a massive expansion project where our skills fit right into his plans. One year after our first visit, Dottie and I were invited to work at SCM. Peace Corps/Philippines approved my request for extension before my contract expired.

BACK IN General Santos in August 1972, I looked forward to my next assignment at Santa Cruz Mission, even as I continued my busy schedule at the community centers. With only four months left in my contract as Coordinator of Social Action at the Dadiangas Parish, I started the process of turning over my role to the nuns and offered help where needed at the *Convento*. Fr. Gabriel Baldostamon, who replaced Fr. James, was working hard at several community projects. One was flood control of the Silway River. His efforts were commendable but temporary and sometimes washed away in the flood before the work was completed.

I offered to help him get some old jeepney bodies that were rotting away in front of every repair shop in town. It had a two-fold effect: clean up the city and, at the same time; help provide a dike for flood control. Fr. Gabe was not ready to implement this new idea and continued to work on a temporary wooden dam.

Meanwhile, visitors flocked to the City of General Santos as though they heard I was leaving and wanted to take advantage of the free services of the self-proclaimed Peace Corps tour guide. I appreciated the activities as it provided new and exciting adventures and an occasion for meeting interesting travelers like the Frenchman I met at a hostel in Manila. He was traveling all over Asia for a $1 a day. It was something I thought I would like to do after Peace Corps.

In early August 1972, I had two visitors who arrived on the same day, Wolf Strehlke and Leslie Savina. Wolf was a German student the same age as I. He got my name and address from Mr. and Mrs. Dedek, the German family that hosted me in Cebu. He traveled through Asia for three months and spent less than a dollar a day. When he moved from one country to another, he budgeted $2.50 to 3 per day due to the cost of transportation.

Leslie,[6] an eighteen-year-old girl from Wenatchee, Washington State, was an exchange scholar for the Rotary Club. She stayed at the Calderon's residence, the same as I, for the first three months of her term. After that, she stayed with other Rotary families for the remainder of the year. She studied at Notre Dame College. On the days that she had no school, she shadowed me on some of my projects.

I told her the Rotarians would show her the wealthy side of the Philippines; I would show her the poor side of town. She designed some potholders for our sewing class and helped at the medical clinic. Leslie made every effort to adapt and learn about the Filipino ways. We did a lot of snorkeling together with her friend Kim Chin, another scholar teaching at the Public School in Dadiangas. Kim was on a U.S. based Study-Abroad program from the University of California Berkely.

My letter to my brother Bud summed up the busy last four months of my stay in General Santos City.

August 31, 1972, 9 AM Thursday.
Dear Enid, Bud and all,

I hope you are well and happy. Since the last I wrote, I had letters from you and Dad, both written on July 31. Everything is going along fine here and busy as usual.

Before I talk about anything else, I would like it if you could do me a favor. Recently, I read in one of the magazines I received about ERTS-1 (Earth Resources Technology Satellite) launched from Vandenberg Air Force Base in California.[7] The satellite flies 570 miles above the earth's surface, takes pictures and collects data about our planet. Information is available to anyone in the world for a price. The article ends by advertising one thing to send for. Could you please write to them to send me one real life-size actual working satellite that can be launched from here with a homemade rocket that weighed two-and-one-half tons and fueled by gunpowder?!

More seriously, they are advertising pictures available on any part of the earth. Please order me a 20"x20" photo of South Cotabato. Just ask Joyce for money from my bank account to cover the cost plus postage. Thank you. I'll quote from the paper: "Those wishing an ERTS picture of any part of the world can have it by writing to the Department of Interiors Earth Resource Observation Systems Data Center in Sioux Falls, South Dakota. The cost is $1.25 for a black and white, 70mm (2 inches)... Blowups to 20 inches by 20 inches are $3.50. Each picture covers an area on the ground 115 miles..."[8]

One of the things that keep me busy lately is the influx of tourists here in General Santos City. I have become a magnet to them; it would seem. Maybe I had mentioned a French student a couple months ago that tried to go to Indonesia from here. I wanted to help him make arrangements but was unsuccessful because the immigration officer would not sign his passport. He had to go back to Davao and leave from there.

Last week I had eight visitors at the same time. On a Tuesday afternoon, Phil Lilienthal, my Peace Corps Regional Director for Mindanao, came. Seven Peace Corps Volunteers were with him. That evening, Phil, and I went up to the Dole housing compound in Kalsangi to visit someone his parents met in the states. We had an all-American meal at the clubhouse, and later Mr. Sink of Dole came and talked with us for a short while.

On the way home, we passed a jeepney that had stalled. We, along with the pickup truck of Coca-Cola, helped a dozen or so passengers get back to Dadiangas. The pickup truck pulled the jeep all the way to the city. We carried some of the passengers in our vehicle – a picture of the "Bayanihan" custom here. There's no Triple-A [American Automobile Association] *to come to your rescue when your tire is flat or the engine stalled, so everyone just pitches in.*

The seven new Peace Corps Volunteers who just arrived will be assigned to various parts of the Philippines but came to General Santos as part of their training program. At the airport, we met two men from the government's Bureau of Plant Industry, who also came to meet the new volunteers. I spent the day with them touring several of the local rice and corn mills, a grain elevator, a farm machinery manufacturer, and a piggery with over 10,000 pigs. One of the real highlights for me was the farm machinery manufacturer called Silayan Engineering. I had seen their sign many times before but never been inside the factory. It is really an old rice bodega (warehouse) converted into a machine shop.

The guy running it is not even a high school graduate but speaks better English than most college graduates. He is a real genius in my book. He designs or copies and improved upon machines, which he makes. He will see a particular device and decide to copy it. In doing so, he finds ways to make it better. On some items, he takes a picture from a book and an idea of how it works and comes up with a working machine. He designed and built a big and modern corn milling operation that we visited. I had the luck of riding in his jeep. He never gets patents for his inventions, and many times competing manufacturers copy them.

The operation is mainly on job order and not an assembly line operation. He has no showroom or sales office. People needing things just come in and order. He can produce and market a feed mixer at a profit of about a third of the price of the mixers sold in the big machinery dealer in town. He has made a new design of corn sheller that does not break up the cobs and shells cleaner than the old model.

Sometimes he gets an idea to make something even if there is no market for it at present, and then he looks for a market later. Like the Micro-Mixer he built for mixing antibiotics and supplements to animal feeds. After developing and making it work successfully, he is now offering it to the piggeries to try. He plans to build a pelleting machine to turn ordinary feeds into pellets. I really have a lot of respect and admiration for this guy, even though he has not finished high school. His drawings are so professional that you would think a first-class engineer did them.

(I regretted not writing down the name of the man I so admired and was crestfallen that I could not even remember his name. Chris Gammon, my tireless sleuth of an editor, was so fascinated by this story that he did further research on Silayan Engineering online. He was determined to find out more about the person, what happened to him, and to give him a name. An entry on LinkedIn led him to more details. The side story took on a life of its own unfolding in a fascinating manner that revealed a remarkable discovery about the phenomenal success of this "Silayan genius." An almost incredible update on this story is found in Postscript: Fifty Years Later).

Concerning my own work here, things will be winding down soon. Our assistance from Catholic Relief Services for the nutrition centers will end on September 30. We do not plan to operate any more nutrition programs. If the Sisters coming in November want to run a program similar to our current center, they will have to look for some assistance. My own personal recommendation is that a modified version of our program with an emphasis on early childhood education would be as practical as the current approach. The savings in salaries and operating expenses would make several modified programs worth the effort.

The sewing cooperative we were trying to organize in Bula is no more. We are still conducting sewing classes at the Convento in Dadiangas. The community center in Bula is currently being used as a school building by the public school. They are supposed to build new classrooms but have not started yet.

Our former handicrafts and kindergarten teacher, Anna Garcia, got a job at the Santa Cruz Mission with Fr. Rex in Lake Sebu on my recommendation. She will be joining Prima and her friend Rosela who had been teaching there since June. She was hired to start at the beginning of next month as the Local Products Manager and will be working with T'boli artisans to develop native handicrafts and market them. Creating a demand for the T'boli crafts provides an economic incentive for the T'boli weavers, brass makers, beaded jewelry crafters, etc. to continue their art form, thus preserving it for the future generation.

At the moment, I think I will begin working at Lake Sebu around January 1973. I will be among friends when I get there. I want to give the Sisters who are taking over my projects some overlap time to familiarize them with the town and the centers. I also want to take a little vacation before I report to work at Santa Cruz Mission.

September 3, 1972, 7 AM Sunday

Yesterday the Calderons and the Rotary Club took Leslie on a picnic to the Dupalco Ranch at Cabo Beach. I was fortunate enough to

go along. The beach, corals, and the shells are not so impressive here as
my other favorite places to go like Tinoto. The Rotarians prefer going
to Cabo as it is closer to the city and because one of the members is
related to the owner.

Yesterday things were doubly sad for beachgoers because the water
and the beach were covered with oil. I am not sure where the oil
came from. They said it was there only for two days now. Perhaps a
tanker ship carrying bunker oil discharged its waste in the middle of
Sarangani Bay. To me, it is a real crime the way the seas and oceans
are being polluted. I read that in Europe, most beaches around the
Mediterranean Sea are closed because of oil pollution. Not only does
the oil ruin the beaches for swimming and recreation, but it also
kills the living things in the sea. I guess shipping lines and the oil
companies believe they won't be around to spend their profit in the
next few years. They also do not care about the possibility of their
children or grandchildren living beyond the next ten years.

Sept. 12, 1972 P.S. I should have put this in the mail last week, but it
just did not happen. So now I'll send it and start a new one in the next
few days. Last week I spent the whole week working with a notable
archeologist and anthropologist here in Asia, Dr. Wilhelm Solheim,[9]
which I'll write about in the next letter. Meanwhile, take care and drop
me a line when you have a chance. Alvin

A week after I wrote the letter to my brother, President
Ferdinand Marcos signed the declaration of martial law on
September 21, 1972. Unlike the assassination of John F. Kennedy,
I could not remember much of what happened the day martial
law was declared except that the airwaves went dead, the
newspaper publications were suspended, and the Military took
over the public utility services, including the airline industry.
Not wanting to take a chance on an already undependable
airline schedules, I canceled my Manila trip. The Voice of
America went off the air briefly but came back on promptly.

In his book, David Searles described the summer leading
to Martial Law. He wrote, "...floods of biblical proportions

struck Luzon's rice fields, and a severe drought ravaged the corn crop in the south. An American resident in Manila, Beth Day, declared that an "unholy alliance [of man-made and natural disasters] had turned the beautiful city into a frightened hotbed of demonstrations and random violence, earning it the doubtful distinction of being one of the most dangerous and lawless cities in the world."[10] Searles continued:

> "It was in these circumstances that Marcos took action one evening to declare martial law. Early the following morning, I received a worried call from PC/W giving me the news. (There were no newspapers that morning because Marcos had suspended all publications, so I was unaware of his declaration). What, Washington wanted to know, was the situation? And were the volunteers safe? My reply was that martial law was less cause for alarm than one might think, that perhaps it could restore some order to a chaotic situation and that volunteer safety was enhanced by martial law, not diminished. My response was fully consistent with the feelings of a large majority of ordinary Filipinos in 1972. Six or seven years later, it would be a different story as Marcos's true nature became widely known, but in the beginning, his declaration of martial law had a broad base of popular support."[11]

It was a big deal in the United States. And many were concerned about Marcos becoming a dictator. However, just as many in the Philippines welcomed it. General Santos was so far removed from the seat of government in Manila that after the initial shock, life normalized again.

The declaration was neither an issue for me, nor memorable. Curfew was probably the most disrupting aftermath causing inconvenience, but the initial impact and fears abated. A good number of people I knew complained about the nationwide curfew in effect from midnight to four in the morning. However, it did not affect me. Apart from events related to my job or to attend parties at my friends' houses or to travel, I could only remember going out past midnight a few times. Once to see a movie with Mr. and Mrs. Oliveros; it was a Tagalog film. I slept through it.

Another time, they took me to Jeanette's Refreshment Parlor a restaurant that featured local bands located along Pioneer Avenue across from Bajunaid Department Store.[12] In front of the restaurant, small stalls were selling delicious barbecued pork skewered on bamboo sticks. Inside, they served the best *halo-halo* - shaved ice mixed with fruit, sweetened beans, milk, and topped with Magnolia ice cream of different flavors, my favorite being *ube* (purple yam). We listened to the band while we ate our barbecued pork, drank San Miguel beer, and stayed until the eatery closed. The nightlife, be it in the cities of Manila, Cebu, Davao, or General Santos, just did not have any appeal to me. In South Cotabato, life settled down to its usual pre-Martial Law conditions in no time at all.

As part of my vacation plans, Ron, a Peace Corps Volunteer assigned in Marbel, and I decided to climb Mt. Parker. We picked a date a few weeks before his wedding. I stayed with Ron at the house he had rented for him and his bride-to-be Delia. We hired T'boli men who claimed to know Mt. Parker very well to be our guides. Stories of a pristine lake inside the extinct volcano crater and breathtaking sceneries lured us. A *jeepney* took us as far as the road would go. Then we hiked a long way until we reached a house that would be our "staging" site. We were told that it would be a two-day hike to Mt. Parker from that point.

The first night we stayed at the T'boli house, where we were served dinner. My troubles began after supper. We slept on the floor in a common living area, sharing the space with the other occupants of the house and their dogs. Well into the night, I could feel the familiar on-set of amoebic dysentery about the same time that thousands of fleas found me. I tried to cover my whole body, including using my extra-long socks as gloves, but it did not stop the critters from leaving their bite marks all over me.

Early the next morning after breakfast, we started our trek for the big push to climb Mt. Parker. Lacking insect repellant, we tried rubbing our skin with garlic. I even ate raw garlic in the hope that I smelled unpleasant to leeches and biting insects, but it was to no avail. A leech attached its sucker on my foot. One of the guides promptly and properly removed it by placing his fingers near the head of the leech and slowly pushed the sucker out of my foot. One was not supposed to just pull the leech off, or it would leave an open wound.

About this time, my amoebic dysentery had become full-blown. I told everyone to continue without me. One of the guides stayed with me while I rested. My condition worsened. The guide and I decided to retrace our steps to the house where we stayed the night before. Ron and the others pushed on, but no one actually made it to the top of Mt. Parker during that trip. Amoebic dysentery made sure of that; Ron got it too. Back at Ron's house in Marbel, we took turns inhabiting the outhouse. No sooner would one of us occupy it would come a knock on the door. It went on like that all night.

In November, the nuns took over much of the operations at the Social Action Office. The staff organized a going-away party and wished me well.

I packed my worldly goods and got ready for my third assignment. Fr. Albinus and a few priests in the area were planning to attend the 40th birthday bash for Fr. Rex scheduled for December 29, 1972. There was no seat for me in Fr. Albinus' jeep, but he offered to take my belongings to Lake Sebu.

I bid adieu to Sarangani Bay and all the friends I met in General Santos. After Christmas, I moved to Santa Cruz Mission to live on the banks of Lake Seluton.

Goodbye, Sarangani Bay.
On a snorkeling trip to the beach with Leslie Savina and Kim Chin.

Hello, Lake Seluton.
Elizabeth "Bo" Duncan, my co-teacher at Cheyenne Sioux Indian High School, South Dakota, visited Lake Seluton in 1977. She donated blood to a T'boli woman who was hemorrhaging.

The Mission Called Santa Cruz   **12**

ON THE MORNING after I fell off Pops Weaver's personnel carrier (December 28, 1972, to be exact), I woke up to the same forlorn chant that lulled me to sleep the night before, but it was accompanied by children's laughter. During the twenty months that I lived in the T'boli neighborhood along the banks of Lake Seluton[1], I reveled at my daily routine of waking up to the musical polyphony of woe and mirth. The melodic chant was coming from my neighbor's hut. Usually heard just as the sun peeked out of the darkness and slowly spread its shimmering rays over the lake.

For the four years that I worked in General Santos City, I stayed with Filipino host families. At Santa Cruz Mission, I lived in the Men's Dormitory that sat on the side of a hill overlooking Lake Seluton. Clusters of T'boli huts dotted the pastoral landscape. From my window, I could see the newly built mission school. The two concrete structures looked so incongruous in its rural setting. From our living room, I could observe my T'boli neighbors going about their activities. The men grooming their horses, kids fetching water from the tanks, women sweeping leaves off their dirt-covered yard, or tending to their cassava, tomatoes, sugar cane, and their children at play nearby. Around me, the roosters crowed, the goats bleated, the birds chirped, the horses neighed amidst the sound of the gongs echoing a deep refrain over the surrounding hills.

Just below the school campus were three newly built structures – a dining hall with full kitchen for employees (we called the "Clubhouse") and two identical dormitories. The buildings abutted the land occupied by the T'boli, living in their ancestral domain before the Mission was established. The dormitories had sixteen rooms: fourteen designated as bedrooms, one bathroom with four stalls (two sinks, two showers, and two toilets), and a living room. The dormitories provided lodging for the single men and ladies termed non-T'bolis working in the administrative offices at the Mission. All of them came from the lowland. The teachers lived in the old dorms with the T'boli children located at the old SCM campus.

Our small spartan rooms had a single bed made of wooden slats on wood frames. A mattress about three inches thick was available to buy or to order on a monthly salary deduction plan. Some employees used mats made of reed. I used the hand-sewn sleeping bag that I designed and created for my own use by one of the mothers at Bula Community Center sewing class.

On nights and mornings when it was cold (and there were many), I slipped inside my sleeping bag, zipped it up to my chin, and stayed comfy within. All the bedrooms in the building had identical built-in writing-table in one corner with a chair. We had indoor plumbing (a welcomed luxury). Running water was piped into the building from tanks sitting on the side of the hill slightly elevated from the structures. The tanks collected rainwater and could be supplemented with water from the springs during the dry season. At least we had flush toilets and showers (albeit frigid water). Electricity was available from five PM to nine PM.

I arrived at Santa Cruz Mission two days before Fr. Rex's 40th birthday celebration held on Friday, December 29, 1972. For meals, I walked for half a kilometer to the old campus since the new Clubhouse was not ready for full operation for another month. I followed the dirt road past familiar places, including Datu Ma Fok's and the Maghari's houses on the hill. The latter's pair of pet geese honked as if to welcome me. It felt good to be back at the Mission, secure in the knowledge that I would be staying for at least twelve months with the prospect of extension should I decide to do so.

At breakfast, I was reunited with Rose, Annie, and Prima. They introduced me to their new circle of friends. It was like the good old days at General Santos, knowing I was among my *barkadas* (buddies) once more. Until the Clubhouse was fully opened for business, all twenty-two of the unmarried staff continued cooking and eating their meals at the Lady Teachers Kitchen nicknamed LTK. A fourth of the building was designated kitchen and dining hall for the forty or so T'boli boys and girls living in the dormitories. Two T'boli women were hired to cook for all the 300 plus school children that were fed lunch during school days. The children who lived in the dormitories got three meals daily.

Like all the other structures in the old SCM campus, the Lady Teachers Kitchen sat on a hillside. Before the new ladies' dormitory was ready for occupancy, all the unmarried women employees (Dottie and Prima included), resided at the old campus where there was no indoor plumbing. No more than five steps immediately below the LTK was a wooden co-ed outhouse-cum-shower room about four feet wide and sixteen feet long divided into four stalls. Two stalls were designated as showers and two for the open-pit toilets. When one took a shower, the water drained down the hillsides.

The latrine was an entirely different proposition. The waste material from the open pit drained down the side of the hill too. That's including excrements, maggots, and all. I used to joke that the best time to use the toilet or take a shower was during mealtime; all the flies were on the dining table.

The administrative staff survived these primitive living conditions until the new dormitories were opened. The first to open was the men's dormitory, the guys moved in by November 1972 before Fr. Rex's birthday bash. The Clubhouse and the ladies' dorm would not be totally operational until a few months later. As for all the unmarried teachers, they never had the luxury of moving into a new dormitory to enjoy all its relatively modern facilities. To their credit, the teachers lived just as happily under the same living conditions when they arrived at the old campus until they left the Mission.

After breakfast, I went to the administration building to meet with SCM General Manager, Quirico Batilaran. He was pleased to see me and informed me that Dottie was coming later in the month. I inquired about the lodging arrangements and meal plans. (I recall that the lodging was free for unmarried employees, but I was not sure how we paid for our meals or if we paid at all. According to Beth Lazo Ledesma, one of the ladies who worked at the accounting office in 1972, our lodging was free. However, all our Filipino co-employees paid for food through salary deduction. The number of employees who ate at the LTK divided the cost of the total amount. This deduction was indicated on their payroll slip. As for Dottie and me, Beth believed that the Mission paid for our share. The employees eating at the LTK formed themselves into groups. On a weekly rotation, each group shopped for groceries and cooked and became dishwashers too. "No, maids!" Beth said).[2]

The following day, the Mission was abuzz with preparations for the birthday party. Recently, Fr. Rex wrote, "I cannot remember the exact date on which I celebrated my 40th birthday, but trying to reconstruct it from the 1972 calendar that you sent me…it is possible that I did celebrate it on the actual 29th birthday…that celebration had 1000 invited guests and another thousand un-invited guests."

The top of the ridge that we unofficially dubbed as the Afus Hill where the clumps of bamboos abound was transformed into an outdoor chapel for the concelebrated mass. His Excellency Bishop Reginald Arliss, C.P., D.D., and Fr. Rex officiated. A Filipino priest assisted them. The communion line was so long and took about thirty minutes or more even with ten priests and laymen giving out hosts to the faithful. Datu Ma Fok and his four wives, many of the Passionist priests, St. Paul Sisters, the staff, and the whole SCM T'boli Community attended. The Afus Hill was covered with guests.

I will never forget the series of temporary bamboo huts built just for the occasion with rows upon rows of pots hanging from the rafters where rice a-plenty and large quantities of side dishes were cooked. According to Ma'am Angeles Maghari, the day before the event the rain came in torrents. The pit that was readied for roasting filled up with water. The charcoals in the pit floated to the surface.

Ma'am Ang continued, "I remember one cow and two pigs were roasted on an open-pit like *lechon*. Two more pigs were butchered, a lot of chickens and ducks too, and were cooked into various side dishes. The cow was the biggest yearling, according to Sir Vir. The birthday party was like the Lemlunay SCM Fiesta.[3] The old T'boli folks were teary-eyed because it was their first time to taste *litson baka* (roasted cow). The cow was undercooked because the bamboo pole used as a giant skewer loosened and the men could not rotate the cow to roast it over the charcoal. Before it was served, the roasted cow was cut up into big chunks and recooked."

As I anticipated, some T'boli men came in their traditional outfit made of *t'nalak*. But almost all the women dressed up for the occasion. A T'boli woman might have two blouses elaborately embroidered. According to Gabriel Casal: "... these embroidered blouses, strikingly beautiful as they might be, are not the ultimate in a T'boli woman's world. Only the *k'gal binsiwit* (embroidered blouse enriched all over with ½ inch triangular shell spangles attached from one point and left free to dangle and reflect their pearly sheen) has this prerogative. To match the elegance of *k'gal binsiwit*, the *tredyung* (or *t'riyung*) is worn – a highly valued, black, pinstriped linen skirt considered an heirloom. The linen was acquired through barter with coastal tribes and is of probable Chinese origin".[4] The *k'gal binsiwit* is only used for special occasions, like at the

T'boli woman's wedding or in this case, for an important feast like the director's 40th birthday.

After lunch was served, the Afus Hill transformed into an amphitheater. The performances of traditional T'boli Dance, the Warrior Dance, and the playing of musical instruments (*hegelong*, *s'ludoy*, and *agong*) warmed up the audience. Then came the main event - a T'boli traditional horse fight. Ah, those horse fights. The writer from U.K. Marcus Brooke described it vividly: "The good-humoured crowd of T'boli seated on the hillside roared with amusement as the defeated stallion raced away. Its victorious opponent pawed the ground and coyly accepted the adulation of the proud owner. The fight, seemingly full of fury, yet signifying little in the way of real violence, was over, and the crowd began to disperse. It had, all in all, been good, clean fun."

Watching the horse fight, I was concerned about the horses getting hurt; a feeling that Mr. Brooke shared. He wrote, "I had been assured that the horses taking part in these fights are never even injured, let alone killed. Sceptic that I am, I had watched in anticipation of a bloody combat to the death, yet never did I see any blood drawn even though the action was ferocious – teeth were bared, hooves flayed, the head and body blows were vicious – and in some contests, one horse might even succeed in getting on top of its opponent. Yet, somehow, the loser, knowing itself beaten, and without any intervention from its owner, would suddenly wrench itself free from the melee and run for its life."

Mr. Brooke continued, "The stallions do not normally fight one another. As ever, it is sex that provides the spark. A young mare is tethered, and two stallions are, in turn, brought closer to her; or alternatively, each stallion will be aroused by a mare of its own and then pulled away from the object of his desire and pitted against its adversary. Sometimes the stallions are slow to be aroused, but in other instances, they are quickly rarin' to go. Horse fighting is to the T'boli what cockfighting is to other Filipinos, and in the same way (quite inexplicable to the foreign mind) that Filipinos dearly love the cocks they pit against each other in mortal combat, so too do the T'boli worship their horses."⁵

Horses were prized possessions for the T'boli. It was the most coveted dowry. Around my neighborhood, they roamed freely grazing on the hills around the Mission. Often, we saw a foal being born outside our window. There was a horse called *Mabuot* (well-behaved) that stood out among the rest. Sometimes on my way home from the office, I'd hear the faint but distinct clip-clop of horse's hooves along the footpath. I'd look up to see Fr. Rex riding behind me. He'd catch up in no time. He'd stop to say hello. As tall as I am, I had to crane my neck to see the face of the rider. He'd ride up the hills and down the valley reminiscent of the old western movies sans a cowboy hat.

I wish now I had taken the time to capture a photo of horse and rider. It was an impressive sight. *Mabuot* was a pedigreed quarter horse that came all the way from a horse farm in southwestern Pennsylvania. He was a part of a group of three; the other two were *Maganda* (beautiful) and *Maisug* (brave).

Curious about the presence of such an animal much bigger than the local horses, I reached out to Fr. Rex, who at the publication of this book still lives near Lem-ehek, Lake Sebu. He is still involved in helping the T'bolis through his Great Work Mindanao project. During his furlough in the U.S. in 1966, he met a group of people in Southwestern, Pennsylvania, who were horse enthusiasts, and they donated horses to the Mission. Fr. Rex explained in an email: "About the horse, *Mabuot*, that was just one of my misguided ventures, and, yes, it was my intention to upgrade the local native horse. The donors thought the American Quarter Horse would be a good choice for our terrain, but it turned out that the native horse had the dominant DNA, and the offspring favored the native breed probably imported centuries ago from Spain or even North Africa."[6]

THE BIRTHDAY party was over too soon. Two days later, it was time to report to work. The Santa Cruz Mission that

I knew in 1971-74 was located in the Barrio of Lake Sebu. (Today Lake Sebu is no longer a barrio, but a first-class municipality).

In 1971, the Santa Cruz Mission service area was over 2,000 hectares. There were 21,000 people within the service area, 3,000 were non-T'boli settlers. There were 18,000 T'boli served by Santa Cruz Mission. Among the Peace Corps memorabilia that I had saved was a 1973 copy of the SCM Fact Sheet called *Santa Cruz Mission*. The Fact Sheet stated that in 1973, "...Tribes untouched by the 300-year Spanish rule or the fifty-year American rule are called cultural minorities or minority tribes. Most minority tribes are non-Christian."

The four-page flyer included dire statistics geared toward raising funds in the United States through our Santa Cruz Mission office in Pittsburgh, PA: "One person out of every three in South Cotabato is a member of a minority tribe. These are Blaan, T'boli, Maguindanao, Kalagan, Ubo, Manobo, and Tasaday. No accurate census has ever been made of the minority tribes because of the inaccessible places they are living in. Most minority tribes now live scattered in the mountain areas. In 1939 the government sent people from other islands to settle in Mindanao. Currently, there are over half a million people in South Cotabato. 90% of the better agricultural land is in the hands of the settlers. 98% of minorities were illiterate. The average T'boli eats only one meal a day, less than five pounds of meat a year, and works twelve hours a day."[7]

The major problems that beset the indigenous people were poverty, illiteracy, disease, and the pressure of disrupting outside influences. Santa Cruz Mission served the Forgotten Tribes through four programs: Education, Health, Economic, and Community Development. The managers were Emma Crespo, Dedicacion Fuentes Maderal, Virgilio Maghari, and Ramonito Crespo, respectively. Ma'am Ang supervised the education department under the management of Education

Manager Emma Crespo. We only had elementary school grades at the Mission at that time.

The high school students attended the Notre Dame High School of Surallah, and the college kids studied at Notre Dame of Marbel College (NDMC). Both schools were located in the lowland. Without public transportation available from the Mission campus to Surallah or Marbel, it was necessary for the students to board and lodge in town. Others were sent to Davao or Cebu City or other places for degrees not offered at NDMC, such as agriculture.

DOTTIE AND I developed a special bond with Virgilio Maghari, the Economic Development Manager, and his wife, Angeles Romero Maghari. (Angeles helped a lot in the research and fact-checking for this book). We fondly called them Ma'am Ang and Sir Vir. Sir Vir oversaw the motor pool, road construction, and maintenance, the Woodworking Shop, the management of the plant operations, and the T'boli Products Store. Dottie worked with Sir Vir at the office of T'boli Products.

The etymology of the Mission's name was explained by Ma'am Ang in her recent email, "Santa Cruz Mission was founded by the Passionists Congregation, a religious order that professed devotion to the Holy Cross (Santa Cruz in Spanish) intending to reach out to the poor communities."

Lem-ehek was one of those poor communities so remote that until 1964, an average T'boli in the area "had never seen a truck and a safety pin was a wonder to them," thus described a Mission brochure. So isolated, it was at least a two-hour ride away from the nearest town of Surallah. Absent any form of evening entertainment in the remote mountains - no movies, no radio, no restaurants, no place to shop except the small mission store - the employees at the Mission had to concoct creative ways to amuse themselves. In early mornings, according to Ma'am Ang, she could get good reception from her radio emanating from DXKI at King's Institute in Marbel.

She lived on the second-highest point on the mission campus, so she was able to listen to music.

Rose and I brought our old record players. I brought with me from the States a good selection of long-playing records by the Lettermen, Kingston Trio, Harry Bellafonte, Herb Alpert and the Tijuana Brass and classical pieces. (Most of these records were gifted to Rose and Ma'am Ang when I left the Philippines).

Prima had a cassette player that she won through her father's subscription to the Readers' Digest magazine. The subscription was a gift from her Uncle Gil Diaz in California who served in the U.S. Navy for twenty years. She filled out a "raffle form" and mailed it. To her pleasant surprise, she won one of the fifty consolation prizes for the contest held locally in the Philippines. In 1971, a cassette player was a "state of the art" tape recorder.

There was no shortage of places to go or things to do in the daytime. On weekends, the Alo Falls was a favorite place for a swim and gather *keting*. Or we'd go boating on Lake Sebu and stop at the only other *sari-sari* store within ten kilometers owned by Santiago Diaz to check if he had other goods that was not available at the Mission store. The Diaz store usually had more fresh vegetables and fruits to sell.

We also went hiking a lot. As though we needed one more mountain to climb, one day, a dozen of us followed narrow trails toward Klubi to visit a newly opened satellite mission managed by our former cook and Clubhouse Manager Ely Cabayao. We picnicked in the forest primeval. We packed marinated pork, cooked rice, bread, and a liter or two of Coke. The guys whittled skewers out of bamboo gathered in the wild, and we roasted the pork barbecue on an open fire. It was like going on a Boy Scout bivouac.

Ma'am Ang and Sir Vir hosted many a night of creative enjoyment for Dottie, Prima, and me. After dinner most Friday nights, we'd climb to the top of the hill to their *nipa* hut. Most often, we gathered to watch Sir Vir and Dottie engage in serious chess combat and in stimulating and spirited conversations. Dottie recalled, "I wonder if I could still beat Virgilio in chess. Those were fierce games that got pretty lively with Anejo rum." Or we played a very competitive scrabble till midnight punctuated by serious challenges to questionable words.

For countless hours one night, we watched a long line of ants carrying specks of granulated sugar across the dining table to somewhere. We made up stories of their journey with such levity we laughed ourselves crazy.

Bro. Louis   Fr. Rex

Dottie & Gabriel   Leslie Savina & author with T'boli Children

Afus Hill was also one of our favorite hangouts. Fr. Rex subtly advised us *Puti or Bukay* (white) people to minimize socializing by ourselves at the exclusion of Filipino employees. During this time, there were four Caucasians at the Mission – Fr. Rex from Pittsburgh, Pennsylvania, Bro. Louis Bouchard from Ludlow, Massachusetts, Dottie Anderson from Maryland, and me. Bro. Lou was of French-Canadian descent. He arrived at the Mission in August of 1969. The SCM brochure: *A Photo Report – Bro. Louis' Challenge* stated: "He came as an apostle of technology to teach the boys and young men of the TAGABILI tribe the basic skills on which to build a modern technological society.[8] At a time of life when most men are calculating their pensions and social security, Bro. Louis has sought and found a man-size challenge to his wide experience and diversified skills." He is still remembered by many staff and the T'boli kids for teaching them how to sing "Alouette" in French.

According to Ma'am Ang, Bro. Lou designed Fr. Rex's *Convento*. She remembers vividly as her father, Potenciano Miguel Romero, the resident carpenter of the wealthy and prominent Dizon family of Marbel, was requested by Fr. Rex to assist in the construction of the *Convento*. As the foreman, Mr. Romero came to the Mission with his team of carpenters. He only stayed for one month. His men completed the job.

Some Sunday afternoons after mass, we'd pack a picnic basket of peanut butter, SkyFlakes crackers, salted garlic peanuts, bananas, and a bottle of warm Anejo rum for Dottie, warm bottles of San Miguel beer for Bro. Lou and me, and we'd hike over two hills to our favorite spot, the Afus Hill. There we'd attempt to solve the problems of the Mission. Failing that, we'd move on to the issues of the world. Failing that, we'd simply enjoy the good old American camaraderie without having to worry about speaking our minds and offending anyone. Later, we added Prima to the circle to accommodate Fr. Rex's terms of being inclusionary. At the end of the day, we'd all stumble down one hill and struggle up the next to get back to our dormitories, sometimes a tad inebriated but ridiculously happy.

Dottie is one lady who lit up from the inside. She had the best-decorated room in the neighborhood. Her zest for life and sense of humor (that can be described to be at the edge of the warped zone) is rather contagious. She promptly corrupted the sheltered and naïve Filipina girls at the dorm by selling them the idea of DHOP (Dottie's House of Pleasure). The girls, eager to be a part of a 'Kana Club, immediately christened their living quarters DHOP Dormitory. The honorable Bishop Reginald Arliss, C.P., D.D., once visited the ladies' dorm accompanied by Fr. Rex. The Mission hosted a four-day Indigenous People Workshop, and the Bishop attended. He saw the DHOP sign conspicuously hanging on the wall of the living room.

"Hmm, does that DHOP stand for something?" he asked.

"It's Dottie's House of Prayer, Your Excellency," one of the girls explained.

As soon as the Bishop and Fr. Rex left, all the ladies praised the girl who came up with the witty explanation. Truth be told, DHOP was an inside joke that Dottie and her friends in the U.S. had carried on for so long. She had a DHOP sign that she brought to SCM, which still exists. The sign aroused curiosity among the ladies at the dorm. Once explained, the ladies lapped it up. (As a testimony to the significant DHOP imprint on the ladies' lives, they refer to themselves on Facebook Group Site as DHOPians to this day).

The night after the Bishop's visit, Dottie donned her Mother Superior caftan complete with a headcover made from a white sheet and gave "communion" to her girls using thin slices of bananas as hosts. As each of the girls received the "host" Dottie being Dottie, "blessed" them and said, "Chinga banana!" Dottie still speaks in fifteen Philippine dialects all curse words! Without such moments of levity, we'd probably all go crazy from the sheer boredom and remoteness of Lem-ehek.

Dottie, artistically gifted, was tasked to expand the market for T'boli Products beyond the mission walls and to find T'boli artisans - t'nalak and basket weavers, brass and bead jewelry makers - as reliable sources of supply. Her experience in finding lucrative outlets in Manila for the Yakan handicrafts while she was working as staff in Zamboanga City proved very valuable to SCM. The connections she established with upscale outlets in Manila provided a ready market for SCM's T'boli products.

Fr. Rex set a goal of ensuring a better future for the T'boli people. It was accomplished through education, securing land titles, improving economic well being, and keeping their traditions and culture alive. Many minority indigenous tribes lose their language, culture, arts, and crafts when they integrate into a broader society. To a large extent, the T'boli preserved their language, culture, arts, and crafts. Dottie's work at SCM deserves the credit for the weaving and other traditional crafts being passed on to the younger generations. Today's generation of T'boli wants to carry on their traditions because they are proud of the items they produce and are also able to earn a living by creating their traditional crafts.

In June 1973, Dottie, our guide Gabriel, and I went to Tacunil, the site of our best brass makers, to film the process of brass making. On our way, we stopped at a spring, a community water source for several hundred people, about half a mile from the Tboli houses. All the water was carried. There were little girls and women fetching water for their family's supply. They used bamboo tubes called *kubong* to carry the water from the spring. The bamboo stem is straight, cylindrical, and hollow. The T'boli fashioned a water container by cutting bamboo stems, leaving a node on each end. A hole poked on the top node allowed water to be poured in and out.

Bamboos are not only used for making *kubong*. It is one of the most utilitarian gifts from nature of notable economic and cultural significance to the T'boli people. They are not only used mainly for building materials, but also as a food source and for making musical instruments like *s'ludoy* (bamboo zither) or *kumbing* (mouth harp). Bamboos belong to the grass family and are some of the fastest-growing plants in the world.

The Peace Corps Volunteer drinking from a spring using a leaf for his cup. A T'boli grandmother and a child walking down the hill to fetch water from the spring below.

T'boli girls had already gathered to fill their *kubong* that came in ageappropriate sizes.

Around the spring, we encountered only women and young girls. According to Zenaida Dorol, who did extensive research of the T'boli people for her master's degree thesis, "Boys did not fetch water. A wife carried the *kubong* (a water container made of *afus*/bamboo) while the husband followed the wife without carrying anything. He just accompanied the wife for security."[9] Ms. Dorol's thesis focused on the "folkways of the T'boli adolescents." She listed the traditional "masculine and feminine" tasks. The boys gathered firewood, hunted, etc. and work in the fields except weeding. Weeding the fields was strictly for girls, as they were considered "light" work. The girls cooked, did the laundry, embroidery, and weaving of *t'nalak*, among others.

In the early 1970s, it was a challenge to find brass makers near Santa Cruz Mission. To film the lost wax process of brass making, Dottie and I hiked for hours with our guide Gabriel to the mountains of Tacunil. The arduous trek led us to the finest brass artisans who became Santa Cruz Mission's dependable suppliers of quality brass products.

The brass artisans lived on the ridge of the mountain. Dottie was on her way to meet them.

The Lost Wax Process of Brass Making

Step 1. Beeswax is used to make the design for a belt buckle. Note the stem leading out from one corner of each half of the buckle.

After this design is encased in clay, it is heated over charcoal. When the beeswax melt, the stem becomes the cavity through which the melted brass is poured. Right: T'boli artisan rolling beeswax to make swirls in the buckle. Note his traditional pants made of *t'nalak* abaca cloth.

Step 2.

The wax design is encased in clay. The clay forms the mold and is heated in the fire to harden. The heat melts the wax and is poured out of the mold, leaving an empty cavity. Charcoal is used with bellows made of bamboo to add air making the fire hotter. Brass is melted in a small clay pot with a spout. When the brass is melted, it is poured into the empty cavity of the mold.

Step 3. After the brass has cooled, the clay is broken off, leaving the brass buckle ready for cleaning and polishing. There will never be two exactly alike because the original wax design is melted, and the clay mold is broken, hence the "lost wax process."(Right): Brass wire is made similarly. Instead of beeswax, bamboo sticks about the thickness of the pencil are layered in clay. After the clay is heated in the fire to harden, the bamboo sticks are removed. Melted brass is poured into the cavities of the mold. When cooled, the clay is removed, leaving brass rods. The brass rods are warmed to soften, then pulled through a series of dies, making the rod thinner and longer.

To pull the rod, a pair of pliers is attached to a rope. The rope is attached to a pole on the other side of the house. Another person turns the pole winding it around to pull the rod through the die. Designs are added to the wire with a hammer and punch. See designs on the man's rings.

Dottie moved into the White House and lived there until the new ladies' dormitory was completed. It was a small hut with a corrugated tin roof, painted white, hence the White House. It was divided into four rooms identical in size, a single bed in each room. She did not have to share her room. Some of the five other staff members doubled up in the three remaining bedrooms. Dottie described her living quarters in an email she sent recently, "I was at the White House the whole time until we moved to the dorm. The RAT story happened at the White House. The building, by the way, had wood windows that swung open for ventilation. The bed was wood slats with a mat on it, and we all had chamber pots. It had a homemade wood chair and table. No electricity. I do not remember where Al lived, but I'm sure that I was very jealous if he stayed in luxury at Rex's place. I, too, remember that the girl's dorm was finished later than the men's dorm."

On Market day (Saturday) at the Mission, some T'boli sold their products at the stalls surrounding the administrative building while others came to shop. It was downtime for the T'boli men as they gathered around in circles to chew betel nut. I assumed they were discussing world issues! On Sunday, the chapel overflowed with the worshiping faithful.

Saturday was a time for socialization too at the open market and a chance for the T'boli families and for us to buy fresh fruits, vegetables, freshwater clams, and the occasional chicken. During weekdays, the variety of food at the LTK was so limited. Market days offered a change of menu. Before the Clubhouse was operational, I remember eating mostly canned goods, SkyFlakes crackers, and bananas cut in half spread with peanut butter.

Many of us competed to buy a chicken at the market. To win the competition, one had to be lucky enough to spot a chicken vendor and be the first to reach him as he came down the hill. Tilapia was abundant at Lake Sebu, and the freshwater clams called *keting* were in good supply. They were an excellent source of protein. So were duck eggs. But one could only stomach a limited dose of all three, not as a regularly recycled portion of one's daily meal. There were a few times when we ate fried duck eggs for breakfast and boiled duck eggs for lunch, always with rice. And there was the famous *pancit bihon* (rice noodles) cooked with canned Vienna sausage, Hormel corned beef, Spam, or Ligo sardines. Sometimes we had normal *pancit bihon* with pork, chicken, or vegetarian. I don't ever remember being served beef at our dining room.

One morning at the LTK, the menu consisted of fried rice, scrambled duck eggs, and fried *dilis* (dried anchovies pronounced as dee-lees). Dottie hated those *dilis*. Not so much because of the smell or the taste as much as how their googly-eyes stared back at her.

Once, she took a *dilis* back to her room, pasted it on her letter to her mother, put it in an envelope, sealed it, and set it aside to be mailed the next day. The following morning, she found her letter was all chewed up and the anchovies missing. A rat raided her writing table and decided to eat the anchovy for its midnight snack.

Life was ever challenging at Santa Cruz Mission, but it was never dull!

The cluster of houses inhabited by my T'boli neighbors behind two dormitories for ladies and men and the Clubhouse. Adjacent to the dormitories and Clubhouse was a community of SCM employees living in standard lowland *nipa* huts. Datu Ma Fok's house stood like a sentry on top of the Lem-ehek hill.

FATHER REX MANSMANN'S 40TH BIRTHDAY PARTY

Top: L-R: Bishop Reginald Arliss, Fr. Rex, and a Filipino priest concelebrated the mass. Behind them were Fr. Hyacinth, Fr. John, and Bro. Louis.

The rest of the photo: My former boss Fr. Albinus, being welcomed by my new boss Fr. Rex. The St. Paul Sisters with staff in front of Fr. Rex's Convento. A musician playing the tnongong, a T'boli woman dressed in her prized and finest k'gal binsiwit, and the performer of traditional war dance.

Prima with her goddaughter Felicidad "Siding" Anggol, Gilda Bangaw (younger lady), and Ma Fok's sister Be Ye Udoy inside the Santa Cruz Mission Chapel after mass.

Gumbay Sulan was the popular player of *s'ludoy* (bamboo zither). Here she entertained customers at the T'boli Products Store. Note brass rings on her toes. Right: A T'boli lady played the *kumbing* (Jew's harp) while another looked on wearing at least 15 brass bracelets. Musicians played the *agong* and the *hegelong*.

The Light is Shining on this Side of the Mountain 13

ALL I really need to know about the Courtship and Marriage customs in the Philippines I learned from Peace Corps Training. On the first day of orientation at the former nudist camp in Escondido, California, Don Berman gave an engaging lecture on the subject. Don was the Training Director for the Philippines based in Hawaii at that time. The information he imparted was so interestingly different from what I was accustomed to.

For example, he revealed that it was widely acceptable between girlfriends to hold hands in public or even put their arms around each other's shoulders while walking down the street. Likewise, it was acceptable for men to hold hands, which, to an American, felt uncomfortable. But a boy and a girl holding hands while promenading in public were frowned upon because it implies that the girl is somehow morally flawed. Making out openly in public is also considered an affront to Filipino sensibilities. A woman who dates more than one guy at a time risks being branded as *malandi* (a flirt). Yet it is okay for a married man to have a *querida* or mistress openly.

In Hawaii, the many hours we spent on Cross-Cultural Studies reinforced the basic facts we learned on said customs with additional lessons from our language instructors. I considered it very valuable knowledge to help me understand the new set of cultural practices I was exposed to as a Peace Corps volunteer. But it had no direct bearing on me. Or so I thought. Never in my wildest imagination did it occur to me that at some time in my future, I'd be digging into the recesses of my brain for Don Berman's tips to avoid a *faux pas* in my quest for a serious romance. Especially when a Filipina was the object of the quest.

In 1973, after four years of living and working at my sites, I heard more about the "olden days" of the traditional courtship in the Philippines, which was very old-fashioned indeed compared to western societies. In general, a suitor just doesn't ask a respectable Filipina to go out on a date as a twosome. Usually, there is an entourage of friends or siblings to provide a modicum of propriety. In the rural areas (I was told that even to this day), the courting usually starts with a *harana* (serenade). If and when the suitor had mustered enough gumption, he visits the object of his affection at her home. There, they would sit in the *sala* (living room) with the woman's parents or a chaperon hovering protectively. With the parents' approval, the couple might be allowed to go out for a walk in a safe public place.

A designated chaperon always accompanied the couple. A couple going for walks by themselves at night or going out to the movies without an escort is taboo. It was also common in the rural areas for a suitor to engage in some form of *paninilbihan* (servitude) - doing household chores like chopping wood, carrying water from a well or river, etc. Some may find these practices unorthodox, but for me, it made so much sense. It conforms with my own deep-seated belief that one gets to know better the ways of the woman and her family and vice versa.

This statement is not based on any kind of scientific research. But I read somewhere that 60% of Filipinos (living in the Philippines and abroad) still cling to their highly esteemed traditions. They practice said traditions to this day. Among them are *mano po* (kissing of the hand of elders to say hello or goodbye), *bayanihan* (spirit of communal unity to achieve a particular objective like moving a *nipa* hut from one lot to another), *harana* (serenade), *pamanhikan* (to go to the lady's house to ask for her hand in marriage), etc.

Out of habit, I still call out *Maayo* to announce my arrival at
a Filipino house instead of knocking at the door. My children
and grandchildren do the same. It is a contraction of the
greetings in the Ilongo dialect *Maayong aga* (good morning) or
Maayong gab-i (good evening). When I came back to the U.S., I
was often asked why not just knock on the door. I explained
that some houses in the rural Philippines have no doors.

THE MANY friendships forged while I was in the Philippines
sustained me through the years. Such close relationships
became a delightful constant in my life at a time when my
familiar support system was ten thousand miles away. None
was as pleasurable as my affinity with the Guipo family, Prima,
and her circle of friends.

Once I went hiking and mountain climbing in Polonoling
with the Guipo siblings in search of staghorn ferns. We brought
home one medium-sized specimen, which we added to the
trunk of their *camachili* tree amidst Mrs. Guipo's flowering
orchid collection. The more sizeable ferns we could only take
home as images in my camera, because they hung on branches
of trees more than twenty feet high, way beyond our reach. On
our way home, we made a stop at a Blaan community.

Another time, Prima's older sisters Nena and Josie, took me
to Malungon near the border of Davao del Sur to visit a village
of Kalagans. Nena was working with the Philippine Rural
Reconstruction Movement (PRRM) at that time as a social
worker (considered as a local counterpart of a Peace Corps
volunteer). She was looking into the possibility of starting
community development programs with the indigenous tribes
of North and South Cotabato. The summer before I arrived,
Nena also spent a month with the Tiruray people in Upi, North
Cotabato. She took Prima along during that trip.

Since the first day that I started teaching at Notre Dame
College, I had been working very closely with a singular
girl. I wrestled with the idea for a long time. I wanted to

court Prima openly but was concerned I'd lose our special friendship if things didn't work out. Eventually, I set aside my apprehensions and determined to openly woo her anyway and in the true Filipino tradition, notwithstanding what I'd heard about a former suitor who came back into her life. Of course, I did the courting my way. I mean sans the *harana* (I couldn't carry a tune) and the *paninilbihan* (the Guipos had running water from the tank and no chopping wood either as they had by this time a propane gas stove). The idea of courting at home had a romantic appeal.

One day in March 1972, I went to see Bro. Henry and requested to speak with him confidentially. Prima was finishing her Bachelor's degree in Education and had to attend a class on Test and Measurement with Mrs. Priscilla Dinopol, the Principal of the Elementary Department. Bro. Henry locked the doors to his office, including the adjoining Dean of Studies. He also closed the privacy curtain over the small glass window on the main entrance so no one would see who was inside. We heard someone turn the doorknob. But realizing it was locked, the person walked away.

Bro. Henry just listened intently as I poured out my feelings for Prima. I came not seeking advice, as much as to share with someone I trusted what I was going through. Since no advice was sought, Bro. Henry did not offer any. I emerged from the office an hour later. I felt better for having unburdened myself to Bro. Henry. Prima was standing across the way at the Book Room. She visited with the book room manager Gloria Saclot while waiting for the door to open. I said a quick hello and went on my way.

Shortly after, Fr. Rex Mansmann came to Notre Dame College to recruit teachers and staff to work at Santa Cruz Mission (SCM). I was overjoyed when he told me that he had just the right job for Dottie and me as part of his expansion plans. During his first recruitment trip the year before, I took Fr. Rex to FNCB and introduced Prima to him. Prima took home an application but did not fill it out. She had other plans. Bro. Henry encouraged her to apply for a Ford Scholarship at CRC (Center for Research and Communications), the kind awarded to her older sister Susan.

Rose submitted her job application at the Mission, interviewed in Marbel, and was offered a teaching job. But before Rose made her final decision, she accepted an invitation from Fr. Rex to check out the mission in Lake Sebu. Prima and Susan, who had never been to the Mission, were excited to join Rose. Since I had visited SCM with Dottie Anderson the year before, I decided to tag along to see the progress that had been made.

Bro. Henry declared at the last minute that with college graduation ceremonies just a week away, he could not spare Prima from the office, so she was not able to go with us. We were all disappointed. The staff at Santa Cruz Mission and the children at the mission school welcomed us warmly. Fr. Rex accommodated me at his *Convento.* We attended the graduation ceremonies on April 4, 1972. On graduation night, Fr. Rex wore a real snappy coat made of *t'nalak,* a T'boli woven fabric.

I stopped at Notre Dame College after we came back from Lake Sebu to give Prima a T'boli necklace that I had purchased at the Mission T'boli Products store.

"Why so glum?" I asked when I saw her at her desk.

"Did you know?" she asked.

"Know what?"

"That Bro. Henry is leaving for his furlough in May? And that he is not coming back to NDDC? He is being transferred to Marikina as the Provincial Treasurer after he returns from Spain."

"No, I haven't heard," I said. "What are you going to do?"

"I don't know yet, but I told him I am not applying for that Ford Foundation scholarship. He's kind of disappointed, but I made up my mind. I have to look for a job."

"Well, I heard they are still hiring at Santa Cruz Mission."

"Ah, too far away from home," she dismissed my suggestion.

Two weeks later, on a Saturday, Fr. James, who was permanently transferred to Marbel, came to visit General Santos. He was starting a Community Center similar to the one he established in Silway and was looking for an administrative assistant. I told Fr. James, that I had just the right person in mind, that she might be interested and had the experience to boot. We hopped in his jeep and went to Prima's house. Although Bro. Henry gave her assurance that she could stay as secretary to the incoming college director; Prima accepted the offer from Fr. James. A month later, Fr. James and I took Prima to Marbel. It was her first time to work or to live away from home.

In Marbel, there lived a couple named Jose and Vance Ang. They owned the KOGENHAS store (Koronadal General Hardware and Auto Supply). To many Peace Corps volunteers, they were simply known as *Kuya* Jose and *Ate* Vance. (*Kuya* and *Ate* are terms of endearment in Tagalog for an older sibling or anyone older). They not only opened their home to volunteers to stay for two years or more, but they also welcomed volunteers with nowhere to go on holidays.

The Angs were ardent supporters of and very active in the Catholic Church; he was a member of the Knights of Columbus, and she was an officer for the Catholic Women's League. Fr. James arranged for Prima to stay with the Ang family. Another Peace Corps Volunteer named Stacey Spillane was also living there. Stacey and Prima became roommates and friends. They had previously met at one of the beach picnics I hosted for the Marbel volunteers.

Fr. James left a few days after he oriented Prima with what needed to be done, mostly filing and organizing his file cabinet and completing forms for non-profit organizations to raise funds for the community center. He went to Manila to procure much-needed financial help for the proposed Center. A natural when it comes *to how to win friends and influence people*, Prima settled in well with the other staff.

WHENEVER I was in Marbel, I always stayed with the Bedfords (Fred & Catherine), who took over the bungalow that my Group 31 friends Tom and Marilyn Perardi used to occupy. A girl named Vilma Bordamonte was a working student for the Perardis and stayed on when the Bedfords arrived. Vilma and I had become friends. I introduced her to Prima. The Bedfords were Peace Corps volunteers in their 60s who taught math and science at Notre Dame of Marbel College, where Vilma was a student. Fr. James informed me that Mrs. Vance Ang enjoyed having Prima around. She read books to the four Ang children, played *sungka*,[1] and they sang while she accompanied with the guitar.

One day, I hopped on the motorcycle to transact business with Fr. James in Marbel. The road was rough. I had placed my razor inside a Tupperware tumbler with lid. My toothbrush was too long to fit, so I cut off the handle to the size of the Tumbler. Razor and toothbrush were placed inside the tumbler and buried in the middle of a tightly packed set of clothing for extra protection. By the time I arrived at the Bedfords, the double-edged razor blade had bounced out of the razor. It had been so dulled from the tumbling action that it could not even cut my finger. So I went unshaven for the remainder of the trip.

The Marbel Parish Fiesta of St. Anthony de Padua was held every June 13. The week before, the *Convento* staff and Prima were busy with preparations for the fiesta. The renovation of an existing building to be used as the Community Center was not completed yet. But Fr. James, who was back to Marbel for the celebration, planned to advertise the Center to solicit patrons during the fiesta. On the Friday before the celebration, Mr. and Mrs. Bedford hosted a birthday and graduation party for Vilma. I was invited, so I went back to Marbel, but I rode the Yellow Bus this time.

On the eve of the party, I had a heart to heart talk with Vilma. I confided to her my feelings for Prima. I danced a lot with Prima at the party and walked her home that night. Under the light of the waning crescent moon and the stars, I told Prima that I was in love with her, that the emotion started when we visited the T'boli country in Kematu, Edwards three years before. My declaration was met with dead silence. I clumsily reached for her hand, but she pulled it back and said, "Can we just stay friends, please?"

An uncomfortable lapse of silence ensued for the next remaining few blocks to the Ang's house, a mile and a half distant from the Bedfords. When I returned to the Bedfords, I wrote Prima a very long letter recalling the three days she, her brother, and I spent together in Kematu, where I first felt affection toward her.

In my letter, I bared my heart and soul and shared with her the story of a girl named Anne back in Pennsylvania who was going to marry someone else. I quoted in the letter the things I wrote about Anne that could be said about her. "*...the many talents, cooking, sewing, honors in school, arts and crafts, the*

collections of little but important things, singing, remembering, love
of people, ability to look beyond a little world so much rolled into one
girl..."

During our trip to Kematu in 1969, I found a pebble.[2] It was
shaped like half a heart that I had kept inside my shaving kit. I
sent the stone with the letter and added a meaningful message
quoting 1 Corinthians 13. "Love is slow to lose patience; it looks
for a way to be constructive. It is not possessive. Love has good
manners and does not pursue selfish advantages. Love knows
no limit to its endurance, no end to its trust, no fading of its
hope; it can outlast anything. It is the one thing that stands
when all else has fallen."

Also, I expressed in the letter a wish that I hoped someday
to go back to the T'boli land to find the other half of the heart.
I ended my letter by confessing that "the light is shining on my
side of the mountain." That if and when she feels the same to
let me know.

"Let's just stay friends," she said. My romantic
prospects dimmed. I wondered if there was someone else.
Notwithstanding, I remained hopeful. My Peace Corps career
looked bright and promising. It kept me occupied while I
sorted out my personal life. My work at the Parish started to
wind down as I began the transition of handing over the Social
Action office to the nuns. I had already signed on the dotted
line as Management Consultant at Santa Cruz Mission and
planned to move to Lake Sebu at the end of the year after I
wrapped up our outstanding projects at the Dadiangas parish.

The day after Vilma's party, I stopped by at the Mission
Office in Marbel to see Fr. Rex Mansmann to let him know
that I would start working at SCM in six months. Afterward,
I went to the Marbel Parish *Convento* to deliver my letter to
Prima before I left for General Santos. I popped into the office
and gave her the envelope. There was a bit of awkwardness
to overcome at first. But Prima and I both shared such
extraordinary friendship that my declaration of the night

before didn't ruin a close personal alliance. We resumed the same comfortable relationship we had developed and appreciated for three years.

I noticed something was amiss as soon as I came into the room. Prima was stunned and sad that Fr. James had just left for Manila and will not be coming back to Marbel. So was I, sad and disappointed. She was well acquainted with Fr. Anthony, the interim priest taking over until a replacement was found for Fr. James. Fr. Anthony was assigned in Lagao Parish when Prima was in high school. He knew Prima well and said she could keep her job while they work out the future of the community center. Prima knew him very well too. She did not really want to stay and work for a grumpy old man. She resigned.

Meanwhile, Fr. Rex had informed me that there were still openings for staff members and teachers at the Mission. I convinced Prima to prepare her resume. Fr. Rex stopped by at the Marbel *Convento* and went back to Lake Sebu carrying Prima's resume. Having done my good deed for the day, I left for General Santos.

Out of a job, Prima went home to General Santos in the middle of June. A few days later, she received a telegram from Fr. Rex to report to the Mission as soon as possible if she was interested in a teaching job. Her best friend Rose had already accepted the same offer. Rose had just come back from a vacation in Bohol when she heard that Prima was joining her at SCM. We celebrated the good news with a trip to the beach. That night, I came to visit Prima at her house. I was determined to do the courting the Filipino way.

I brought a dozen roses from Mayor Barney French's garden in Polomolok and Hershey bars. I handed it directly to Prima in the living room full of people where the family gathered, including her cousins. My action revealed for the first time to her family that I was courting her. Embarrassed by my open display of affection and in her discomfort, she dropped the box on the floor. But she picked it up when her mother eyed her with displeasure. I maintained my composure. She apologized later and explained that everyone assumed I was interested in one of the other sisters.

Another night, I came to visit after I had gone on a picnic on the yacht named The Buccaneer owned by Dole. Josie, Prima's older sister, had resigned from Notre Dame and was teaching at the Dole School in Kalsangi at that time. Prima was invited, too, but did not join us. I arrived on my bicycle after dinner, but Prima went to bed early. For three years that I had been a friend to the family, I had made it a habit to bring Magnolia ice cream whenever I visited.

"So, Al, did you come back to help us eat the ice cream you brought the other night?" Mr. Guipo asked.

Caught by surprise, I must have turned the color of my hair when I stammered, "Oh no, I did not come just for that. I am here for other reasons too." As soon as I said it, I realized I had put my foot in my mouth as there was a daughter in the living room, and it was not Prima.

As if that was not enough, on my way home to the Calderon's house on Quirino Avenue a few kilometers away, just past the Emergency Hospital that abutted the Guipo's lot, a pack of guard dogs belonging to the Denoga family (Guipo's neighbor) decided to chase me. With only the faint bicycle headlight to illumine my way, I pedaled as fast as I could. Thank goodness the owner hushed the dogs and called them back just in time before they could take a bite of me.

ROSE AND Prima left for Lake Sebu to start their teaching jobs at the end of June 1972. A week later, I followed to attend the orientation for newly hired employees held during the three-day General Meeting. The Mission's Fact Sheet of 1973 noted, "The mission is professionally organized by the latest management techniques, following the system of Program, Budgeting, and Management by Objectives as adapted to Sta.

Cruz Mission by Planning Dynamics Inc. of Pittsburgh and the Corporate Management Services, Inc. (CMSI) of Cebu City, Philippines."

Fr. Rex had invited a Management Consultant Group of three men and one lady from CMSI to moderate an employee seminar and orientation of incoming staff members.[3] Our new group employed for the year 1972-1973 was the largest cohort of twenty-two incoming young men and women to join the Santa Cruz Mission staff.

The CMSI management group led by Renato Kintanar discussed the goals of the mission, its expectations of its employees, accommodations, among other things. General Manager Qric Batilaran gave a general overview of the operations of the Mission. Each of the Managers also described the programs at the mission – education, health, economic development, and community development. It was followed by a question and answer (Q&A) session.

During the Q&A, the question was raised about the restrictions placed on non-T'boli employees of the Mission. They were prohibited from buying or owning land located in Lake Sebu or within the Santa Cruz Mission service area. Angeles Maghari explained the rationale behind this policy in a recent email: "Fr. Rex believed that the land should be preserved for the T'boli as their ancestral legacy. But some T'boli who were not loyal to SCM sold their pieces of land to rich and entrepreneurial non-T'boli people from Surallah, Marbel, and other neighboring towns."

"Why aren't we allowed to buy land when other non-T'boli who are not employed by the Mission are acquiring land as fast as they could," asked one long-time employee during the meeting.

Fr. Rex explained that if the Mission employees were allowed to buy land, it could be construed as a blatant conflict of interest. Here we are trying to preserve the culture and the ancestral domain of the T'boli, yet we take away from those whose interests we were trying to protect, their most valuable possession - their ancestral land.

"Well, they are selling them to the non-T'boli anyway, wouldn't it make more sense that we buy their land instead?" reasoned another long-time employee.

The discussion got heated from thereon. Renato tried to diffuse the situation, but it escalated instead. I should have kept my mouth shut at this point. But I couldn't help it. I raised my hand to be recognized, stood up, and spoke my piece in defense of Fr. Rex and the mission's policy. Well, that got me off to a good start with the long-time employees of the Mission. The hostile attention was deflected from Fr. Rex and was now aimed at me. After the seminar, Fr. Rex took me aside. He appreciated my concern, but he requested me to apologize to certain employees who took umbrage at my action. I did so immediately and learned my lesson in diplomacy from Fr. Rex.

At the end of the seminar, before the Management group returned to Cebu City, two administration staff with Prima, Rose, and Siony, took Renato and his group on a boating excursion at nearby Lake Sebu. I was invited to go along. The weapons carrier took us to the edge of the lake. A small boat picked us up. We ate our supper on the boat while the light of the full moon above illuminated the lake.

Although I was not officially working for the Mission yet, every now and then, I'd go up to Lake Sebu to help Annie Garcia find a market for the T'boli handicrafts. To bring awareness of the plight of the T'boli artisans and craftsmen, I organized an Exhibit of T'boli Handicrafts in some private homes in General Santos City, like Mrs. Estela Tan (owner of MarTan Trading) and at the Dole Clubhouse. I also managed to send a care package for Rose and Prima, filled with chocolates and their favorite SkyFlakes crackers. Many times, I wanted to send them fresh fish from Sarangani Bay, but refrigeration during transit was a problem.

Every chance I had from June to December, I visited Lake Sebu. I kept my promise to Prima to stay friends. I gave her space to get to know me better too. She told me that she did not want her pupils and the staff to talk unkindly about us when we were together. She insisted that it was better to keep our relationship platonic. We exchanged friendly letters now and then.

On one of these trips, I was able to catch the last Mission vehicle for the day. It was getting dark when we started. By the time we reached the Allah Valley River, it was pitch dark. The T'boli driver, Boning Landusan, realized that the lights on the weapons carrier had malfunctioned. He deemed it dangerous to cross the river without the lights on.

No problem. One of the T'boli kids took a bottle of coke from the case. He popped the lid with his eyetooth, a common practice in the Philippines, even when there was a can opener available. Then he passed the bottle around for everyone to take a swig. Once empty, he took a screwdriver and punctured two holes on the top of the five-gallon can of kerosene. With the help of another T'boli kid, they filled the empty coke bottle with kerosene almost to the top.

"Hey, Sir Al," said one kid. "May we have some pages from your magazine?"

I gave him the cover of TIME and a page or two that I had already read. He rolled it into the shape of a cigar, stuck one end into the bottle, and lighted the other end – he had a kerosene lamp. The T'boli kid sat on the bumper of the weapons carrier, extended his arm as far as it would go, and held the kerosene lamp in front of him. Farther down the road at a logging camp, one of their drivers had some extra wire. He hot-wired the lights directly from the truck battery. Whew! Not perfect but safer than a T'boli kid sitting on the bumper holding a Molotov cocktail!

In October 1972, I received letters from Rose and Prima. They were full of news about their first four months of teaching at Santa Cruz Mission.

Dear Sir Al,

Rose and I are enjoying the SkyFlakes and Hershey bars that you sent. We received the package through Annie. Thank you for the goodies and the letter from Nanay and Tatay [mother and father in Pilipino language]. *It is like the good old times in General Santos all over again here with the three of us working at Santa Cruz Mission. Annie said you would be joining us in January. By the way, that was so thoughtful of you to go to my folks' house to inform them you were sending a box to us and to include a letter from them. Salamat.*

Teaching has been okay, but I struggled. So did my co-teacher Morit Jugar. He has a degree in math and science; however, he was assigned to teach English. I only took the required math and science subjects in college and have a minor in English, but I am teaching science. We went to our Principal, Ma'am Ang Maghari, who submitted our proposal to switch roles to the Education Manager Ma'am Em Crespo. Ma'am Em approved it.

I now teach English from Grades Four to Six and am assigned as a homeroom teacher for Grade Six. It is a bit of a challenge because I don't speak the T'boli dialect well yet. The T'boli, in general, don't speak Tagalog. It's a good thing the kids understand my Ilonggo dialect. So we manage somehow. As much as I enjoy being with the kids, I am happy that I won't be teaching for long. As a teacher, I feel so inept and ineffective.

Last August, Fr. Rex attended our teachers' monthly meeting. He had this wild idea of finding sponsors for the pupils in all our mission schools (500 kids plus). The Mission is erecting new schools. Fr. Rex predicts our pupil population will hit the 1000 mark next year. He plans to create something similar to the Sponsor-a-Child Program of World Vision or UNICEF. He explained the concept to us. For $5 a month, someone in the U.S. can sponsor a child for a year ($60 annually). The amount will pay for the complete schooling and living expenses of an elementary school child. This includes the running costs for medicines, uniforms, food, and clothing. In return, the sponsor will get a photo and profile of their "adopted" child, and we will provide them with a progress report twice each school year. We will target sponsors in the U.S. first, then introduce the concept here in the Philippines.

Fr. Rex gave us homework to write a profile for each of our students. The first thing I did was to provide sixteen pupils in my Grade Six class a simple questionnaire: Name, Age, Birthday, Number of brothers and sisters, Distance of house to school, Favorite things to do, Parents name, alive or dead. It was easy then to write their profile using the information they provided. Many don't know their exact birthdays. Without birth certificates, there is no way to find out. Sad no?

We all submitted our homework to Ma'am Ang and Ma'am Em. Two weeks later, Fr. Rex asked me if I'd be interested in helping in the Office of Promotions. It is a new department being created under the office of Fr. Rex. I will also help as his secretary to take dictations and type his letters mostly. The goal of the Promotions Department is to raise funds mainly through the Santa Cruz Mission Office in Pittsburgh, PA. An SCM office to be established in Manila is in the plans.

I had been working with Fr. Rex since September putting into action his concept for the Sponsor-A-Child Program. We will also create brochures and flyers. Eventually, we will prepare slide presentations that Ma'am Em can use when she goes to Davao, Cebu, and Manila to solicit sponsors at various Universities there. (I will be putting into good use what you taught me about creating slide shows).

Once the construction of the new elementary buildings overlooking Lake Seluton is finished, my sixth-grade classroom will be converted into the Promotions Office. It's next door to the office of the Manager of Education and the Director. So it will make it very convenient to collaborate with Ma'am Em and Fr. Rex. A new teacher will be hired to take my place, and I will work full time as in charge of the Promotions Office starting December. My cup of tea!

Last month, Rose (she's homeroom teacher for Grade 5), Siony (Grade 4), and I went together on our monthly house visitation. The first time we went in July, we were sore all over as we walked all day from one mountain to another to visit our pupils in their homes. This is mandatory for all teachers for us to get to know our pupils and their families. Also, for us to observe what their family circumstances are, so we may be able to give allowance when a pupil is late, for instance, or if he's sleepy or tired in class, etc. Some of these kids have to walk three hours or more to school. They have the option to stay at the dormitory, but for some, they'd rather endure the long trek than be away from their family.

One of our students who lived the farthest felt so sorry for us that he borrowed his uncle's horse for us to use. Rose and Siony enjoyed the ride, saddleless. But I'd rather walk than nurse a sore behind.

It is so heartwarming how much regard the parents have for "mistulos" (teachers). They served us merienda when they have barely enough for themselves and their children to eat. I need to learn T'boli fast - I want to be able to talk to the parents on the next visit. I can understand a lot, but I am so frustrated that I could not speak their language as well. Our pupils are more than willing, in fact, proud to be interpreters.

It gets rather chilly, especially in the mornings and when there's a breeze. The cold air streams through the bamboo walls and floors. Rose and I share a single bed that takes half the space of our tiny room. We have a small table where Rose has her record player and my cassette recorder, a pitcher of water, and two Tupperware tumblers for our toothbrushes and toothpaste, that's about it. She brought her guitar that's hanging on one wall of the room.

We were able to cram our traveling cases under the bed. We live out of our suitcases, so to speak. Food is still scarce. The unmarried employees like us residing in dorms cook our own meals. I did not have much practice cooking at home with three older sisters, but I am learning fast. The other day, I was taking dictation from Fr. Rex. He *was writing to his friend Jim Ryan, one of our biggest donors. He said Mr. Ryan and his family own the Ryan Homes Company in the U.S. I thought Fr. Rex described our food situation aptly. "Around here, we scrounge for food."*

By the way, my sixth-grade class is planning a field trip to the beach in General Santos in February next year. Ma'am Em approved it. With all my siblings away from home, my parents offered to host them at the house in Lagao. You should be here by then, so Rose and I were hoping you could help as a chaperon. And you also know which beach would be best-suited and safe for sixteen sixth-graders. We take the students who live in the dorm to the rivers and lakes here for weekend excursions, but for some, this would be their first time to go to the beach and visit the city of General Santos.

After it was announced yesterday, Sonia, one of three girls in my class, came to talk to me. She was so sad and was crying. A marriage was arranged for her while Sonia was still very young, about five to a man ten years older. She is now fourteen, and the husband wants her. She has no choice because if she runs away, which she had considered a few times, her father would have to return the dowry. He has no means to do so. She asked me if I could talk to her father, but we were instructed during our teachers' orientation that we should not get involved in matters such as this. It breaks my heart.

When I told her about our position on the matter, she asked if I could at least convince her father to let her stay until after the field trip. She probably will not even be allowed to wait for her graduation ceremony. I am hoping that her father and the man she was promised to would at least let her go to the beach.

Another sixth-grade pupil Bert Sman took some T'boli kids and me to Lemdalag, the sitio bordering Lem-ehek. One of his relatives had died of an unknown disease. He thought it would be nice to pay our respects. As we were going down the hill to the valley, we saw the thatched roof house, but Bert told us that we shouldn't go any farther. He was afraid we'd get infected. From a distance, we watched people gather around the T'boli house. We waited for about an hour. Then the house with the dead body inside was set on fire. We left after it was totally burnt to the ground.

I am learning a lot about the T'boli culture just hanging out with my pupils. I know Filipinos are very superstitious, but some of the things that are taboo here I have heard for the first time. In the T'boli dialect, a taboo is called "lii" (pronounced as lee-e). It has been educational for me. For instance, it is taboo to strike up a conversation with a t'nalak weaver while she is weaving, and single adolescent girls must avoid eating twin bananas as it is believed to "cause" twin babies and having a twin is a sign of bad luck.[4]

We had a scare last night. I don't know whose idea it was, but Annie decided to de-louse ten-year-old Elena, who is living in our dorm. The common practice employed here in the past is to douse the headful of hair carefully with kerosene, then wrap the head with a thin white towel. Let the kerosene soak overnight. It had worked very well without fail. The following morning, we'd unwrap the head and find dead lice on the towels. Then we give the kid's hair a good shampooing. Except Annie did not factor the fact that this kid loves to read. So Elena read and must have fallen asleep with her reading candle still on. We were so glad that the kid woke up when the corner of the towel started to burn! Siony always kept a pitcher of water on her bedside table.[5] She emptied the water on the girl's head. Elena is free of lice, at least, for now. Like you are fond of saying, "all's well that ends well."

Okay, the warning lights just flickered. Again thanks for the goodies. I will give this letter to Nong Ronnie Vergara in the morning to drop at the Mission's office in Marbel.

Cheers, Prima

THREE MONTHS after I received the letter from Prima, I moved to Santa Cruz Mission in time to attend Fr. Rex's birthday, and I was hanging out with her, Rose, Annie, and Siony. Also, I began to familiarize myself with the lay of the land, made a point to introduce myself to the guys at the dormitory, and get to know them better. I volunteered to help in the training of the Clubhouse staff. It did not take long before I eased into a pleasant daily routine.

There's something to be said about Lem-ehek and the unhurried rhythm of life where a spectacular sunset or a rainbow arching over Lake Seluton was the main event of the day that demanded one's notice and begged to be savored. The nights came swiftly. Even before the mission lights switched off at nine, Mother Nature started to display her countless stars. When it was totally dark, the stars seemed brighter and glittered more.

It was the perfect place for the time described in the song *The Green Leaves of Summer* by the Brothers Four.[6] "A time just for planting, a time just for ploughing, a time to be courting a girl of your own." Romantic alliances were forged and cemented at Lem-ehek that happily resulted in marriages among the staff that came and met at Santa Cruz Mission. Seeing Prima every day made me think of what could have been or what could still be.

Two weeks after his birthday party, Fr. Rex briefed me as to his expectations from the new Management Consultant. He shared his vision for SCM to start offering various services outlined in one of the brochures. Such as Management training, Consolidated promotional program, Personnel recruitment and orientation, Motor pool including cargo trucks and road-building equipment, Auditing Services, and Consolidated marketing and purchasing facilities. Fr. Rex notified me that my position would be a part of the "Consolidated promotional program."

The Promotions Office was officially launched in December with Prima in charge under Fr. Rex's direct supervision and in tandem with Ma'am Emma Crespo, the Education Manager. I was to help with research, writing of feasibility studies, and submission of project proposals to various charitable non-profit organizations in the Philippines, the United States, and

Europe to raise funds for the mission. To that end, I would be collaborating with the Promotions Office for administrative support.

Also, I volunteered to assist in other projects where help was needed. Ely Cabayao, the Clubhouse manager, began setting up the kitchen and dining hall before I arrived at the mission. While some of the appliances were still in transit, the clubhouse was scheduled to be fully operational in February. My first assignment was to provide training for the all-T'boli staff (boys and girls) hired to help out at the clubhouse. I also created a work schedule for Ely's workforce. This kept me busy for most of January.

Before the month ended, Fr. Rex informed me that it was time to take our General Manager Quirico Batilaran to Manila and Baguio City for some much-needed exposure and procurement of materials. It was one of my favorite perks of the new job. I relished playing the role of tour guide, as it was Sir Qric's first trip to the big cities in Luzon. A very amiable man, Sir Qric was married to Manang Elise who managed the Mission Store. Like all the pioneering teachers of the Mission, he started as a teacher and worked his way up the managerial positions. In Manila, we stayed at a Youth Hostel.

He and I shopped for the mission's supplies in various shopping centers in Metro Manila. We stopped at the Peace Corps Office and had lunch at one of my favorite restaurants frequented by American expatriates. We visited tourist spots to soak in the sights and sounds of the business capital of the Philippines. One night, we took in a show at the Philippine Cultural Center.

The bus trip to Baguio City, the summer capital of the Philippines, where the weather was cold, and the terrain so hilly reminded Qric of Lake Sebu. We went on a boat ride at Burnham Park, visited the Mine's View Park, and ate a lot of strawberries that we bought at the Public Market. He was so fascinated by the woodcarvers. At the end of our trip, he just kept shaking his head in disbelief and he wore a grin from ear to ear all the way back to the Mission. All the while thanking me profusely.

It was during this ten-day trip I realized in consternation that I had too much time to think. It became difficult to ignore a situation that had been nagging me since I moved to the Mission. Before Sir Qric and I left for Manila, I saw Prima daily at mealtimes and during office hours. She was always at the Sing-Along sessions. It had been a year since I made the conscious decision to court Prima. My feelings remained unchanged. Her constant presence began to diminish my resistance and resolve, leading me to debate with myself, as I had never done before. Do I perpetuate the status quo or do I break a promise to stay friends and find out where I stand?

The tours and the business activities with Sir Qric kept my head occupied during the day. But the nights left me alone with my thoughts. My contract was good for eight more months. I had been toying with the idea of going to Graduate School after my Peace Corps contract was up. I filed the plan on the back burner. I decided I had enough time to just enjoy the moments and make an intelligent and informed decision as the future unfolded. When we got back to the mission, I immersed myself in the daily routine.

Once a month, the employees at the Mission were entitled, as part of their contract, to a long weekend break. The unmarried ones who reside in dormitories left the mission early on Friday morning. They went home to their respective barrios to recharge, and back at Surallah before noon on Sunday to catch the truck bound for the mission. Leaving the Mission, the massive Reo truck was usually loaded with sacks of rice and corn. The staff would sit on top of the sacks and made sure they held on for dear life as the truck went downhill on Canahay Road. It was a miracle that the Mission never had a serious accident, ever!

On February 23, 1973, the employees' weekend off, Prima took her Grade Six class to General Santos City for a field trip; all fifteen of them, thirteen boys and two girls. I asked Prima about the disproportionate number of boys versus girls in her class. She explained. In first grade, one would notice that the ratio between boys and girls in a classroom was almost even. Then in later grades, the ratio skewed in favor of the boys until in Grade Six, it is almost predictable that the boys would outnumber the girls by a long shot.

The reason was simple. A girl could be promised in marriage to a man who could offer a dowry. By the time the girl reached puberty or even before, the intended groom could claim his intended bride. Prima struggled with this custom and told me about the heart-wrenching story of her fifth-grade student Sara. She was only eleven years old. She had to quit school because the groom threatened to confiscate the dowry. The father of Sonia, one of the three girls in Prima's sixth-grade class, yanked Sonia out of school before the field trip to the beach.

I was glad to chaperon and take the kids to the beach. The whole class plus one of the chaperons, Annie Garcia, stayed at the Guipo's house. Annie took some of the pupils shopping at the Public Market to buy food provisions for the weekend and for the picnic. The boys and girls took over the Guipo kitchen to cook their meals together and to prepare the picnic baskets. It was a novel experience for all of the T'boli kids.

Early on Saturday morning, we all went to Tambler Beach. For some of the T'boli children, it was their first time to be away from the Mission. For many, it was their first trip to the city and to go swimming in the ocean.

Rose remembers one of the kids exclaimed, "What kind of a lake is this? Can't drink it, too salty!" Another boy saw the big rolling waves for the first time. When the waves rushed to shore, he ran, sheer terror on his face, yelling, "Bless me, Dwata. The lake is chasing me!" (*Dwata* is the T'boli word for God). We waded in around the coral reefs, combed the beach for seashells, built sandcastles, and had a wonderful time. All the kids were so pleasantly docile that disciplinary measures were unnecessary.

When in General Santos City, I always stayed at Don and Socorro Partridge's house in Lagao. Don was then an executive at Dole Philippines and Socorro, a practicing physician. Socorro's brother Boy Mayol accompanied me that evening to the Guipo's house to bring ice cream and cookies for everyone. The spacious porch was filled with merrymakers. There was a lot of singing. It was plain to see that the T'boli kids were having such a great time. Prima's high school and college classmates happened to be at the house visiting, too, including her boyfriend from high school that I had seen hanging around at Notre Dame College on many occasions.

Flor Congson, a benevolent lady who was introduced to me by Fr. James at the Bula Community Center, donated a crate of fish to take back to Lake Sebu the following morning. When we got back to Lake Sebu, Prima told me that someone sent her to ask me what to do with the crate of fish. I told her that it really didn't matter to me what they did with it, as long as it was shared with everybody at the LTK, including the T'boli kids staying at the dormitories.

After that conversation, Prima started avoiding me all of a sudden. It was a situation I did not quite understand. It left us not quite on speaking terms. Two days later, I heard from Dottie that Prima was so upset with me about the crate of fish because she thought I was brusque in my response to her question. She felt I spoke with a raised voice as though I was angry with her for no reason, and that I did it in front of a group of people close by who heard what transpired.

For a day or two, I tried to talk to her, but Prima wouldn't relent. I sent a letter via Rose, but she did not respond. One evening, I attended mass at the chapel. Prima walked in, like the pied piper with a bunch of T'boli kids in tow, a familiar sight that I had grown to appreciate. Our eyes met. After the mass, I was able to convince her to give me at least five minutes to explain. I apologized profusely, and all was well again. A week later, on March 4, 1973, Prima left the mission for an indefinite medical leave without telling anybody but Fr. Rex, Dottie, and me. I was disheartened. I wrote her a long letter. I gave it to her just before she boarded the weapon's carrier for Gen Santos. The subject of the message must have sounded like a broken record. But I needed to remind her about "the light that continued to shine on my side of the mountain." I repeated that if and when it does happen on her side, I would be waiting. She went to Manila. No one heard if she had plans to come back or if she was coming back at all. When Fr. Rex hired Linda Basadre in April as his new secretary, I had a sinking feeling Prima was not coming back.

After the trip with Sir Qric to Manila and Baguio early in the year, I came back to the Mission energized. Armed with ideas and plenty of materials that I had picked up at the Peace Corps Office, I started to envision projects specific to the Mission's Community Development programs.

Fr. Rex's new secretary, Linda was kept very busy attending to the Promotions Office, helping Fr. Rex with his correspondence while learning her job. Linda finished her secretarial course at Notre Dame of Dadiangas College. She told me that although she did not take any of my Economics classes, she had seen me around campus and during school events. I got to know her better as she tried to manage the Promotions Office in Prima's absence.

Unusually tall and fair-skinned for a Filipina, Linda was a beautiful girl with long hair reaching past her waist. Her face was always lit with a big smile. Very artistic and diligent, she was a perfect fit for the Promotions Office. Her English was impeccable too. And her excellent administrative skills and work ethics were added pluses. Linda assisted me in typing the feasibility studies and filling out forms for the project proposals that we submitted to the non-profit organizations.

The Promotions Office received a considerable order from the U.S.-based Santa Cruz Mission, Inc. (SCM/US) for more Sponsor-A-Child leaflets. SCM/US was a non-profit charitable organization established by the Mansmann Family and friends along with the Passionists Provincial Monastery in Pittsburgh, PA. Santa Cruz Mission in Lake Sebu was financially supported in large part by SCM/US.

MRS. BETTY GESK, the office manager in Pittsburgh, was our conduit for finding sponsors in the United States, with the help of the family and friends of Fr. Rex. (I would later meet Mrs. Gesk when I went back to the U.S. She had kept in touch with my dad, who sponsored three children, sequentially over ten years, until my dad died. For many years after my return to the States, I continued to campaign for the Sponsor-A-Child program of the Mission. I organized slide presentations using my Peace Corps experience as RPCV that resulted in sponsorships from friends, relatives, and members of our church).

The Sponsor-A-Child leaflet was hand cut from a piece of *cartolina* 22"x 28" into eight pieces of 7"x 11" and folded in half.[7] It included a picture of the T'boli child and a brief profile. It was distributed to anyone who signed up to sponsor his or her education. We called this leaflet a *bi-fold*. Hundreds of this handmade *bi-fold* had been designed and prepared in advance by Prima. However, Linda needed photos of the children to complete the materials. Upon Fr. Rex's request, I assisted Linda by taking pictures of the children.

The *bi-fold* outlined how the plan worked. We did not have a printer, so even the typewritten texts were not mimeographed, each leaflet an original. Fr. Rex contended that the leaflet was more effective when it had a hand-made look. Our graphic artist Linda Basadre simulated the intricate designs of the *t'nalak* on the borders. The template for the Sponsor-A-Child Program started in 1973 with low budget but personalized promotion material became the bread and butter for the Mission's Education Program that lasted for over thirty years. The goal of the program was summed up in this message. *Our hope is that these children will one day; lead their people to a better life.*

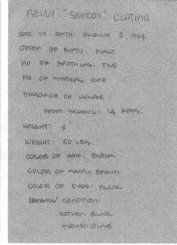

(It has come to pass that these T'boli children now lead their people. Two pupils at Notre Dame of Lake Sebu SCM, Samuel Loco, and Antonio Fungan, Sr. served as Mayors of Lake Sebu, and another Floro Gandam, Sr. is the Mayor as of the publication of this book. Those who served as Vice-Mayors were Eugene Temen, Dominador Baay, Remie Unggol, and Nena Twalang, the first T'boli woman to hold a government office. She was the wife of one of our very able drivers name Dindo. Others have become teachers who are now teaching their own people, community organizers, agriculturists, social workers, and government employees serving at Lake Sebu Municipal Hall.)

In addition to being the photographer, Fr. Rex directed me to conduct feasibility studies on various ways we could monetize some of our Economic Development Projects. As mentioned in Chapter 8, the Peace Corps had successfully implemented New Directions at this point. The main thrust of New Directions was to transition from its former focus on education to the promotion of community development programs, including everything agriculture. The goals of the Mission and the Peace Corps were perfectly aligned. The partnership between the host (SCM) and Peace Corps (represented by Dottie and me) could be viewed as a "poster child" that proved New Directions worked.

Fr. Rex and the Community Development Manager Boy Crespo had been working with the Agriculture Department to help the T'boli farmers to transition from the production of seasonal crops like rice and corn exclusively, to permanent cash crops like citrus, mangoes, coconuts, bananas, etc. I played a role in the transition.

The Mission implemented the Sponsor-A-Livestock Program similar to the Heifer Project International during this time. A sponsor could pay for the cost of a healthy animal donated directly to a T'boli family. An animal husbandry extension worker supervised the program, ensuring a maximum benefit to the farmer. When an animal is fully grown and had a baby, the baby was returned to the Mission. It was distributed to another family. Thus, the sustainability of the program was guaranteed.

In March, I shadowed our Agriculturist, Forting Espada, to help me understand what the best crops were for our area and to meet the T'boli farmers. While Forting was an excellent agriculturist, he was not so enthused about becoming an extension worker or organizing the T'boli farmers to buy into the Mission's innovative projects. The Mission hired two more capable persons, an Animal Husbandry major Rey "Bebot" Bugante and Agronomist Bert "Nonoy" Dapulang. I later worked very closely with Nonoy and Bebot as they proved to be excellent assets for the mission as agricultural extension workers. (Bebot is now in the U.S. He visited us a few years ago).

After studying the information we gathered in the field, I concluded that the best project with which to start was to plant citrus. *Calamansi!*[8] Fr. Rex and Boy Crespo approved. The fruit was in demand; it had a long shelf life and could be transported easily to the market. It bears fruit after two or three years from saplings. Part of the plan was to convince the T'boli farmers to set aside a portion of their land for *calamansi* so they would have a steady income all-year-round. Then we'd find non-profit organizations to fund the initial capital for saplings, and the necessary barbwire fencing around the perimeter to keep the free-roaming domesticated animals from divesting the young *calamansi* plants.

On one of my trips to the barrios with Forting, I bought a bunch of ripened bananas from a T'boli farmer. It was a big bunch, so I requested the farmer to divide the bunch into two. Using a piece of bamboo similar to a milkmaid's yoke, I carefully distributed and suspended the bananas from each end of the yoke. I carried the load over my shoulder back to the Mission. Walking along the road carved on the side of the mountain just below Datu Ma Fok's house wearing my T'boli hat, I saw a lady half running toward me. She was coming from the community of homes built by the Mission for the married SCM staff.

"Can I buy some bananas?" she sent her question ahead of her, speaking in Ilongo. I understood "saging", Ilongo word for bananas. She switched to T'boli in case I didn't understand. As she got closer, she realized it was the volunteer 'Kano.

"Oh, so sorry, Sir Al, I didn't recognize you," said Manang Baby Evangeline Crespo, the wife of Antonio "Jun" Matillano, the brother of Sir Qric's wife. (*Manang* or *Manong* is a common endearment in other dialects for anyone older similar to *Ate* and *Kuya* in Tagalog. Jun, Boy, Girl and Baby are also common and favorite nicknames).

"Okay lang, *Manang* Baby. Gusto mo ng saging?" I replied in Tagalog. (No worries. Do you want some bananas?)

Manang Baby and I had a good laugh. I gave her a few hands of bananas and deposited the rest at the Clubhouse for Ely to share with the staff.

By the middle of April, Fr. Rex and I had identified and prioritized the projects that we considered had the best chance of being funded. Fr. Rex set an ambitious goal. He and I worked on multiple project proposals that would benefit the Education, Health Services, and the Agriculture departments at the mission. I immediately went into overdrive. I started to conduct feasibility studies to build a high school and a college at the Mission, a hospital, and the livestock and *calamansi* projects simultaneously. Fr. Rex set a deadline. His goal was to submit these proposals to non-profit organizations no later than June 1973.

Personally, I was agonizing over another deadline. My contract with the Peace Corps was ending on August 15, 1973. I knew that by the middle of May, I had to make a vital decision – to leave or to stay. If I were to extend for one more year, I needed to submit my request right away. I chose not to discuss the matter with Fr. Rex until I made the final decision. I know I could prepare all the proposals on his wish list and submit them by his self-imposed deadline. I had no other outstanding projects, having just successfully helped to set up the bakery and the Clubhouse, which were both in full operation. So I could concentrate on the feasibility studies already on my plate.

At supper one night, Dottie mentioned that she was going to Manila on business for the Mission. We both had not heard from Prima. That night before I fell asleep, I reflected on what it would be like without Dottie and Prima around. The picture looked bleak. By morning, I decided I was not going to renew my contract. I was moving on. Eight months prior, while I was still working at the Dadiangas Parish Community Centers, I met Dr. Wilhelm Solheim, who explored caves around Kiamba, Maasim, and Maitum. He was an American Anthropologist "recognized as the most senior practitioner of archeology in Southeast Asia and as a pioneer in the study of Philippine and Southeast Asian prehistoric archeology." [9]

Always up for an adventure, Leslie Savina and I volunteered to be his assistants for one week. We did not know what we were doing, but he was a good teacher. Digging for physical remains and the analysis of artifacts that followed appealed to me. A few weeks later, I attended a Peace Corps Conference in Davao City. Dr. Solheim discovered a cache of pottery and artifacts nearby and set up a camp to dig and sort pottery shards, bone fragments, and other objects. I told other volunteers about Dr. Solheim, and we all went to visit him. We tried our hand at assembling pieces of pottery together like fitting interlocking board puzzle pieces, one of my favorite past times.

Reading up about archeology and anthropology, I discovered a highly recommended program at the University of Oregon in Eugene. I decided to go back to school after the Peace Corps. It was too late to apply for Graduate School for the year 1973-74. I planned to do some traveling after I left the

Philippines, get a job, and aim to start the Graduate School Program the following year.

Dottie left for Manila on a business trip. I told her before she left about my future plans. She was not too happy about it, but she wished me luck. I decided to leave Santa Cruz Mission by July 1973. It would give me time to travel around Asia before flying back to the States and to apply for Graduate School.

Having made my decision, a heavy burden was lifted off my shoulder.

Looking for artifacts around a rock shelf in Maasim, South Cotabato, with Dr. Wilhelm Solheim II and Leslie Savina.

T'boli Hear Me Come 14

IT WAS the middle of May 1973. I faced a recurring dilemma – to extend or to terminate my Peace Corps contract. I was at the pinnacle of my career as a Volunteer, where the level of personal job satisfaction was at its highest point. My current occupation that began as an idea for a summer project evolved into something I could never have imagined. Here I was, working side by side with Fr. Rex Mansmann, the director of Santa Cruz Mission. This remarkable missionary had dedicated a decade of his life not only to minister but also to improve the lives of the T'boli and the indigenous people of South Cotabato. I was proud to be a part of an organization serving the community of T'boli, Blaan, Ubo, Manobo, Kalagan, and Maguindanao.

For the first time in four years, I could truly identify with my preconceived notion of what an ideal Peace Corps Volunteer was supposed to be - roughing it in the remote mountains, scrounging for food, and devoid of many of the comforts of modern life. The allure that the T'boli people had cast on me in Kematu four years prior had not waned; it only intensified since I started working and living with them. Yet, I realized too that there was a time when a man must move on. Having made my decision to pursue Graduate School, I could not find the courage to tell Fr. Rex that I had no intention of renewing my contract. I was fully aware I had to let him know sooner or later, but I kept on postponing the inevitable. I put all my energy into finishing the tasks he assigned to me instead.

Crafting my own workload (based on Fr. Rex's expectations and the goals he had outlined for my new position) lent excitement to the job and a welcomed distraction. Prima was gone for more than two months, and no one had heard a word from her that I knew of. Dottie left too for a business trip to Manila in the middle of May. Deprived of their company that I have grown so accustomed to, I would have been at a loss without my job to keep me occupied.

I appreciated the increased physical activity and the busy schedule, but I ran myself ragged. Inevitably, it weakened my resistance. The old chronic amoebic dysentery came back with a vengeance during this time. I have read so much about this disease since I contracted it during the first week of training in the Philippines.

I have taken every precaution, but whenever my resistance is low, it seemed to recur. The Peace Corps doctor told me that people come into contact with this Entamoeba histolytica parasite by "...drinking contaminated water, eating contaminated food, or touching others that have the infection and are unclean."[1]

Some countries in Asia use human feces as fertilizer, where the parasite thrives. The parasite invades the large intestine, lives there, and can cause severe damage. It could stay in the system for months or years. The symptoms manifest only after the parasite has burrowed through the wall of the colon. It can spread to other parts of the body through the bloodstream, including the liver, the heart, and the lungs. In very severe cases, it is fatal.

Toward the end of May, my condition worsened. I had severe diarrhea that contained blood and pus. I lost a lot of weight. People infected by amoebic dysentery can pass ten to twenty liquid stools daily. In less severe cases, it could be up to eight soft stools daily. I decided to go to General Santos to see my doctor and personal friend, Dr. Venancio Yap.

Looking back now, it is hard for me to imagine how I managed to travel in my condition for no less than three hours from Lake Sebu to Surallah to Marbel without restrooms along the way. I remembered being so weak that I couldn't make it to General Santos without stopping halfway in Marbel. I made a stop at the Reisen's house in Bolul. Andrea served me some home-brewed tea and crackers, just enough to regain my strength.

When I finally reached General Santos, I made a special request or perhaps begged was the word for the Yellow Bus driver to drop me off at the Yap's Clinic. Unlike the *jeepneys,* the buses usually do not make a special delivery. But after I explained my situation, the bus driver let me off right in front of the clinic. As soon as Dr. Yap saw me, he ordered his driver to take me directly to the Doctors Hospital in his Mercedes Benz. He called to tell Sister Joan that I was on my way. I was admitted, wheeled into my room, and soon after, Dr. Yap arrived.

I stayed at the hospital for a few days. The fever, severe chills, pain under my right rib cage, cramps, and every amoebic dysentery symptom were more serious than I have ever experienced. Worst, Dr. Yap poked me at places where "the sun don't shine." All the time, by my bedside looking in, were the pretty Sister Joan and the St. Paul Sisters who knew me from the Community Center. I was too weak and too sick to care. Dehydrated, I was fed intravenously for a day or two to give my digestive system some rest. It was no picnic. I missed eating real food, I was miserable, but the kindly St. Paul Sisters more than made up for it by pampering me. By the time I left the hospital, I had lost twenty pounds.

After the hospital discharged me, I stayed with Don and Socorro Partridge in Lagao for a few more days. They were one of those couples that took volunteers and other expatriates in as they would their extended family. We would just show up at their doorstep without notice. Dottie and I often marveled at their hospitality and generosity.

Feeling re-energized again, I returned to Lake Sebu. The bus ride was uneventful except for the usual bumpy roads, the heat, thick swirling dust, and passengers packed like sardines. For the first time in a long while, my mind wandered to springtime in Bethlehem, Pennsylvania, and what it would be like to be home again. I imagined the paved highways, driving a car of my own, no more bus rides, being with family, hanging out with childhood friends, and eat all the food I've been craving. And I was hopeful that I'd be rid of the suffering from amoebic dysentery!

The past months I'd been relishing the novelty of working directly with the T'boli in the new community development projects at the Mission. It was very fulfilling. Before I got sick, I vacillated many times between renewing my contract or not. However, that wasn't the case anymore. The latest bout of amoebic dysentery fortified my resolve to go home to the States.

Back at the Mission, I slowly climbed up the hill and went straight to the office of Fr. Rex. Still feeling weak, I was short of breath by the time I entered the door. I informed Fr. Rex that I made the final decision not to apply for an extension. He was understandably disappointed. I shared with him my plans to travel around Asia and to go back to graduate school. I assured him that I would complete all the pending projects and help him identify a current staff that could take over my position. We have two months and a half to execute the plan.

I did not even stop at the Promotions Office next door because I knew that not seeing Prima there would only dampen my day. I went down to the Administration building to inquire about the exit process. As I was walking past the motor pool where the trucks and the Mission vehicles were parked, I saw a familiar person with long black flowing hair, her back toward me. She was with some T'boli boys and Bro. Louis, who had started heading toward the Woodworking Shop. I hurried to their direction and tapped her shoulder with my rolled-up TIME Magazine. Bro. Louis and the group waved to me as they walked away.

"You're back," Prima said, surprise written all over her face. "Siony told me you left for good."

"Oh, that's a case of misinformation. I was in General Santos for over a week and spent a few days at Doctors Hospital. Yeah, the usual," I stammered.

She understood what I meant. I was so happy to see Prima. From her demeanor, I could not discern if she was pleased to see me too. But her beaming smile was encouraging.

"Amoebic dysentery again, huh?"

"Yup!" I said. "When did you get back?"

"May 29 in Gen. Santos, did some errands and came straight here two days later. If I had known you were in the hospital..."

"I was out of the hospital around that time," I said. "I stayed at the Partridges for a few days after I was discharged."

She was all business after that. "Before I forget," she said. "Would you be so kind as to help us take photos of the kids for the Adoption Program as soon as you have free time? We received requests from the St. Paul Sisters in Manila and the Pittsburgh office to send more packets of the children's profile for sponsorships."

"I'd be glad to do it," I said. "When do you want me to start?"

"Would tomorrow be too soon? If you're up to it, that is. Linda is running out of photos. We need to get the packets out in the mail as soon as possible. Let's meet in my office tomorrow whenever you're ready."

And with that, we parted ways. I went back to my dorm room, filled with mixed emotions all over again. What to do? It's the first week of June. My contract ends on August 15. I need to notify PC/Manila three months in advance if I wanted to extend or re-enroll. Without a doubt, I was so happy to see Prima back at the Mission. But dare I hope?

At the Clubhouse for dinner that night, I noticed everyone seemed so genuinely happy to see me. I joined the table where Prima, Rose, Siony, and Annie sat. Rose and Annie had just returned from summer classes in Manila. It was just like the good old days as we talked about the picnics at the beach on Sarangani Bay, about Bro. Henry, Fr. Albinus and Fr. James, and about the people we knew at NDDC and at the Community Centers. After dinner, somebody brought out a guitar. We all trooped to the top of the hill in front of the Clubhouse. Music filled the night again after two months of silence. We sang songs, and we all went back to our respective dorms just before the lights went out at nine o'clock.

I reported to the Promotions Office the following day. It was the beginning of the school year. Prima had prepared a schedule for the photoshoot of 500 plus pupils in three mission schools. The timetable started at Lake Sebu, on to Lemakulen, and then Bolul. She coordinated with the teachers to let the children out of the classroom according to grades beginning from Grade 1. So as not to disrupt their studies too much, she instructed the teachers to let out five kids at a time, no more than ten. With kids in tow, we went to nearby Lake Seluton, around the clusters of T'boli huts, and by the hillsides where the T'boli lived for a variety of backdrops for each child to ensure no photos were alike.

As soon as the school opened, we started taking pictures of the children. Working together again, Prima and I recaptured the camaraderie I cherished. I was elated. The photo sessions were interrupted when Prima contracted an infection from staph germs, which caused a boil on her left leg. There was a prevalence of the spread of the bacteria among the T'boli children living in the dormitory. Proper hygiene alone does not guarantee safety from contamination.

Our Health Manager, Manang Diding, promptly told Prima that an antibiotic was inadequate in treating an abscess. The primary treatment was hot packs and draining (lancing) the abscess, but only when it was soft and ready. The lancing could resolve it plus other home remedies. We suspended the photo taking when Prima's pain became too intense to walk comfortably. Four days later, Manang Duding deemed the boil ready for lancing.

I walked Dottie home from the office to the DHOP dormitory at the end of the day. I delivered a can of SkyFlakes I bought from the store along with three pink roses stolen from Ma'am Ang's garden. Prima's room adjoins the dormitory's living room. "Maayo!" I called out as soon as we entered the door. She came out walking gingerly. Prima informed us that earlier in the day, Manang Diding came to the dormitory with a Coca-Cola glass bottle filled with hot water from the Clubhouse. She let the hot water stand for ten minutes, poured it out, and positioned the bottle upside down over the eye of the boil. She held it in place for ten minutes.

"It sure was painful with the hot bottle against the skin," Prima continued. "Thankfully, it worked on the first try. The vacuum drained the abscess. After the pus had drained out, Manang Diding applied antibacterial cream, covered the wound with wide gauze, and gave me some antibiotics."

Before I left, I watched Dottie write with a black marker on the edge of the medical gauze, DHOP, and a smiley next to it. Then she added, "wounded in action" underneath.

WE RESUMED taking the pictures of the kids on June 18. I reported to Prima's office ready to tackle the day's schedule. She seemed a bit edgy and distracted. Not her usual bubbly self. It was so unlike her. I chalked it up to the pressure of preparing all the packets to meet her self-imposed deadline and her frustration over the boil that set us back a week. Dedicated and one-track minded about deadlines to a fault, there was no dissuading her to take things easy.

Camera cases in hand, we made our way toward the elementary school half a kilometer away. We started making small talk. Then, as casually as I could, I told her something I had meant to share with her since she came back.

"I don't know if Dottie or Fr. Rex have mentioned this to you, but I did not renew my contract. I will be leaving in two months".

"Dottie told me as much," was all she said before she lapsed into a disconcerting silence.

I could not read anything from her reaction. She remained silent and pensive as I chattered about my post-Peace Corps plans. I paused to elicit her response, but she did not make any comment. I continued telling her about going back to Graduate School, etc., etc. Just as we were on the footpath between the clubhouse and the Dottie and Al trees, about to climb the hill halfway to the school buildings, she stopped dead in her tracks and looked straight into my eyes.

"I have something to ask you," she said nervously. Before I could say anything, she blurted what sounded so rehearsed in such a softly modulated voice without any preamble and out of context. "Would you believe, and if you do, would you care if I tell you that the light is now shining on my side of the mountain?"

I stood there. Stupefied. Mouth agape. Rooted to the ground for what seemed like an eternity.

"What did you just say?" I managed to ask to be sure I heard her correctly.

"And yes, of course," she said. "You'd make me repeat it knowing the effort it took me to say it the first time." But she repeated it just as rehearsed as the first time as her brown eyes gazed at me amusedly.

How we got through our schedule for the day, I had no recollection. She walked back to her office. I went to find somebody to talk to, or I'd burst. I found Dottie, who would tease me to this day that I walked on cloud nine during those first few weeks after Prima's declaration.

I told Prima that I shared our little secret with Dottie. She was okay with it but told me to keep it between the three of us until we adjusted to the idea. We made a pact to write to each other so as not to arouse suspicions. We had an excellent excuse being together during office hours now that I was officially the photographer of the Promotions Office, and she formally was my boss.

For two weeks, Prima and I succeeded in keeping our secret under wraps. Outside of work, we did not meet more than the usual sharing of a table at dinner or joining the sing-along that happened after dinner. She wouldn't even let me walk her from the Promotions Office to the DHOP dorm unless Dottie or Linda happened to join us. We planned to reveal our secret only to close friends, her family, and mine by July 4th - the symbolic Filipino-American Friendship day.

I was curious about her change of heart. Longing to ask her, but feeling timid, I tried to wait for the right moment. At the same time, I was feeling a profound need to make her realize that I was past petty romances. I wanted to ascertain where I stood. There's also the Peace Corps extension or no extension that I had to consider with a sense of urgency.

Hesitant to spoil the mood by being too inquisitive, I nevertheless drilled Prima with questions that, to her credit, she promptly answered. One lengthy letter explained everything. We both were getting to know each other more intimately now that we were free to speak of our love for each other, albeit in letters only. It was very liberating for her. Based on my experience, most Filipinas were usually disinclined to discuss their feelings and emotions verbally. Prima was the worst of the lot. Thankfully for me, she loves to write. Her letters became my window to her heart, her reservations, her aspirations, her dreams, her fears, and her enviable sense of humor.

June 22, 1973
Dearest Sir Al,

I had never used that salutation with such a feeling until now. The warning lights just flickered, so in thirty minutes, I will have to continue this letter writing by candlelight. Kind of romantic, don't you think?

You asked a lot of questions in your letter that I got this morning. This will be a kilometric response, consider yourself warned. Yes, they were all fair questions. However, I'm afraid I have no black and white answers to all of them. But I will do my best. And nope, I do not mind this means of communication as we adjust to this new level of our relationship. I totally agree with you about the heart having less chance to get in the way. Besides, my pen is more eloquent than my mouth.

You asked how sure am I about my feelings for you this time. I had never been so sure of anything that I'd even marry you to prove it. There, there. Two proposals for you in five days!

Why did I leave, and why did I come back? *"You" are the answer to both. I had such a schoolgirl crush on you the first time we met, just like so many girls at Notre Dame College. We dubbed you "crush ng bayan" (town's heartthrob). Tall, good-looking, strong square jaw with a kind smile, brown eyes, and that red hair!*

Did you ever wonder why your class always had the maximum number of students allowed? And there are more girls than boys? Although you professionally kept a respectable distance, you were always friendly, the best-dressed faculty member with your tie always knotted perfectly. And the polo barongs become you.

Remember the movie "To Sir With Love" that was showing in town the summer you arrived? You got many of us singing with Lulu, the movie's theme song. Some thought you are somewhat aloof, almost snobby. But those of us, who got to know you, know better.

For me, the crush blossomed into something more affectionately intense when you invited my brother Toto Felipe and me to the T'boli land of Kematu. During our hike to the PANAMIN settlement, you opened a window into yourself, and I saw the image of my father whom I adored – selfless, principled, empathetic, generous. To whom little things mean a lot, among many other admirable traits.

You told me about growing up at your family farm, helping your dad and brothers with the chickens and farm animals, and baking cakes and cookies with your mom and sister. I was fascinated by your stories shoveling snow in the wintertime, hayrides with your nephews and nieces in autumn, and hunting for asparagus along the fence of your farm in the summer. And the time you decided to live at home, even though it meant hours of a long commute to work and to attend graduate school, so you could be with your mom when she was dying of breast cancer. I saw a glimpse of the endearing side of the earnest, distant college professor we all had placed on a pedestal...that trip later inspired me to work with T'boli people.

I did write a lot of poems for you, some were even published in the Vox college paper. Later in a national teen magazine Homelife a few copies of which were available at the college library. It still amazes me that you never caught on. "AH...AUBURN NIGHT," for instance, was a dead give-away, I thought. How many A.H. did you know at the college had auburn hair? But then again perhaps you never read the Vox or liked poems.

I firmly believed then that even if I got lucky to attract your notice, any relationship between you and me could have never progressed into something more meaningful as I had wished it to be. So I suppressed the feeling as best I could. Racial, cultural, religious, and other barriers (six-and-a-half years age gap) seemed insurmountable for a nineteen-year-old that I was.

Besides, working as a secretary to Bro. Henry, I knew about you more than you could ever guess - like your engagement to a certain JM! It was on your resume in your personal faculty file that I had access to. I was not snooping by the way; I did not have to. Right there on the first page of your resume sent by Peace Corps to Bro. Henry, on the third line below your name, Marital Status: Single but engaged to Jane Miller, *you printed. Then there were those letters that arrived regularly from a lady in Quezon City, and the one with a beautiful penmanship from Vassar College, New York. (I sorted mail at Bro. Henry's office, remember?) How was I to know that you had broken up your engagement while in training in Hawaii? Or that any of the other ladies who wrote to you often was out of your life?*

Then came the clincher. You stopped by at the college one night to tell me that you were dating a mutual friend, who confirmed a few days later that you and she "were more than just friends," her words exactly. To her credit, she did not know anything about my crush on you. I was actually happy for both of you. I figured that if you got married, at least, I would still be a part of your orbit. But, I think that was the moment I willed myself to get over you. Here's someone in flesh and blood, pretty, accomplished, and intelligent, that you are actually dating and who was obviously in love with you, not just some faceless girls I imagined writing letters to you. Was I jealous? Not jealous but acutely saddened by the possibility that I might lose our special friendship.

Remember the poem I wrote T'boli Hear me Come?[2] I gave you a copy of the Vox, where it was published. You included the essay in one of your newsletters for mass mailing to your friends and family in 1970. Reread it. T'boli was a metaphor for you. I wrote a sequel after your revelation about the Filipina girl you were dating. I submitted it to Homelife teen magazine. They published it. I kept a copy if you wish to read it. At least I got paid P10 pesos for my heartache. I have to ask, though, why did you invite me to be your chaperon when you took her out on the motorcycle rides to Olaer's Resort and other places for your dates?

My knowledge (baseless and judgmental perhaps) about the presence of these ladies in your life was the root of the prejudices that kept me from entertaining your romantic overtures this past year.

By the way, Bro. Henry, my confidant, could attest to all of these confessions. He was the only person to whom I confided my secret love. Not even Rose knew. When she interviewed in Marbel, Rose and I stopped at Notre Dame College and ran into Stacey, who told me that you were thinking of getting married. Then when your friends Diane and Janet stayed at our house after your picnic in Tinoto, they repeated the same news that they heard through the grapevine. Guess who they told me the girl was? Me! Which, I knew to be untrue because it was news to me. So I deduced there must be someone else.

Do you remember that time you were inside Bro. Henry's office; I turned the knob when I came back from Mrs. Dinopol's class, and it was locked? Bro. Henry has never done that to me before. He might have closed and locked all the doors, but he never closed the privacy curtains on me, not once since 1968! I was so miffed because my purse was inside and I was hungry for merienda. I borrowed money from Gloria Saclot for my snack. When I returned, the door was still locked. I waited in the Book Room for another half hour.

Then you came out, and guess what ran through my mind? Hmm, maybe he was really getting married! But the next day, I asked Bro. Henry if he has heard the rumor. He assured me he had not. While he was listening to your confession, he must have been having his fun at our expense. I wonder what would have happened if he had just hinted to you or to me about our mutual affection? Would it have hastened the process and save us years of heartaches? I cannot wait to tell him about this new development! He'd flip!

Bro. Henry wrote that he would be visiting Dadiangas in early September. Let's surprise him and have the last laugh. One more thing, I requested him to concoct that story about being needed to prepare for the graduation ceremonies to give me a reason not to go to Santa Cruz Mission with you, Rose, and Susan. I was concerned about being in very close quarters with you thinking that even after your profession of love, there were at least four other girls in your life. (May God forgive me for putting my boss in a position to tell white lies on my behalf.)

When you finally came to work here at the Mission last January, and after our misunderstanding, you reminded me again about the "light shining on your side of the mountain." The repercussions had I revealed my true feelings scared me so, having to leave my family was foremost. It wasn't as though I was not tempted to reciprocate. I just was not ready for any romantic relationship, and most importantly, I was so afraid our friendship would suffer if things didn't work out. I needed to get away from you to think things through.

My sister Susan and I rented an apartment in Quezon City, and I started the process of applying to FNCB Makati and even went for an interview at a travel agency that Susan recommended. For almost three months in Manila, I convinced myself I was finally over you.

And I was doing okay too, until the phone call from Dottie. I had left a message at the Peace Corps Office for her to call me at my cousin's house in Makati when she arrives in Manila. She returned my call promptly, and after some tsismis [gossip in Tagalog] *from the mission, she told me that you were not renewing your contract and that you were leaving in July.*

It seemed ironic that only when I was faced with the inevitable – parting - I realized how much you meant to me. It hit me like a ton of bricks. I agonized about it. Then one day, I realized you had become an essential part of me, that you were the one for me.

I couldn't bear to let you leave without letting you know that "the light finally was shining on my side of the mountain." It didn't matter anymore if it went unrequited; I needed to let you know. Susan advised me to just send you a telegram - if you didn't care anymore, I could stay in Manila and save myself a boat fare. But I wanted to do it in person, that's the reason why I came back. Besides, after three months of living in a zoo called Manila, I knew I could not live there to work. At least, if I were back at the Mission, a job that I love was waiting for me.

The boat ride back to General Santos gave me plenty of time to rehearse what I wanted to say when we met… I practically breezed through Lagao, stayed two days at our house to do laundry, and to shop for necessities. I rushed back to Lake Sebu. Imagine my utter disappointment when I arrived at the Mission. Siony told me that you had packed all your things and had left for good. She even said to me that Nonoy Dapulang had already put a bid on your room. Whew! I am glad that, as you are fond of saying, "all's well that ends well."

Circling back to your questions. Could I live in relative poverty all my life? *Why do you think I turned down Aristotle Onassis?*

What would I do if I could not live in the Philippines for the rest of my life? *Well, live elsewhere, I guess, but surely live.*

What about cross-cultural factors? *For starters, let's take out the burdensome "cross" and tackle the cultural factors without it!*

Flippancy aside, I had thought about all these very carefully since you verbally professed your love for me last year after Vilma's party. The fact that I came back to tell you about my certain kind of light should be proof enough for you that I am willing to face and surmount these barriers with you.

What are my plans? *At this writing, I could honestly say that I do not want to settle down yet. Thank you for not asking for any commitment. About your question on commitments and past experiences, I guess it's a fair question since you already confessed that you have no current romantic engagements, including JM, the lady in QC, lady at Vassar, our mutual friend. I have no boyfriend at present if that is what you mean. What I experienced in high school was puppy love that never progressed beyond the "walk-me-home-from-school" stage.*

When I was in college, there was this guy who reminds me so much of you. He is a prolific writer too and says it with roses, Cadbury chocolates, and poems – he was the one who sent all my Lettermen long-playing records. He was studying to be a lawyer at San Beda College, Manila. We tried to make a long-distance relationship work through letters.

Last year, after losing touch for months, he sent me a card for my August birthday as he always does, addressed to Notre Dame. But I moved to Lake Sebu in June, remember? The letter reached me in October after Martial Law. He asked if I had a boyfriend. No, I wrote back. In December, I received a message from him saying that since he had not heard from me for five months, he believed I had forgotten about him and was not interested anymore. He decided to go steady with a mutual friend he courted in high school- they made plans to get married.

What do I want from life? *I plead the fifth, as I don't believe in giving all the information during the first stage of interrogation.*

You said you want to go back to school after the Peace Corps. You have my blessings.

You asked about religion. You were raised Lutheran, I was raised Catholic. Martin Luther was once a Catholic priest. That's an excellent place to start.

To your question, "Who wishes that I shave my beard?" I have to admit; I think you'd look younger without it. But if you have a good reason to wear it, I have no objection. My father, however, might have something to say about it. Just so you know.

What if Peace Corps disapproves my request for an extension? *Let's cross that bridge when we get there. You could go home to the U.S. Go back to school as you had decided before I muddled your plans by coming back into your life. I could stay here. I have a job that I genuinely love, so I'd be okay. We could always continue to correspond and decide where this new journey will lead us. I have a renewed sense of confidence that together - the two of us - can resolve any issues that come our way. If the "lights" have not been extinguished these past four years, I believe that it would continue to shine forever no matter where you are or where I am.*

Lastly, as to the "Sir" bit, it became a habit all these years; it would be hard to drop it just like that, especially when everyone else all around us addresses you that way. Think of it this way. If I slip, consider "Sir" as an endearment and take it as "d-e-a-r." They kind of rhyme. Deal? You signed ALways. I sign PRIMArily yours.

ON JULY 4th, Filipino-American Friendship Day, I decided to shave my very long beard. The reaction was mixed. Some who knew me from General Santos had seen me without it. But most of the Mission employees had not. Prima wrote: *"I sure feel guilty. While I was not entirely thrilled about your beard, I did not want you to shave it if you really did not want to. Anyway, it's gone now as in the case of spilled milk. Although unlike spilled milk that is irretrievably lost, you could always grow it back, couldn't you? Dottie would be disappointed, though. But all the Pinays at the dorm prefer your chin naked."*

Although Prima had given me many good reasons to assuage and quell my nagging doubts about our relationship,

I continued to debate with myself about renewing my contract. After a long talk with Fr. Rex, he asserted and assured me that the mission needed my skills and services. I scrambled to apply for an extension. I dispatched my request to the Peace Corps Office in Manila. The wait was agonizing.

Meanwhile, Prima's brother Tito was hired by SCM to open and manage an office in Manila. He came to visit the Mission at Lake Sebu for a week, and he arrived on July 7, 1973. Fr. Rex wanted him to get a feel for what our Mission was all about, meet the staff with whom he would be dealing directly, and see in person the T'boli way of life. Prima was beyond pleased. In the past, some members of her family tried to talk her out of working at the Mission. Her mother let it be known that she preferred that Prima stayed working at the air-conditioned FNCB bank, more glamorous than the backwoods of Lake Sebu. Notwithstanding, Prima was earning more at the Mission. Tito just completed his CPA review and was waiting for the result. His employment at the Mission from Prima's point of view was a validation of her decision to work with the T'boli. Santa Cruz Mission Office in Manila was opened in September 1973. Tito and Fr. Rex promptly hired an office manager, Ding Dominguez, and his wife Lorna as secretary. (But as soon as Tito passed the CPA board exams in December, he left the Mission. He was pirated by SGV - Sycip, Gorres, Velayo Company, a prestigious accounting firm in the Philippines).

In addition to our workload at the Promotions Office, Fr. Rex received a request from Fr. Felix Miller in Bolul. Prima was tasked to help launch the Bolul Sponsor-a-Child Adoption Program. Dottie's job was to find Blaan artisans and to help market their handicrafts. I came along as the photographer for both projects. Dottie was in Manila on official business when the trip to Bolul was approved along with the expense budget. Prima insisted on waiting for Dottie before we set out for the Blaan Mission so we have a chaperon. A few days after Dottie came back, we were off to Bolul.

There were two resident Peace Corps volunteers in Bolul assisting the Blaan Mission's agriculture program - a husband and wife team, Mathias and Andrea Reisen. Located closer to the town of Marbel, Bolul was not as remote or isolated as Lake Sebu. Food and entertainment were readily available in Marbel. Matt and Andrea came from Pennsylvania, not far from where I grew up. (Their story is found in Postscript – Fifty Years Later at the end of this book).

Matt and Andrea "went native" and built their own *Bahay Kubo* in Marbel when they arrived. It was a convenient stopover for me from Lake Sebu to General Santos. On many occasions, I would stop at Matt and Andrea's house. One day, I knocked on their door to rest up overnight as I was suffering from another bout of amoebic dysentery. I decided to use Katol (a coil incense used to repel mosquitos) instead of a mosquito net. I was sound asleep when my head felt hot, and I smelled something burning. Suddenly, I realized my hair was on fire after getting too close to the Katol. A few pats on the head, and the fire was out. It singed my red hair!

On the first two days of our business trip, Prima and I worked with Delia Malaga, the Mission Secretary, and her sibling Edna, a teacher. We briefed them about the Sponsor-A-Child Program and took photos of all the school children. On the third day, it was muggy and hot. Having finished with our tasks, Prima and I accompanied Dottie in her search for crafters and basket weavers.

As we were leaving the mission, we were introduced to a Blaan lady who embroidered blouses. She knew some basket weavers in her area. None of us spoke Blaan. However, Prima spoke rudimentary T'boli enough to get by, and fluent Ilonggo, a dialect that was a language familiar to most Blaans of Bolul. The Blaan lady was still shopping, but she gave us directions to her house near where most of the crafters lived.

We started our trek through the vales and dales, past rice paddies, bamboo forests, banana clumps, gullies, and streams until we came to the foot of a steep hill. We started our arduous climb. The Blaan lady we met at the mission caught up with us. She was carrying a load on her back, a large basket laden with foodstuff, and supplies bought at the Mission store. The rope handle of the basket was slung on her forehead and supported by her back, leaving her hands free. She smiled and greeted us, went past us, and up the hill. She didn't walk, she moved with springy steps; then disappeared on the crest of the ridge as we lumbered and continued our climb.

Thirty minutes later, we stopped at the house of our first crafter, who embroidered Blaan blouses. The man of the house welcomed us. When we entered, next to the earthen fire pit in one of the corners of the house, squatted a Blaan lady. The same lady we met who was shopping at the Mission store and who passed us at the foot of the hill. She had boiled bananas ready for our *merienda* (snack). We also visited a few basket weavers and needlework artisans in the same area that the Bolul Mission staff had recommended.

We heard of the Blaan's *mabal tabih* woven cloth. *Mabal* is the Blaan term for the abaca weaving process. *Tabih* is the term for the finished hand-woven fabric, and it also refers to the traditional Blaan tubular skirt. Natural dyes from endemic plant species in the community are the source of colors for different designs of this indigenous textile. But our search for a Blaan cloth weaver yielded no positive result; even the Mission staff did not know any weaver that existed within the service area of Bolul Mission.

The search for the *Mabal Tabih* weavers reminded me of the trips that Dottie, Prima, and I did in Lake Sebu looking for *t'nalak* weavers. Gabriel S. Casal, a Jesuit priest, inspired by his encounter with the T'boli during a visit to Santa Cruz Mission, wrote his Master's thesis on *T'boli Art – In Its Socio-Cultural Context*. He stated: "All authentic and truly traditional T'boli *t'nalak* (abaca cloth) is always woven entirely out of abaca fiber. The secret of abaca weavers lies in the carefully selective preparation of the fiber used... T'boli women do not sketch or draw the design on the warp before them but merely follow a mental picture of the traditional design... The weaving of the *t'nalak* usually takes about a couple of months, or more, depending on whether or not the women's help is needed in the fields, as in the case during planting or harvest time..."[3]

Thanks to Fr. Rex Mansmann and Dottie Anderson for helping to save the art of weaving *t'nalak*. Its revival at the service area of Santa Cruz Mission in the early 1970s ensured the preservation of the art for future generations. It also provides a dependable income for the T'boli of Lake Sebu and beyond. (At the time of publication of this book, there are a good number of T'boli weavers, according to Cecille L. Castillon-Weinstein,[4] Mrs. Philippines America 2019. Her father was a teacher at the Mission, and her mother, Juvy Palces Castillon, worked at the Promotions Office from 1986 to 1994.)

The *t'nalak* fabric is available to avid collectors and for use in many items for the tourist trade. Also, there is now a living T'boli Museum in Lake Sebu and a Cooperative of Women in Health and Development (COWHED), an organization that promotes the T'boli Arts and Crafts.

The *T'nalak* weaving process is quite complex. During the time I was working at the Santa Cruz Mission, each buyer of the *t'nalak* was provided a brochure that described the simplified process. I documented the stages of the weaving process in photos, which required going back to the same weaver for months to complete the story.

In 1978, when our small business Crafts 'n Baskets was operational in Tampa, Florida, we sold T'boli arts and crafts. Our buyers of *t'nalak* and brasswares were limited to museums and art galleries in Florida and Pennsylvania. The T'boli and Blaan baskets had a more universal appeal. I deemed it valuable enough to share in the following pages, the process involved in making the *t'nalak* as described in the brochure created by our Promotions' Office team.

"The *T'nalak* is a natural fabric made by a centuries-old process by the women of the T'boli Tribe, Mindanao, Philippines," stated the opening line of the brochure that our Promotions Office prepared in 1973. Prima and I put together the catalog in collaboration with Dottie and Fr. Rex.

The Process of Weaving *T'nalak*

The fiber is carefully selected from a fruit-bearing abaca plant about eighteen months old and at least ten feet tall. The fibers are stripped by hand from the soft wet pulp of the abaca stalk. By repeated combing and sun bleaching, the fiber becomes pliable and flaxen. The design on the *T'nalak* is exactly the same on both sides. Only cloth processed by the method of tie-dyeing can produce this phenomenon, one of the most tedious methods of putting a design on cloth.

Photo 1   Photo 2

The refined fibers are laid out on the simple loom (photo 1). The fibers stretched out on the loom are tied with other fibers that have been rubbed in beeswax. All the areas covered by the waxed string will not be penetrated with the dye. It is in this process of tying that the real artistry lies. The women work deftly knowing beforehand the results of their work. The cloth makers use no measuring instrument. Yet the patterns will emerge with almost perfect precision. Measurement is done with finger joints, the length from the index finger to the elbow, etc. Once the fibers are tied, they are ready for dyeing. The black dye is made from the leaves of *k'nalum* tree and the red from the roots of *loko* trees.[5] The fibers are placed in a "double boiler" (photo 2). The steam carries the dye to the fibers. The dark color is dyed first then some of the waxed strings are removed. The newly exposed areas are now dyed red, the lighter colors.

The remaining waxed ties are removed, exposing the undyed areas making three colors in the design – black (or dark brown), red, and the cream or the flaxen color of the natural fiber. When the dyeing process for the red is completed, the bundle of fibers is removed and rinsed. The dyed fibers are then again laid out on the loom, ready for weaving. The design is already evident (photo 3).

Photo 3 Dottie interviews the weaver,   Photo 4 (top) & 5
Prima interprets.

The weaver sits on the floor with her feet against a bamboo brace fitted for the purpose. A belt of woven rattan fits around her hips and is fastened to the loom (top photo 4). With this very simple backstrap loom, she weaves in the standard way. A shuttlecock is an instrument used in weaving to carry the thread back and forth from side to side through the threads that run lengthwise. Held in her left hand by the lady in bottom photo 5, the shuttlecock had black or dark brown color fiber that had been dyed with the other threads.

After the cloth is woven, it is removed from the loom. If it is to be made into a large blanket (the "true" T'nalak), three lengths of the cloth are sewed together edge-to-edge, not overlapping. If the sewing is well done, a person will have to look carefully to find the seam.

The cloth is now pounded with a mallet and rubbed with a special cowrie seashell. This gives the cloth a waxen sheen. The cloth is now finished. The entire process from the beginning to the end takes about three months for a piece of fabric about eighteen feet long. It is then hung over the special window in the house dedicated to drying t'nalak. The weavers sell their finished products to the Mission Store.

Wherever we went during that Bolul trip, we were received warmly and were offered ripened eating bananas, boiled peanuts, or broiled sweet potato. Around four in the afternoon, we retraced our way back to the Mission. As it always happened in the mountainous regions like Lake Sebu and Bolul, the weather turned for the worst without warning. The skies darkened, and the rain started pelting down. As we were negotiating the footpaths on top of the ridge, lighting illuminated our way. The thunder was louder from the height we were at and reverberated over the mountains.

I made sure the airtight camera case was appropriately shut every time we went on a photo shoot. Thankfully it was in the waterproof case this time. The wind swirled wildly; causing the wheat-colored grasses that covered the ridge to sway in rhythm to the wind. It was a sight to behold, but I knew it would be folly to take the camera out to capture the moment.

By the time we reached the footpath down the side of the steep hill, it was so muddy that we were slip-sliding away. Dottie and Prima were such troopers; we were all laughing and giggling like kids having fun playing in the rain and mud. We got back to the Mission, totally drenched, and exhausted. Andrea and Matt had a hot meal and hot drinks ready for us. We slept soundly that night. Fifty years later, the three of us would still recall this trip vividly.

A few weeks later, we went back to Bolul to follow up on the collaborative projects. Another volunteer, Sue Bienkowski, who was assigned in Marbel, met us at Matt and Andrea Reisen's house. Dottie, Sue, Prima, and I went on a day trip to find weavers and basket makers. We came upon a group of Blaan chewing betel nut. We accepted their offer to try it. I spat out sooner than Dottie and Sue; they must have "bitten off more than they could chew." They were a bit high and were giggling all the way back to the Reisen's house.

SHORTLY AFTER the Bolul trip, I took our newly hired Marketing Manager Rudy Pastor to Marbel and General Santos City. I introduced him to various merchants that the Mission dealt with in the city - our suppliers of beads and cloth at Kimball Store, construction materials at Carlos Hardware Store, film, and Kodak photocopying at Rams Bombay Bazaar, etc.

Rudy recalled that we went to Cotton Bowl Grill for dinner. He emailed, "Sir Al ordered steak. Rare. When I cut it, it was oozing with blood. I only ate one-fourth of it!" We were supposed to be away for two days only. However, the rains played havoc on our schedule, and we could not get back to Lake Sebu. On the third day, it took us seven hours to go home, and three hours of it, we traveled in the dark. Prima was so happy to see us back, partly because we brought her a lot of packets of photos.

Before I took over the photography at the Promotions Office, a visiting Brother from the Maryknoll Order did the job for Fr. Rex. He was a professional photographer, who used Hasselblad cameras, the best in the business. I was overjoyed to shadow him and be his tour guide. We walked from *sitio* to *sitio* (village) looking for T'boli subjects. We captured on film their singular way of life unfiltered and unrehearsed – women weeding the corn and rice fields while their husbands chewed betel nut with their friends, children fetching spring water from a homespun bamboo pipe, a Datu and his six wives, etc.

I carried the Maryknoll Brother's photographic equipment and, using my own Minolta SRT 101, I photographed the same durable portraits of the T'boli and their way of life alongside him for my own personal use. (It was a decision that paid dividends. My slides and photos are the only surviving images taken during that session). The Maryknoll Brother shared many tips, but I remember the most notable. To get one excellent picture, a photographer must take at least twenty shots or more. Before digital technology, however it was rather expensive having to take rolls and rolls of film only to be discarded after the best shot was chosen. We created presentations using his slides for promotion purposes. Later, the staff that took over my job after I left the Mission used the same slide show template to promote the Mission outside of South Cotabato.

We celebrated Prima's 23rd birthday at the Clubhouse with a slide show. I taught Prima how to operate the slide projector, but she took the production process to a higher level and ran with it. She just didn't put slides together; she created a theme and arranged the slides accordingly. Then she produced a compelling story. The new set of slides that I had brought back to the Philippines from home leave two years prior was incorporated into the presentation. The kids enjoyed seeing the changing of the seasons, most notably the snow.

I popped some corn bought from Mr. & Mrs. Felix Chiew's Maricel Grocery store and served it with Dole pineapple juice.

Earlier in the morning, we serenaded Prima at dawn - the teachers, pupils, co-employees, and I. For a present, I offered to give her my college ring. She told me it fits her toes but might prove uncomfortable inside her shoes. That night, I strung some beads into a necklace and used my ring as a pendant. I gave it to her as a birthday present. However, she refused to wear it lest people would get suspicious. We wrote to each other every day, sometimes twice or more, depending on our moods.

On August 3, she wrote:

Dearest Al,

That's an improvement, wouldn't you agree? No more, Sir. Thank you for all you did – slide presentation and popcorn! It was the best birthday yet. Everyone enjoyed seeing on the big bedsheet screen, you raking the autumn leaves and you shoveling snow. The kids asked when we could do another slide show again...

You asked how I feel about your "primature" question as you called it. Let me answer with a question. Was the question that followed, "what do you think about going on a honeymoon in the U.S. for New Year," part of the proposal?

Would you be so shocked if I told you that I would consider saying yes to marrying you in December? At first, I thought it was too soon, won't leave us room to prepare. But tonight, this is how I feel. I realized that "I can't last a day without you" as Linda next door continually reminds me of her singing of the Carpenter's song. Sorry for the melodrama...

I am so happy about the good news from Peace Corps regarding your extension. When you spoke about going home to the States this afternoon, I could glean between lines that you might be getting homesick. Anyway, is your refusal to go on home leave by yourself having anything to do with me? You earned that vacation. Why not take advantage of it? What's a week or two or even a month being apart?

Now here's a counter-question. Would you consider taking your home leave if I went with you? Yes, I know exactly what that means - I have to marry you before we could travel together. I will give this letter to you at breakfast, please read it before you report to work, so we can discuss it at length when we walk to Bon's house for the photoshoot. We still have five months before December. If we finalize plans before we leave for Lemmakulen next week or during the trip there, perhaps we can process the visa paperwork, as you suggested...

I am so inspired I have a lot of subjects lined up for you to photograph. I'm thinking of finishing the story of Bon to include in the next slide show. Let's add a stop at her house on our itinerary today.

Al, I won't be able to sleep well tonight - you can pat your back for it. (It's a compliment!) Put on your record player on low volume, play the Special Request by the Lettermen, guide the stylus to Secret Love, and let the crooners finish this letter for me..."and my secret love's no secret anymore!" Guinahigugma ko Ikaw, Prima [I love you in Ilongo dialect].

P.S. My cassette is almost out of battery, but I am playing the Lettermen's Secret Love just the same.

Linda was in the Promotions office busy preparing the adoption *bi-folds* when I finally reported at the office the next morning after reading Prima's letter. Prima had just finished placing the last of the photographic equipment by the door when I came in. The adoption leaflets, along with the packing materials, were strewn all over Prima and Linda's desk. The packet had to be mailed to the Manila Office and SCM Pittsburgh when the truck went down to Surallah at ten o'clock. I was in and out of the office as I followed Prima out the door to give Linda space and time to finish her packing.

We spent a few hours taking pictures of the children by the banks of Lake Seluton. On our way to Bon's house, we discussed the letter that she gave me at breakfast. The picture-taking session finished for the day, we retraced our route back to the Mission before lunch.

When we arrived at the Mission, I took Prima's picture in front of Fr. Rex's *Convento* for posterity.

Around her neck, she was wearing the engagement ring that I had made for her.

The T'boli kids getting ready for their individual photoshoot along the banks of Lake Seluton and Prima wearing the engagement ring.

The kids often crossed the hanging bridge built by the community over *Lo El* (the River) to go to school.

Sunrise Sunset Over Lake Seluton   **15**

THERE WAS a special place on top of a hill overlooking Lake Seluton that was bare except for a few trees. Two prominent trees stood out; the *bong* tree (*bong* means big in T'boli) and a tall, skinny coconut palm. The T'boli kids named the trees *Dottie and Al* after we both moved to Santa Cruz Mission. Not only because we frequented the hill but also because the trees matched our profiles. There was no undergrowth, no bushes, and no shrubs, just a carpet of green grass covering the knoll where the horses and cows of my T'boli neighbors grazed. From my room, it was the first of many inspiring views that met the eyes when I opened my window every morning.

In 1973, a gazebo intended to be used as an altar during the September 13 Mission Fiesta called *Lemlunay* (paradise in T'boli) was under construction. But it was unusually rainy that year, and the gazebo, not being on the top of the priority list, was not finished until December.

The gazebo became our favorite stage for a Sing-Along. After dinner, especially on weekends, we'd gather under the gazebo. Sometimes the guys brought bottles of beer or Tanduay rum and coke. But mostly, they came to lend their voices and a profusion of memorized ballads to the homespun musical entertainment. It was amazing how almost all the members of the staff loved to sing. They were even familiar with Broadway hits from *The Sound of Music, My Fair Lady, Man of La Mancha, Fiddler on the Roof,* etc. They would bring their guitars and those of us who couldn't carry a tune spent hours just listening. I never grew tired of those spontaneous events. It was our respite from the spells of isolation.

The knoll was one of my favorite places to capture the spectacular sunrise and sunset, the serene lake below, or a rainbow or two with my camera. There was nothing to obstruct the view. In broad daylight, it was one of the many places in the area that never ceased to inspire.

On moonlit nights the knoll was idyllic. With Mother Nature dressed up in her very best, falling in love was easy. In fact, Ma'am Ang, with the help of other former SCM staff provided me with a list of the many like-minded men and women who came to work at the Mission, courted, fell in love, and wed there. It resulted in an inordinate number of marriages (25! as of the last count) among non-T'boli employees from 1966-1988. I was not immune. My name was added to the list.

After we announced our engagement, I wrote to my dad and family and told them about our wedding plans. I was elated when we received my father's response. I wrote back:

October 3, 1973
Santa Cruz Mission, Lake Sebu
Dear Dad and all,
Your very longed-for letter arrived today. We were delighted to hear the words you said about accepting Prima and her family. I

was not really worried because I know my dad is kindhearted, open-minded, and understanding. Prima's parents were very concerned, however, about whether my family would accept her. Now I can show them your letter, and they will be fully convinced. Prima was so happy to receive the little extra special note that you included for her. You said just the right things to her. She plans to write to you to be added to this letter. She is quite a good letter writer when she gets started. She has currently about twenty pen pals from all over the world.

I just stopped to reread your letter. I just can't help thinking about how you are such a great Dad to us all...Finding the right person to spend one's life with is sure a hard task. It took me long enough to find my one true love, but this time I am very sure that I have found the best there is. It is certainly worth the wait. Anyway, back to your being a great Dad, it is also nice that you accept and respect my decisions. After all, you and Mom struggled to get me through college, and I end up working in the Peace Corps all these years when I could be earning a good salary in the states and helping to repay all you have done for me...

Life here is hectic, as usual. Last weekend, Prima and I spent a few days with her family in General Santos. Prima stayed in the city while I went to Davao for a Peace Corps Conference. Tuesday, Prima took the bus to Surallah, and I flew from Davao to Surallah. There we met the mission truck and came back to Lake Sebu. Shortly after the vehicle hit the road, the rains came. The road was very slippery, muddy, and we had to winch most of the way. The trip took us about four hours (to travel fourteen or so miles!) ... A week before that, there was a landslide. Sir Vir had to send a bulldozer and a crew to repair the road. It took them three days to unblock the way. The rainy season really plays havoc with the roadways and transportation here. The rains are beneficial to the farmers and their crops, though.

I hope you will be able to come to our wedding. I would appreciate your presence than a check. You are not replaceable for the wedding but the money we could do without. Please do try your best to come. Take care now, and we wish you the best. Alvin

If it were left to Prima and me, our engagement period would not have been filled with many twists and turns as the Canahay Road. But we both understood that when we married, we also marry into two sets of families with two sets of cultures and traditions. Many adjustments and compromises had to be made to make everyone happy; something that was so important to someone so selfless as Prima. With her seven siblings scattered all over the Philippines, just deciding on the date for the wedding became a big challenge. I sent her a few more points to ponder. She wrote back: Big wedding or small wedding? *I really would like to get married here in a small, intimate wedding. Walking down the church aisle in a lacey white dress with 1,000 eyes gawking at the bride is probably every girl's dream. I hope it comes true for every bride who wishes it. But it is my idea of torture.*

Lagao or Lake Sebu? *In a perfect world, I'd prefer full T'boli regalia for a wedding dress, get married at sundown on the hill near Lake Seluton, for the reception, a bonfire as you suggested. You are more popular than me in General Santos. So could you imagine having to pare down your guest list without offending many of your friends? Besides, most people who are important to me are here at the Mission. The staff, Datu Ma Fok, and the T'boli kids might not all be able to attend if we hold it in Lagao. But there are the wishes of Nanay and Tatay to consider.*

Would you want a diamond for an engagement ring? *I'm ecstatic and proud of my engagement ring. I'm not into jewelry, so I'd only trade the one you made for me if you mine the diamond in Africa yourself.*

About your P.S. What do you mean??? Is it really the woman's family who pays for the wedding in the U.S.? Who thought of such a crazy idea? A man, I bet!!! Hmm, I think I want to change my mind. Just when I thought I know everything there is to know about American wedding traditions and agreed to marry you, you tell me this? Datu Ma Fok offered ten horses and a few cows for Dottie if she married him. You mean I won't even get a horse out of this deal? Kidding aside now, please tell me the rationale behind the idea. There's got to be a good reason for it? There better be. [Traditionally in the Philippines, the groom's family pays for all the wedding expenses].

Having made our decision to get married in December, Prima and I discussed everything we imagined we needed to consider about our wedding plans. I wanted to do the next step, the Filipino way - *Pamanhikan!* It is a Filipino custom I thought deserving of high regard when a man's parents visit the girl's house to ask for the hand of his intended. Not having my parents, Prima suggested that we invite Angelo and Sonrisa along as buffers if needed.

Prima's older brother Angelo worked for Bishop Reginald Arliss under the auspices of Fr. Hilarion's Parish. Angelo and his wife, Sonrisa (who taught at Notre Dame of Surallah High School), lived in Surallah. They honored me as godfather at the baptism of their first child Glenn Michael Angelo.[1] Diana, the youngest Guipo sister, came home from St. Paul School of Nursing in Davao City to be the godmother.

Prima and I visited Angelo and Sonrisa in Surallah to enlist their help for the *pamanhikan*. We synchronized our schedule to meet in Lagao. Mr. Guipo, Mrs. Guipo, Angelo, and Sonrisa were gathered together when we arrived. All went smoothly until religion came into the picture.

"Mixed marriage? What does that mean?" Mr. Guipo asked.

"Al is not a Catholic," Angelo responded.

I interposed before Angelo could go any further. "Prima and I have discussed this at length. I am willing to convert. I have already talked to Fr. Rex about it. The service will be done at the Mission."

The *pamanhikan* turned out not quite as nerve-wracking as I thought it would be. Mr. Guipo delivered the family's request that we got married in the church where Prima was baptized and confirmed in Lagao, Sts. Peter & Paul Parish, and that the reception would be held at their house. We assured them that we would make all the necessary arrangements per their wishes. I then shared our plans to go to Pennsylvania on New Year's Day for our honeymoon, dependent on Prima's visa. My family planned a wedding reception for us.

To make this happen, we had to process Prima's passport and visa in Cebu City, where my regional director lived. I assured Mr. & Mrs. Guipo that proper measures were employed for us to travel together before we were married without a chaperon. It was to ensure that Prima's reputation was not compromised. Brian Furby offered to help facilitate the processing of the visa. We would stay at their house.

Also, I mentioned my plan to attend the Peace Corps Training in Baguio on raising rabbits for protein in late October. I invited Prima to go along so she could shop for her wedding dress in Manila. Susan already wrote to us that we could stay at her apartment. In Baguio, my female Peace Corps friends rented an extra bed for Prima at the Teacher's Camp. Mr. & Mrs. Guipo had no objection and gave us their blessings.

Prima and I took care of a few errands before heading back to the Mission. We went to the Local Civil Registrar office to apply for a wedding license. The clerk, Ella Dumagat, was one of my students in Economics II. She helped us fill out the forms and even stood as one of our witnesses. (Ella, Judge Arne Elma, and Dr. Jose Alvarado signed our marriage certificate).

We stopped at the Lagao Parish Church to inquire about a church wedding and were told we had to go through the Pre-Cana seminar for three weeks. We explained that we both worked at Santa Cruz Mission in Lake Sebu, some six hours bus ride from the Lagao Parish Church, and longer if it rains. Logistics would prevent us from physically attending the one-day per week seminar for three weeks.

Mr. Juanito Espejo suggested that we get a dispensation from the Bishop and do the Pre-Cana in Lake Sebu instead. Knowing the Bishop personally, we assured Mr. Espejo it would be done expeditiously. We registered for the wedding. However, he reminded us that there was no getting around the Banns of Marriage to be read on Sundays for three months before the wedding. It was a legal requirement. (Banns of Marriage are the public announcement in a Christian parish church or in the town council of an impending marriage between two specified persons).[2]

While we were in General Santos City, we found out that our former boss Bro. Henry Ruiz, who was at this time the Marist Provincial Treasurer based in Marikina, Metro-Manila, was visiting Notre Dame College. We went to the Marist Convent to see him. Neither Prima nor I had seen him for a year. Prima had kept up her correspondence with Bro. Henry. But she made a conscious decision not to mention anything about our relationship. She wanted to surprise him. As she told me, "Wait till, Bro. Henry hears about us, he'd flip!"

Over the *merienda* that Mang Carling served us, I thought I'd shock the man who knew our secrets but never let on to either of us that he knew both sides of our story. "Bro. Henry," I said, "I want you to meet my future wife."

"What took you both so long?" was Brother Henry's rejoinder. His face lit up in a big smile, and we had a lively conversation after that recalling the circumstances behind our love story to which he was privy.

WE WENT back to Lake Sebu, thinking about how uncomplicated life would be if we got married at the Mission. But Prima was dead set on honoring her parent's wishes, a decision I totally supported. We started the invitation list. Counting very close friends only and members of the Guipo family from both sides, the total was way past our 300 maximum numbers of guests. On the family column, only first-degree cousins were included, which by themselves numbered up to 200 plus.

I requested Prima to prepare the budget and told her that I would pay for the catering. She wouldn't hear of it. We would share. We went back to General Santos City on her next weekend off in September. Her sister Josie met us at the Guipo house. We went to see Mrs. Puring Obed, the most sought-after caterer in town. Yes, she would be happy to cater for our wedding.

I was staying at the Partridge house and was not present when Prima discussed the catering arrangement with her mother after I left that evening. Mrs. Guipo had a previous unresolved disagreement with Mrs. Obed when Mrs. Guipo's niece got married. She made it clear she did not approve of Mrs. Obed and wanted us to find another caterer. We had a very narrow window of opportunity to do so, considering we lived in Lake Sebu. Mrs. Guipo won't budge.

Prima thought her mother was being unreasonable. She lost her cool and told her mother that she was doing everything that they asked of her as she had done all her life. In her frustration, she blurted, "I didn't want to get married here in Lagao anyway. Maybe it is better to hold the wedding in Lake Sebu." The argument escalated out of control, something so unlike Prima. For the first time in her life, she asserted herself. Mr. Guipo had to play referee. Mother and daughter reached an impasse.

I went to the Guipo house early the next morning for breakfast as planned. Mrs. Guipo was taken to the hospital for elevated high blood pressure. Prima was so upset she was in tears. All she wanted to do was to run back to Lake Sebu. It took a lot of coaxing to convince her to visit her mother at the Canda Clinic before we left.

She acquiesced only after I told her about my father and mother's spat. When I was in college, before my mom was diagnosed with cancer, my Dad got upset about something that my mother said or did. It was a petty misunderstanding. He did not speak to my mom for a few days, which really hurt my mom. I saw her cry over it. I felt so sorry for my mom, but I could not interfere. They made up later. It never happened again. That taught me a lesson never to let the sun go down on a misunderstanding. It festers. It becomes more difficult to make up.

Prima and I went to the Canda Clinic. Mother and daughter made up. But Mrs. Guipo's parting words were, "I hope you don't mind if I don't attend the wedding. I still would like to throw a wedding reception at home after your wedding in Lake Sebu." It was not a request; it was a given. It was her attempt at a peace offering. We accepted. With the wedding date just over a month away, I wrote to my dad.

November 16, 1973
Dear Dad and all,

I owe letters to Enid and Bud, Joyce and Earl, but I'll write to you instead and let you pass the word on. Prima and I have set our big day for December 22 at sundown. You will get an invitation soon. They are at the printers now. I'll save the details of the wedding and reception for Prima to tell you.

Concerning our recent trip to Baguio City for my Peace Corps Seminar, we were able to begin the application for a passport for Prima in Manila and Cebu City on our way home. I applied and was granted the capacity to marry from the U.S. Embassy – it's a U.S. government requirement. Last weekend in General Santos City, we filed for a marriage license (ten days waiting period). We will get that next weekend and probably have a civil ceremony just to get the paper saying we were married. The marriage contract was requisite for Prima's passport and visa. It was necessary to get the documents started, or there would not be enough time before we wanted to go for home leave. Our goal was to get to the states by New Year's Eve.

Under Martial Law, Philippine citizens are prohibited from leaving the country for tourism.[3] It was necessary to apply for an immigrant visa. For that, an affidavit of support was required. Since I am not currently employed in the U.S., I am not qualified to provide that affidavit of support. So, we would like to ask if you could prepare and send one to us for Prima. Enclosed is the paper explaining the requirements. We will all have to forgive the U.S. government for its bigness and bureaucracy. They write everything so legalistic and impersonal, it is hard to understand.

Prima and I had been on a picnic with the vice-consul in Cebu. We visited him in his office, and he came to see our slide show about the T'boli at Brian Furby's home. We still had to go through all the same paper routines as everyone else. By the way, Brian Furby is the Peace Corps Staff Representative. He is married to Cely (a Filipina), and they have two children. We stayed at their home. Karl Danga the vice-consul is a young man who was formerly a Peace Corps Volunteer in Africa.[4]

Dad, I was saddened that you could not make it for our wedding. Another volunteer in Marbel, David Baggott, is getting married to Cecille de Pedro. His parents couldn't make it either. She is the daughter of the Governor of South Cotabato, and they are having a big wedding. They invited us to their wedding, which is a week before ours.

Below is a sample of the Affidavit of Support. I want to get this in the mail right away to give enough time to prepare everything...By the way, the last time we were in General Santos, I requested Prima to read your letter to Mr. & Mrs. Guipo. They were pleased and said, thank you. I gave them your address. Take care, Alvin.

P.S. from Prima. You asked about our weather here these days. Well, it's supposed to be the dry season, but it rains almost every day. Actually, when Al and I got back from Manila on Tuesday, November 6, we hiked about fifteen miles on the muddy road uphill on Canahay! Our day started by waking up at five in the morning to be at the airport on time to catch our flight from Cebu to Davao City. (We stayed in Cebu for two days to process my passport and visa).

At the check-in counter, the Philippine Air Lines rep told us that our connecting flight from Cebu to Davao was okay. However, from Davao to Surallah was canceled because of a storm and the airstrip is flooded. We wanted to be in Surallah on the same day for this big conference at the Mission for all religious and laymen involved with cultural minorities. Even the Bishop is attending. Anyway, when we got to Davao, we had to take a bus to Surallah (eight hours ride) with stops to change buses. We got to Surallah at six in the evening. All the transportations to the Mission had already left. Al tried to persuade me not to go any farther. But I was one of the organizers. I felt I had to be there.

We grabbed a quick supper and started out at seven o'clock. We met up with eight of our high school boys studying in town on their way home to attend the seminar and three other T'boli women working at the Mission. Together we hiked back to the Mission. It was fun for the first few kilometers of the level terrain talking with our fellow hikers. We crossed the Allah Valley River without incident; at least it was not flooded.

The road gradually became punishing just before Canahay. It had rained in the area before we arrived, making the road muddy on a hilly region just as it turned dark. With sheer determination, I tried to keep up with the kids who were used to walking long distances. My legs started to get sore. I didn't give up until the last few kilometers. Just before Lo El, the second river we have to cross before the Mission, my right foot became swollen. I could hardly manage a step anymore.

Al was a real sport. As tired as he was, he gave me a piggyback ride. 100 lbs. of me vs. his 125! He never said, "I told you so," either, which I believe I deserved. At sunrise, we arrived at the Mission after ten hours hike! The eight-hour bus ride alone was a killer! Our hiking story is just one of countless adventures on Canahay Road. One time we even got stranded overnight - a truckload of us stayed at a stranger's house in a logging camp along the way. They even fed us dinner using the provisions we were transporting back to the Mission. But ours is not an isolated story. A majority of mission staff has a ten-hour-hike tale to tell. We rested for four hours, then we both were on our feet again, and we did not miss a day of the three-day seminar.

Yes, we bought the materials for my wedding dress in Manila. My two aunts who are both professional seamstresses are sewing the shirt and pants for Al and the dress for me. Al had suggested a bonfire for the reception, and I like the novelty of the idea. It's in the plans, unless it rains, of course. We are expecting about a hundred guests for our wedding, mostly SCM employees, our T'boli neighbors, and the kids

living in the dormitories. We have no room for accommodations for
out-of-town guests; therefore, we limited the number of guests who
doesn't reside at the Mission. I hope we'll have good weather, though.
Okay. Al wants to send this off today. Cheers, Prima.

I TURNED thirty at Santa Cruz Mission three weeks before
our wedding. As happened when I arrived four years prior,
my colleagues, including the T'boli staff and the T'boli kids,
serenaded me by candlelight at dawn. It was such a stirring
Mañanita moment knowing the trouble they went through to
get up before the crowing roosters on a very chilly Monday
morning. What a gift! I know I would be hard-pressed to wake
up at dawn unless I really like the person. I got serenaded twice
during my Peace Corps stint - at my first and last assignment.

Soon after my birthday, we received good news from General Santos City that Prima's mother was attending the wedding after all. Invitations were extended to Mr. & Mrs. Guipo's siblings only. A reception was planned at the Guipo's House after the wedding. For that reason, the rest of the members of the clan were invited to that affair. About thirty of Prima's family, wedding sponsors, and bridal entourage were added to the confirmed list. Datu Ma Fok, Bishop Reginald Arliss, and some Passionist priests I worked with were invited. My dad and stepmom could not make the trip from Florida. Nine Americans - Peace Corps volunteers in Marbel and friends at Dole - stood for the members of my family.

The "committee" for accommodations found a place for all of our guests to stay at the Mission. The staff, both men and women, gave up their rooms at the dormitories and stayed at the houses of other married employees on campus for the weekend. The SCM family pooled their resources together to turn our wedding into a memorable event. Even Fr. Rex and Bro. Lou found accommodations elsewhere and offered their *Convento* for the bridal suite. It was very heartwarming.

The National Geographic magazine featured the Tasadays in its August 1972 Issue, *The Stone Age Men of the Philippines*.[5] A week before our wedding, Fr. Rex led a group of T'boli and non-T'boli staff from the Mission to check the veracity behind the Tasaday story. After a two-day hike walking from six in the morning to five in the afternoon each day with minimal rest along the way, the group arrived at the Ubo community. They did not go any farther. The Tasaday village would have taken them another day of hiking. Some of the Ubo in full regalia came back to the Mission with Fr. Rex a few days before our wedding. (The Tasaday story was later proven to be a hoax).

Our Ubo visitors had never seen a cassette tape recorder (playing in Prima's office) or a typewriter. Timid and shy, they watched with fascination through the window slats as I typed a letter to my Dad. One of them came into the office to borrow the *hegelong* (a two-string T'boli guitar) hanging on our office wall.

I found out that they were staying at the Mission for a few days. I decided to record some of their music on cassette and to take their pictures. Salic, the man who borrowed the hegelong also played the *flendong* (bamboo flute). I requested Salic, and he agreed to play at our wedding. The wedding service was a fascinating blend of American, Filipino, T'boli, and Ubo customs and traditions. Our exceptionally diverse guests represented five different provinces, six states of the U.S., and at least six different tribes of the Philippines.

Ely Cabayao, our Clubhouse Manager, assured us that he would take care of the wedding reception and literally warned us to stay out of the kitchen. We didn't have to lift a finger to help. Our friends organized a committee for everything from decoration, mass service, transportation, music, food, accommodation, cake, photography, etc. All we needed to do was show up on our wedding day.

We chose the gazebo on top of the hill overlooking Lake Seluton as our wedding venue. Sunrise and sunsets were spectacular from this vantage point. Once I captured on film a double rainbow just behind the *Dottie and Al* trees. On some moonlit or starry nights, we'd just sit quietly on the hill under the gazebo and listen as gongs, hegelong, Jews harp, and ladies chanting filled the air. It was a place like no other that I would remember for the rest of my life. The gazebo was Fr. Rex's idea, according to Ma'am Ang Maghari. She wrote: "The Mission's fiesta falls on September 13. Fr. Rex wanted to have a more spacious place than the chapel to say mass. But due to constant rain every day it was not finished. The foreman was Fred Fontana, and some T'boli men helped him. I clearly remember what Fr. Rex said, 'Vir that gazebo could be used for any occasion.' It was finished in December very much on time for your wedding. Fr. Rex had a hearty laugh when he came to our house one afternoon just to tell us that the gazebo would be the venue of a lovely occasion."

As our wedding day drew near, Prima and I can't remember going through the typical before-the-wedding jitters as our married friends shared with us. Maybe, it was because we had no lingering doubts about our decision to spend our lives together forever. Or perhaps, there was no time for the jitters. We were so busy preparing materials for Fr. Rex, who was scheduled for his April to September furlough. He planned a big media blitz to promote the Mission while he was in the States. We plotted and outlined enough project proposals so I could continue working on said proposals and submit them while Fr. Rex was away. Bro. Louis Bouchard was to take over as Acting Director.

Prima and Linda cranked up their production of the Sponsorship brochures. They prepared drafts of Fact Sheets and handouts for Fr. Rex to take to our SCM/US office in Pittsburgh for printing. We also prepared slide presentations. It was an extremely hectic period for the Promotions Office.

The week before the wedding, the rains came in torrents. We thought the rain would never stop! We had planned to have a bonfire for the reception. We played it safe and moved the party to the Clubhouse. Our biggest concern was for our guests who had to endure the mud on Canahay Road.

On the morning of the big day, the sun rose and bathed Lake Seluton with its sparkling rays. Prima wanted to wear full T'boli regalia for our wedding. However, her mother thought it was going native too much. A compromise was made. For our official wedding photo, taken along the banks of Lake Seluton, we wore our T'boli outfit.

The Mission had just installed a commercial oven at the Bakery Shop. We were so excited to test it for our wedding cake. Early in the year, a Nutritionist Ninfa Dapulang was hired to help with the Nutrition Program for both the school pupils and the dining hall. She offered to decorate our two-layered wedding cake if someone would do the baking. She and Prima sat down and designed it. Our Peace Corps friend Andrea Reisen had a favorite white cake recipe and offered to bake two 24" x 36" rectangular layers.

We both worked till noon on our wedding day. Before five o'clock, the guests started to assemble. Others gathered at the DHOP Dormitory to join the bridal procession. I waited on top of the hill with my best man Matthias Reisen, groomsmen Rudy Pastor, and Prima's brother Tito. Unmindful of our special day, the neighbor's horses grazed around the gazebo.

The services started at five. Fr. Rex officiated wearing his chasuble appliqued with T'boli design. By the time Salic played the flute, it was dusk, and the haunting sound of the flute filled the air. Not many dry eyes among the guests. During the offertory, three T'boli Girls – Maria and Dolores Loco and Joanna Landusan – performed a T'boli dance. Siony sang the Hawaiian Wedding Song. We also observed the wedding customs filled with Filipino symbolism: the giving of the arrhae (coins), we had sponsors for the veil, the candle, and the cord. At the end of the ceremony, our primary sponsors (godparents called *ninong and ninang*) signed the marriage certificate – Gene Ryman, Ramonito "Boy" Crespo, Qric Batilaran, Mrs. Remedios Ferrariz, Mrs. Lucia Valencia, and Ma'am Emma Crespo.

WHEN I was growing up in the Bethlehem-Allentown area of Pennsylvania, I hung out with kids who were friends of my older brother Bud. One of them, Don Turick, got married first. Soon everyone found their mates, and they too got married, leaving me the only bachelor in the mix. One day, I asked Don, how does one know when one finds the right girl?

"You'll know," was all he said. Looking back now, I could explicitly state that for me, communing with the special girl on the hills of Kematu was the "You'll know" moment that Don Turick prophesied.

I recalled the time I found a stone shaped like half a heart on my first visit to T'boli land. I gave that piece of stone to Prima. (She calls it her precious stone that she has kept to this day). I told her then that I wished I'd find on T'boli land the other half of the heart someday. And I did.

As Fr. Rex read our wedding vows, I repeated after him, "... to love and to cherish until death do us part."

I knew that was the moment when my heart was complete.

The day after the wedding, all the guests left for their respective homes. Canahay Road, on rainy days, turned into an adventure too exciting for comfort for some of the guests. Many times they had to get off the vehicles and walk on muddy roads, a Canahay Road experience like no other that gave them something to talk about for many months after the wedding. In fact, they are still talking about it to this day. Prima and I went home to Lagao with the family. On December 24, inviting only close friends and members of the Guipo-Grana family, Mrs. Guipo feted us to a second reception at the Guipo's house.

Everything worked according to our plans, except we had to cancel the honeymoon in Pennsylvania. We didn't anticipate that Prima's immigrant visa would take so long. Prima cajoled me into going home alone so I wouldn't lose an earned home leave. But I was just as determined not to go without her. We went to Cebu City for our honeymoon instead. The Management Consultant Group for the Mission that was based in Cebu threw a party for us.

I proudly showed my new wife the city's tourist attractions. On our way back to the Mission, we flew to Cotabato City so Prima could meet my friends. We stayed with Mr. & Mrs. Lim. On New Year's Eve the dark skies of the city plaza lit up with a spectacular fireworks display. The following day they took us on a city tour stopping at parties hosted by their Chinese friends and relations. Coming from the remote, isolated village of Lem-ehek, the trip was an incredible change of scenery. And the biggest surprise, none of our Philippine Airlines flights was canceled!

Four months before our wedding, we began planning for our living quarters. Our dream house was a two-room *nipa* hut. I drafted the plan and sat down with Prima to discuss our proposed little house in Lem-ehek. There wasn't much land to build at the new community near Lake Seluton, but there were open spaces below Datu Ma Fok's house. We had hoped to get a home lot in the vicinity with room for vegetable and flower garden. I calculated costs and prepared a budget for it.

Before I could even finalize the plans, Prima already "planted" her rose garden in the imaginary yard. Ma'am Ang had given me some cuttings from her roses. I planted them in empty Dole pineapple cans to start the young plants – pink and red roses. I figured by the time we moved, they would be ready to transplant. Prima could not wait to start her garden. But first, we needed a small patch of land, the size similar to other married couples' home lot. We met with Fr. Rex to secure his approval and to request a lot on which to build it. As soon as he saw the plans and the bill of materials, Fr. Rex exclaimed somewhat incredulous and in a teasing mode:

"Al, are you serious?" he said, grinning widely. "What would her parents say? All of that for P700 pesos too! Commendable. But I tell you what, why don't you let the Mission build you one. After you leave, your home could be turned into a house for other employees or an office. We will try to get it done by December."

We didn't refuse the Director's generous offer. A beautiful site was assigned to us on an open space at the base of a small ridge opposite Afus Hill. We had no neighbors in close proximity. Across from us on a higher hill was Datu Ma Fok's residence, where he lived with his four wives. Construction started soon after the conversation with Fr. Rex took place. But the rains slowed the process. If the house was not ready for occupancy after we came back from our honeymoon, our contingency plan was to stay in my room at the Men's dormitory. And that was what happened exactly. We stayed in my room at the Men's Dormitory and slept inside a cozy sleeping bag spread on top of a single bed for a month.

The thirteen men living in the Men's Dorm did not mind having Prima around. They had always considered her "one of the guys." But we made sure to always go together to use the bathroom so I could ensure no one entered while Prima was inside. Or no one was inside when she went in!

In the mornings, she'd wait until after everyone had left for work to use the bathroom. When she had to go early to her office, she went over to the DHOP dorm to shower and get dressed. One day, Fr. John, a priest from out of town, was visiting the Mission. He stayed at the Men's Dorm. Because Fr. John did not belong to the Passionist Order, we did not know him too well.

The usual daily din at the dorm of banging doors, heavy and hurried footsteps, and the loud banter echoing through the hallway hushed as the last of our doormates left the building. It was the signal for Prima and me that the bathroom was ready for her to use. She went inside and pushed the door of one of the stalls. Lo and behold, Fr. John, was there ensconced on the commode!

Prima couldn't wait until we moved to our own house!

The Ubo people visited Santa Cruz Mission for the first time in December 1973, led by Sgalang (man on the right), their self-proclaimed chief, and his wife (left).

Many of the women had blackened teeth. They believed that it made them superior to animals; keep their teeth strong and healthy, and added beauty and prestige. A few also exhibited signs of goiter.

THE WEDDING ALBUM

The bridal entourage led by primary sponsors called Ninong and Ninang (l-r) Emma Crespo, Lucia Valencia, Boy Crespo and the SCM employees and family. Lake Seluton in the backdrop.

During the Offertory, Maria Loco, Dolores Loco (not visible in photo), and Joanna Landusan performed a T'boli dance as part of the offering.

Salic, a member of the Ubo tribe played his flute. The Ubo men wore earrings long before it became fashionable. Made of brass, these earrings are quite heavy.

In the background, (l-r) Dottie, Dave Delasanta, bridesmaids Diana Guipo, Bing Ferrariz, & Puring Limjap Bongolto and Mr. Guipo.

Madam Dottie and The DHOP Girls, our honored guests.

Mr. & Mrs. Guipo and family with Bridal Entourage and Datu Ma Fok (extreme right).

The Grana & Guipo Family

An all-day wedding reception was held at the Guipo family's lawn. The photographer (Angelo) could only fit a hundred family member on the porch for this picture. A second picture was taken with the rest of the relatives and friends.

Our Bahay Kubo Our newly constructed house was relatively upscale compared to the other homes at the mission but it had no indoor plumbing. Our outhouse and shower room was located behind it.

Peace Corps: No Source of Pride More Real[1]   **16**

I really love being a Peace Corps volunteer and very proud of the work we do. Peace Corps has done a lot for me, especially in terms of showing me that the American way of doing things is not the only way, nor always the better way. It is humbling. And that the trappings of wealth are not always the answer to happiness; a simple way of life can be a source of utter joy and fulfillment.
~ Alvin J. Hower in his letter to his dad.~

NOTHING EVER went my way entirely in the Philippines. Or so it seemed. As a result, I learned to roll with the punches – a very significant take away from my Peace Corps experience. And to be ready with an alternative for when plans go awry. Like the countless times, I arranged a beach picnic with my friends who did not show up after I'd waited for hours, I went alone. Traveling by air in the Philippines back then was so unreliable and frustrating. One must always be ready for flight delays and cancellations. So I learned to get used to it without rancor, accepted it with a hefty dose of patience as the new normal, and find a creative way to get from point a to b. Like the time when the last leg of my flight from Davao City to Surallah was canceled, I took an eight-hour bus ride, followed by a ten-hour hike to get back to Lake Sebu.

My last eight months at the Mission was the perfect example of things gone awry as our letters would attest. I forewarned my family in the U.S. *Our plans for the future – they are quite flexible, and I'm sure we will have to bend with the will and the wind as time goes on.* I realized with great surprise that the Filipino *bahala na* (fatalistic) attitude that drove me nuts during my first year as a Peace Corps volunteer had somehow seeped into my own value system. Most surprising, I was okay with it. I even found myself invoking "Que sera, sera" more often than my Filipino colleagues. Rolling with the punches was a life lesson that would serve me well as a Returned Peace Corps Volunteer.

January 9, 1974
Dear Joyce, Earl and all,
   We just got back to Lake Sebu from our honeymoon. We are moving to our house tomorrow, and reports are that it is frigid inside the house with bamboo slats for walls and floors. That being the case, we will need extra coverings. I was wondering if there are any extra comforters or quilts from over at the farm. If not, we can buy blankets here, but I have not seen comforters or quilts.
   Prima also likes magazines like Good Housekeeping, anything about home interior decorating and gardening, fiction books, and memoirs. She only has a subscription to Reader's Digest Asia edition. If you have old copies of magazines, would you be willing to donate them plus postage to the Mission? Also used board puzzles, dominoes, and decks of cards for the Clubhouse would be much appreciated by all...
   We did not move "tomorrow," as I predicted. There were some issues with the electrical wiring. Also, I decided to install a water-sealed toilet in the outhouse before we moved in. Instead of the standard open-pit toilet used in the Mission houses, I poured a reinforced concrete slab to cover the deep open pit. In the center of the slab was an opening for the waste to go down. Over the opening, I added a locally made concrete toilet bowl (without the tank). After the concrete was cured, water was added to the toilet bowl, and we had the first flush outdoor toilet in the Mission. We saved the drain water from our kitchen sink to flush the toilet.
   On February 5, Prima wrote to my family: *Hope dashed again! Our house is not quite ready. Al can't wait to move in. He keeps*

himself busy with preparing our garden and raising rabbits for protein so we can be self-sufficient. He hopes it would rub off on the neighbors, and they'd join the Rabbit for Protein Program. The biggest challenge for him will be to convince the T'bolis to eat such cute looking animals. He has eight rabbits already. Fr. Hilarion is giving him two more for a wedding gift...

On February 9, she wrote: *Hurray! We finally moved to our house! It is almost completely furnished. We bought a two-burner propane gas stove (a luxury here) when we were in the city last week. The wedding gifts completed our household needs except for little things like peelers, can openers, etc. Wish me luck on my first cooking adventure in our new home...*

In January, I started to till the black, fertile soil of our yard, one shovel full at a time. I planted some carrot seeds and the leftover uncooked potatoes that we had bought from the *palengke* that had started to sprout. Lem-ehek was located in a high rainfall zone of Surallah. Mother Nature watered our plants. The plants seemed to grow much faster in our garden than in the lowlands.

Since we lived quite a distance from the Mission's water supply, I had to figure out how to get water from the Mission's supply tanks to our house for drinking, cooking, washing dishes, and bathing. Enter what I called our "running water." There was this enterprising middle-aged T'boli man who ran from house to house over the hills to deliver water at minimal cost using a milkmaid's yoke. He filled two cans from the Mission's water tanks, fastened the containers to each end of the yoke, and balanced the yoke on his shoulder. He poured the water into a twenty-gallon can with a faucet at the bottom sitting atop the side of our outdoor kitchen sink.

Until we left the Mission, we continued to scrounge for food. But food, especially meat, was always plentiful after a trip to the city. During this trip, Prima's sister Josie gave us steaks that she bought from Dole where she was teaching. Mrs. Flor Congson also gave us fish. Since we did not have refrigeration at the Mission, Prima cooked the fish to extend its shelf life. They were fried, salted and dried, or prepared as *paksiw*. I bought a small Styrofoam cooler and buried the steaks in ice to transport back to the Mission. We invited Dottie for dinner and served her an honest to goodness American meal: steak, steamed carrots with margarine, and boiled potatoes from our garden. She brought her Anejo rum.

By April, we finally settled comfortably in our little house. A neighbor loaned us a single bed, and we continued to snuggle inside my sleeping bag (under a mosquito net) to keep warm on those nights when it was very cold and damp. We added a wooden dining set for four bought from the Mission Woodworking Shop and got two extra chairs. I purchased pieces of wood pre-cut to the desired length. Without proper tools, I managed to build a shelf for our living room. Our six dining room chairs doubled as living room furniture. Life was simple.

BEFORE EASTER, DHOP Madame Dottie announced she was leaving the Mission, having finished her one-year extension. The DHOP girls were just as devastated as we were. The girls asked us if they could hold a surprise *Despedida* (going away) party for Madame Dottie at our house. We gladly said, yes. They prepared a program that was a total surprise, even to us. Each brought their food ration from the Clubhouse. I butchered one of our chickens for the occasion. Linda and Nenen stretched the meat by cooking recipes that called for a lot of vegetables like *chop suey, pancit bihon,* and *tinola* (chicken soup) with lemongrass and green papayas.

Dottie had her instructions to come at six-thirty PM. All the girls arrived at six, and they commandeered our second bedroom to prepare for the party. Fr. Rex was unable to attend, as he was busy preparing for his U.S. furlough. Bro. Lou and Sir Qric arrived fifteen minutes before Dottie. As soon as Dottie entered the front door, we placed her on a prominent chair

in the living-cum-dining room flanked on either side by Bro.
Louis and Sir Qric.

Prima played her cassette tape. The Beatles upbeat song
All You Need Is Love filled the room. On cue, the DHOP girls
paraded out the bedroom, and down the plight of stairs. Linda
Basadre came out first, the pirate with two pregnant wives.
The rest followed – two pacifists Nuns and the activist, the
Hollywood actress and a rock n' roll star, a nun, the grandma
and a baby. They were all wearing costumes so outrageous,
fashioned from mosquito nets, bed sheets, *luwek* (T'boli skirt),
etc. Their stirring tribute was a testimony to how much they
treasured Dottie as being one of them. Those DHOPians, they
were special folks.

We laughed so hard tears were streaming out of our
eyes. There was a contest for the best costume judged by Sir
Qric, Bro. Louis and Dottie. The winner was awarded a prize
purportedly donated by the General Manager, Sir Qric.

When Grandma Odette Maghari opened her gift-wrapped
box for the best costume, three giant Hawaiian toads leaped

out of the box and hopped all over the room before they were shepherded out the door. Linda and companions had caught the frogs from the rice paddies along Lake Seluton. The festivity was topped with a delicious dinner. The girls brought their Tanduay Rum and coke too. Everyone left before the lights went off at nine. We were folks starved for entertainment, but definitely, there was no shortage of creativity. (The DHOPians keep in touch to this day on their own private Facebook Group Site called LTK Survivors of Lake Sebu).

Being married to Prima was like having my own private secretary. Soon she took over my correspondence and wrote to my folks more often than me. It freed up my time to enjoy my hobbies of raising rabbits, taking care of the laying hens, and gardening. On April 20, she wrote:

Dearest Dad, Gladys, and all,

As Al and I were walking home from work this afternoon, we saw two rainbows arched beautifully over the top of the hill where our wedding was held. Al believes he captured the scene with his camera. I will send a photo. This is one of the wonders of Lake Sebu, aside from the falls, lakes, rolling hills, rivers, and streams. The Milky Way seemed more prominent here at night too. The full moon, the stars when the sky is pitch black, and sunsets are just simply beautiful. It's hard to find the right words to describe. Sometimes Al and I stay late at night stargazing or wake up early just to catch the sunrise. We'll really miss this place when we leave. But Al assured me that there would be sunrise and sunsets as spectacular in the U.S. too.

Your letter that arrived today was handed to us inside our "movie house." Yes, our very skilled electrician Danny Reyes fixed an old movie projector that was donated to the Mission long ago. It was a Filipino film that was premiered last night. It was standing room only. Al and I had more fun watching the T'boli audience, young and old, who has never been to a movie before! Rather hard to believe, huh? Considering that men have been to the moon and back. Anyway, this movie was the first ever to be shown here.

Bro. Louis and Danny ran the same film five nights already. The scenes with horses got the most applause! The movie was in Tagalog, and most of the T'boli in the audience do not understand the national language. But they seemed to know what was going on, or at least they laughed at the right moment...

Our Director Fr. Rex left today for the U.S. Dottie left for Manila on the 15th. She hopes to come back someday, though. She's quite amazing. In fifteen months, she revived the dying T'boli arts and crafts and found lucrative outlets to market them in Manila. She trained the Filipino and T'boli staff to take her place.

Al is going to be quite alone with only one other American around, Bro. Louis. We are already missing Dottie...We are both well. On the 28th, we are going home to my folk's house in General Santos for a one-week vacation. We plan to go snorkeling again. Al misses the beach so much. Hello to all. Love always, Prima

P.S. from Alvin. I'll just say we are doing fine and then to something you are all waiting to know about – our plans for the future. Basically, we would like to spend another year at Santa Cruz Mission. Our work here is so satisfying, and we are accomplishing a lot for the mission, primarily in terms of getting funding for our projects. My real goal, though, is to go back to school to study Anthropology or Archeology after Peace Corps. After some course work, we would probably come back to the Philippines to do research. Beyond that, we have not really made any real plans.

At present, we are working on my application for an extension with the Peace Corps for one more year (from August). We will not know until June or July if that extension will be granted. As of now, things are tight with the Peace Corps. I heard they are trying to cut down on the number of volunteers in the Philippines, especially in our area. There is trouble brewing in Kematu between the settlers and the indigenous tribes over land ownership, according to Doris Porter,[2] a Wycliffe Bible translator who visited the Mission recently.

We had already discussed our plans to stay for one more year with Fr. Rex before he left for the U.S. He was the one who encouraged me to request an extension as our Promotions Office is really kicking into high gear. We have so many feasibility studies in the works plus proposals already submitted to local and international agencies, including Misereor in Germany, to build a much-needed hospital, a high school, and college here in Lem-ehek. Currently, our students go to Surallah and Marbel to study in high school and college. We spend a lot of money for their schooling, board, and lodging. In the long run, having a high school and college here would be cost-effective and beneficial for the T'boli.

As to the need for a hospital, I had to write justifications for the funding organizations. A pregnant mother of two died recently from bleeding. The weapons carrier took the T'boli mother to St. Joseph Hospital owned by Dr. Jose SF Velasquez[3] in Surallah. She did not survive. Our friend Ma'am Ang, who came to the Mission six years before me, also told us the story of two T'boli girls attending school who were married and pregnant at an early age. They did not notify the teachers of their marriage or pregnancy. Their "hilot" (tribal medicine man or woman) treated them. Both died but might have survived if they were treated at the hospital.

The incident prompted Fr. Rex to build the dormitory so the teachers could keep an eye on the girls and intervene before it was too late. We could have avoided tragic happenings like that if we have a hospital on campus. Our small clinic is not equipped to do more than the basic check-up, patching up minor wounds, and dispensing pain or cold medicine, etc. Once in a while, our Health Manager invites a dentist who donates his services pro bono.

Fr. Rex offered to provide me with necessary financial support in case Peace Corps Manila disapproves of my extension. If that happens, we may have to figure out what to do about my visa. But we are looking into it and Fr. Rex promised to help. Everyone is praying for an extension, it's so heartwarming.

I really love being a Peace Corps volunteer and very proud of the work we do. Peace Corps has done a lot for me, especially in terms of showing me that the American way of doing things is not the only way, nor always the better way. It is humbling. And that the trappings of wealth are not always the answer to happiness; a simple way of life can be a source of utter joy and fulfillment.

Every day I see and hear this around me watching the T'boli and non-T'boli go about their daily lives. My T'boli neighbors are chanting all the time as though they don't have any care in the world. My colleagues always sing and so full of joy as though they'd burst if they didn't. When I present a slide show, the laughter of children is infectious when they see themselves on the big makeshift screen fashioned out of bed sheet.

I am looking into applying for teaching positions as a fall back in case all these plans do not materialize. Our best man, Matt Reisen, recently gave me an application for job openings at the Indian Reservations. Prima encouraged me to apply to one in South Dakota. They are looking for a business teacher. Regarding our planned trip to the states to use my earned home leave, we are not sure of that yet. So far, we still do not have Prima's visa. Frustrating.

We had a memorable Easter celebration here. The services were conducted mostly in T'boli. Fr. Rex, who is fluent in Ilongo as well, translated the Easter ceremonies into English so we non-T'boli speakers could understand. We had Agape Mass on Holy Thursday, where everyone eats a meal together. On Good Friday, the students had a drama portraying the crucifixion. It reminded us of the movie Jesus Christ Superstar. (Prima and I saw it in Cebu during our honeymoon). After the drama was a mass. Saturday evening was baptism. It starts with a bonfire using bamboo, which crackles and explodes like firecrackers.

From the fire, a candle is lit, representing the new fire. It was followed by the procession to the chapel. This year Sir Vir and his woodworking crew built a fountain outside in the ground next to the chapel.

The candle is dipped into the water as a sign of fertilization of the water. Then the school-age children are baptized by submersion. There is a lot of meaningful symbolism. The mixing of the fire and water represents the candle (man) fertilizing the water (woman). The submersion in baptism using the "fertilized" water symbolizes a new birth into the church of God. Following the baptism, we had mass and a meal.

The thing I like so much about Fr. Rex is the way he puts the mass into a context that the T'boli can relate to. It is spiritually uplifting to me. It might behoove you to consider the possibility of coming to the Philippines to visit us during a religious holiday like Christmas or Easter.

Prima has already written to you that Fr. Rex is on his way to the States. I gave him your address and also Joyce's. If he happens to call, please give him every courtesy, and if you can open your home to him, that would be nice. He is truly a wonderful and remarkable man. Only getting to know him can tell you that, though. I'll close for now because I want to write to Joyce, Dean, and Bud before the lights go off at nine.

Take care now. Oops, I almost forgot to tell you about our promotional campaign. Fr. Rex wants us to spread the word about Santa Cruz Mission and our work for the T'boli tribe. Prima wrote some newsworthy articles about the contributions of Peace Corps volunteers like Dottie and me. We are getting some pictures together. We will be sending you under a separate cover in a week or so.

Gladys, since you work at Tampa Tribune, could you submit it to them for publication? They are always looking for human-interest stories about the Peace Corps volunteers abroad.[4] Enid and Bud successfully got three stories about my work here published in papers in the Lehigh Valley area. If Tampa Tribune publishes our story, please send us five copies of the article. Please make sure to include the entire page where the article appears and dates and name of the newspaper for future reference.

If Prima's visa is issued soon and my extension request is approved, we'll take my home leave in July or August. Take care, Alvin

P.S. Our garden is thriving. We have squash that is now crawling all over our roof and bearing fruit too.

I installed a twenty-gallon can with a faucet atop our outdoor sink. The water from washing dishes was collected into a bucket below the sink and recycled to use for flushing our toilet. We designated a corner in the outhouse as our "shower" room with a five-gallon can always full of water for bathing. We took a "shower" by using a small can as a dipper and practiced the "pour and wash" method. Slowly but surely, we became self-sufficient, but our access to a steady supply of meat, especially beef and fish from the ocean via Canahay Road, was still limited.

THE CANAHAY Road never ceased to amaze me, not only because of the inherent danger every time one traveled, but because during the existence of Santa Cruz Mission, there had not been any major accidents with the Mission's vehicles. Once Pops Weaver's personnel carrier rolled down a ravine, as it started the climb on Canahay Road. It landed belly up! (It was the same vehicle mentioned in Chapter 1 from which this 'Kano had fallen after I had dozed off).

We were on the same road a few hours after the accident happened and saw the mangled body of the truck at the bottom of the ravine. Sir Vir told us that the passengers were able to jump out of the sides. Thank goodness for the roofless cab. Nobody died, just broken bones, cuts, and bruises. From the looks of the aftermath, it was a wonder that anyone survived.

Not only were the roads dangerous. The Mission trucks would certainly not meet American safety standards. Because every trip to town included a journey through the Allah Valley River, the brakes on the vehicles were deemed useless and, therefore, not maintained. The brake pad did not last because the lining got wet regularly. The mud stuck to it. We only had two vehicles during that time, the weapons carrier, and the Reo. One of these vehicles went down to Surallah at least three times a week and crossed the river twice on each trip.

To stop a vehicle, the driver shifted down and coasted to a stop. If needed, the driver could turn the key off, and the vehicle would come to an abrupt halt. One day, Bro. Louis was driving up the steep Canahay hill with its S turns. The transmission slipped out of gear. Bro. Louis sped down the mountain for a mile going backward. Amazingly there was no accident, and no one was hurt. Muddy or not, the Canahay route was one of the trickiest roads to navigate.

Another time, Prima and I were on our way to the city. Boning Landusan, a young T'boli driver barely five feet tall, was at the wheel of the weapons carrier. Seated next to Boning were two American ladies - Doris Porter, a Wycliffe Bible Translator from Sinolon, and the sister of Rev. Jared Barker, the Director at King's College of Marbel. They came to visit the Mission to look into some sort of collaborative project to translate the Bible to T'boli.

The trip was uneventful until we came to the bottom of the muddy hill. The road was level but slippery with a ten-foot ravine to the side. As the truck started sliding toward the drop-off, the two American ladies in the front seat turned extra white and started praying. Those of us on the back of the truck prepared to jump off. Boning had it all under control. He downshifted, turned off the ignition, and the weapons carrier skidded to a stop at the edge of the ravine. Without pausing, Boning started the engine, backed up to the middle of the road, and we continued on our way.

By the end of May, Prima reported the most attention-grabbing headlines of our letters to my family.

May 30, 1974
Dearest Dad, Gladys, and all,

We are going to have a baby! Dr. Yap confirmed it. I'm in my third month, and thank God I did not suffer any discomfort like nausea, morning sickness, etc. Al fusses over my diet, though, as I am a picky eater. But I am trying hard to be compliant for the baby's sake.

Linda Mai (yes, we are quite sure it's going to be a girl!), per doctor, will be arriving early December. Wouldn't it be nice if she were born on Al's birthday? We are naming her after our best friend Linda Basadre at the Promotions Office. Linda, in Spanish, means pretty. Mai is the name of the Datu Tuan (chieftain or leader) at the PANAMIN Settlement. (There's also a T'boli princess here in SCM nicknamed Mayang – May for short and pronounced "my" same as Mai). Pretty princess leader she'll be. After the visit to the doctor, we snorkeled among the beautiful corals at Tambler, something we had not done for a while. My mom was concerned because of my condition, but Dr. Yap said snorkeling is a good exercise.

End of April and the first week of May, we attended Al's Peace Corps Conference in Davao City. From there, we went to Cotabato City to see Becky Hsu (David's wife), who is on vacation from Boston. I appreciated her sharing her impressions of the U.S., joys, as well as challenges. She was in the U.S. for three years before she was able to come home for the first time. Al promised me that I could go visit my family after three years too.

We just came home from the Orientation of new employees and the annual SCM General Meeting. Al lectured about our work at the Promotions Office...he looked quite snappy wearing the shirt from our wedding. Our staff is growing in number. I think we are close to

300 now – mostly T'boli and eighty non-T'boli. Till the next letter, Prima

Meat - beef, pork, or chicken - was still very scarce at the Mission. But compared to the year before I arrived, the meat supply had improved considerably. The SCM Piggery Department butchered meat on market day (Saturday) to make them available to the T'boli as well as employees. Or we'd "hunt" for meat. Hunting entailed being the first to spot a T'boli coming down the hill during the market day carrying a basketful of freshwater clams or tilapia, or the most prized meat of all – chicken!

I can only remember two instances that I got lucky. Once, just before a T'boli vendor reached the market, I met him halfway as he came down the hill and bought the old rooster he was carrying. Prima prepared the scalding pot for the removal of the chicken feathers. When the hot water was almost ready, I tied the chicken's feet securely (or so I thought). My wife ran inside the house the moment I positioned the chicken on the chopping block. She did not have the heart to watch a chicken being butchered.

I gave the rooster's neck a whack with a sharp *bolo*. A commotion followed. Prima came out of the back door, laughing hysterically as she watched the chicken, feet untied, literally "running around the yard with its head cut off." It flew over the barbed wire fence and kept on going, still flapping its wings in the field behind our house. When the old grisly, headless rooster finally stopped, I went over to the other side of the fence to pick up its limp body. We enjoyed a good meal for a few days.

Another time, we invited the DHOP girls and some guys over for a party. At dinnertime, someone asked, "Sir Al, how many chickens did you butcher? I counted at least four drumsticks."

After the guests were all sated and dinner was over, I took a poll. "How many of you liked the adobo tonight?" All hands went up, followed by a chorus of, "Delicious, yummy, 'love them."

I fessed up. "I only butchered one chicken. But it had four legs!"

"Oh, the poor rabbit," they lamented when they caught on. The ladies did not stop coming to our house, but I don't remember if they ate rabbits again after that.

We also had five laying hens that were the subject of our visitor's scrutiny one night. "Hey Sir Al, how come you always have eggs from your chicken? You don't even have a rooster."

"Hens lay eggs without a rooster," I replied.

"We don't believe you. You must put some kind of special potion in the feeds to make them lay eggs."

Even Prima was incredulous the first time I told her that the hens produce unfertilized eggs all the time. "It's only when the farmer wants chicks that a rooster comes into a hen's life," I informed her.

THE SCHOOL year in the Philippines is in June to March and summer vacation in April and May. The T'boli high school and college students either came home to the Mission or to their families. Bert Sman, a high school kid who was a pupil of Prima in sixth grade, came back to the Mission to earn some money after visiting his mother and siblings for a few days. Prima's fifty-year-old and unmarried aunt, Eyay Eya, came to live with us that summer. She practically ran the Guipo household since 1947 and raised Prima, her younger brother, and sister while Mrs. Guipo taught in public school.

Although Eyay Eya only speaks Ilongo and I only know Tagalog, somehow, we understood each other. Mr. Guipo's father, Mateo, and Eyay Eya's father were brothers. Mateo adopted Eyay when her parents died during World War II. She was sixteen. After her only sister Charing got married and migrated to Mindanao with her husband, Eyay followed to live with them. Charing died in childbirth shortly after Eyay arrived. Orphaned, Eyay moved in with Prima's family and lived with them for the rest of her life.

While barely legible, she learned to sign her full name Eulogia Inego Guipo, but that was it. Eyay was about four-feet tall, had no formal education, but she was intelligent. She cooked very well too. To keep herself busy, she mended all my socks and shirts and did our laundry. She also enjoyed working with Bert in the garden.

Among my Peace Corps memorabilia, I found a letter that I wrote to my family about Eyay Eya and Bert Sman. Bert was a skinny boy with a fragile physique whose face looked older than his age. He was a very intense kid who didn't seem to know how to relax. Bert worked on projects non-stop. He epitomized the T'boli children whose biggest dream in life was to go to college.

June 4, 1974
Santa Cruz Mission, Lake Sebu
Dear Gladys, Dad and all,

All our plans are in a state of suspension at the moment. The Peace Corps hasn't notified us about my extension. We should hear this month and will promptly update you.

There is a topic I started in a letter to Joyce but did not finish. Roberto Sman, nicknamed Bert, is going to second-year high school. Bert is our "adopted" T'boli son. It started with my sponsoring him in the mission's school adoption program. I pay P15 monthly to help support his schooling. (U.S. adoptions are $15 monthly for High School and $5 for elementary. Prima's office manages this Sponsor-A-Child program).

Bert's father died when he was still small. His mother worked hard so Bert and his sister could continue their schooling. Bert attended the Mission school grades 1-6 and stayed in the mission dormitory since his mother's home is a full day's hike from here. Another family, Ma'am Ang and Sir Vir Maghari gave Bert the family support he needed from third grade through sixth grade.

This summer, Bert worked around our home. He and I planted our entire lot with all kinds of vegetables. Together, we built the chicken cages out of bamboo and scrap lumber. He fixed some of the rabbit hutches for me and fenced our house with bamboo poles to keep stray cows and horses from eating our plants in our garden.

Bert is also a big help in the kitchen. He'd get lunch started before we came home from the office, and always offer to wash the dishes and did other work around the house. Bert is really industrious. On Saturdays, he would go to the market and cut hair for 70 centavos (10¢ US dollar) per person. Instead of foolishly spending his money, this boy would give it to us to save for him. He has P27 pesos deposited with us ($4 U.S.).

During his summer vacation, Bert ate his meals with us and, in the end, even slept in our extra room. We bought Bert his clothes and school supplies and paid for his enrollment for high school this year. We also plan to give him some spending money from time to time. One weekend we gave him some money and sent him home to visit his mother. He came back with two young chickens for us.

Last month, we brought Bert to Dadiangas when we visited Prima's parents. We really had a good time at the beach. Especially Bert – that was only his second time to swim in the sea. The first time was when he was in Prima's sixth grade class, and she took the whole class for a field trip...I gave him his first snorkeling lesson.

Last Saturday, Bert had all his worldly possessions packed in two small cardboard boxes. With a big smile on his face, he boarded the truck and went off to Surallah for another year of high school. We sure miss Bert around here – not just for the work he has done for us but because he is such a good boy, honest, polite, and well-meaning. We sure wish him all the best there is and hope he can continue his schooling through college.

Prima's aunt is still living with us. She was diagnosed with TB. I doubt the accuracy of the diagnosis because she is not showing any symptoms. She has kidney issues, however, and was given medication. Not being able to read and write, I had to fashion something to help her take her medication regularly. I found an old calendar and wrapped

each of her pills in plastic and pasted one for each day of the week.
She follows instructions very well, she now takes her medication even
when she is alone at the house, and we're at work… That's all for now.
Take care. Alvin

(We sponsored Bert through high school and college. He wrote
to us regularly. During the summer breaks, he stayed with
Mr. & Mrs. Guipo in General Santos and earned extra money
helping Mrs. Guipo sell coconuts from the twenty-four trees
growing in the Guipo's yard. When I waved goodbye to Bert
before he left for high school, it was the last time I saw him.
Sadly Bert died of complications from pneumonia while he
was in college. However, Prima went home with our daughter
for a month in May 1977. Bert stayed at the Lagao house to be
with Prima for three weeks. He enjoyed babysitting for Linda
and her cousins and going to the beach).

THERE WERE days at the Mission that just stood out among
the rest. The day described in my letter below was one of
them. It started as one of those ordinary days. I got up, fed
the chickens, had breakfast, got ready for work, and by eight
o'clock, I was at the Promotions Office poring over a table laden
with project proposals that had been reviewed by the non-
profit organizations and were returned for minor revisions.
On top was a letter from the Peace Corps. My ordinary day
ceased to be.

June 28, 1974

Dear Gladys, Dad and all,

Good news and bad news. The bad news first – Peace Corps did
not grant the extension I requested. That means my contract ends on
August 15, one month and a half from now. At first, we considered
staying on our own until our baby is born and take Fr. Rex's offer to
support us financially. But there's the issue of my visa. I don't know if
it can be extended if I were not a Peace Corps anymore. Fr. Rex won't
be back until September. I am not sure how much help he could give

us regarding my visa, considering he is still in the U.S. Last night, we made our final decision.

The good news we are going to see you sooner than we expected! Our target date is the last week of October or the first week of November. That may seem like a long time. However, for us, time is drawing short because we plan to leave the Mission before August 15.

Bro. Louis is beside himself. He sent a cable to Fr. Rex in the States who responded and reiterated his offer for us to stay. Our friends here, both T'boli and non-T'boli, are so sad, we are sadder. Our General Manager Qric told us that many of the staff offered to donate a certain amount from their own salary toward my financial support just so we could stay.

We have so many projects in the works I really hate to leave without giving the Mission time to train anyone, not only to take over my job but, most importantly, to find a replacement for Prima. We met with Sir Qric and Bro. Louis to strategize our next move. There are potential candidates that we have identified, but we have to train them immediately. We only have a month and a half to do it. Fr. Rex would like to try and contact the Peace Corps on my behalf to see if we could buy some time. I sent Fr. Rex the contact information for Barry Devine, the new country director, who took over a month ago.

Just a few words about the Mission and our work that is so heartening. Another project proposal I submitted was approved. This is to help sixty T'boli farmers pay off what they owe the Mission Co-op, buy work animals, and plows for developing their land to rice and corn. The amount is equivalent to $50,000 (P6 to a $1) and comes from the Philippine Business for Social Progress, a Filipino foundation. The other proposal that was funded before this was for the Calamansi Project for $69,000 equivalent in dollars. Also, from a Filipino non-government foundation, the name of which escapes me now. I sure would like to see all these projects implemented before I leave. However, the personal aspect of my life now takes precedence.

Last weekend, we were in Bolul Mission. Fr. Felix loaned me a Travel Trailer magazine to read. I got excited to travel again and remembered the Volkswagen Campers I used to own. I suggested to

Prima that we leave after August 16 and travel via Europe on our way to the States. In Germany, we can buy a VW Camper and bring it to the States with us. We can use the camper for a rolling house when we visit friends or go job hunting.

Crazy idea, I thought, but Prima really liked the idea and said, "Let's go!" We also figure that we can put $1000 that we would spend here to have the baby and to live on, into a car, which we will need in the States. Either way, I would probably have to look for a job upon arrival in the States.

Take care now. Oh, by the way, we plan on being in the States for a few years. I still want to go back to school to take a master's in Anthropology. If you still want to visit the Philippines, maybe we can make that trip together. Love, Al and Prima

While we lived in Lake Sebu, Prima and I wrote a lot of letters to my in-laws too. Sometimes we'd arrive at their house before the message. This is the only one that survived from that period.

July 21, 1974

Dear Nanay & Tatay and all,

This is just a rush note to inform you that we have to make a quick trip to Cebu City for the mission's Promotions Program. We will be flying all the way. We expect to be back in Lagao on August 1 but may be delayed a day or so depending on the transportation and our getting things packed here. We will spend a week or so finalizing things in General Santos (police clearance, etc.) and say goodbye to friends. Then we'd be on our way to Manila. Please tell Eyay Eya to be packed and ready to leave around August 15.

This trip to Cebu is not on our schedule and puts a tight squeeze on our time, but we have worked things out. I think everything will be okay. It may also work to our advantage since Prima can possibly work on her security clearance in Cebu. We received a wire that my Peace Corps representative in Cebu picked up Prima's passport. He will forward it to Susan in Manila.

That's all for now. Prima is at home this morning while I am in the office. Someone will bring this message down. I'll take advantage of writing this note even without any word from Prima. Take care. See you all on August 1. Alvin

July 30, 1974
Lagao, General Santos City
Dear Dad, Gladys and all,

I hope this letter finds you all well and happy. We are all fine here. You may, however, think we're crazy. We changed plans again—all the sooner to be in the U.S. and see you.

We are at the Guipo's house right now. We recently learned that Prima would have to go straight to U.S. soil because of her immigrant visa. We decided to scrap the idea of going to Germany and tour Europe in a Volkswagen van. We're going to Hawaii instead to visit for about a week. I will check on the possibilities of going to school there. (Dr. Solheim, the archeologist that I had a chance to go on a digging escapade just outside of General Santos two years ago, teaches at the University of Hawaii).

From there we would like to visit friends on the west coast. We have not made any arrangements yet. From the west coast, we may take either a bus or plane, depending on circumstances, to the east coast, PA, or Florida depending on time. All the volunteers in my Group 31 did some traveling on their way home around Asia, the Middle East, and Europe. I'd like to do the same to treat Prima and myself after over five years in the Peace Corps.

Actually, we will be here at the Guipo's house for another week or two and then in Manila another week or two. I need to process my exit papers at Peace Corps/Manila and may have to follow-up on Prima's visa to find out what's the hold-up. We plan to go by ship from here to Manila...We were out to the beach this morning to snorkel and gather corals and shells. If I don't get back to this letter, we will try to write again on the boat to Manila. Love, Al and Prima

July 30, 1974
Dear Joyce, Earl and all,

As I had written to Dad, we have to go directly to U.S. soil because of Prima's immigrant visa. We also found out that the airlines won't allow pregnant passengers to travel after seven months...

The letter you sent from Florida arrived last week. In it, you sounded like you were disgusted with the mechanical difficulties on the airplane and the thirty-minute delay it caused you. I sort of laugh inside because that happens here almost anytime we fly.

Last week, we took a plane to Cebu City. Going there, we had a stopover in Davao. We were delayed for mechanical difficulties too. Coming back, the flight from Davao to General Santos was canceled because of the rain. So, we took the bus from Davao to here – only five hours this time on the new route. I'll let Prima tell you what we did in Cebu.

This is Prima. It sure is clever of Al to talk me into finishing his letter! Anyway, our recent trip to Cebu City was one of those last-minute arrangements. Bro. Louis received a telegram from our Management consultants that they needed someone from the Mission to speak at the Fund-Raising Gala at P30pesos a plate ($5). We had no plans to go because we barely have enough time to get ready to leave the Mission no later than August 5 – less than a week from now. But nobody else was available or willing to do it at such short notice. Since the fund-raising campaign is under the purview of my office, Al and I went.

The experience is something to write home about. For one, we only brought one set of casual clothes for the weekend, and for the gala a barong for Al and a T'boli outfit for me. Upon arrival at the airport, our host, who picked us up, said we were going to appear on TV that evening and live during the newscast to advertise the gala. It sure shook both of us! Here we are, Al in his muddy and holey old shoes to appear on TV. So we frantically went shopping. Al bought a shirt for him; I got a blouse for me, and shoes for us both. To top it all, the unexpected shopping blew our personal budget. Luckily, the Mission *gave us money for the business trip. We have to refund them when we get back.*

Al confessed that he is suffering from another cultural shock. Being with very successful young professionals of his age, riding in their Mercedes Benz, seeing their big and beautiful houses, in professions with high-paying jobs, or running their own business, Al felt so poor next to them. My husband is ready to go home to the States and earn money, not necessarily to get rich, just enough to live comfortably. I pointed out to him that there are colleagues at the Mission who probably view us in the same light as he sees these successful, wealthy people we are mingling with. It's a matter of perspective, I suppose. But I must admit, he is right. Someday when we write our life story, Chapter 5 will be titled, "Country Mice Went to Cebu City."

The TV show turned out very well, considering that we were not prepared. Last year, when we appeared on TV, they gave us more prep time. Al looked competent and confident in his new shirt and new shoes. The TV news director requested that I wear my T'boli attire because she wanted me to look authentic. She thought I was a T'boli, so I played the part.

Al was so nervous a few hours before the show. Once it started, he fared so well. I was calmer because I was just in the background as they interviewed the star. A handsome star if I may say so. (They loaded my face with make-up and told us that no matter how intense the camera lights are, not to wipe our face or neck, etc. We did not see the footage of the newscast, but I was soaking wet by the time we finished filming live).

At the gala party the following night, Al showed slides of the T'boli Way of Life. We both created the slide show. Usually, our Education Manager, Ma'am Em, presents them to universities and civic organizations in Manila. This was the first time we viewed our own slide show inside a big hall on the big screen (not using a bedsheet!). While Al was presenting the slides, I sold T'boli handicrafts that the Mission had shipped for the purpose. We had a great time. The gala was well attended. The leader of the management group wants to make this an annual event.

Al's Peace Corps regional boss and his wife – Brian and Cely Furby, attended the dinner. She is a Filipina too, and she wore a T'boli costume like I did. We stayed at their house, and I had a ball tasting the American dishes that her maid prepared. Although we had visited them before, I was acutely more observant of their American way of life now that I am married to an American.

Right now, we are back at my folks in General Santos City. We snorkeled all day at the beach below the Monastery that belongs to the Passionist Priests. It was kind of secluded and very private. The underwater life was fantastic. I was tempted to touch the lionfish – they were that close - but Al warned me they were poisonous. We plan to do more snorkeling before we leave for the U.S.

We are leaving very early tomorrow to go back to the mountains for a week or so. It will be a sad affair to say goodbye to everyone at the Mission and our way of life here. But there's so much to do yet so I won't have time to wallow in sadness. My friend Linda Basadre, who had been working with me for over a year, will take over my job. She is highly qualified, but she worries about writing and editing articles. I assured her that Fr. Rex would be back soon. He can do that part of her job as she learns.

An administrative staff named Flor Gabato is replacing Al. She'll have a steeper learning curve, but she will be fine. She already knows how to operate the SLR camera and attachments after a few days of working with Al. That's half of the job. As to researching feasibility studies, writing concept papers, and preparing budgets for project proposals for funding, it is a learned craft. Fr. Rex can also guide and instruct.

Al and I try not to think about leaving our house, our garden, the Mission, and the friends we treasure. Or we'd just break down and cry. We look forward instead to what lies ahead in the U.S. Take care, Prima

P.S. from Al. Here's an update to our schedule. Leave Lake Sebu on August 5. Leave General Santos August 15 or before. Leave Manila Sept 1 or as soon as Prima's passport and visa are ready. I hope you don't mind too much that we keep changing plans and that our dates are so open because plans must often change due to circumstances we cannot control.

WE WERE back in Lake Sebu the following day. Two days later, our friends celebrated Prima's birthday, combined with the going away party at the Clubhouse on a Friday night. It was bittersweet. On the eve of our departure, our very close friends came to our house. We butchered two hens. I gave the other three live ones to Sir Vir.

On Monday, August 5, we said goodbye to our life with the T'boli. Boning eased the weapons carrier out of the motor pool shed. Bro. Louis, Sir Qric, and the employees standing by the Administration office waved at us. We waved back as we both tried to hold back the tears, quite unsuccessfully.

We stayed in General Santos for ten days. Half of the time, we invited friends to the beach where we said our goodbyes. Prima's four siblings were living in Manila. Mr. and Mrs. Guipo decided to follow us there. Tito, who was a Comptroller at San Miguel Beer Company in Davao City, also planned to join us in Manila. Angelo and his family and the youngest sister Diana, could not go because of work and school. They spent the night at the Guipo house for a mini-reunion before we left.

During martial law, all passengers boarding a plane or a ship had to present some form of identification. Since Eyay Eya was going with us, we discussed this kink in our plans with Angelo. Eyay Eya had to produce an I.D. She was listening intently with a worried look on her face. Angelo mentioned that any identification form like a *cedula*[5] would do. When Eyay heard the word *cedula,* she ran upstairs and came back with a piece of brown paper covered with creases. When she migrated to Mindanao in 1947, she had to get a *cedula.* We looked at the document that she held in her hand. It was dated 1946, bearing her signature Eulogia Inego Guipo. Eyay had kept her I.D. inside her wooden *baul* (trunk) all these years, and it was still valid.

Our ten days in General Santos City was over too soon. As M/V Filipinas pulled out of Sarangani Bay, Prima and I stood hand in hand by the stern of the ship. We watched the imposing Mt. Matutum fade away at sundown. I stayed transfixed with wonder until the darkness of night swallowed Sarangani Bay too. The lights from the city slowly faded as the fastest ship in the Philippines picked up speed.

We retraced our way to our cabin. The mixed emotions were gut wrenching. I comforted myself with the knowledge that wherever Prima and I end up, we will always have a special place in our hearts for Lake Sebu, General Santos, Sarangani Bay, and Mt. Matutum, the people who inhabit them and who enriched our lives.

Prima wrote to my father on his 59th birthday:

August 25, 1974
Quezon City, Philippines
Dear Dad and all,
   On your birthday we are thinking of you!
   We are here in Manila now. We are staying at my sister Susan's two-bedroom apartment. It is a bit tight with ten folks but the crowdier the merrier. Filipinos are used to it. Al had adjusted. My parents arrived last Friday with cousin Francisco "Noning" Sumatra.[6] He just finished his studies as a Merchant Marine. We are proud of him. He is one of those typical hardworking Filipinos who seek a better life so he can help his family overcome poverty. He will stay with my sister while he applies for jobs at international commercial shipping companies. My brother Tito and his son Ian will join us just before we leave on September 5. (Mother is playing gin rummy with Al – he just lost!).
   Our boat ride from General Santos City was satisfactory. We were delayed twelve hours because of a terrible storm. The boat had to seek shelter close to an island after we left Cebu. The streets of Manila were flooded when we arrived and continue to this day. Classes are

suspended, so my siblings are home. It's just like growing up in the old house being together here.

Al's training director Mr. Mel Beetle took us to our first Japanese dinner at a restaurant last night. It was definitely upscale, with a manicured Japanese garden at the entrance, waiters, and waitresses in Japanese costume, and you have a choice of sitting by a low table, shoes off, and seated on the floor or on a regular chair by a dining table. We chose the latter. We were given chopsticks to eat. Al was finding it darn hard to pick up rice with two thin sticks. After trying with little success for a few minutes, he finally gave up and asked for a spoon and a fork. I did too!

Joyce's letter was waiting for us here in Manila. She and Enid had arranged for our baby to be born at the Allentown Hospital. Dean was so kind to offer us to stay at his place until such time that Al finds a full-time job. Al was apprehensive about the future, but having all these essential things settled before our departure lifted a load off his shoulder. We are truly grateful for having a supportive and caring family such as yours. When our baby is old enough, maybe I could find myself a job too. I will leave room for Al to finish this letter. See you soon.

August 28...letter from Al.

Happy belated birthday, Dad! I woke up at four this morning and could not sleep. Yesterday, Prima got her visa, finally! While she sat waiting at the U.S. Embassy, I went around to a dozen airlines and travel agents. I was able to come up with a discounted fare on Air Siam that will save us $113 on the transportation to the west coast. The route will permit us to stopover in Hawaii for a few days with no extra cost for the airfare. The hotel and food would cost a lot, so we decided to cancel our visit to Hawaii this time.

Yesterday, we also were visiting with Barry Devine, the Director of the Peace Corps in the Philippines. Someone I consider a friend. We've been to dinner at their house, and he has always been supportive of my work. He and his wife Sue were invited to our wedding. However, it was during Christmas, and they couldn't come. He advised us that

Los Angeles is about the best place to buy a car and especially if we're interested in campers. He also suggested that it might be cheaper to drive across the country than take a bus.

August 30...I made our final reservations for our flight yesterday. We are now booked on Northwest Orient Airlines for Thursday, September 5, at 11:15 AM, leaving Manila. We change planes in Tokyo and then on to Honolulu and Los Angeles arriving the same day (we cross the International Dateline we gain a day). We will stay in California for five days to buy a camper and adjust to the time change.

We will travel through California, Oregon, Washington. Included in our stops are the University of Oregon (to check on the Anthropology master's program and visit Gene Ryman, our godfather at our wedding from Dole), and Space Needle in Seattle on to Spokane, WA visiting friends along the way. And the good news, I also received a job offer to teach at the Indian Reservation in Eagle Butte, South Dakota. We plan to check it out if we decide to drive cross-country.

Mr. Guipo is helping me build the crates for our stuff. The crates we're packing will be sent to Philadelphia. It will be easy for us to pick up from Allentown. Bud and Dean will help me. They can also help turn the crates into furniture. We used the variety of hardwood called Philippine red mahogany. See you soon. Alvin

P.S. At the moment, Prima's younger brother Felipe is playing the guitar that I bought for her in Cebu. Felipe is an excellent guitarist; he should make a successful performer. He plucks the guitar like Chet Atkins. We are so happy that he is taping an hour's worth of our favorite songs for us. Prima plays the guitar also. I promised her one before leaving for the States. That will have to replace the TV or stereo that most Americans would have.

NO SOONER had I finished the last paragraph of my letter than the Guipo siblings broke into a hearty rendition of *Leaving on a Jet Plane*. The song tugged at my heart; I could not hold back the tears.

I recalled the time I reported at the former nudist camp in Escondido and again in Hilo, Hawaii. A group of volunteers would gather at night and sing the same song. *"All my bags are packed, I'm ready to go. I'm standing here outside your door, I hate to wake you up to say goodbye...Cuz I'm leaving on a jet plane, don't know when I'll be back again..."* [7]

Prima and I went to bed that night with our minds and hearts all set to leave for the United States of America. "Nothing could stop us now," I thought to myself.

The following morning, on a dismal and stormy day, we received a telegram from Fr. Rex. JUST ARRIVED STOP PLEASE MEET ME ASAP STOP, it read.

A driver picked us up at Susan's apartment and took us to the Passionist House in Loyola Heights, Quezon City, about twenty minutes away.

"You would never guess what I have to tell you," was the first thing Fr. Rex said when we arrived at the House. "I went to see Barry Devine at the Peace Corps Office as soon as I arrived. He said you could stay for another year."

Prima and I just looked at each other wide-eyed and in total amazement. I went through the emotional wringer all over again, albeit briefly. Mixed emotions washed over me. Stay? Or Not?

On the one hand, it felt so good to know that the Mission still needed our services enough that Fr. Rex would go to such trouble. On the other, I felt like a heel having to let Fr. Rex down and not easy. But there was no time to debate with myself this time.

We told him that we had made our final decision, bought our tickets for L.A., were leaving in a few days, and the two crates filled with our worldly goods were on their way to the Port of Philadelphia. Fr. Rex was obviously saddened as we were, but he did not try to talk us out of it. He understood.

We were walking toward the Passionist House exit gate when we heard the bells of the *sorbetero* (mobile ice cream vendor). Fr. Rex flagged him down and bought each of us an ice cream cone. It was a plain, ordinary, simple *merienda*, yet the moment was indelibly seared into my memory. Fr. Rex recalled the moment too, he recently wrote: "And I can never forget the two of you, newlyweds meeting me in Manila before your trip home, bedraggled and underfed but happiest two love birds."

Fr. Rex gave us his sister Pat Mansmann's address in Pasadena, CA, upon hearing that our port of entry was Los Angeles. He said he'd call Pat and their younger sister Joey to arrange to pick us up at the airport. We hugged and said we'd keep in touch.

On September 5, 1974, Prima's family bid us goodbye at the Manila International Airport.

As the Northwest flight was on its way to Tokyo, I reached across the seat for Prima's hand. This time she clasped my hand back as though her life depended on it.

"You know I was just thinking..."

"No wonder I see smoke coming out of your head," I teased.

"I thought that goodbye is the saddest seven-letter word."

"I agree. It is worse than culture shock."

"Worse than amoebic dysentery?" she asked.

"Yeah," I said. "At least with amoebic dysentery, I could take medication and get some kind of relief."

She squeezed love into my hand as we watched the flight stewardess walk down the aisle, giving out menus for lunch. I welcomed the interruption. My wife was on the verge of tears, and I was not far from the brink myself.

"Wow, they even have menus?" Prima exclaimed. "And look at this, steak, Cornish hen...hmm, I think I will order Cornish hen."

"You're passing up on the steak?"

"I've had steak before, but I have never tasted a Cornish hen," was her reply. "You think I'd like it?"

"You'll never know until you try, right?" I mimicked her favorite expression when a new Filipino dish was put before me to try. She looked at me and smiled. The flight stewardess brought our meals.

"Oh my, look at this, real silverware!" Prima said, wonderment written all over her face. "You think I can ask for a pair for a souvenir?"

After lunch, Prima looked pensive. I held her hand and asked, "Still feeling sad about the goodbyes?"

"Yes, but it could be worse," she reasoned. "At least, to each other, you and I, we don't have to say goodbye."

"So why the pensive look on your face?"

"The stewardess forgot to bring the silverware that she promised," was what she said. I could not help but smile.

I thought of the thick steak, mashed potatoes, green beans, salad, and roll that I ate for lunch. What a meal! It reminded me of the first flight I took when I reported for training five and a half years before. My Peace Corps experience had come full circle.

Unlike on my first ever airplane ride, I was not alone. I have Prima as a reminder of the unforgettable and rewarding segment of my life – the Peace Corps years.

And it's not only for a moment but daily, for the rest of my life.

POSTSCRIPT
Fifty Years Later

DAVID SEARLES was the Peace Corps Country Director in the Philippines for three of the five and a half years of my stint there. On the last page of his book *The Peace Corps Experience - Challenge & Change,* he wrote: "Did the Peace Corps make a difference? The answer must be a resounding yes. First, the Peace Corps experience changed those who were part of it... At the same time, the American image in the Third World has been softened, humanized, and made more representative of the country at its best..."[1]

I can unequivocally say that my Peace Corps experience changed me for the better. I can only hope that I did represent my country as best I could.

In this chapter, my goal is threefold: to provide then and now pictures, to share a glimpse into my life after Peace Corps, and to highlight the compelling stories of five Returned Peace Volunteers who served with me in the same province of South Cotabato. As Searles opined in his book, "...Finally, the Peace Corps has made a difference in the way development is practiced and in the way that many in the Third World live their lives."[2]

The stories of my RPCV friends illustrate the assertions that Searles has made in his book. Our narratives have a common thread. We all wholeheartedly admit that Peace Corps changed our lives. However, we have always wondered how much difference we made on the lives of the individuals we served. Writing this book, we encountered many of the men and women whose lives we have touched. Thanks to the Internet and social media that reconnected us to the people from our past. I included some stories of their updated lives here. They all agreed that the presence of the Peace Corps in their lives had made a positive influence.

It is difficult to quantify my impact on more than 500 students at Notre Dame College, who attended my classes. But the teaching experience sure had a profound effect on me. The warm sense of belonging is still palpable from the time that I taught there. It serves as a constant reminder that there is still so much we could do as Returned Peace Corps Volunteers.

My gratifying experiences in the Philippines and the desire to give back propelled me to assist Prima in establishing three Children's Libraries at the Notre Dame Schools. In 2004, my family sponsored the first Children's Library - The Trinidad and Doroteo Guipo Learning Center at Notre Dame of Dadiangas College (NDDC), where I had taught. A visionary Marist Brother and then President of NDDC, Bro. Willy Lubrico made this collaborative project possible.

We sponsored two more libraries later. The Hower-Bates Library at Notre Dame-Sienna College in partnership with the Directress, Sister Mailyn Bolivar in 2017; and in 2019, The Alvin & Prima Hower Library at the Notre Dame of Marbel University again working with Bro. Willy Lubrico after he transferred to Marbel as President.

All three libraries are dedicated to children and young adults from one to eighteen years old. I would not have seen the need nor appreciated its import on the lives of the Filipino children had I not joined the Peace Corps. A majority of these kids have never owned a book.

Our biggest donor of books is the Barrington Public Library in Rhode Island. Monetary donations used to partially subsidize the cost of shipping come from The Friends of the Hower-Bates Library. The Friends network includes former colleagues of Prima at Brown University School of Engineering and the University of South Florida College of Nursing. Support also comes from the Notre Dame University Alumni Associations, my children Linda and Lee, and their circle of friends, and strangers who heard about our advocacy.

Our granddaughters, on their birthdays, request their guests to donate new or gently used books in place of gifts. (Prima affirms, *A book no matter how old is new to one who hasn't read it.*) In addition to the three family-sponsored libraries at the Notre Dame Schools, we supply books to thirty other libraries in the barrios and the public schools located in Luzon, Visayas, and Mindanao. Three of these libraries have high enrollees of indigenous people; one is dedicated to T'boli kids exclusively.[3] In 2018 and 2019, we sent over 25,000 donated books to the Philippines.

THEN AND NOW.

Through Prima on Facebook, I receive progress reports from a number of my students at Notre Dame of Dadiangas College. I have met many of them at alumni reunions held in the U.S.A. One of my former students, Roberto Borromeo, wrote:

> In 1970, I enrolled in Economics 1, which was a required subject in the Bachelor of Arts (A.B.) curriculum. I thought the first session would be uneventful, just like any of my classes, which were handled by instructors, with whom my classmates and I were familiar. We were in for a surprise when an 'Americano' came in. Initially, I thought he was a Marist Brother recently assigned to Dadiangas. But after the brief introduction, I found out that he was a Peace Corps Volunteer. Like any typical Filipino, most of us in the class were in awe as this was the first time we would be in a class handled by a foreigner.
>
> This 'Americano' had a way of simplifying complex concepts, making everyone at ease and encouraging even those who had difficulty with the English language to speak up and participate in class discussions.
>
> At the cognitive level, it was in that Econ 1 class, where I learned about the essential factors of production: land, labor, and capital. Knowledge about these factors remains relevant to me when I discuss productivity in the New Economy with my graduate students. It

facilitates an understanding of productivity in an era where intellectual ability, creativity, and technology have overshadowed land, labor, and capital in the process of productivity and wealth creation.

At the affective domain, Mr. Hower's class, characterized by respect for each person and opportunities for everyone to be heard, shows that learning is possible in a 'relaxed' classroom.

Thank you, Sir Al, for laying the foundation for my understanding of Economics. (The basics helped me when I did a course on Economics of Education in De La Salle University-Manila and in London). And for helping instill in me the value of respecting every learner in the classroom.

Roberto Borromeo, Ph.D., became the Vice-Principal of Marist School Manila, the President of FAPE (Fund for Assistance to Private Education), also Associate Professor and Dean at De La Salle University in Manila, and the current President of Elizabeth Seton School in the Philippines (as of publication).

The two teachers that I replaced Miss Vitaliana Cabatingan and Mr. Leonardo M. Yu received their Masters in Teaching Economics. They are both happily retired after successful careers in academia, business, and government sectors. I heard from Nards Yu recently:

Your writing a book about your happy and unforgettable memories of your sojourn in the Philippines as a Peace Corps Volunteer and as a professor at the Notre Dame of Dadiangas College is an attestation of your deep understanding and affection for the Filipinos, its culture and cultural heritage. You have more than proven this when you embraced our traditions and married Prima, our best friend.

I do appreciate and thank you for unselfishly and ably taking my place as a professor in Economics at NDDC in 1969-71. Otherwise, I could not have obtained my MA in Teaching Economics from the Ford Foundation Scholarship.

Kahlil Gibran says: a man who shares his fortune with others is a good man but a man who shares himself – his time, efforts, and knowledge is a great man!

Mabuhay ka Al, my friend. You are much, much more than "great" for me, for my wife Beth, and my family.

May God grant you all the time, wisdom, strength, and inspiration to accomplish *No Greater Service*, as it would be a lasting legacy for your family and for the future generations in the Philippines, in the U.S., and for the rest of the world.

Leonardo Yu taught at Notre Dame College for many years, concurrently serving as the Registrar, after I transferred to the Parish Social Action office. He left Notre Dame, and the Philippine Port Authority in Manila hired him as one of its executives. Nards Yu's claim to fame is the invention of the award-winning Challenge 21. It is a fun-to-play multi-layer board game intended to enhance mental skills through the formation and/or blocking of nature-inspired shapes and patterns with mathematical logic. It won the Gold Medal award from the World Intellectual Property Organization (WIPO) of Geneva, Switzerland & *Tuklas* Award (Outstanding Invention) awarded by the Department of Science and Technology of the Philippines.

Notre Dame of Dadiangas College[4] is now a university and boasts of 1800 solar panels on its roof, a brand new air-conditioned school bus, offers masters and doctorate degrees, and college enrollment of 2,854 (2019-2020 school year). There are five colleges –Architecture/Engineering & Technology, Arts & Sciences, Health Sciences, Education, and Business. The latter has the highest enrollment at 868. To put that in context, the total population of Notre Dame College when I taught there in 1969-1971 was about 700. There are numerous active alumni associations in the United States, Canada, and in the Philippines with group websites.

When I think of Notre Dame, I think of Bro. Henry Ruiz. One of the buildings at NDDU is named after him. Bro. Paul Meuten, who met me at the airport when I first arrived in General Santos City in 1969, and who now lives in New York, wrote an article about Bro. Henry.

> Bro. Henry was a kind man. Students remember him for help with mathematics and accommodation if their financial resources did not enable them to pay school fees on time. Testimonies even point out those students would borrow money from him. The reasons that were given varied. Some borrowed for "personal necessities," such as food or "facial enhancement items" (these generally covering other terms of dire necessity), or the release of official school records, as such required full payment of all school obligations based on a promise that their first salary would be used to repay their account.

Bro. Henry gave special discount to faculty members who supported many relatives in school, according to Bro Paul. "They were told under the strict order of confidentiality on an individual basis...And one such beneficiary told the writer that she could not join a faculty strike in later years because of Bro. Henry's kindness. As a host, Bro. Henry always had a piece of better meat in the refrigerator for visitors."

Born in Palencia Spain on March 23, 1910, Bro. Henry was on family visit when he got caught up in the Spanish Civil War.

Bro. Paul continued, "...he was conscripted as a translator on the Franco side...reproduced excerpts from two of his letters in 1939, Bro. Henry briefly describes the situation at the national and family level, corresponding with his sister, who had to use a pseudonym through an address in Paris."

At age fifty, Bro. Henry volunteered for the Philippine Mission, arriving there on October 21, 1960. His first assignment was at Notre Dame of Marbel College (NDMC) as a teacher and became NDMC director in 1961. In 1966, he returned to Spain for a family visit and upon his return became the director of Notre Dame of Dadiangas College in 1967. He returned to the United States in 1996, retired in Florida, and died on October 22, 2000. "He loved short wave radio", Bro. Paul concluded.

In writing this book, I indulged in the recollection of my former friends and colleagues with a tinge of nostalgia. I tried to reach out to as many of them as I could find. A cousin of the late Mrs. Flora Kaiser recently informed us that Mr. Kaiser did return to Germany with his fourteen-month-old son. He lived with his parents and had remarried. I am so happy to hear this as I lost contact with Mr. Kaiser. The same cousin who lived in Switzerland had visited Mr. Kaiser and his son in Germany. Then they lost touch when she moved to the U.S. But now the cousin is trying to reconnect with Mrs. Kaiser's family, and hopefully, I'd hear more updates about them.

Also, I had wondered about the family of Mr. Nicolas Galas. When he died, his wife and ten children survived him. A month before the submission of the final draft of this book to the publisher, George, one of his kids wrote to my wife:

> I just found you on Facebook. Mr. Nicolas Galas was my father, and I am a member of Notre Dame High School Class 1970. Your cousin Mr. Victorio Guipo was my physics teacher and close friend, his brother Jose,

was my classmate. I have little recollection of how you look now because I am a little bit confused – there were so many Guipos at Notre Dame College when I was a student there.

However, Mr. Hower, even though my memory is now fading, still exists and fresh in my memory bank. I could vividly recall that day in May 1970 two months after my father died.[5] Mr. Hower set foot inside our modest house on Sampaguita Street. He was lugging several Dekalb chickens and gave them to my mother so that we could raise them on our farm in Banga, South Cotabato. The Dekalb chickens were huge compared to our native chickens on our farm. Our neighbors were amazed and wondered from what planet they came.

George ran away from home in early 1972, sensing no opportunities for him in Banga. He landed in Manila, and his life was full of struggles as a young high school grad kid trying to survive in Manila. He said, "But that's a long story for another book. I joined the Philippine Navy in 1976, retired in 2008, and today I am a Senior Vice President at the Navy Bank. I am married to Nelia; we have two daughters. Pamela is a pediatrician married to a surgeon, and the younger Madonna is a lawyer and a senior State Prosecutor married to a lawyer. I left General Santos in 1972 and went back for the first time thirteen years later in 1985. A few of the Dekalb chickens (or perhaps their descendants) that Mr. Hower gave my mother were still there. To celebrate the coming home of the prodigal son, my mother cooked me a hearty meal of *tinolang* Dekalb!!!"

THERE IS an inspiring update coming from the city of General Santos that is of particular interest to me. Malnutrition was prevalent in the underserved areas, particularly in Bula and Silway, during my service. As discussed in Chapter 10, the

Catholic Church, through its Social Action Program, brought this issue to the consciousness of the City Government during the term of Mayor Antonio Acharon. In 1969, Mayor Acharon made the reduction of malnutrition among children a vital part of his legacy in line with his mantra *"Una sa lahat ay tao"* (People First).

The Malnutrition rate of prevalence remained high in General Santos City until 2000. The recent statistics are very encouraging, in fact, astounding. From 38% in 2000,[6] it was down to 4.4% in 2019.[7]

On a personal level, writing this book reconnected me for the first time in fifty years with the people I met in General Santos City and the staff who helped me at the Community Centers. The Manager of the Bula Nutrition Center, Teodora "Dula" Pacomo Gomez is now married, retired from the Public School, and works as a Principal for the Passionist Technological Institute Inc. at Calumpang, General Santos City. Sadly, according to Dula, Ligaya Saavedra, who managed the Silway Center, had died. Dula does not know the whereabouts of Liberty Caderao, the manager of the Coca-Cola Center. Dra. Teresita Catapang, our volunteer dentist, is now eighty years old and still reports to her Dental Office at the Parish Center, according to Angie Catapang-Bongcawil (her niece) and Lucina Tapucar, (who helped in the research for this book). We made every effort to locate Dra. Pancho, nurse Grafilo, and especially Fr. James but quite unsuccessfully.

As to Fr. Albinus, I did not know (as I am sure his countless Parishioners) his remarkable personal story before he came to Dadiangas until I found his obituary online. Born in June 1912 to a father who was a business leader in Auburn, New York, and a mother who was a teacher, Fr. Albinus was ordained a priest in May 1941. He was a military chaplain in the United States Air Force from 1945 to 1956. According to the article: "One source says that he was the first priest to fly over the North Pole and often accompanied pilots on experimental flights.

During the 1950s, he served in the Philippines as a military chaplain. It was there that he met Apostolic Nuncio Vagnozzi, who requested that Father Lesch seek out the possibility of bringing the Passionist to the Philippines."[9]

He joined the first missionaries to the Philippines in 1957 after he left the Air Force and after he served as an assistant pastor at St. Michael's Monastery Church in Union City, New Jersey. He was assigned to the coastal parish Kiamba in southern Mindanao. In 1964, he transferred to Our Lady of Peace and Good Voyage Parish in Dadiangas. During that time, "the parish served 100,000 Catholics and more than twenty-five outstations."

Fr. Albinus believed that developing a Christian community was essential. To this end, he spearheaded the construction of the largest center in the city, which also became the cultural and social center. The article continued, "At the same time, Fr. Albinus had to contend with local warlord Adan de las Marias who was known locally as 'Octopus' and had a private army. Fr. Lesch penned a letter against the local warlord in the local parish bulletin entitled 'Who Runs Our Town' in 1973. In 1989 he began to suffer from strokes, which eventually hastened his death on December 26, 1989."[10]

The once sleepy, underserved barrio of Bula is now a very prosperous sector of General Santos City. It is home to one of the best fluvial (water) parades in the country and many of the city's shipping magnates. Marfenio Tan, Notre Dame University Alumnus 1964, is one of them. As the person in charge of the 2020 fluvial procession, Mr. Tan "invited personnel from the Philippine Coast Guard, Philippine Navy, and Maritime Police to serve as the parade marshals."[11]

The photos I took of the modest Isda-Isdaan Festival parade in 1972 now look quaint compared to the massive tourist attraction it has become. The event draws 100,000 devotees and visitors annually. For its 42nd Anniversary Festival in January 2020, "the local government and the festival organizers deployed a thousand security forces to ensure peace and order. The Sto. Nino Fiesta celebrates the founding of the Bula parish. The event began as the Isda-Isdaan Festival of Barangay Bula in the 1940s."[12] It evolved into the spectacular present-day extravaganza with the participation of the numerous hugely prosperous tuna fishing companies that originated in Bula. According to MindaNews: "Fishing companies and fishermen in the area mainly believe that their devotion to the Señor Sto. Niño has brought blessings to their operations."[13]

General Santos City also boasts of having the second biggest Fish Port in the country.[14] Listed as the top destination in the city on TripAdvisor©, it is the center of the fishing industry in Region XII. The thirty-two-hectare fishing complex in Tambler generates millions of foreign exchange earnings. It is processing 750 metric tons (1,500,000 pounds) of fish daily and provides 8,000 jobs. It was awarded the Guinness World Record Certificate, according to Avel Manansala. The largest Guinness fish display, the certificate read, "...consisted of 25,594.49 kilograms of yellowfin tuna. It was achieved by the City of General Santos (Philippines) in General Santos City, South Cotabato, Philippines, on 11 September 2014." [15]

IN CHAPTER 11, I noted that in September 1972, Phil Lilienthal, my Regional Director, came to General Santos with seven Peace Corps Trainees from the agriculture group. I accompanied them on a tour of piggeries, rice, and corn mills, etc. One of our stops was at the Silayan Engineering Works, a small company making farm implements. The leader of the workers there so impressed me. I wrote to my brother Bud and my family about him. My editor Chris Gammon was doubly impressed. He researched the company online. Chris found an entry on LinkedIn for an engineer named Oscar Bustmante, Jr.,[16] who worked at Silayan Engineering. However, Mr. Bustamante started there in July 1973 a year after I visited the site, so Chris deduced it was not the Silayan genius that I was looking for.

Chris was undeterred. His persistence paid off when he came across the website of the Samir Fouzan Group (SFG), which led to the identity of the Silayan genius. SFG listed Vercide Engineering Works, Inc. as one of its "Alliances" and profiled the company that opened in 1979 under the name Vercide Integrated Engineering. "A sole proprietorship engaged in metal fabrication, mills installation, & general construction that Mr. Atanasio T. Vercide acquired from Silayan Engineering Works, Inc, a business partnership that opened in 1969. He started with a workforce of five, including himself. Now, with another factory in Cagayan de Oro City together with his engineer sons and sons-in-law, he now commands a workforce of more than 960 and exports some of their products as far as the United States, Papua New Guinea, Indonesia, Malaysia, and some subcontracting jobs for high-rise buildings such as the Jing-Guang Center in Beijing, China, and the sixty-six storeys UOB [United Overseas Bank] Building, the tallest in Singapore [tallest during its construction and before 2016.]"

Through Facebook, we contacted Orman Ortega Manansala, President of the Federation of Notre Dame Alumni Associations. He just happens to be a classmate and friend of Salem Vercide. Salem confirmed that Mr. Atanasio Vercide was indeed his father – the Silayan genius I was looking for. Sadly Mr. Vercide passed away in 2016.

General Santos City is now one of the top twenty fastest-growing cities in the Philippines. It has numerous four-star hotels, an upscale SM Mall (Shoemart), and gated communities comparable to the cities of Davao, Cebu, and Manila. One can browse online for affordable rental vacation places to rent a one-bedroom or an entire six-bedroom house on Airbnb©, complete with hot showers, Wi-Fi, and modern amenities. General Santos International Airport has a state-of-the-art air traffic control tower. Funded by the Philippine Government and USAID (United States Agency for International Development), its sprawling airport ramp accommodates large airplanes simultaneously. The Boeing 747-400, as well as Boeing 777-300 ER, Airbus A 320, A330, and A340 pick up tuna and other cargos plus an increased number of passengers daily.[17] There are fifty private schools, more than 100 public schools, and three universities. The University of Santo Tomas will open a campus in General Santos City in 2021.

The isolated beaches where I used to snorkel (and not encounter a soul all day) are now lined with upscale resorts frequented by local and international tourists. In Chapter 7, I mentioned that the tourism industry is one of the biggest income producers of my host country, as well as the province of South Cotabato. The incentive is high among the national and local governments to preserve the beaches and the marine life for the tourist trade. Sarangani Bay is a fertile ground for marine eco-tourism. There is now a Tuka Bay Marine Sanctuary in Kiamba. The Kamanga Marine Eco-Tourism Park and Sanctuary in Maasim was named one of *Para el Mar (For the Sea) Awards* Most Outstanding Marine Protected Areas in the Philippines."[18]

My favorite Tinoto Beach still holds its charm. Just past Tinoto Beach is a resort called *Lemlunay* (paradise in T'boli). It is located in Maasim, owned by the Partridge family (my former hosts in Lagao Don and Socorro Partridge). As part of its business practices, *Lemlunay* made it their priority to preserve the natural beauty of marine life along the Tinoto Wall. According to its Manager, Paul Partridge, eco-friendly water sports like Scuba Diving with PADI affiliations (Professional Association of Diving Instructors), snorkeling, kayaking, etc. are available.

ON SEPTEMBER 5, 1969, four months after I arrived in my host town, I participated in a parade celebrating the 1st City Charter Anniversary of General Santos. All the private school students and faculty marched in the parade. There were floats, marching bands, and hundreds of spectators lining Morrow Boulevard and Pioneer Avenue. The ceremony culminated at the city plaza, highlighted by the ROTC pass and review before the government officials and guests seated at the stage erected for the purpose.

Fifty years later, in 2019, the event has become one of the biggest and most spectacular, and well-attended events in the country now called the Tuna Festival. Expatriates from the U.S., Canada, Europe, Australia, and other foreign countries go home to General Santos, Philippines, during this weeklong festival to partake in the celebration and gorged themselves with the best tuna in the world. Expatriates living in many continents can buy frozen tuna processed and packaged in General Santos City at their neighborhood Oriental store.

AS TO Lake Sebu, it is no longer a remote, isolated, and stagnant barrio; it is a thriving municipality. The bumpy National Highway that I used to take from General Santos to Marbel to Surallah is paved. And air-conditioned buses with thick padded seats and Wi-Fi ply the route! There is now a permanent bridge over Allah Valley River and a concrete roadway leading into the heart of Lake Sebu. *Jeepneys*, cars, SUVs, even tricycles and *habal-habal* (a regular motorcycle turned into a taxi and used beyond passenger capacity, up to six at the least), can easily traverse the road. Lake Sebu provides its population with 24/7 electricity, three cellphone towers, a hospital, and a public market with meat, fresh fish, vegetables, and fruits daily, among many other amenities. Lake Sebu has a dominant presence in the Internet world because of its eco-tourism, three lakes and Seven Falls, and one of the highest zip lines in Asia at 180 meters (590 feet).

Mayor Floro Gandam, Sr., elected in May 2019, is the third T'boli student of Santa Cruz Mission to hold the highest municipal office in Lake Sebu. Aquaculture and eco-tourism are the top two industries. It is a well-known tourist destination (highly visible on TripAdvisor©) with spectacular views, famous local *tilapia* cuisine, and offering water sports like river tubing, boating, kayaking, canoeing, etc. Miss Universe 2018 Catriona Gray placed Lake Sebu on the world stage. She wore a T'boli inspired outfit (*t'nalak* design) during the Miss Universe competition. She released a video on YouTube© filmed partly in Lake Seluton and T'boli land; *This is Mindanao: Tradition and Spirituality.*

Santa Cruz Mission (SCM), on the other hand, underwent a major administrative "changing of the guards" in the early 1990s, causing the demise of the Mission, as I knew it. I was told that a bitter and irreconcilable conflict arose between the T'boli and non-T'boli employees of the Mission. It resulted in the unceremonious ousting of the latter. Perhaps at that point, for better or ill, the time had come for the T'boli people to manage their own affairs. And from all indications, they are managing relatively well. There was resentment on both sides for quite some time. Recently the parties had again come to work together for the common good.

But just like many towns in South Cotabato, Lake Sebu is experiencing "growing pains". Some T'boli friends lament the bygone days when the lakes were not polluted, before the tourists came in droves to disrupt their peace and quiet, and families of three generations lived together in one house taking care of their elderly population, etc.

Santa Cruz Mission was initially established by Fr. George Nolan to provide education for the T'boli people of Lake Sebu. Fr. Rex Mansmann took over in 1963 and expanded the programs. Of the four programs at Santa Cruz Mission

(1970-1994) – Education, Health Services, Economic, and Community Development - only Education now exists offering six Elementary schools, two High Schools, and a College according to the SCM website. The old High School structures were built in the late 1970s and still standing in 2020. According to Gerry Hingco, who became a principal, the seed money for the school buildings, came from the early fundraising we did at the Promotions Office.

The Notre Dame of Lake Sebu, as we knew it, is now called Santa Cruz Mission School, Inc. The College Department has offered a degree in Bachelor of Science in Community Development since 1989 in collaboration with the Notre Dame of Marbel University. Dedicated solely to T'boli, its Mission Statement includes, "Actively support the IP's in their continuing struggle for self-reliance and self-determination."

After 1994, the T'boli staff took over the management of the schools. It now employs T'boli administrators, faculty, and support teams. The President of Santa Cruz Mission School, Inc., Maria Loco Gandam, is the wife of Mayor Floro Gandam, Sr. She has a degree in Social Work. The first T'boli Mayor of Lake Sebu was her brother, the late Samuel Loco (B.S. in English). Their youngest sister, Dolores Loco Agor, is now a teacher and community organizer.

FLOR GABATO, who replaced me when I left, was promoted as Administrative Manager of SCM in 1980s. Consequently, Ma'am Emma Crespo took over the management of the Promotions Office, which brought in millions of dollars for the Mission, according to Gerry Hingco, who managed the Education programs until 1993. "You guys laid the foundation, developed valuable connections with non-profit organizations, and provided the templates that made it easy for us to have projects approved and to manage the Promotions Office," Gerry texted.

Juvy Palces Castillon worked at Santa Cruz Mission's Development Office from 1986 to 1994 (formerly called Promotions Office pioneered by Prima). Juvy emailed: "The Promotions Office was split into two departments – the Development Office where Sir Gerry Hingco and I continued the project proposals to secure funds, and the new Sponsorship Office under Ma'am Em and her team, Doding Drilon, Vivian Faldas, & Mila Luces." According to Juvy, the Sponsorship Office partnered with the Japanese Foster Parents Association (JOFPA), headed by Mr. Fujiwara. "JOFPA became the most significant donor and helped the Education Program. Mr. Fujiwara frequently visited the mission until 1994. JOFPA also became a conduit in the reforestation project of 659 hectares and provided the mission with a Komatsu Grader."[19]

MISEREOR, (a German Catholic Bishops' Organization for Development Cooperation), funded the proposal to build a hospital that Fr. Rex and I submitted before I left. In 1977, Prima visited the Philippines with our daughter Linda and my co-teacher, Elizabeth "Bo" Duncan from Cheyenne Sioux Indian School in South Dakota. They stayed at the Mission for a week and saw the hospital in operation where they met the St. Paul Sisters. Bo donated blood to a T'boli lady who was hemorrhaging during that visit.

Flor Gabato now lives in Australia. She visited us in Rhode Island in 2018. She emailed:

"I can't remember the exact date that the hospital was built. But it should have been around late 1975 or early 1976 because the St. Paul Sisters came at the end of 1974 soon after you left and your house became the Sisters' Convent. Sir Al initially submitted the project proposal for the hospital."

According to Flor, she maintained the records and correspondence during the life of the Misereor projects and coded them as MH-Misereor Health for the hospital. Misereor, also donated money for road constructions to the villages under the account called MRC – Misereor Road Constructions. Flor continued, "USAID and Oxfam funded-projects came later. President Corazon Aquino also championed government programs for the Indigenous People that benefited SCM in the millions of funds. By the way, when Mayang [Maria] and [Mayor] Floro Gandam got married, Fr. Rex asked me to be the photographer. I was a nervous wreck because I knew that if I messed up, there was no chance to retake the pictures, unlike taking photos of the school children. Thanks, Sir Al for your tutelage, all the wedding photographs came out fine."

After I left the mission in 1974, six more Peace Corps volunteers served in the Mission, including Dottie Anderson, who went back in 1976 to 1977. There were also British Volunteers like Chris Atkins, who married Cecilia Molina, the Manager of the T'boli Products. Fr. Rex recently emailed Prima: "The early days of Al in Lake Sebu are very clear in my mind, as is your marriage on the hilltop and your work at your Promotion Office. Unfortunately, all the photos that we had there were swept away, along with other historically valuable documents after I left the Santa Cruz Mission. And yes, I would love to have copies of the digitized photos that Al took during his time in Lake Sebu. FYI, PCV Mike M. lives in Baltimore. Surely, you must remember Dr. Gervaise Hamilton of London, U.K. Talk about diverse species! We surely had a great cast of characters. One could make a movie out of that."

In December 1998, I went back to the Philippines for the first and only time to celebrate our 25th wedding anniversary. Prima and I visited Santa Cruz Mission with my daughter Linda (twenty-four), her then-boyfriend now-husband Bruce Bates Jr., my son Lee (twenty), and their cousin Kimberly Hower. The late Mayor Samuel Loco and his staff greeted us with a rousing welcome to the Town Hall in Lake Sebu and took us out to lunch at the Punta Isla for some broiled *tilapia*.

We visited the Mission that was so unrecognizable. The administration building seemed to have shrunk. The T'boli Products Store still sold gift items for tourists and visitors. However, the forest reclaimed the open spaces in the old campus, and almost all of the wooden structures were no longer there.

Walking down the footpath leading to the dormitories and the clubhouse (turned into offices), I could not see Datu Ma Fok's house on top of the hill; calamansi trees, coconut palms, mangoes, and bananas, etc. obstructed it from view. Vegetable gardens abound in the community as well, a marked improvement. Our house was barely visible from the road; the jackfruit tree that I planted was taller than the house. It spread its branches and framed our home and its old and tired roof.

The gazebo where we were wed was long gone from the hilltop overlooking Lake Seluton. T'boli houses now stood in its place. A deep emerald swathe of corn covered the hillside, and overgrown trees provided shade for horses tethered to the trunks. There was no trace of the once imposing *Dottie and Al* trees that were conspicuous in the once vast open landscape.

Prima took a picture of our daughter, Linda, along the footpath at the bottom of the hill in May 1977. In the photo, the *Dottie and Al* trees stood as backdrop stately and proud. Sadly, the trees were later chopped down to make way for progress. Electric poles and wires now crisscross over the new campus. T'boli houses covered the hilltop where the descendants of our previous neighbors live. The new residents sent us photos of their current neighborhood. Surrounded by resorts, they lament that Lake Seluton is polluted. The lake is being choked by water lilies purposely brought in to provide an attractive ambiance for tourists photo-ops to post on Facebook© and TripAdvisor© website.

If you ask Dottie and me, as much as we appreciate progress, the last photo of the bong and coconut palm nestled closely taken in 1977 is the image that we'd rather preserve in our memories.

Last photo in my possession of the *Dottie and Al* trees taken in May 1977.

Notre Dame of Dadiangas

Notre Dame of Dadiangas College in 1969 with Mt. Matutum as a backdrop. The grass reminded me of the field of wheat at our farm.

2019 - Notre Dame of Dadiangas University now occupies the whole five-acre campus. The High School and Elementary Departments were transferred to the Notre Dame of Lagao campus. Photo provided by Ruben Tugari, University Alumni Coordinator from the archives of Notre Dame of Dadiangas University.

Dadiangas Parish Center

1971 - The dream project of Fr. Albinus Lesch. He believed "developing a community was essential." The Parish Community Center became the hub of gatherings – sports, social and cultural, weddings, graduations, etc.

2019 - The Parish Center continues to function as Fr. Albinus had envisioned. Note the cell phone tower behind the building. Courtesy of Lucina Tapucar.

The Bula Señor Sto. Nino Festival

1971. The fishermen take time out from their daily grind to bring their families in their *bangkas* to enjoy the Isda-Isdaan Festival fluvial parade.

2020. The fishermen still take their families to enjoy the fluvial event with 100,000 devotees and visitors. But fishing boats of all sizes now dominate the fishing industry in General Santos, replacing the old dependable *bangkas*. Courtesy of Ronald Velasquez, professional photographer.

General Santos City

1969 General Santos City Pioneer Avenue & Plaza. The photo was taken by Narcie's Studio owned by Mr. Tony Cascaro (deceased), with permission from Narcisa Reblando Cascaro Santos, daughter of the studio owner

2019 General Santos City Pioneer Avenue & Plaza. Courtesy of Joery Duco using a drone.

In 1969 Tinoto Beach was accessible only by *bangka*. Today Cesma Cliff (owned by Prima's childhood friend, Celia Parica Esma) is the closest resort to this location pictured here.

1998 *Lemlunay* Resort, Maasim, Sarangani Province just past Tinoto Beach.
Paul Partridge (left) took Bruce Bates, Jr. (right) scuba diving along the Tinoto Wall.

September 5, 1969 - The message translates to "Mabuhay – First Anniversary of General Santos Cityhood. MarTan Trading and the house of Estela and Marino Tan Sr. in the background.

September 5, 2019 - This is one of the spectacular floats at the Tuna Festival depicting fishermen "hauling" in a tuna along Pioneer Avenue. Courtesy of Ronald Velasquez, former Tuna Festival Director, and professional photographer.

1970 - Datu Ma Fok, with Ye Lo, (one of his four wives), was the T'boli Chieftain at Lem- ehek when I was there. Datu Ma Fok wore the traditional T'boli outfit made of t'nalak fiber. Many of Datu Ma Fok's grandchildren are now the young professionals in leadership roles at Lake Sebu.

Photo from Santa Cruz Mission Archive permission to print by Rex Mansmann, Director.

2019 - Floro Gandam, Sr. the Mayor of Lake Sebu with his wife, Kenaban (Princess) Maria Loco Gandam, at the Helobung Fiesta Parade held at Lake Sebu Poblacion. Helubong means "endless joy and merrymaking".

Maria, daughter of Datu Loco Legal, is a direct descendant of Datu Ma Fok. Samuel Loco, her late younger brother, served as a Mayor of Lake Sebu. Both Samuel and Floro were Prima's pupils at Notre Dame of Lake Sebu, Santa Cruz Mission.

Photo courtesy of Maria Gandam.

Santa Cruz Mission

1970 - The old campus. The T'boli children were cleaning the open space around the flagpole.

1985 – The new campus. Eleven years after we left, Prima went home to visit Santa Cruz Mission. She took this picture of the high school and college buildings.

The Santa Cruz Mission Hospital donated by Misereor, the German Catholic Bishops' Organization for Development. Bo Duncan and my daughter Linda Mai visited the Mission in May 1977.

As Fr. Rex predicted, our house was repurposed after we left. It became the convent of the Sisters of St. Paul.

A Glimpse of Life After Peace Corps

Life as a Returned Peace Corps Volunteer (RPCV) was, and still is, in itself, another kind of adventure.

In her journal, my wife summarized my first year as an RPCV in the words of Charles Dickens. Prima wrote her thoughts on the same thirty-five-cents Stenographer's Note Book that I used when I joined the Peace Corps.

She noted: *1975 - It's June now. Since December, I can describe our life by the famous twelve words in the novel A Tale of Two Cities by Charles Dickens. "It was the best of times; it was the worst of times."*

I was married to my dream girl with long, black flowing hair that bore me a lovely daughter. We lived in America, so much in love, had a roof over our heads, owned a car, surrounded by a caring family, and could eat any food we wished: *it was the best of times*

Yet I felt sorely wanting. The America that welcomed me back in 1974 was not the same America I left behind in 1969. I did not expect it to be. I just never imagined a culture shock so severe when I first arrived, considering America was my home for twenty-five years before I went to the Philippines. Peace Corps had changed my worldview so much and for the better.

Prima and I arrived in Los Angeles on September 5, 1974. Fr. Rex had arranged for his sisters Pat and Joey Mansmann to host us for five days as we shopped for a used Volkswagen Camper. (Pat and Joey have since moved to their ancestral home in Pittsburgh, Pennsylvania. We keep in touch).

They took us to the Fisherman's Wharf for a fancy dinner one night and a baseball game at the massive Dodgers Stadium another day. The sports fanatic Prima couldn't hide her excitement as we climbed what seemed to be endless stairs to our seats. When we got home, she promptly wrote to her mother and sent her the ticket stub from the baseball game. (Mrs. Guipo was a softball star when she was a student).

The mundane things that I took for granted were mind-boggling to Prima, but she lapped them up with sheer delight. She could hardly suppress her exciting observations as she narrated them to me every night at bedtime. She was so fascinated when Joey placed an order before a voice box at McDonald's drive through window, and the pre-packaged dinner appeared a few minutes later ready for Joey to pick-up. "Joey didn't even have to get out of her car," she said amazingly.

Then there was Aunt Verna's magical gadget she carried in her car consul that automatically lifted the garage door open with a mere click of a button from a block away. My wife wrote lengthy epistles to her family and friends during those first few months in America. And just like my dad and siblings, her family kept her letters. Her father meticulously filed them all in chronological order in folders, the date of the letter's arrival noted on the envelope, a storybook in waiting.

After we bought our VW camper, I took the vehicle for a test drive. It felt strange at first, as it was the first time in five and a half years that I drove a car. We explored the city of Los Angeles, blanketed by smog. It was hard to breathe, and we never saw sunshine. We visited the La Brea Tar Pit and Museum. About this time, I was still seriously considering getting into a graduate school to study Anthropology.

We traveled for a month across the country, stopping at various locations in California. We visited Prima's neighbor, the Paredes family in L.A., and her uncle Gil Diaz and his family living outside the Naval Air Station in Lemoore. (Gil served in the U.S. Navy for twenty years; his two sons, Gil Jr and Scott, graduated from the U.S. Naval Academy in Annapolis and the youngest son, Peter, from the Air Force Academy in Colorado).

Also included on our itinerary were RPCVs Dottie Anderson, Tom and Marilyn Perardi, and Allen and Annie Spencer. Dottie, Prima, and I were together again at Yosemite National Park. The newcomers were totally awed by the iconic El Capitan, the Bridalveil Falls, etc. Dottie guided me while I drove my VW camper up, up the winding and steep mountainsides making stops at natural lookouts. We stayed in the Yosemite Valley for a few days, picnicked, and ate lunch by a brook. It was just like the old days. The year before, I ate lunch with Dottie by a spring in Tacunil, Lake Sebu. With the Perardis, we rode the cable car and listened to live singers at a folk bar in San Francisco for dinner one night. We strolled along the beach with the Spencers.

Our journey took us on the highways and byways of fourteen states,[20] sometimes stopping for a few days, or for a quick tour, or just passing through. Tony and Ella Savina living in Wenatchee, WA hosted us for a few days. (Their daughter Leslie was away at college. She was the Rotarian Scholar who was my housemate in General Santos City when I was staying at the Calderon's house). The Savinas drove us to Lake Chelan Dam Hydroelectric Plant. We watched the salmon climb the ladders on their way to their spawning ground.

One day, Tony and Ella included an apple orchard on our itinerary. It was such a joy to watch Prima beaming at her purchase of a bushel of apples for four dollars! She told Ella, "We only get to eat apples at Christmas imported from Japan, and they were expensive! My mother would buy half a dozen and cut them in halves so all ten of us could have a piece." We picked grapes and pears too from the Savina's backyard. The couple taught Prima how to can pears.

Ella worked in the city's social services office. She arranged for us to visit a Community Center for Senior Citizens to show a slide presentation of my Peace Corps experience. The lecture held at lunchtime was well received. I fielded a lot of questions. After the show, an elderly lady shuffled toward me, reached out with both hands, and planted a five-dollar bill on my palm and closed my hand over it.

"When my husband and I traveled as missionaries," she said almost in a whisper, "someone gave us money that helped us a lot." She told the story of how crossing the southwest desert, their old car had two flat tires and only one spare. A kind passerby helped them on their way. I was so touched my eyes welled as I thanked her.

THE NEXT day, I felt adventurous. I showed Prima the map, and we decided to take the "road less traveled" to see the countryside. Instead of taking Interstate 90, I chose the northern road parallel to it – Route 2. In the middle of nowhere, between Wenatchee and Coulee City, Washington, our VW camper broke down. A couple, total strangers and out for an afternoon drive casing an excellent place to hunt for pheasants, came to our rescue. They drove me to a Volkswagen garage in Moses Lake about seventy miles one-way.

Prima decided to stay in the camper to catch up on her reading. We had stopped at a thrift shop in LA, and she bought all the books that she could find of Mark Twain, Jane Austen, Louisa May Alcott, and the Nancy Drew series, which were later sent to the Philippines. (Prima told me recently that if she knew then what she knows now, she would never have stayed in that isolated, less traveled road by herself. But those were the good, innocent days of old when folks hitchhiked and arrived at their destination safely in one piece and unharmed).

The owner of the VW dealership towed our camper back to his garage. He gave us a choice: he could put a new engine for $800 and be on our way, or he could rebuild the engine for $400, but it would take two days. This RPCV's financial resources were dwindling; I had to call my dad to loan me the $400. The owner of the Volkswagen dealership allowed us to sleep in our camper while they rebuilt the engine. We used the dealership bathroom.

Across the street from the dealership was a Chinese Restaurant where we ate our meals, as they were relatively cheap. We also took in a movie showing *The Absent-Minded Professor*. I had seen the film shortly after its release ten years before. There were about a dozen folks in the audience. (It is worth noting here that by sheer happenstance, Prima's sister Nena lived in Moses Lake for three months five years prior, as a 4-H Ambassador of Goodwill).

Three days later, we were on the road again. We stopped at Butte, Montana, per the advice of the VW mechanic to have our rebuilt engine checked. Following Interstate 90 east, the snow started to fall as soon as we hit Wyoming.

All her life, Prima had been dreaming about snow that when it began falling from the skies right before her eyes, she was so excited she was like a kid in a candy store. I, on the other hand, discovered the windshield wipers did not work. Driving slowly, I opened the windows every so often and reached out to scrape the snow off by hand.

The weather worsened. I was so concerned that we'd get caught in the blizzard-like condition I did not even stop to take my wife's first picture in the snow. (She still harps over that to this day just to tease me. But the travails from that 1974 cross-country trip are for another story). Our plan to check out the job offer at the Cheyenne Sioux Indian High School in Eagle Butte, South Dakota, was scrapped due to inclement weather.

Our next stop was Neenah, Wisconsin, to visit my mom's sister, Aunt Verna, and her husband, John Garis. I had corresponded with Aunt Verna all the years I was in the Philippines. They took us apple picking too. Aunt Verna showed Prima how to bake an apple pie. Prima cooked Filipino dishes for them as she did for every American that we visited along the way. There was a plaque on the wall in the bedroom where we stayed that read; *You cannot repay kindness, so pass it on,* a notable takeaway that we try to practice.

In Michigan, we spent three days to reunite with an RPCV from Marbel, Ron, and his wife, Delia. Ron had returned to Law School at a university in Detroit. He took us to the campus one beautiful autumn day. I saw a group of protestors holding a sign, *Down with Gay People.* "Ron, why are they upset with happy people?" I asked. Ron had to explain the pop lingo to this clueless RPCV.

We arrived in Pennsylvania on October 11, 1974. My dad and stepmother flew from Florida to welcome Prima and to attend the wedding reception that the Hower-Judd family organized. A month later, our daughter, Linda Mai, was born at the Allentown Hospital. My sister Joyce and my sister-in-law Enid took Prima under their wings and guided her through the challenging first year of motherhood.

My youngest brother Dean invited us to live with him until such time that I found a full-time job. Well, the full-time job did not materialize until ten months later. Looking back now, the readjustment process as an RPCV would have been more severe without the excellent family support system.

For ten months, I struggled to find work and jumped from one tedious and meaningless sales job to another. About this time, I had given up the idea of going back to graduate school. *It was the worst of times.*

IN SEPTEMBER 1975, one year after we came back to the U.S., I accepted a teaching job at the Cheyenne Sioux Indian High

School in Eagle Butte, South Dakota. Interestingly, it was the same position I declined the year before. Two years of living on an Indian Reservation was like being in Lake Sebu, remote with wide-open spaces, a lot of mountains in the Black Hills, and very rural. We'd explore the area around Mt. Rushmore and somewhere under the canopy of pine trees and within the gaze of the four presidents; we'd camp in our Volkswagen Campmobile for the weekend.

"Downtown" Eagle Butte was a sight reminiscent of an old Western movie set. There was an assortment of ramshackle buildings – a run-down theatre that showed movies intermittently, a small grocery store, a fabric shop that sold crafts and gift items. A truck stop for a restaurant completed the scene.

The biggest shopping "mall" (a Kmart Store) was 180 miles distant west of Eagle Butte, located in Rapid City. One can drive the seemingly unending stretch of highway without running into a stoplight, and where no one ever observed the speed limit of seventy-five miles per hour. There was no traffic cop on that stretch of road to give out a speeding ticket to a driver.

We learned how to make our pizza dough and egg roll wrappers because the nearest Pizza Hut and the Oriental Store were in Rapid City, 180 miles away. There were Sears and J. C. Penney in Pierre; the state capital ninety miles away that carried a minimal stock of merchandise on the premises. However, one could order from the catalog and pick up from the store. Big appliances and furniture were delivered.

We had two TV channels in Eagle Butte. The program offerings were slim pickings. On Saturday nights, both channels ran the same programs – the Lawrence Welk Show, followed by Hee-Haw. The channels went off the air at ten PM.

Life was easy and uncomplicated in Eagle Butte, population 303. It was an ideal place to raise children in a very close-knit community of professionals. The employees of the Bureau of Indian Affairs (BIA) populated our section of town. Our house was located at one of the clusters of dwellings provided to teachers, administrators, coaches, office support teams, etc. by BIA for minimum rent. One could borrow a cup of sugar from a neighbor and use their washer and dryer in their basement until Sears Company delivered the washing machines that one ordered.

Ranches surrounded the town. We befriended the Vrooman family, who owned thousands of sprawling acres where they raised 300 or so cattle. In the winter, they'd invite us to their pond to go ice fishing and skating, in the summer we went horseback riding and watched the prairie dogs go in and out of their burrows in the grasslands. In Eagle Butte, we even hosted a seventeen-year-old exchanged scholar, Julio Lopez, from Nicaragua for three months.

To earn comp time at my job, I volunteered to work at rodeos. Prima and Linda tagged along to watch the bucking broncos, steer wrestling, bareback riding, and roping. Some of my high school students were consistent winners at some of these contests. We also attended cultural shows sponsored by the Indian community held annually at the high school basketball court. The Pow Wow was one of the best ways to experience the Native American culture. The costumes were spectacular heightened by dancing, singing, food offerings, and crafts.

The stimulating experience and the happy two-year stay in the little town of Eagle Butte helped me tremendously. It cushioned my transition from the backwoods of Lake Sebu to a fast-paced life in a highly urbanized America. Working at the BIA high school and earning more money than comparable positions in Lehigh Valley, restored my sagging confidence. Most importantly, I was doing something more meaningful, teaching the high school kids in an underserved Indian Reservation, instead of peddling encyclopedias or household products for Jewel Tea Company.

We spent two Christmases in Florida with my dad to get away from the blizzards of the mid-west. In July 1977, we moved to Tampa to be close to Dad and my stepmother. (Four years later we bought the house next door to them). Our son was born in Tampa in 1978. We wanted our children to grow up knowing at least one set of grandparents since Prima's family was half the world away. Later, we were able to sponsor Mr. & Mrs. Guipo to come to the U.S. They lived with us for two years in Tampa. All of Prima's siblings also visited us except Angelo and Felipe. Nena and Diana immigrated to Florida, and Tito, Susan, and Josie came as tourists to attend our daughter's wedding in July 2003. They stayed for six months.

Before leaving South Dakota in July 1977, we decided to provide an outlet in the United States for the handicrafts from Sta. Cruz and Bolul missions. We invested our life savings mainly on T'boli and Blaan baskets. For variety, we ordered smaller quantities of *t'nalak* weaving, beaded jewelry, brass figures, and other souvenir items.

A month after we arrived in Tampa, we registered our small business under the name Crafts 'n Baskets in August 1977. We sold our baskets to boutique gift shops and collectible items such as the *t'nalak* woven fabric and brass items to museums. Without a high demand for the T'boli and Blaan gift items, we diversified and added Prima's handmade crafts to our line of merchandise.

For the first two years of Crafts 'n Baskets, I taught as an adjunct professor at the Hillsborough Community College in Tampa and St. Leo College in San Antonio, Florida, to augment our income. (St. Leo College was the alma mater of Lee Marvin, the actor.)[21] We barely broke even on our investment on the T'boli and Blaan products. The indigenous people's baskets, while decidedly superior in design and durability, couldn't compete with comparable items from China. Sadly, after we sold all the T'boli and Blaan items, we did not reorder.

But all was not lost. It was the stepping-stone to the realization of Prima's dream to establish a cottage industry. Through the era of macramé, soft sculpture, and eventually floral design, Crafts 'n Baskets flourished for twenty-seven years until we voluntarily closed it in 2004. I could write a book about that segment of my life. My family and I regularly traveled to ten eastern states peddling our crafts at street art festivals, convention centers, shopping malls, and theme parks like Busch Gardens and Sea World of Florida and Ohio. We attended arts and crafts shows thirty-five weekends in a year. We also supplied Craft Stores and gift shops in the Tampa and Orlando area. In 1981 and 1982, we exported wholesale our macramé gift items to a couple in Kuwait whom we met at the Sea World Florida Festival.

I've had a string of careers other than Crafts 'n Baskets. I was a business manager at Independent Day School in Tampa that my kids attended, a tax preparer and accountant for doctors at the University of South Florida School of Medicine and a Supervisor at a nuclear pharmacy, Anazeo Health, for six years until my retirement in 2010. I hold my Peace Corps experience at the top of the list as my favorite job. If we did not have grandchildren, Prima and I would have joined the Peace Corps after our retirement. In fact, in 2004, we extensively researched the Peace Corps online and sent for the Peace Corps application forms. For now, though, the granddaughters are our "cause".

LIFE HAS treated me well. Our daughter Linda Mai married Bruce Bates (Jr), son of Ellen and Bruce Bates (Sr). An alumna of Wellesley College '96, Linda works as an HR Process Manager at Gilbane, Inc. Linda and Bruce have two daughters - Zoe and Lexi. Our son Lee graduated with dual degrees from the University of Pennsylvania School of Engineering and Wharton in 2000, where he was the Student Speaker at his graduation. After working as an early employee at PayPal/eBay, Lee became a member of the founding team at *LinkedIn* and a Co-founder/Partner of *NextView Ventures*. He is married to Heather Meg Dixon, daughter of Judi Dixon and the late Michael Dixon. Lee and Heather have a daughter named Summer.

The girl who said without hesitation that she could live with me in relative poverty all her life didn't do too badly either. She has a fondness for handwritten letters and wanted to be a mail lady. For eight years, she worked for the U.S. Postal Service, starting as a mail lady and later as a management trainee. She resigned before she finished her Postal Management Certificate to manage our floral design business full time. She wanted to own a small business; she did as my co-owner and manager of Crafts 'n Baskets. She racked up seventeen blue ribbons at Arts and Crafts Shows for her original designs and won purchase awards too.

She wanted to go back to academia. For five years, she was the Administrative Assistant to the Deans at the University of South Florida School of Nursing until we moved to Rhode Island. She worked at Brown University School of Engineering in Providence for seven years. She resigned at the pinnacle of her career as the first Faculty Affairs Coordinator to become a full-time "*Lola* Nanny" to our granddaughters, Summer, Zoe and Lexi. (*Lola* is grandmother in Pilipino).

IN DECEMBER 1993, during our 20th wedding anniversary, I surprised Prima with a ticket to see The Lettermen in Florida. During the audience participation, the founder of the Lettermen Tony Butala called on her to stand up. When asked about her favorite song, she replied, "In 1974, you performed in Manila during the Miss Universe Pageant. You sang our Filipino Love Song, *Dahil sa Iyo*. May I dedicate it to my husband on our wedding anniversary?" The audience broke into applause. The Lettermen said, "Happy Anniversary," and serenaded us in Tagalog. One other exciting moment of her life was to see Paul McCartney (her favorite Beatles) perform live in concert in

Tampa. Most recently, her friend Darlene Dilangalen Borromeo arranged for her to present a welcome bouquet to one of her teen pop/rock idols Gary Lewis (of the Gary Lewis and the Playboys) and his wife Donna at the Newark Airport. Prima danced with friends and Donna while Gary and his Playboys performed on stage at the Fiesta in America in Meadowlands, New Jersey. (Gary's first wife was a Filipina).

My brother-in-law Earl Laudenslager taught Prima the intricacies of football. She became a big fan overnight. I'm still not a fan, but I watch to cheer for her team.

She loves snow. In 2010 the year after we moved from Florida to Rhode Island, two feet of snow fell. She built seven snowmen in our yard - the Berenstain Bears Family of five and a couple dressed in Florida get-up. She also learned how to ski cross-country and enjoys snowshoeing. An avid gardener, she tends to her bulb, peony, and hydrangea gardens as well as landscapes our kids' yards.

Prima is active in the Notre Dame Alumni Association, a non-profit organization of alumni from all Notre Dame Schools of General Santos City. She helped organize the association in 1993. In May 2019, she attended its Silver Anniversary Reunion in Seattle, WA, along with over 200 alumni, teachers, and mentors. After the reunion, off she went with fifty-five members of the association on a seven-day Alaskan Cruise to cross off Alaska from her "Visit 50 States Bucket List". She hopes to visit Arkansas, Colorado, and New Mexico - the last three remaining on her list.

IN OCTOBER 2019, I participated in a Cultural Exhibit of Indigenous People (T'boli, Blaan, and Maguindanao) at the Philippine Embassy in Washington, D.C. in collaboration with the lead exhibitor, Craig Diamond. His extensive collection of indigenous artifacts is museum-worthy. *The T'boli Way of Life – Expressions in Photography,* showcased my photo collection of T'boli portraits and their way of life.

In 1972, I helped to promote and market T'boli handicrafts in General Santos City. Mrs. Estela Tan, the owner of MarTan Trading and other benevolent parishioners, invited me to their homes to display the products for the community to buy. We also exhibited and sold at the Dole Clubhouse.

In October 2019, I explained the process of weaving and brass making to a guest at the Indigenous Tribe Exhibit at the Philippine Embassy, Washington D.C. Many of the images I showcased at the exhibit are included in this book. (Photo courtesy of Allan Chan, Sr.)

Prima chaired and produced the event with her colleagues from the association SOCKSARGEN USA, Inc., sponsor of the exhibit, and the host of the venue Philippine Embassy and staff. SOCKSARGETN USA, Inc. is a non-profit organization based in the United States. Members of this association are former residents of South Cotabato (Region XII) living in the U.S. The organization's stated mission is to promote Filipino culture and values.

My Tagalog is a bit rusty now. But, it comes in handy as an icebreaker when someone responds at a call center in the Philippines or when I meet Filipinos at the grocery store. Prima is the cook at our house. We seldom eat out, as she treats us to a variety of Pilipino and Asian dishes, exotic and familiar. Rice is still a dominant part of our diet. Sometimes, I'd roast a chicken with all the fixings, and I do most of the baking. Since 1974, I can count on my one hand the times Prima roasted a turkey, but she bakes a killer apple pie, and prepares *lumpia* (egg rolls) by the hundreds!

I don't mind when she fries *bulad* or *dilis* inside the house (although they still smell like a dead rat to me). And I will probably eat these salted and dried fish if it's the only thing available to survive.

RPCVs and the 50th Reunion

LIKE COUNTLESS Returned Peace Corps Volunteers, my RPCV friends and I try to find ways to contribute as best we can to America that we now inhabit. Looking back fifty years, our experiences in South Cotabato, a place once unknown to all of us, may not be as vivid anymore. However, the feelings associated with those experiences are palpable still. Now and then, we relive our Peace Corps days through social media, email exchanges, and mini-reunions.

As mentioned in the Introduction, March 11, 2019, marked the 50th year that I officially joined the Peace Corps as a volunteer trainee. I organized the Golden Anniversary Reunion for PC/ Philippines Group 31 held in Warren, Rhode Island, on June 14-16, 2019. I invited other Returned Peace Corps Volunteers from different groups assigned in the Philippines and their RPCV friends who live in New England.

Basking from the euphoria of reliving the fond Peace Corps memories with fellow volunteers, I started on this book project after the reunion. In 1993, I received a letter from David Searles requesting contributions from RPCVs who served during his term as Country Director/Philippines from 1971 to 1974. His letter gave me the idea to solicit stories from RPCVs. David expressed in said letter that he wanted "a reader to understand the reality of the Peace Corps experience."[22] I wish to achieve the same and not only from my perspective.

I invited RPCV friends to share their experiences. After all, our stories are closely intertwined. Each of them could fill up a book with their own colorful lives and Peace Corps adventures. Even if we inspire just one reader to become a volunteer, the production of this demanding project would have been worth all the effort.

THE 50TH REUNION

Group 31/PCP Reunion to celebrate the 50th Anniversary of our joining the Peace Corps

(March 1969-March 2019) in Warren, Rhode Island. L-R: Dottie Anderson (Group 23, who was Administrative Assistant at our Regional Office), Author, Patty Flakus Mosqueda, Nancy Nicholson, Marilyn Maze, and Tom Perardi.

2019 Peace Corps Reunion in Warren, Rhode Island. Standing l-r: David Delasanta (RPCV), Alvin Hower (RPCV), Scott (RPCV) & Mary McCaffrey, David Chan, Dottie Anderson (RPCV), Kathleen Ursin, Patty Flakus Mosqueda (RPCV), Marilyn Maze (RPCV), Angelita Altea (PC/P staff), Andrea Reisen (RPCV), Jim Barfoot, Matt Reisen (RPCV), Tom Perardi (RPCV).

Seated l-r first row: Prima & Anthony Delasanta

2nd row: Marc Forte (RPCV), Nancy Nicholson (RPCV), Guada Shaffer (Language Instructor), Michaela Delasanta

3rd row: Brenda Delasanta & Steve Shaffer (RPCV)

My response to David's 1993 letter was a summary of my Peace Corps stint. It is followed by fascinating stories from Matt and Andrea Reisen, Marilyn Maze, Tom Perardi, and David Delasanta. I wish to thank them all for generously adding their "grain of sand" to the pile.

June 25, 1993
Dear David,

About your book: Yes, I would find the task enjoyable...

I must start by saying my Peace Corps experience was the best part of my entire life. I look back and think, "I must have been crazy to leave a secure job and all the comforts of home to go to the Philippines." Maybe youth does that to a person – no, it can't be since many retired persons joined the Peace Corps. Perhaps it was the desire for adventure in a far off land. Or was it a desire to be different from the crowd? Those may all have contributed to my decision. Personally, the overriding factor was a desire to make a better place for all. That is a pretty lofty goal, and I may have achieved only a tiny grain of sand's worth, but if everyone were to add just one grain of sand, we would soon have a big pile.

To that end, here are a few grains of sand from my Peace Corps experience added to the pile. Eight indigent children with a single or double cleft (harelip) were operated on to close the cleft in the palate. The surgery certainly improved their appearance and self-esteem. Six doctors volunteered their time; three hospitals volunteered their facilities; neighbors volunteered their transportation and other assistance. Each gave a little of his time and skill made for a very noticeable difference.

My former students at Notre Dame College reflected that their economics classes enhanced their lives. It may not have been the lessons on economics that they learned as much as the communication skills and the broadening of a worldview. They are now teachers, administrators, managers, agriculturists, owners of their businesses, government officials, etc.

The hundreds of children, pregnant and lactating mothers that were educated and fed at the nutrition programs in General Santos City hopefully had more healthful lives. The grains of sand: USAID for food commodities, Catholic Relief Services for partial funding and coordination, CARE for some equipment, local parishioners for building material and labor, drug companies for medication, and the local parish church for continuing the work after I left.

Working with the T'boli people of Lake Sebu was the most singular assignment of my Peace Corps years. The colorful costumes and rich culture left an indelible and lasting impression. Under the title of Management Consultant, I wore many hats. The job offered an opportunity to examine and discover myself and contribute skills that I thought irrelevant or took for granted, like working as a photographer for the Santa Cruz Mission promotions. Set-up bakery and cafeteria, train local managers in various phases of economic production and write feasibility studies, budget, and project proposals for funding development projects.

Leaving in August 1974 with many things hanging in the balance, I often wondered if any of those ideas ever succeeded. Through correspondence with colleagues, they assured that some things did, and some things did not. The bakery and the cafeteria closed. The person I taught to do photography took over and trained others. A hospital, high school, and college building were built and staffed through a proposal I worked on initially. Agricultural projects for T'boli farmers were funded, and the proposal template I originally wrote used as a model for future project applications.

That condenses the work I did in the Philippines as a Peace Corps Volunteer. There is certainly more to tell: the harrowing, the heartbreaking, and the humorous encounters. But that will have to wait for another time.

Sincerely yours, Alvin J. Hower

MATT AND ANDREA REISEN[23]
Group 50 PC/Philippines 1972-1974
Avoca, New York

I thought it was going to be the end of me. I was a Peace Corps volunteer in the Philippines when my leg swelled one day after working at the rice terraces at the Bolul Mission. The Mission was located in Marbel, South Cotabato.

I was running a high fever and was taken to the De Jesus Clinic in Marbel. Dr. De Jesus diagnosed my condition as phlebitis. Fortunately, the Cessna plane belonging to the Wycliffe Bible Translators at Edwards, Surallah, did medevac me to Davao City. At the Davao airport, my wife Andrea was beside herself when she was told there was no seat in the plane for her, our toddler daughter Christina, and me.

She started bawling, and Philippine Airlines accommodated us. We arrived in Manila, and I was taken directly to a hospital. To this day, no one seems to be able to diagnose my medical issue; it is not phlebitis I was told. It flares up when the condition is right.

Andrea and I were in PCV/Philippines Group 50 in 1972-1974. The Peace Corps New Directions policy was being implemented in full force with a new emphasis on community development rather than education. I was part of the Agriculture Program sent to the Philippines as a Feed and Grain Technician. I was tasked to help in the production of corn, sorghum, and soybeans for animal feeds. During this time, piggeries with up to 10,000 pigs or more were sprouting all over the province of South Cotabato. We were sent to one of South Cotabato's inland towns called Marbel to work at the Bureau of Plant Industry (BPI). We arrived in October of 1972.

Unfortunately, it was not a good match for me. I basically sat at the desk for four months, as my BPI host did not know what to do with me. Through Ate Vance Ang and her husband Jose, we met Fr. Felix Miller. He was a Passionist priest who was the director of the Bolul Catholic Mission, serving the Blaan, one of the many indigenous people of South Cotabato. We processed my transfer, Peace Corps approved, and I became the Mission's Conservation Agriculturist. I served out my two-year term in full.

The Blaan farmers had been battling erosion on their hilly land for many years. Together we built mini-rice terraces so they could continue planting rice on the hillsides. I also introduced other sources of protein and cash crops like mung beans. We raised chickens and goats.

Andrea and I attended language training in Ilongo. We did not speak the Blaan dialect. There was a male teacher at the Mission School named Hermie who acted as our translator when we went from village to village to work with the Blaan farmers. He was indispensable.

My wife Andrea came as a "nonmatrixed" spouse per Peace Corps jargon. As part of the New Directions, a new vocabulary emerged including one that Searles mentioned in his book, *The Peace Corps Experience and Challenges*, "...the widely abused, misunderstood, and unfortunate term nonmatrixed spouse..."[24]

Basically, a nonmatrixed spouse meant that if the spouse of a volunteer did not meet the necessary skills to be added on the "matrix," they were referred to as "nonmatrixed." Although they were just as committed and motivated, the Peace Corps had no mechanism in place to absorb them in any of the programs.

Before the implementation of the New Directions, the volunteers were expected to keep quiet, do as they were told, or be sent home. Searles continued, "It is to their lasting credit that most nonmatrixed spouses did find their own way and did make lasting contributions to the Philippines, to the Peace Corps –and, one hopes to themselves."

In the 1980s, only the couples with the skills that meet the Peace Corps need were accepted into the program, thus ending the usage of the word "nonmatrixed spouse." Searles lamented,

"They did so much to make the volunteer contingent truly representative of the United States that their present absence is a decided negative."[25]

When we arrived in Marbel in October 1972, we built a beautiful *nipa* hut and lived there. Four months later, we moved with our house (literally) to Bolul Mission. With the help of other volunteers, we transferred our house from Marbel to Bolul Mission in the true *Bayanihan* fashion. The nipa house was disassembled, hauled on a truck, and reassembled.

During our tour of duty, there were other Peace Corps Volunteers in Marbel and Tupi that we knew personally– Sue Bienkowski, Frank Tuma, David Baggott, David Delasanta, Billy the Kidd, Stacey Spillane, and Dr. & Mrs. Bedford. Once the Kennedys, a couple who were doing research on the monkey-eating eagle, visited us in Bolul Mission. A dead eagle was brought to the Mission. Fr. Felix preserved it inside his refrigerator freezer. It came in handy as a specimen for the Kennedys.

Andrea devoted her time to the high school students teaching them how to cook healthy nutritious meals. She also collaborated with the Department of Public Health in Marbel on the birth control program and helped in the handicraft projects at the Mission.

Al used to stay with us when he was in Marbel and later when he came down from the mountains of Lake Sebu. When Peace Corps volunteers get together, there's always the fun of comparing our culinary adventures. Al told us that finding food, especially meat, was a challenge for him at the Mission; it was not for us. We grew our own diversified garden and raised goats and chickens.

There were also unwanted animals like rats crawling in between the *nipa* walls of our house. I'd get up in the middle of the night, find the location of the rat, and stabbed them with a *bolo* (machete). I created holes on the wall, but it was better than listening to Andrea scream all night. Al told us that he had an aversion for rats. While in Pampanga, he was fed a broiled rat that was caught by his farmer host in the rice paddies. He also ate monitor lizard the Filipinos called *bayawak*. None of us ever tried *balut* or durian. Interestingly Andrea ate a snake in Manila. I was fed locusts and dogs. An article on a blog called *The Dog Visitor*[26] stated, "Though there is no law explicitly banning the eating of dog meat, Philippine laws make it illegal to trade dogs for their meat or to kill them. Based on the amended Meat Inspection Code of the Philippines (RA 10536), meat dogs and other "non-food" animals are considered "hot meat" and cannot be sold or distributed."

Challenges? Andrea and I went through the typical experiences of a Peace Corps volunteer - culture shock, the challenges of adapting to a new language and a different way of life, etc. Andrea fared very well and in no time at all. However, my biggest challenge was "not fitting in," as in not fitting in locally sold shoes and clothing. And entering doors! I am six-foot-six tall. I had a tough time finding shoes, shirts, and pants in the Philippines. When I walked into a house, I had to stoop rather low. So when we built our house, we made a conscious decision to make the entrance doors taller than usual.

I was honored when Al asked me to be the best man when he got married. It rained a few days before the wedding. Riding the weapons carrier from Surallah to Lake Sebu was quite an experience for us, although we also lived on a remote and hilly Bolul. We were walking more often than riding on the weapons carrier during the climb to the top of the mountains of Lake Sebu over 3000 feet above sea level.

Andrea was so glad to be a part of the joyful event too. She baked the 24"x36" two-layer wedding cake. Andrea forgot to factor in the altitude and did not allow for it in the process. The cake did not rise to the level expected. But no one noticed after the cake was placed on risers.

In the Philippines, we adopted a beautiful girl named Christina. The three of us came home to America in 1974 after traveling through Thailand and Germany. We lived in Mt. Bethel, Pa. Later we had our own daughter Juanita and adopted another girl Lyn Li and two boys Billy and Travis. Sadly Lyn Li died when she was only eighteen years old.

We never lost contact with Al and Prima since we all came back to the U.S. in 1974. In the 1980s, Al and Prima sent their children Linda and Lee, to visit us at our farm in Avoca, NY. Our daughters, Christina and Juanita, visited the Howers in Florida and had a great time at Disneyworld.

We currently own a forty-acre farm in upstate New York, where we run our business called *The Healing Spirits Herb Farm & Education Center.*[27] Andrea and I founded our company in 1991. It is located in the Finger Lakes Region of Western New York. We sell the majority of our products online. Andrea is a student of numerous healing modalities, including CranioSacral, Reiki, and Therapeutic Touch. She is also certified in Zero Balancing. She has studied with Brooke Medicine Eagle. Andrea's love for nature is infectious.

I hold a Bachelor of Science degree in agronomy and worked as an agricultural agent. I love to tend all the herbs, flowers, and vegetables at the *Healing Spirits*. I channel my intense spiritual energy to enhance *Healing Spirits'* ethically wild-crafted and organically grown herbs. Andrea and I graduated from Rosemary Gladstar's apprenticeship program and have studied nature awareness and philosophy at Tom Brown's Tracker School. Healing Spirits manufactures and produces Sage Mountain herbal products.

Shortly after we came back to Pennsylvania in 1974, I received a phone call from the Peace Corps to report at a hotel in the Catskills, New York, for a photo session. It was my claim to fame to be chosen as a "poster" volunteer for a Peace Corps ad. Along with a female nurse and another volunteer, we were taken to a farm in Connecticut for the filming.

I was "paid" two months equivalent of Peace Corps/ Philippines pay, an 8mm film, and my face plastered on a 60-second TV ad, and in newspapers and magazines mostly all over the northeast from New York to Boston. Andrea's brother is a pilot. He called one day and said: "There's a full-page ad of Matt the Peace Corps Volunteer in our Aviation Magazine." The experience was more than payment enough. I was glad to be able to give back to the Peace Corps for what it has done for Andrea and me.

We joined the Peace Corps because we wanted to experience another culture aside from our own and to do something good in the process. Peace Corps completely changed how we viewed the world and changed the way we live. We realized that we could enjoy life as a minimalist without all the gadgets of convenience we were used to in the U.S.

In the last ten years, I have done five "Farmer-to-Farmer" projects in Belarus, Nepal, Jamaica, Colombia, and the Dominican Republic. "The USAID-funded John Ogonowski and Doug Bereuter Farmer-to-Farmer Program provide technical assistance to farmers, farm groups, agribusinesses, and other agriculture sector institutions...The main goal of the program is to generate sustainable, broad-based economic growth in the agricultural sector through voluntary technical assistance. A secondary goal is to increase the U.S. public's understanding of international development issues and programs...".[28] These were usually two to three weeklong stints helping with a particular project.

Andrea summed our memorable experience for both of us, "We never once regretted our Peace Corps years. They were the foundation that helps with the rest of our life."

Our nipa hut in Marbel, Philippines.

The Healing Spirits Herb Farm & Education Center in Avoca, New York.

MARILYN MAZE[29]
PC/Philippines Group 31
Maryland

After Tom Perardi and I left the Peace Corps, we traveled for a year before we arrived back in the US. We headed north as far as Japan, then south to the ASEAN countries, then India to Turkey by bus, and took the Orient Express to Germany. We traveled around Europe in a Volkswagen van.

We settled in San Francisco, where Tom became an APE (Air Pollution Engineer) for the Bay Area Air Pollution Control District. After a couple of years of climbing smokestacks to measure emissions, he moved to the Planning Department. He specialized in computer modeling to answer the question, How will X affect air quality? Where X could be a shopping mall, amusement park, new highway, etc.

I went back to school and earned a master's degree in Career Counseling. We divorced. I took entry-level career counseling jobs in schools, and then entered computer-assisted career planning. I worked for EUREKA, the California Career Information System. I started my own business paying programmers to write career-planning software that I designed. I then accepted a position at ACT (the college entrance exam company) working on DISCOVER, a computer-assisted career planning program that served millions every year. I considered this the pinnacle of success in my field because few companies hire career planning software developers, and ACT paid the best of those who did. With their support, I earned a doctorate in counselor education. I married an astronomer, Holland Ford, who worked on the Hubble, built the Advanced Camera, which is still in use in the Hubble and is credited with proving the existence of black holes.

I helped a friend start a new professional association in 2010, the Asia Pacific Career Development Association (APCDA). My background in software, websites, and business start-ups all came in handy. ACT downsized in 2015, and, at seventy, I was free to volunteer full time for APCDA. I now put on a conference every year in a different Asian Country and help APCDA grow in any way that I can. I have selected my successor and put enough savings in the APCDA bank account, so with the approval of the Board, I hope to turn over my job to a paid Executive Director in 2020. I also run a small counselor-training non-profit called PsyCoun that provides workshops for counselors in Maryland.

As a Peace Corps Volunteer, I took over the job of a math teacher at Notre Dame of Marbel College who went to Manila for a master's degree in math. I had twenty-four hours of preparation each week during my first semester because all but one of my courses were singletons (thirty students who planned to be math teachers). Instructors were expected to teach twenty-seven hours a week. After two years of teaching the same students all the various math subjects, I supervised them in their internships. This was very rewarding for me because I knew I had a real impact on the way they taught and what they understood about mathematics.

When we arrived in Marbel, the Peace Corps thought that, as a married couple, we needed our own house to live in. They rented a very elegant house for us. Except for the broken glass on the top of the wall around the house, it could have been featured in House Beautiful Magazine. Our big house was supposed to be a meeting place for all of us stationed in Marbel, but it did not work out that way.

Peace Corps volunteers Patty and Bill each lived with families, and even in Marbel, we found different ways to spend our spare time. We did invite Paul Lagakus, a PCV teaching math in a nearby barrio, to spend a summer with us. He enjoyed being with Americans because his level of isolation in the barrio was much higher than ours. We enjoyed getting to know Bob and Bev, PCVs who came to Marbel in our second year, and built a *nipa* hut so they could have the full Filipino experience. And we really enjoyed the visits to Zamboanga and the Wycliffe ladies, where we met the local tribe-people the T'boli, who they worked with.

During my first semester in Marbel, the doorbell rang one day. Vilma Bordamonte had come to ask if we could help her. She explained that she had to drop out of school because she had no money to pay tuition. Later, our first helper quit, I found Vilma and invited her to be our housekeeper. She protested that she had no money for books, clothes, etc., and we promised to take care of her needs.

We also hired another student to keep her company, but Vilma was like a daughter to us. I bought a Filipino cookbook, and she tried each of the dishes until she found the ones we liked. When we left, we took her with us to Manila, her first trip out of Mindanao. She was then hired by our Peace Corps replacement [the Bedfords] and later started an import/export business from Manila to Mindanao. Then she joined the Peace Corps staff, met Lon Laack, and finally (after their first child), married him and returned to Wisconsin with him. He recently passed away (cancer). Vilma now lives in La Crosse, Wisconsin, where her youngest son also lives. She loves to have visitors but does not travel for health reasons.

In the Peace Corps, I learned new ways to do everything. I learned how to wax the floor by putting the wax on the rough side of a coconut husk and pushing it across the floor with a barefoot.

I learned how to make copies for my classes using gelatin, glycerin, and ditto masters. The lesson of frugality and inventing makeshift solutions has served me well in my many start-up businesses. Living in the Philippines taught me to understand the perspective of others from the viewpoint of a minority. This has been invaluable in Asia Pacific Career Development Association (APCDA), where I seem to get a new lesson in cross-cultural sensitivity each year. I still love to travel, and still love Asia more.

Marilyn attended our cultural exhibit at the Philippine Embassy, Washington D.C., along with my high school classmate Ronald Klayton (the guy who encouraged me to go to college). L-R: Ronnie Klayton, Author, Marilyn Maze, Janet Klayton, and Prima.

Exhibit Hall at the Philippine Embassy, Washington D.C. Docent Shirley Zolina Victa is Prima's childhood friend. Photo courtesy of Allan Chan, Sr.

TOM PERARDI[30]
PC/Philippines Group 31
California

Inspired by Kennedy, I was in two separate Peace Corps programs, Bolivia 1964-66 and Philippines 1969-71.

I'm now in Oakland, California, retired, enjoying leisure life with my partner Kathleen Ursin. I met her in Boston while I was at the Massachusetts Institute of Technology (MIT). She was at Boston University, and she lived in a small BU dorm next to my fraternity house on Commonwealth Ave. After college, we went separate ways each married then divorced. Got back together much later, when I was 50. We went on a safari in Tanzania. We're in the Oakland hills now, with a beautiful view of San Francisco, just across the Bay. Most recently, an executive recruiter, Kathleen, is also retired. Currently reading to pre-school kids to support learning skills.

I got a B.S. degree in Chemical Engineering in '64, then spent two years in the Peace Corps in Sucre, Bolivia, teaching science and engineering courses in Spanish at a historic Jesuit university.

Bolivia, a landlocked country of 4 million people in 1964, was half indigenous Quechua and Aymara speakers in the highlands. Hardscrabble agriculture and tin mining were survived with coca leaves and cane alcohol from the Amazon lowlands. My posting was to Sucre, the old and fading capital city at an altitude of 9000 feet. The Jesuit University founded there in 1624 (that's 12 years before Harvard) was launching an engineering curriculum. With my fresh Chemical Engineering degree from MIT and intensive language training, I taught several engineering courses in Spanish. One of the old Jesuit teachers had invented his own unique version of the Periodic Table, so we had to work around that.

Students ranged from a bright European-looking young man who had spent a year in the US, to a slim brown-skinned man with indigenous features. He was teased and called Indio or Geronimo by the mestizo students, but his family owned a trucking company, so he could probably buy and sell the others. I occasionally went out with the students to little bars where we ate chicken stewed in chicha (corn beer), drank good German-inspired beer in big bottles, heard terrible jokes, and lamentable politics. And were impressed by those who could swallow hot chili paste by the spoonful. Bolivia had averaged around one revolution per year since independence from Spain in 1825. Another occurred during my term. A lot of noise but thankfully, very little violence as Victor Paz Estenssoro was ousted. (Oddly enough, he came back to be president again in 1985-89.) A fascinating country and a rewarding job!

Some travel, and then back to MIT for my Master's degree. I worked for a year at Oak Ridge National Lab (Tennessee), where I met Marilyn Maze.

We got married and lived in a little rural house on Dogwood Lane. I bought my first car, a '68 Camaro SS with a big V8 and 4-speed manual. (Right, uncomfortable and impractical, a wild oat. Now know better: Toyota Highlander.)

We went into the Philippines Peace Corps Program and were assigned to Notre Dame of Marbel College under the Marist Brothers. We were impressed that it was one of the very few officially accredited higher education institutions in the Philippines. The Brothers seemed serious about education. I taught science courses. Faculty and students were friendly and supportive. We were fortunate to have a modern house from the College. Bathroom, small fridge, fan! Electricity most of the time. Even better, we found two students, Vilma Bordamonte and Florencia Principe, as live-in helpers, to handle cooking, cleaning, etc. We felt some colonial guilt but didn't refuse. (Vilma was a hard worker, independent with an entrepreneurial streak. She married a Peace Corps Volunteer, had kids and family life in Wisconsin.)

Leaving the Philippines, Marilyn and I spent about a year traveling through Asia and Europe, finally returned to the U.S. We bought a rusty old Ford van in Boston, fitted it out as a homemade camper, and drove across America to California.

I got a job in San Francisco, working for the Bay Area Air Pollution Control District. So my professional career was dedicated to reducing air pollution in the nine counties around San Francisco Bay. Our agency was a pioneer in the field before the California Air Resources Board, and before EPA. Starting as a test engineer, I got into computer modeling of the atmosphere and ended up as Director of Planning for the agency. Air quality was much improved over the years, and I retired in 2004.

Marilyn and I, within a few years in California, had drifted apart, then separated and divorced. We still meet on occasion and exchange holiday newsletters and good wishes.

My main interest these days is my art/antique collection ... mostly Asian art, including some from the Philippines. In recent years I've worked with volunteer support groups for the Asian Art Museum in San Francisco and the UC Berkeley Art Museum. But I spend a fair amount of time on home maintenance and cutting back the jungle that seems determined to overwhelm the house. We also enjoy travel. Some favorites are Santa Fe, New York, Amsterdam, and southern Utah. We've made several trips to Asia, where high points were Bangkok, Angkor Wat (Cambodia), Pagan (Burma), the Shanghai maglev, and Wulingyuan (China), Halang Bay (Vietnam), and the Diamond Mountains (North Korea). By the way, our trip to North Korea was perfectly legal. And it was pure coincidence that Kim Jong-Il set off his atomic bomb test three days after we left. Travel in Asia inspired my long-term interest in Asian art, history, religions, and cultures.

So what has my Peace Corps experience meant to me? I'm extremely grateful for the opportunities and adventures. In my case, I got to see two significant parts of the world, Asia and

South America, from tribal societies to archaeological marvels to great modern cities. Priceless education and expanded world view. (I only wish that more Americans, including elected officials, shared it.)

One of the basic lessons was the universality of human experience. How similar the aspirations and how remarkable the adaptations to different environments physical, social, and political. I came to appreciate the skills developed in all societies to cope with the challenges of life. At the same time, incorporating art and beauty, from primitive to refine forms.

From the Peace Corps teaching itself, it was rewarding to find bright and ambitious students, working hard for a better life. I hope I helped a bit to educate and inspire them.

My current do-good work is very limited, mostly modest financial support for a few causes I admire. It's clear that there are more needs and problems in the world than I can solve. And I'm much saddened by current events here in America and in the Philippines. But I feel good that I spent a few years of my youth trying to make the world a little better.

Kathleen Ursin and Tom Perardi

DAVID DELASANTA[31]
PC/Uganda and the Philippines
Newport, Rhode Island

My remarkable Peace Corps adventure took me from one assignment that became life-threatening to another that was one of my most rewarding and defining life experiences, plus astounding visits to three continents – Africa, Asia, and Europe.

My desire to contribute, to do something good, and to travel to another country was why I joined the Peace Corps. In 1960, John F. Kennedy was running for President of the United States. While campaigning in Michigan, he stopped at 2 AM on October 14, 1960, in Ann Arbor to rest. As they were passing the University of Michigan campus, the campaign team noticed 10,000 students waiting for Kennedy to speak. It was there at the steps of the Michigan Union that he delivered his speech pitching a novel idea of a Peace Corps. [32] JFK said:

> I want to express my thanks to you as a graduate of the Michigan of the East, Harvard University... How many of you who are going to be doctors, are willing to spend your days in Ghana? Technicians or engineers, how many of you are willing to work in the Foreign Service and spend your lives traveling around the world? On your willingness to do that, not merely to serve one year or two years in the service, but on your willingness to contribute part of your life to this country, I think will depend on the answer whether a free society can compete. I think it can! And I think Americans are willing to contribute. But the effort must be far greater than we have ever made in the past."[33]

JFK won the presidency, and during his inaugural address, I was one of the millions riveted to a TV screen watching his famous speech. (Three months later, he signed an executive order for the creation of the Peace Corps). I was ten years old.

Born and raised in Rhode Island, I attended Cumberland Hill Elementary School and Cumberland High School. Fresh out of Providence College and armed with Physics major, I joined the Peace Corps in June 1972.

I remember telling my Dad that I was going to join the Peace Corps. I was an only child, and my father worked very hard to send me to college, something that he did not achieve for himself, having completed only an eighth-grade level of education. I told him that I wanted to join the Peace Corps to do something good for those less fortunate. My father didn't understand why I did not just want to teach, earn money, and stay home.

"So how much are they paying you," he asked.

"Oh, the same salary as my counterparts are receiving from the school," I replied.

"And how much is that?"

"Something like 120 dollars."

"A week?" he asked.

"No," I replied. "A month."

It did not go too well with my dad and Mom. Enter my Cousin Skippy, the family counselor, and a source of great knowledge. When Cousin Skippy graduated with a Ph.D. from Brown University, an Ivy League school, his opinion was highly regarded and sought after. Cousin Skippy interceded for me. He pacified my dad saying that it's only for two years and assured him that the experience would do me a lot of good. Mom and Dad, albeit reluctantly, gave me their blessing.

Peace Corps assigned me to Uganda as a science and math teacher. Our eight-week Peace Corps training started in Philadelphia. Cross-cultural classes, Peace Corps, related information sessions, practice teaching, and language training in Swahili continued in Kampala, the capital of Uganda.

In-country training proved invaluable in avoiding embarrassing cross-cultural faux pas. Walking around Kampala one day, I noticed signs for "Zebra Crossing." Curious, I asked the trainers, "How does the zebra know where to cross?" After all, Kampala was a good-sized city, wouldn't a car hit them? All the trainers howled with laughter. After several minutes it was pointed out to me that in Uganda, pedestrian crosswalks were painted black and white stripes like a zebra.

I started my Peace Corps assignment as a high school science and math teacher in August 1972 in Southwestern Uganda at Kigezi High School near the Towns of Kisoro and Kabale.

Although it was forty-eight years ago, I still vividly remember the beautiful boarding school campus in Southwestern Uganda, on a mountain surrounded by rolling hills five thousand feet above sea level. It was ten miles away from the Rwandan border and the Mountain Gorilla sanctuaries in Zaire (now the Democratic Republic of the Congo). Ugandan Grey Crowned Cranes flew between the hills as I was having my morning tea. I was provided free housing, a wooden house with a porch, and a lush garden. It was an idyllic place, and the students were eager to learn.

Our students were all boys. It was mandatory for students to live in the boarding school that was government-funded and supplemented by financial aid from Britain. Ugandans and British expatriates taught at the school. I was the only American. For fun and recreation, soccer, basketball, boxing, and other sports tournaments were played each weekend between students and teachers.

Competition among the students to advance to a higher academic level was fierce. Only 10% of Advanced high school students were admitted to the University. One of my tasks was to visit each dormitory at 10:00 PM to ensure that all lights were out. Often I would find students under blankets studying past curfew with flashlights that I would have to confiscate.

In many ways, I lived much better than my blue-collar family back in Rhode Island. I had three servants, a brilliant and skilled man who ran my household, cooked my meals, laid out my school uniform of shorts and knee socks each morning, and, more importantly, gave me advice on how to fit in with my coworkers and students. There was also a lady who washed and ironed my clothes and a gardener.

Having servants in my "employ" (yes I paid them in Ugandan shillings out of my Peace Corps allowance of $120 a month) was too much of "colonial exploitation" for my taste but Peace Corps encouraged us to employ servants as was the local custom and it also provided jobs in an area where good-paying jobs were scarce. When I joined the Peace Corps, I imagined I would help a poor country and people grow and prosper and not live a luxurious life. I was very uncomfortable with my Peace Corps position in Uganda as a result.

On September 17, 1972, all of this changed. It was a Sunday, and I was looking forward to a restful weekend when the fighting began between current President Idi Amin and recently overthrown President Milton Obote. Our school was cut off from the capital city Kampala and also the rest of the world. In the United States, the news of the attack was everywhere on the pages of The New York Times, The Associated Press, and The Washington Post. But the news in my Ugandan town was spotty and unreliable as it was passed on by word of mouth. A description of the fighting from the Associated Press said:

> A force of some 1,000 troops, believed to be a guerrilla army composed mainly of exiles loyal to former Uganda President Milton Obote, attacked Uganda from Tanzania September 17. The invaders were repulsed by September 20 after briefly occupying several small towns. One American was killed in the fighting, and several others, as well as nationals from Britain and France, were detained.[34]

Louis Morton of Houston, Texas, an American Peace Corps volunteer trainee was killed. More than sixty foreigners and nine other U.S. citizens were arrested in Uganda (Peace Corps volunteers, missionaries, and Associated Press correspondent, Andrew Torchia). According to the State Department spokesman, Morton and another former Peace Corps volunteer, Robert Freed of Madison, Wisconsin, were en route from Mbarara to Kampala Sunday, "apparently unaware of the fighting in the area." The two were stopped twice on the road, but allowed to continue. Despite this permission, they were shot at. Morton died. Freed, slightly injured was picked up by soldiers and taken to Kampala.[35]

Louis Morton was in my Peace Corps training group from our start in Philadelphia, where we assembled before traveling to Uganda and through the eight-week training program in Kampala. At the end of the training, Louis decided not to continue as a volunteer. I remember him as fun, smart, and very pleasant, a friend to everyone.

On Monday following the attack, classes were canceled. My servants did not show up that morning, and I had no food. So I walked down the mountain to the town below to buy some eggs for my breakfast. It was not the wisest decision I ever made. As soon as I got into town, a small, green Peugeot car stopped beside me. Two men that I believe were Idi Amin's secret police grabbed me shouting "British spy." I explained that I was an American only to learn they did not speak English. I tried Swahili that I learned in my Peace Corps training, but they did not speak that language either. One of them shoved me in the back seat and sat on top of me.

Clueless as to what was happening and unable to resist the men, I was terrified. They then took me to the local magistrate and police office, where I sat alone in a room for about an hour.

The two policemen then brought me to the Magistrate. In English and in a loud voice that anyone outside his office could hear, he accused me of being a British spy sent to undermine the authority of the new President Idi Amin. The verbal abuse went on for another hour, and then he sent the policemen out and shut the door. He leaned over to me and whispered, "I know that you are an American, and I am going to release you. Go back to school as soon as you can. You are not safe here." After a few more minutes, he called back the policemen and explained he interrogated me and declared that I was not a British spy but an American teacher and then released me. I picked up my bag of eggs (surprisingly none were broken), and walked back to my school.

One of my students had seen me being roughed up and shoved into the car. He informed the Headmaster at the school. The news of the incident quickly spread around the school. I met with the Headmaster, who assured my safety and told me to stay on campus. The fighting stopped four days after it began, and I resumed teaching when school restarted.

Three weeks later, a bus came to take me away from my home with only my shirt on my back, my passport, and important documents in my pocket. All my other belongings were left behind. Along the way, the bus made frequent stops and picked up other Peace Corps volunteers. On our way to Kampala, our bus was stopped at sixteen roadblocks. We were interrogated at each stop. At many of the barricades, a soldier put a gun to my head. He said he was going to kill me. At one roadblock, I was so scared I almost peed in my pants. But by the end of the trip, I was angry, and by being angry, I was less scared about what was going to happen. I started to mouth off to one of the soldiers, much to the dismay of a fellow volunteer. I thought if it's out of my control, I could at least die unafraid. It was rash, but I still feel good about it today.

Back in Kampala, I found myself stuck in a dumpy hotel for prostitutes for a couple of weeks, waiting for the Peace Corps to evacuate us. Meanwhile, the Peace Corps office in Kampala processed the exit of 118 volunteers and their dependents. Respecting the position of the U.S. Government and the Embassy "not to antagonize Amin," Peace Corps evacuated us out of Uganda in small groups. Stanley Meisler of the Los Angeles Times described the plan[36], "...Instead of officially pulling out, the Peace Corps adopted the subterfuge of withdrawing its volunteers and dependents in small groups and informing anyone when asked that the volunteers had made personal and individual decisions to leave."

The Peace Corps gave me a letter stating that I was a courier of medical records of the persons listed in the letter. If I were asked, I was to show this letter for safe passage to Ethiopia. Once evacuated and safe in Ethiopia, Peace Corps representatives met with volunteers and gave us a choice to leave the Peace Corps or transfer to another country and assignment.

Those of us who wanted to finish our two-year term were shown a list of countries and jobs to choose from. I read a job description written by a Marist Brother named Bro. Paul Meuten about an opening for a Math and Science teacher at Notre Dame of Marbel College in South Cotabato, Mindanao, Philippines. The position was to work for a newly formed Regional Science Teaching Center (RSTC) for Western Mindanao. The RSTC mission was to bootstrap a science education in the region by teaching teachers how to teach science. Western Mindanao was underserved in the sciences.

Only a few high school and elementary school teachers in the region had any science education background. Often a school asked their English teachers to also assume the responsibility to teach science because they could read the American textbooks that were donated to the school.

The position included a three-year summer training program for teachers plus instruction in constructing science equipment from local resources. And as a part of the local college, the job included starting a new major, Bachelor of Science in Secondary Education, major in Physics. It was just what I wanted to do! I could have a considerable impact, and in the Philippines, there was no war or civil unrest. I chose the Philippines.

From Ethiopia, I was sent home to Rhode Island before I went to the Philippines. During the fighting and my evacuation, my parents did not hear from me and were only told by Peace Corps that I was safe, so they were still worried. My Mom called the office of Rhode Island Congressman Fernand Joseph St. Germain to get help in finding me. A week after I arrived in Rhode Island, my mom received a telephone call from Congressman St. Germain informing her that I was safe and evacuated to Ethiopia. My Mom replied, "Congressman, I do not need you to tell me where my son is, he is sitting right here in front of me." Congressman St Germain spent the next few minutes profusely apologizing to my Mom, who was not very forgiving of the Congressman.

I was only home for a few weeks. The academic semesters in the Philippines started from July to November (first semester), November-March (second semester), and May-June (summer session), and the school wanted me there for the start of the second semester. My parents were disappointed that I could not stay home for the Christmas holidays. After Thanksgiving, I left for the Philippines in time to teach for the second semester.

I was in Manila for a few days to take care of Peace Corps administrative matters, medical stuff and to meet the country director Mr. David Searles, then off to Koronadal (Marbel). I arrived in Marbel and met with Bro. Paul Meuten, President of the Notre Dame of Marbel College (now a University). My first tasks were to teach Physics to a class of six college students and to help Bro. Renato Cruz, in developing the curricula for the summer courses and an instruction manual for constructing science equipment for the RSTC. Peace Corps Volunteers Sue Bienkowski, Fred, and Catherine Bedford were also involved in the center.

I temporarily lived with a local family while looking for a permanent host family. After Uganda, I had wanted to live with a family to get a better cultural experience. I had my own room and a bathroom. The first night I was there, I got up to use the bathroom, turned on the light, sat on the toilet, and looked up to see a six-inch-long spider. Hairy.

I abandoned the bath, and the next day I talked to Bro. Paul and the family. I was told the spider was safe, ate mosquitos, and was quite helpful. It was clear that Hairy Spider had dibs on the bathroom. The college made arrangements, and I went to live with Nonong DeJesus and his family, where I stayed for the duration of my assignment in Marbel.

I learned a lot from the Nonong DeJesus family. As an only child, I did not know how to interact with siblings on a daily basis. The family had five kids, many grandkids, plus servants, other relatives, and workers in their family businesses. At lunch, there were often twenty people communally fed at the table. I learned how to get along with everyone and fix problems that arose. I learned about marriage. Mrs. DeJesus (I called Mamung) would confide in me her strategies and tactics for managing Mr. DeJesus. Mr. DeJesus would do the same.

Soon I realized Mrs. DeJesus was a better strategist. Mamung counted all the money from the family businesses and would skim 10% every week to keep in a secret place. When times were bad, she would put the money back into the business. She confided to me that Nonong was unaware this was going on and thought that he was just a good businessman. There was great love between Mr. and Mrs. DeJesus through tough and good times.

Mr. DeJesus was also a City Councilor and would take me along on his visits to his constituents in the surrounding barrios. Nonong would explain why it was important to be a part of each community's fiestas, weddings, and bad times. Being a public servant meant that you served with an open heart.

Early in 1973, Muslim guerrillas of the Moro National Liberation Front attacked Marbel. A family of nine was killed, and their bodies were displayed in the town center. There was widespread panic. Many people evacuated the town. As the attacks continued, I became concerned, but I didn't evacuate. When the fighting slowly abated, Bro. Paul came to me and said it was time to visit schools in western Mindanao to assess what their science teaching needs were. He told me not to worry that the Muslim rebels were educated in their Marist schools, and the Marists would let them know I was coming. I was game, and off we went. I had a driver and a Land Rover, and we passed by town after town of burnt homes, mosques, and churches. I visited over twenty schools without a problem. Without my Ugandan experience, I do not know if I would have taken that trip.

My biggest challenge in the Philippines was parasitic diseases. Amoebic dysentery I had through my entire term characterized by extreme diarrhea, fever, and weight loss. I could not get rid of it. When I went to the Philippines, I weighed 167 pounds and over six feet tall. At one point, the dysentery was so bad that I dropped down to 127 pounds. At the insistence of Bro. Rey and Sue Bienkowski, I went to Manila to see the Peace Corps Doctor. When I walked into the Peace Corps Office, the Doctor was playing guitar, and other Volunteers were sitting around talking and singing. At first, the Doctor did not recognize me, but when he did, he jumped up and sent me immediately to the hospital where I stayed for three weeks.

After my two-year contract expired, I extended for another year and continued to teach at NDMC and the RSTC. I completed my one-year extension in March 1975. Finally, I felt that I could not do anything more to make it a success. It was time to go home. After I left the Philippines, I traveled to Asia and Europe. I went to Indonesia, took a coastal freighter to Singapore then a train to Kuala Lumpur, Malaysia, train to Bangkok and Chang Mai in Thailand. Plane to Bombay

(Mumbai) then a one-month train around all of India, Nepal, and back to Bombay, off to London and then to New York City.

When I arrived back in Providence, Rhode Island, two of my Aunts met me at the airport. Both my mom and dad were not there. My Aunt Sue told me that my Mom had a bad heart attack three weeks earlier and may not make it. We drove to my home in silence. When I walked in, my mom and dad were standing in the kitchen. We all burst into tears.

After my Peace Corps experience, I realized that I really did not want to be a science teacher anymore. I had succeeded at that job, and it was time for new challenges. While in the Philippines, I saw the environmental degradation from slash and burn agriculture and heavy pesticide use. I decided that I wanted to do something about it. After teaching one year at Cumberland High School, I received a scholarship to pursue my Masters in Technology and Human Affairs at Washington University, St. Louis, Missouri, and study global environmental issues.

After graduation, the newly passed Clean Air and Clean Water Acts positioned me for a career in an area that aligned with my passion and career goals in a wide range of specialties from air and water pollution, clean energy, and much more. My first job was in Washington, D.C., on the economic justification of rebates for energy-efficient appliances, a program that still exists today!

I also got to return to the Philippines in 1982 on a NASA project to commercialize photovoltaic energy in the country. It was wonderful to be back and see my former students, friends, and the De Jesus family. I moved to California in 1984 and continued to work on air, water, solid waste, and hazardous materials environmental problems. It was a very satisfying career, and I was able to make the United States a cleaner, safer, and better place for the next generation.

I met my wife, Brenda, in California. Brenda is smart, funny, beautiful, and very talented. She is an auditor, a singer, and a terrific Mom to our three kids. My wife is very special and a joy to me. She is also African-American. Again my mom and dad were concerned. There was the requisite trip to see Cousin Skippy. With Skippy's approval, my mom and dad reluctantly approved of our marriage. Not surprisingly, Mom and Dad soon understood why I loved her. Over time they came to love her too. If I had not had my Peace Corps experience, I wonder if I would have been able to see how wonderful my wife is. As my parents aged, we moved back to New England to spend more time with them. Finally, in 2015, I retired.

How do I measure my contribution as a Peace Corps Volunteer? It is difficult to quantify the impact I had on my students, but I know for sure that I fulfilled the mission of the RSTC (Regional Science Teaching Center). Later a Summer Science Institute was established for math and science teachers to get credits toward their master's degree.

As to the impact on individual students, Al and Prima reached out to the six students in my first math and science class, members of which still keep in touch with me to this day and visit me when they are in the U.S. Two of them joined the Marist Religious Order, Bro. Rosendo Yee and Bro. Paterno Corpus. According to Bro. Pat Corpus, "...in 1973, the Notre Dame of Marbel College (now a University) opened a new major in its program in Bachelor of Science in Secondary Education, major in Physics. Six students were invited to enroll in the new program. I was lucky to be one of them. The teachers who taught the Physics subjects were Mr. David Delasanta, Ms. Susan Bienkowski, and Brother Renato Cruz.[37] Dave Delasanta became one of the most significant teachers who influenced our lives. The concrete proof is in how we, his six students, became successful in our professions. Dave taught us not only Physics but to believe in ourselves. He bolstered our self-confidence. He always emphasized the value of hard work and perseverance in whatever we do. Those lessons he imparted, we learned and used in our life and work. Dave's legacy as a teacher is manifested in the lives of his six former students.

Bro. Pat wrote: "After they graduated from Notre Dame of Marbel some of Dave's students pursued graduate studies. *Uldarico Lanado*, a Civil Engineer, became a distributor of computer-related products. *Renerio Jover*, a respected executive of Dole Philippines, represented the company to attend meetings in the U.S. and other countries. After he retired at mandatory age of sixty, DolePhil retained him as a consultant. *Edgar Ambulo*, taught higher math subjects to engineering students at ND Dadiangas even before earning his degree. He received his Master in Computer Science at De La Salle University and became the head of the CS Department of Notre Dame Marbel until he retired. As a Consultant for the Commission of Higher Education Region 12, he was tasked to validate the compliance of Schools that offer IT Programs. *Nelfa Parreno* became a successful Physics and Chemistry teacher at ND Marbel University. From a working student in the Physics Lab she has come a long way. *Brother Rosendo Yee* is a well-respected Marist Brother. He holds a Masters in Theological Study from Ateneo de Manila University. He became a Physics teacher, Director of Aspirants, Vocation Director, Director of Notre Dame of Cotabato. Just like Dave, Bro. Ross became a volunteer teacher in Mainland China for ten years.

I was the sixth student in Dave's class. After becoming a Marist Brother, I was assigned as a teacher in different Marist Schools in the Philippines. I earned a Masters in Theological Studies from Ateneo de Manila University, a Certificate in Psych Spirituality and Formation from St. Louis University, St. Louis, Missouri, and a Doctorate in Education from De La Salle University. I am currently the President of Notre Dame of Dadiangas University.

These are the former students of Dave Delasanta, whose lives he greatly influenced. Dave taught us, "How to think." Like Dave, all six of us worked to improve the lives of others. As his students, we are most grateful to Dave. The same regard is accorded to Sue Bienkowski and Bro. Renato. We always remember Dave as a great mentor, a teacher, and a friend, according to Bro. Pat.

After my Peace Corps experience in the Philippines and Uganda, I felt that I could face any adversity, handle any problem, improvise solutions, and, most importantly, befriend people of different backgrounds and cultures. The limited time I spent in Uganda did not allow me many opportunities to travel in the country and get to know its people better. But I will never forget the students who broke the rules to study longer, people who cooked my meals, washed and ironed my clothes, and took care of the garden.

Family and friends who heard about my life-threatening encounter in Uganda asked me why did I not just go home. I completed my service in the Philippines because I really wanted to serve in the Peace Corps. I believed in its lofty ideals. After my Ugandan experience, I felt that I didn't get a chance to fulfill my hopes to make a difference and for people to see Americans as friends and not enemies. It was the best decision. The years I spent in the Philippines were some of the best years of my life.

Today, I wear my title as a Returned Peace Corps Volunteer with pride; it's my Badge of Honor.

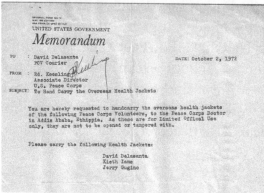

I was an only child. When I lived with my host ,the Nonong DeJesus family, I became a part of a three-generation-family living together. Twenty or more people eat together at lunchtime in this household.

My letter of escape.

After contracting amoebic dysentery, I was reduced from 160 to 127 pounds at over six feet tall. The photo was taken at Sarangani Bay, General Santos City, courtesy of David Delasanta.

DAVID SEARLES asked, "Did the Peace Corps make a difference?" After reading the stories of my fellow RPCVs and what they had accomplished, I agree with Searles that the "answer must be a resounding yes." But Searles also cautions us, "...One must be careful not to exaggerate these accomplishments, however, because the job is far from complete."[38]

On one of my visits to Pennsylvania, I was requested to address teenagers at Sunday school class. I had served as a Youth Fellowship advisor for this church before and after my Peace Corps service. We were living in Florida at this time. As an RPCV, I had done similar lectures and slide presentations at the schools that my kids attended (these days includes grandkids), and other institutions in the Tampa Bay area. It is my hope the message I was trying to convey in this letter reaches the next generation of future volunteers that they too may join the thousands of volunteers to teach a skill and spread the Peace Corps brand of goodwill around the world.

Perhaps then, they will continue to do the job that "will always be far from complete."

March 6, 1988
The Lower Junior Class
Dear Friends,

It makes me feel good to hear that you shared some of what you have with friends in need at the New Bethany Ministries.[39] Sharing, caring, making others feel good, and ease some burdens in their lives is what life should be all about.

Yes, I did spend more than five years in the Philippines, helping others. Have you looked on the globe to find the Philippines? It is on the opposite side of the world from the United States.

The Philippines, like many "third world" and "developing countries," has a multitude of intertwining problems such as poverty, illness, and political corruption. Sometimes the problem is so big it seems impossible to overcome. Each little step that I may have taken to bring food to a hungry family seemed so small by the huge population of the hungry. But each little step is a start and an example to build on, just like your gifts to the homeless at New Bethany Ministries.

Yes, I did "help" in the Philippines by teaching in a college, operating nutrition feeding programs for preschoolers, aiding the needy in finding medical care and writing proposals to fund community development projects. But these were not the greatest of my accomplishments.

The most significant accomplishment, in my view, was building a bridge. This bridge connects people to care and to share so that all might find harmony and peace. The best way to do this is to walk a mile in someone's shoes. If you spent a day and a night with a homeless family, you too would know what it is like to be a Peace Corps Volunteer. You would give up the pleasures and comforts of everyday life to fully understand what it is like to be homeless.

The next time I visit Pennsylvania, I will bring some pictures and share some harrowing and hilarious stories about my time in the Peace Corps. Until then, take the time to walk a mile in someone's shoes. Share your life with a brother, a friend, a neighbor, a grandparent, or someone in need.

Love and Peace, Alvin J. Hower

So how do I view my contribution as a Peace Corps Volunteer? John F. Kennedy crystallized it for me:

> The Peace Corps gives us a chance to show a side of our country, which is too often submerged – our desire to live in peace, our desire to be of help. There can be no greater service to our country, and *no source of pride more real* than to be a member of the Peace Corps of the United States.

I couldn't be any prouder!

MARAMING SALAMAT

A thank you note is due to all the special people who helped
to make this book happen. Any omission is inadvertent.

On March 26, 2019, David Searles responded to an invitation for
the 50th Peace Corps Reunion that I organized for my Group 31. My
wife had mentioned to David how, for many years, she has been
after me to share my Peace Corps experience. David emailed back,
"Please tell Al that I found writing the Peace Corps book a very
satisfying experience. I had specific points I wanted on the record,
but also I needed just to spend time reliving a significant part of my
life." He then suggested that I make a list of what the Peace Corps
experience did for and to me and what others should know about
the Peace Corps. And that once I do that, "it's a matter of filling
in the blanks," and added a note "not that it is easy, but it can be
rewarding." His message was prophetic. It was the impetus I needed
to write this memoir. His book *The Peace Corps Experience – Challenge
and Change* - was an invaluable resource. I am grateful.

To Dottie Anderson and Chris Gammon, I could not thank you
enough. No better professional editors I could have found because
you offered more than just the "dotting of the i's and the crossing
of the t's."

Dottie, your insight coming from the perspective of having
served as a Peace Corps volunteer in the Philippines three years
longer than me (eight years!) proved significant in keeping me
honest. But more than that, your friendship of more than fifty years
has been like the much-desired rhubarb ingredient in my favorite
strawberry rhubarb crumble – it spiced up my otherwise nondescript
life. You embraced not only this volunteer whom you met on his first
week of Peace Corps training in the Philippines, but also my wife,
my children, and grandchildren.

Chris, you are the most techno-savvy guy I have ever known who
demonstrated an editorial sensitivity that is very much appreciated.
There were many times that you highly suggested to chop off a
paragraph here and there to protect my interest, yet when I explained
my reasons for their inclusion, you respected my decision and
helped me to present it in a better light. In a gardener's term, "you

pruned to perfection." You did not only edit the manuscript, but you also fact-checked everything. Your discovery via LinkedIn and the Samir Fouzan Group (SFG) about the man from Silayan Engineering (that is now the globally recognized Vercide Engineering Works Inc.) is one of the wow moments in writing this book. And you being married to my wife's childhood friend Leilanie Zerrudo is an added plus as she offered you and me an additional perspective on the Filipino way of life.

Charles H. Toll, my daughter-in-law Heather, Brenda Delasanta, Robert and Marilyn Yamnitz, read through the entire manuscript. Chuck - your comments and review were extremely useful, your friendship cherished (Jodi and Spencer included). Heather, like you, I am a big fan of anecdotes and photos in books. Brenda much obliged for the final touch up. Bob and Lyn thank you for believing.

William "Bill" Lang thanks for being my third brother and Estelle Lang for the indispensable computer assistance, among many other things.

Thank you, Allan Chan, Sr., Maria Luisa "Lulut" Palacios Chan and family for the generous gift and our continued partnership in worthwhile projects, *No Greater Service* included.

Ramon Cuenco, Soledad Santos Cuenco and family, your contribution to the *No Greater Service* project, and all our advocacies, including the Children's Libraries, are treasured. Your grandfather Major General Paulino Santos would have been so proud!

Deserving mention and profound gratitude are my colleagues and friends. Thank you for your permission to include snippets of your stories, testimonies, comments, photos, your encouragement, and for "doing errands big and small":

- My host families in General Santos City: The Romeros, Oliveros, Santos, Gavilans, and Calderons.
- Notre Dame College: Leonardo M. Yu, Roberto Borromeo, Pat de Leon Matthew, Ronald Velasquez, Rey Velasquez, Jess Mendoza, Rose Tina Dimamay, Herlina Sogon Castanares, Orman Ortega Manansala, George Galas, Joey Odicta, Moner Bajunaid, Manuel Reblando, Narcisa Cascaro Santos, Belinda Gavilan Colon, Arsenia A. Bumgardner, Rolly and Rene Pamintuan.

- OLPGV Parish Church: Teodora "Dula" Pacomo Gomez and Mark Rumel Lorca Polea.
- Santa Cruz Mission: Rex Mannsman, Angeles and Virgilio Maghari, Rosela Datoy Reyes, Asuncion Bolano Panceles, Flor Gabato Tagalog, Gerry Hingco, Floro and Maria Gandam, Dolores Loco Agor, Myrna Bebing Pula, Lawrence Abid, and Michael Angelo Yamboc, Maria Cecilia Bandala.
- Friends: Craig Diamond, Merrit Kimball, Phil Olsen (PC Regional Director), Marc Forte (RPCV), Angelita Altea (PCStaff/Language Instructor), Becky Hsu, Joery Duco, Paul Partridge, Juvy Castillon, and Cecille Castillon-Weinstein.
- To Lucina Tapucar, Evelyn dela Cerna Taylor, and Rose Cababat Jackson, your initial feedback and contributions meant a lot.

Thank you, PC/Philippines Group 31, RPCVs, PC Staff, and Language Instructors for sharing your Peace Corps memories. Nancy Nicholson *salamat* for your generosity in giving me full access to letters to your family, photos, and copies of P/C Handbooks and *Volunteer* Newsletters. To RPCVs David Delasanta, Marilyn Maze, Tom Perardi, and Matt and Andrea Reisen, your stories added color to this book. Thanks.

To all the dedicated and hardworking LifeRich Publishing staff at Reader's Digest, it was a pleasure working with you.

Remembering Linda Basadre, Annie Garcia, RPCVs David Hsu & Muriel Cooke - gone, but will not be forgotten.

Maraming salamat goes to my family for the unconditional support and inspiration. To my wife of forty-six years and personal administrative assistant for fifty years, the girl with long black hair, Prima, you are my dream fulfilled.

The Hower-Bates Family
Summer, Zoe, and Lexi
Lee, Heather, Bruce Sr, Ellen, Bruce Jr, Linda, Prima, Alvin
To enjoy the photos in color, visit us at:
www.alvinandprimahower.com

ENDNOTES

Introduction

1 Kenneth MacLeish, "Help for Philippine Tribes in Trouble," *National Geographic*, August 1971, p. 220.
2 Philippine Statistics Authority, "Population of Region XII-SOCCSKSARGEN, 2015. Retrieved from URL 15 May 2019.
3 Matt Reisen, PC/P Group 50, and my best man at our wedding gave me the information about jobs at the Bureau of Indian Affairs (BIA) a few months before I left the Philippines.
4 Group Travel.Org. "Class Reunion Statistics". Retrieved from URL 15, May 2019.
5 Thank you note from Marilyn Maze, PC/Phil. Group 31 RPCV.
6 Peace Corps, "About," Retrieved from URL, 16 December 2019.
7 Peace Corps, "Fast Facts," Retrieved from URL, 16 December 2019.
8 In his search for T'boli photos taken before 1985, Craig Diamond and I met. He saw a photo credited to Dottie Anderson in a book by Thelma Newman entitled *Contemporary Southeast Asian Arts and Crafts*. He googled Dottie online that led him to David Searles, former Deputy Director, PC/Washington. David connected us through Dottie who was aware of my extensive photo collection. In October 2019, Craig and I collaborated on the Indigenous Tribe Exhibit titled *Of Sacred Mountains and Ancestral Plains –Artistic Traditions of Southern Mindanao – The T'boli, Blaans, and Maguindanao*. It was held at the Philippine Embassy in Washington, D.C. Craig's fascination with the T'boli tribe started when he was a Rotary Exchange Scholar at Notre Dame of Marbel University in 1984-85.
9 Email sent by Maryrose Grossman, AV Archives Reference Desk, JFK Foundation, AV Archives Reference, John F. Kennedy Presidential Library, and Museum, June 24, 2019.

1 – On My Way to the Land of the T'boli

1 P. David Searles, "The Peace Corps Experience, Challenge and Change, 1969-1976," (Kentucky: The University Press of Kentucky, 1997), p. 118.
2 Peace Corps, Philippines Volunteer's Handbook, November 1973, No 3, p. 13.
3 "Survival," *Volunteer*, The Peace Corps, Vol. viii Nos 7-8, July-August 1970, p. 30.

[4] Ibid. p. 30.

[5] Jeepneys are ubiquitous taxis fashioned out of jeeps left by the U.S. Military after WWII. Tricycles are motorcycles with sidecar, calesas are horse-drawn carriages, Bangkas are canoes made of wood and fitted with outriggers, and the REO was a vintage twelve-wheeled military truck owned by Santa Cruz Mission, a remnant of WWII.

[6] Peace Corps Volunteers were offered subscriptions to U.S. newspapers or magazines. I chose TIME and continued my subscription to the present.

[7] Passionist Historical Archives, 14 October 1985, Retrieved from URL, 12 December 2019.

[8] "Forgotten Tribes of Mindanao," *Fact Sheet*, Santa Cruz Mission Brochure, Pittsburgh, USA 1973. Prima and I assisted Fr. Rex Mansmann in writing and producing the brochure.

[9] Ibid. p. 2.

[10] "Biography, A. L. Kroeber," *Encyclopedia Britannica*. Retrieved from URL 17 May 2019.

2 – Life Before Peace Corps

[1] "Bethlehem Marks 50 years since JFK delivered a speech at Moravian College," *Lehigh Valley Live*, October 2010, Bethlehem, PA. Retrieved from URL May 19, 2019.

[2] Email from First Lt. Domenico Sciubba. Dom met my cousin Aletha Reigel after the blizzard incident, and they got married in November 1963 after JFK was assassinated.

[3] Cathy Hut, "First Peace Corps Volunteers to Bolivia Reunite in Blanco," *Blanco News*, 24 April 2019, paragraph 8, Blanco County News, Retrieved from URL 16 December 2019.

[4] Nancy Jane Fiedler Bowman and Prima-Angeles Guipo Hower, "The Lloyd Clarence Hower Story (His Life, His Ancestors, and His Descendants) A Family Celebration 2000," p. 74.

[5] The Amptennian, 1934, p. 11, yearbook of my dad Clarence E. Hower Sr.

[6] I recently googled Fegely and found Fegely Signs in Maxatawny, located along Rt. 22. I called the number and talked to Mr. Alvin Fegley's grandson, who now co-owns and manages the business. In October 2019, my wife and I drove through Maxatawny and saw the building for Fegely Signs.

[7] P. Davis Searles, "The Peace Corps Experience, Challenge and Change, 1969-1976," (Kentucky: The University Press of Kentucky, 1997), p. 39.

[8] Ibid. p. 9.

[9] Ibid. p. 86-87.

[10] James Beebe, "Those Were the Days," (California: Peace Corps Writers Oakland, 2014), p.6.

[11] The Peace Corps Handbook, Sixth Edition, November 1968, p. 27.

[12] Peace Corps/Philippines Volunteer's Handbook, November 1970 No. 3, p. 24-25.

[13] Nancy Nicholson, *Howdy*, May 16, 1969 letter to her parents. Nancy gave me access to her personal letters to her parents and other valuable memorabilia like the Peace Corps Handbooks, copies of *Volunteer* Newsletters, and photos, etc.

[14] Craig Diamond mentioned in passing that he bought on eBay some indigenous artifacts from a certain Dr. Merritt Kimball and gave me an email address. Prima contacted Dr. Kimball now 92 years old. It's the same Dr. Kimball of the Ford Foundation who spoke at my PC Training days in Cotabato City 50 years ago. He provided more information for this book.

3 – The Wild Wild South

[1] "About Us," *Marist Brothers*, Retrieved from URL. "The Marist Brothers are an international religious community of more than 4,000 Catholic Brothers dedicated the education of young people, especially those most neglected."

[2] "The LawPhil Project," *Philippine Laws, and Jurisprudence Data Bank*, G.R. No. L-29354, January 27, 1969, Arellano Law Foundation, Retrieved from URL, June 2019.

[3] A network of Notre Dame schools in the Philippines established in 1963.

[4] *Mang* is a Filipino word used as a form of respect. Carling was the first name of the driver.

[5] Top Stories 2017, *Names of Road in Gen. Santos after WWII Hero*, 6 November 2017, Mindanao News, Retrieved from URL July 2019. Morrow Boulevard was renamed Acharon Boulevard after the former mayor of General Santos.

[6] Andrea Villano-Campado, Ph.D. "Thesis: The Tuna Country At the Southern Edge of Mindanao General Santos City 1939-2000," *Notre Dame GenSan Alumni USA*, Retrieved from URL, 15 May 2019.

[7] "Philippines – Adult (15+) literacy rate, World Data Atlas Philippines. Retrieved from URL 26 December 2019.

[8] Arthur Amaral, "The Awakening of Milbuk, Diary of a Missionary Priest," (Indiana: AuthorHouse, 2015), p. 136-137.

4 – A Host of Settlers at the Melting Pot

[1] "Apr 27, 1521 CE: Magellan Killed In Philippine Skirmish," *National Geographic* 27 April. Retrieved from URL June 2019.

[2] "History of Education in the Philippines," *K12 Academics*, Chatham, VA, Retrieved from URL, 26 December 2019.

[3] Ibid.

[4] "What Language Do They Speak In the Philippines," *World Atlas* 24 July2018, Retrieved from URL. 2 August 2019.

[5] Retrieved from URL. *Utang na loob* is a core Filipino value, a profound obligation to repay a person for a favor rendered. *Apo* means grandchild used for both genders. *Maliit na Gagamba* is the Filipino version of Itsy Bitsy Spider.

[6] Nancy Nicholson, "Mr. Castro", letter to her parents, May 16, 1969.

[7] "Forgotten Tribes of Mindanao," *Fact Sheet,* Santa Cruz Mission Brochure, Pittsburgh, USA 1973.

[8] Ferrel, Robert H. ed., "The Eisenhower Diaries," (New York: WW. Norton & Company, 1981), p. 10-11.

[9] Santos, Paulino P., "First Report of the Manager," *General Santos Philippines: National Land Settlement Administration: 1989* reprinted by the Children of Gen. Paulino Santos, AFP (Ret), 1989. p. 2.

[10] Ibid. p. 6.

[11] Prima Guipo Hower, "Tio Doroy's Field," (Florida: Marakesh Publishing Company, 2004), p. 241.

[12] "Population of Region XII-SOCCSKSARGEN 2015," *Philippine Statistics Authority.* Retrieved from URL, 15 May 2019.

[13] "Senators Profile - Hadji Butu Abdul Bagui," *Senators Philippine Government.* Retrieved from URL 30 July 2019.

5 – The Notre Dame Spirit

[1] PCV Cottage photo by Philip B. Olsen, Regional Director of Mindanao, Philippines in the mid 1965-67 and Director of PC Training Camp Hawaii, 1967-1972. Miguel Dominguez found the photo on Flick'r. Dominguez, former Governor of Sarangani province (2004-2013) shared it with Edwin Espejo, a journalist. Espejo posted it on Facebook and tagged my wife. We located Mr. Olsen online and he granted permission to include the photo in the book.

[1] *"The Alma Mater: Hymn of Hope,"* University of Notre Dame Alumni Association. Retrieved from URL 4 July 2019.

[2] Ibid.

[3] "Who Are the Missionary Oblates?" *Missionary Oblates of Mary Immaculate,* Retrieved from URL 17 December 2019.

[4] Prima Guipo Hower, *"The History of Notre Dame Schools in General Santos City."* About us, Notre Dame of General Santos City Alumni Website, 2003. Retrieved from URL 2 August 2019.

[5] P. David Searles, "The Peace Corps Experience, Challenge & Change, 1969-1976," (Kentucky: University Press of Kentucky, 1997), p. 11.

[6] MSN Entertainment, *Sidney Poitier Movies: 20 greatest films ranked worst to best.* Retrieved from URL 18 July 2019.

[7] Email sent by Bro. Willy Lubrico, President of Notre Dame of Marbel University, and former President of Notre Dame Education Association (NDEA).

6 – When it Rains it Floods

[1] P. David Searles, "The Peace Corps Experience, Challenge & Change, 1969-1976" (Kentucky: University Press of Kentucky, 1997), p. 109.

[2] Ibid. p. 109.

[3] Ibid. p. 111.

[4] Mike Tidwell, "The Ponds of Kalambayi" (Connecticut: Lyons Press, 1990), p. 257.

[5] George Packard, "The Village of Waiting" (New York: Farrar, Straus & Giroux Edition, 2001). Previously printed by Vintage Books 1984.

[6] Information about Mr. Galas was provided by his son George.

[7] In writing this book, I discovered that Dr. Merritt Kimball who spoke to us at the training in Cotabato City, assisted Allan Rothenburg and the Peace Corps in arranging the practice teaching component of our training. When Allen returned to the U.S., Dr. Kimball was transferred to Manila and "inherited" the Rothenburg apartment. Through a mutual friend, Craig Diamond, I got reconnected with Dr. Kimball online after 50 years. Small world!

[8] "Looking Back At The Three Catholic Popes Who Have Visited The Philippines" *Esquire Magazine* Retrieved from URL, second paragraph, 16 July 2019. The Pope arrived in the Philippines on November 27, 1970 in the wake of three typhoons. He survived an attempted assassination by Bolivian expatriate Benjamin Mendoza.

7 – Once There Was M/V Filipinas

[1] Joyce Anne Rocamora, "PH kept 'high profile' in world tourism radar: DOT," *Philippine News Agency*. Retrieved from URL, 24 August 2019.

[2] "The Philippine Coral Reefs – Amazon of the Sea," Unico Conservation Foundation, paragraphs 1 & 2. Retrieved from URL 24 August 2019.

[3] Sen Nag, "Countries With The Longest Coastline" *World Atlas*, Jun. 18, 2018, Retrieved

[4] "M/V Filipinas, The Flagship Wars in the Manila-Cebu Route," *The Philippine Ships Spotters Society*, 20 Aug 2016. Retrieved from URL October 2019.

[5] "Everything Cebu, Mandaue City," *Eversley Child Sanitarium*. Retrieved from URL.

[6] Juan M. Flavier, a country doctor who wrote the book *Doctor to the Barrio* was the President of PRRM (Philippine Rural Reconstruction Movement) during this time. Nena would later follow Dr. Flavier when he became President of IIRR, International Institute of Rural Reconstruction in Silang, Cavite.

[7] I still have this Trim Jim. Since I bought it, I have not been to a barbershop. I still use it to cut my own hair with my wife's help.

[8] Doris Fell, "Lady of the T'boli," (New York: Christian Herald Books, 1979). Doris Fell described Gadu as the essential translator of the Bible to T'boli language. On September 15, 1974, the Wycliffe Ladies were airlifted to Nasuli, Bukidnon when the settlers versus the T'boli tribe conflict escalated in Sinolon. Gadu went to Nasuli with the Ladies. He stayed with the Wycliffe Ladies until the work was done.

[9] Ibid. PANAMIN Settlement was created in 1968. Datu Mai Tuan's story is included in the book about the Wycliffe Bible Translators by Doris Fell.

8 – My New Directions

1 P. David Searles, "The Peace Corps Experience, Challenge & Change 1969-1976" (Kentucky: University Press of Kentucky, 1997), preface viii.
2 Ibid. p. 26-26.
3 Ibid. p. 72.
4 Moritz Thomsen, "Living Poor A Peace Corps Chronicle" (Seattle&London: The University of Washington Press, 1969).
5 P. David Searles, "The Peace Corps Experience, Challenge & Change 1969-1976" (Kentucky: University Press of Kentucky, 1997), p. 86.
6 Andrea Villano-Campado, Ph.D. "Thesis: The Tuna Country At the Southern Edge of Mindanao General Santos City 1939-2000" *Notre Dame GenSan Alumni USA*, Retrieved from URL, 15 May 2019.
7 "Cleft Lip and Cleft Palate," *Patient Care and Health Info*, Mayo Clinic, Retrieved from URL 16 August 2019.
8 DiMartino, Jay. "To Remove Sea Urchin Spines From Your Feet". *ThoughtCo*, 22 August 2019, Retrieved from URL 17 December 2019.

9 – Home Leave

1 The Peace Corps Handbook, Sixth Edition, November 1968, p. 4.
2 Wikipedia. Retrieved from URL 21 September 2019. *Pasalubong* in Tagalog is literally "something for when you welcome me", a Filipino tradition of travellers bringing gifts from their destination to people back home. *Pasalubong* can be any gift or souvenir brought for family or friends after being away for a period of time. It can also be any gift given by someone arriving from a distant place.
3 "47 Statistics that explain Typhoon Haiyan" *Washington Post World News* Retrieved from URL.
4 "Airplanes of the Past" *Tampa International Airport*, Retrieved from URL 21 September 2019.
5 "The Happiest Cruise Ever Sailed" *Disneyworld Magic Kingdom*, Retrieved from URL.
6 Roger Deitz, "If I Had a Song A Thumbnail History of Sing Out! 1950-2000... Sharing Songs for 50 Years," *Folk songs Sing-out! Magazine*. Retrieved from URL.

10 – Social Action: Adventures, Pitfalls and Rewards

1 Arthur Amaral, *"The Awakening of Milbuk, Diary of a Missionary Priest"*(Indiana: AuthorHouse, 2015), p. 30.
2 "Cultural Concepts Filipino Culture," *Tagalog Lang*, Retrieved from URL. *"Bahala Na!* is a Tagalog expression that perfectly encapsulates the typical Filipino attitude toward life. The phrase *Bahala Na* is a form of fatalism, a belief that one lacks a sense of control, and one doesn't have the power to affect change in their lives."

[3] Peace Corps Handbook, Sixth Edition, November 1968, p. 10. The new Country Director was no other than P. David Searles. He took over the helm of the PC/Philippines office while I was on home leave. He had the right to be huffy. If I had taken to heart the Peace Corps Handbook, I would have known the rules right on page 10, Customs Regulations. "After your initial entry, you will be fully subject to your host country's import duty restrictions, both on goods which you bring in personally or should leave the country for some reason and return…"

[4] "A True Story: The Most Explosive Story to Hit the Headlines and Shock the Nation with Shattering Impact" *Octopus (1980) IMDBTV*, Retrieved from URL.

[5] Andrea Villano-Campado, a Ph.D. Thesis: The Tuna Country At The Southern Edge of Mindanao, General Santos City, 1939-2000, *NotreDameGenSan Website*, Retrieved from URL.

[6] Arthur Amaral, "The Awakening of Milbuk, Diary of a Missionary Priest" (Indiana: AuthorHouse, 2015), p. 136-137.

[7] Ibid. p. 31-32.

[8] "Fire destroys Manila's Airport building, Killing 6" *New York Times*, 22 January 1972. New York Times Archives. Retrieved from URL. 3 October 2019.

11 – Goodbye Sarangani Bay, Hello Lake Seluton

[1] "Kenneth MacLeish, 60, of National Geographic" *New York Times Archives*, 7 August 1977, Retrieved from URL 18 December 2019.

[2] "Santa Cruz Mission," *Fact Sheet* published in 1973. I kept copies of the 1973 and 1974 brochures published by the SCM office in Pittsburgh, PA. The Promotions Office at SCM Lake Sebu and I assisted Fr. Rex in the preparation of these fact sheets.

[3] Marcus Brooke, "The T'boli of Mindanao, Text, and photographs by Marcus Brooke," May 1977.

[4] Ibid.

[5] I gave Prima my half of the T'nalak as her graduation gift in April 1971. It now graces one of the guest rooms at our son's house, the room aptly named *Mindanao*, decorated with T'boli handicrafts.

[6] Leslie Savina and I still keep in touch. She is a lawyer now and married to another lawyer John Milne. They live in Seattle, Washington. The couple visited us in Florida in the 1990s. In May 2019, my wife and Leslie attended the Notre Dame Alumni Reunion in Seattle, WA. She provided some of the photos of me in this book.

[7] Boyce Rensberger, "Science", *New York Times*, 30 July 1972. Retrieve from URL 1 April 2020.

[8] My brother, Clarence Hower Jr and his wife Enid, actually sent for the map that I requested. But the copy sent to them was of North Cotabato (showing Cotabato City and Bongo Island) and not South Cotabato. It was nice to know anyway that there really was such a map taken by a satellite, a precursor to GPS, Google Map, etc.

[9] *Wikipedia*. Retrieved from URL 12 December 2019.

P. David Searles, "The Peace Corps Experience, Challenge & Change 1969-1976" (Kentucky: University Press of Kentucky, 1997), p. 91.

[11] Ibid. p. 91.

[12] Lucina Tapucar informed us that Jeannette's Restaurant was owned by the Leyva family and named after their daughter.

12 – The Mission Called Santa Cruz

[1] The lake had always been spelled Seluton during my stay at Santa Cruz Mission. According to Angeles Maghari, the Principal at the school at that time, the Wycliffe Bible Translators started spelling it Seloton, and it stuck to this day.

[2] Elizabeth Lazo worked at the SCM accounting office and is married to Dante Ledesma. Dante was the Administrator of SCM, when I was working there.

[3] *Lemlunay* means paradise. Every September 13, SCM celebrates its Lemlunay Fiesta. It started small and has grown since into an extravaganza that attracts thousands of visitors.

[4] Gabriel S. Casal, O.S.B., "T'boli Art – In Its Socio-Cultural Context" (Philippines: DBI Printing Services, July 1978), p. 38.

[5] Marcus Brook, "The T'boli of Mindanao, Text, and Photos by Marcus Brooke" 1977.

[6] Fr. Rex Mansmann sent the email.

[7] "Forgotten Tribes of Mindanao" *Santa Cruz Mission Fact Sheet*, Pittsburgh, PA, 1973.

[8] "A Photo Report – Bro. Louis' Challenge", *Sta. Cruz Mission Fact Sheet*, Pittsburgh, PA, 1974.
When I first heard of the T'boli, the settlers also referred to them as "Tagabili" and "Tiboli." Recently, some members of the indigenous tribe dropped the apostrophe and now call themselves Tboli. I decided to keep the spelling T'boli for consistency. It was the spelling used during my tenure at SCM. All brochures and my correspondence used T'boli.

[9] Zenaida Formon Cardinal, "Traditional Folkways of T'boli Adolescents in Relation to the Parents' Educational Process," *Notre Dame of Marbel College*. May 1982.

13 – The Light is Shining on this Side of the Mountain

[1] *Sungka, aka chongka*, Learn Tagalog Online, Retrieved from URL 19 December 2019.

[2] Prima and I kept this stone shaped like half a heart for fifty years along with the message I wrote in a paper that I cut into a shape of a heart.

[3] Fifty years later, we tracked through Facebook the three gentlemen – Renato Kintanar, Ernesto Garilao, and Cesar Ledesma (but not the lady). Prima's friend Gloria Jumamil Mercado confirmed and provided us updates on Ernesto and Cesar.

4 Zenaida Formon Cardinal, "Traditional Folkways of T'boli Adolescents in Relation to the Parents' Educational Process," *Notre Dame of Marbel College*. May 1982.

5 Siony recently emailed, "I remember taking the girls to the river. We'd shampoo their hair five times with a bar of soap used for laundry. We sure went out of our way for those kids, but those years were so enjoyable."

6 The Brothers Four, *"About the Brothers Four,* Retrieved from URL 19 January 2020.

7 My dad kept three of these bi-fold leaflets. My stepmother Gladys gave them to me after Dad died in 1987.

8 Ruby Bayan, "What is a Calamondin" Garden Guides, Retrieved from URL 19 December 2019. Retrieved from URL.

9 "Dr. Wilhelm Solheim (1924-2014), *Wikipedia,* Retrieved from URL.

14 – T'boli Hear Me Come

1 Bobbi S. Pritt, C. Graham Clark, "Amebiasis" *Mayo Clinic & Elsevier,* 2008, Retrieved from URL.

2 Prima Guipo Hower, "T'boli Hear Me Come" Chapter 3, last page.

3 Gabriel S. Casal, O.S.B., "T'boli Art – In Its Socio-Cultural Context," (Philippines: DBI Printing Services, July 1978), p. 141.

4 *Hello Cecille,* the website of Cecille L Castillon-Weinstein, Mrs. Philippines America 2019 supporting the T'boli Dreamweavers of Lake Sebu. I recently met Cecille L Castillon-Weinstein at the Cultural Exhibit at the Philippine Embassy, Washington, D.C. According to Cecille, at the Gono Hofo Heritage Center alone, there are twenty resident women weavers.

5 Gabriel S. Casal, O.S.B., "T'boli Art – In Its Socio-Cultural Context" (Philippines: DBI Printing Services, July 1978), p. 144.

15 – Sunrise Sunset Over Lake Seluton

1 Glenn Michael Angelo Guipo is now a nurse living in New Jersey with his wife Lisa (also a nurse) and two boys, Andrei and Aidan. His youngest brother Matt and his wife Renee (a physical therapist), and daughter Mahalia also live in New Jersey.

2 Michael Ray, Associate Editor, Encyclopedia Britannica, Retrieved from URL 7 January 2020.

3 James Bebe, "Those Were The Days" (Peace Corps Writers 2014, Oakland, CA.) p.119. In his book, James Bebe mentioned that his wife was able to get a tourist visa in less than two weeks in 1970. After the Martial Law in September 1972, a tourism visa was suspended. In 1974, we had to apply for an immigrant visa for Prima that took a year to complete.

4 Through the magic of the Internet, we were able to locate Mr. Karl Danga almost fifty years later. We thanked him for his help in procuring Prima's visa. He visits the Furbys every year and gave us the Furby's contact information.

[5] Kenneth MacLeish & John Launois, *Stone Age Men of the Philippines*, National Geographic Magazine, August 1972 issue. Retrieved from the URL 19 December 2019.

16 – Peace Corps: No Source of Pride More Real

[1] JFK Foundation, AV Archives Reference, John F. Kennedy Presidential Library, and Museum, June 24, 2019. Email sent by Maryrose Grossman, AV Archives Reference

[2] The Wycliffe Ladies had to be evacuated in September 1974 by air to Nasuli, Bukidnon, as the conflict between settlers and the T'boli of Edwards had escalated. The gunfire was too close for comfort.

[3] Dr. Jose SF Velasquez owned the St. Joseph Hospital in Surallah. A Notre Dame Alumni, Dr. Jess Mendoza (NDD1964), recently emailed: "I was the assistant physician of Dr. Jose "Tato" Velasquez from mid-1973 to mid-1975. I did attend to several T'boli patients at that time, the more serious ones sent from Santa Cruz Mission in Lake Sebu by Fr. Rex Mansmann to our hospital. I was always fascinated by the T'boli customs and culture; I even bought several of their necklaces, bracelets, etc. Great people. According to Dr. Jose's brother, Dr. Rey Velasquez, St. Joseph Hospital was closed in the late 1990s and sold. Dr. Velasquez transferred to General Santos City, where he founded one of the leading hospitals SOCSARGEN before he died of cancer in 2005. Mayor Datu Dibu Tuan of T'boli municipality posthumously recognized Dr. Jose Velasquez with an award for his medical services rendered to the T'boli people

[4] Gladys Shoemaker's request to publish our article in the Tampa Tribune newspaper in 1974 did not materialize. However, on the 25th Anniversary of Peace Corps, March 1, 1986, Tampa Tribune ran a full-page feature about my Peace Corps experience, *The Hardest Job You Could Ever Love* written by Staff Writer Gwen Fariss and photos by Doug Cavanah, Monday, June 30, 1986 issue.

[5] *Cedula*, Merriam Webster Dictionary, Retrieved from URL. Any of various official documents or certificates in Spain, Latin America, or the Philippines.

[6] Francisco Grana Sumatra Prima's cousin came from a small barrio in Iloilo, worked for an international shipping company until he retired as the ship's Captain.

[7] *Leaving on a Jet Plane*, John Denver, Last FM, 7 August 2009, Retrieve from URL 19 December 2019.

Postscript: Fifty Years Later

[1] P. David Searles, "The Peace Corps Experience, Challenge & Change 1969-1976" (Kentucky: University Press of Kentucky, 1997), p. 221.

[2] Ibid. p. 221.

[3] According to Dolores Loco Agor, *Falel Kesbung* is a school managed by the Department of Education for Indigenous People. It is hoped that a library can be established at *Falel Kesbung* someday for T'boli kids age six to eighteen.

[4] Ruben Tugari, NDDU Alumni Coordinator, provided the latest statistics for the Notre Dame of Dadiangas University.

[5] George Galas vividly recalled that in May 1970 I gave his mother a few Dekalb chicken. That was precisely the time when I was trying to sell 400 chickens from the Kaiser's farm after Mrs. Kaiser died on May 3, 1970. The people that populated my world during my Peace Corps years have "come to life" in my present world through their children, grandchildren, or connections through social media. Theirs are stories just waiting to be told. Some were unknown faces from faded photographs or a mere name on a page of a fifty-year-old letter.

[6] Andrea Villano-Campado, Ph.D. "Thesis: The Tuna Country At the Southern Edge of Mindanao General Santos City 1939-2000," *Notre Dame GenSan Alumni USA*, Retrieved from URL, 15 May 2019.

[7] "SoCot [South Cotabato] to reduce malnutrition cases" Manila Bulletin, Philippine News Agency, 8 August 2018, Retrieved from URL 20 December 2019.

[8] Ibid.

[9] "Father Raymond Francis Albinus Lesch" *FindAGrave & Ancestry.com* 26 December 1989, Retrieved from URL, 10 February 2020.

[10] *Ibid.*

[11] "Fluvial procession ready for GenSan's Sto. Nino fest" *MindaNews*, 14 January 2020, Retrieved from URL 5 February 2020.

[12] Ibid.

[13] Ibid.

[14] "General Santos Fish Port Complex" *Philippine Fisheries Development Authority*, Department of Agriculture website. Retrieved from URL 11 January 2020.

[15] Avel Manansala, "GenSan nets Guinness World Record for Largest Fish Display" *General Santos News Online Magazine*, 12 August 2015, Retrieved from URL 20 December 2019

[16] "Eric Bustamante, Jr." *LinkedIn*, Retrieved from URL.

[17] "General Santos International Airport" *Wikipedia*, Retrieved from URL.

[18] "Sarangani's Kamanga Marine Eco-tourism Park and Sanctuary cited as one of Philippines best" *Philippine Star*, 22 November 2015, Retrieved from URL, 1 January 2020.

[19] Juvy Palces Castillon (mother of Mrs. Philippines America Cecille L Castillon-Weinstein) sent an email.

A Glimpse of Life After Peace Corps

[20] Our 1974 cross-country trip included 14 states: California, Oregon, Washington, Idaho, Montana, Wyoming, South Dakota, Minnesota, Wisconsin, Illinois, Indiana, Michigan, Ohio, and Pennsylvania.

[21] Lee Marvin was known for his role in "The Dirty Dozen." Retrieved from URL.

RPCVs and the 50th Reunion

[22] Letter from P. David Searles, June 15, 1993.

[23] The Peace Corps Experience Story, Matthias and Andrea Reisen, was approved with full permission from Matthias and Andrea Reisen for inclusion in the book.

[24] P. David Searles, "The Peace Corps Experience, Challenge & Change 1969-1976" (Kentucky: University Press of Kentucky, 1997), p. 144.

[25] Ibid. p. 191.

[26] "Is it illegal to eat dog in the Philippines?" *The Dog Visitor*. Retrieved from URL. 11 October 2019.

[27] Mathias and Andrea Reisen granted the author full consent to include their story in the book. Matthias and Andrea Reisen's herb business is on Facebook under the name *healingspiritsherbfarm*.

[28] "About Us" *Farmer-to-Farmer*, Retrieved from URL 20 December 2019.

[29] Marilyn Maze submitted her story to the author with full consent to include in the book.

[30] Tom Perardi submitted his story to the author with full consent to include in the book.

[31] David Delasanta granted the author full consent to include his story in the book.

[32] University of Michigan, Ann Arbor, Retrieved from URL 9 January 2020.

[33] "The Founding Moment" *Peace Corps Website*, Retrieved from URL 9 January 2020

[34] "African Affairs: Uganda Invaders Defeated; Other Developments" *Stanford News*, Issue Date: September 23, 1972, Retrieved from URL 9 January 2020.

[35] "One American Killed in Ugandan Fighting" *Associated Press quoted by The Cornell Daily Sun*, Volume 16, No. 89, 20 September 1972, Retrieved from URL 9 January 2020.

[36] Stanley Meisler, "Despite Abuse of Americans in Uganda, U.S. Sticks to Policy: Don't Antagonize Amin" *Los Angeles Time*, California 12 October 1972, Retrieved from URL, 9 January 2020

[37] Bro. Renato Cruz died of leukemia in 1977. It was a grave loss to the Marist Brothers Community. He was regarded as a genius that traveled the world to give lectures. He received his Master's degree from Wayne University in Michigan.

[38] P. David Searles, "The Peace Corps Experience, Challenge & Change 1969-1976" (Kentucky: University Press of Kentucky, 1997), p. 221.

[39] "Our Mission" *New Bethany Ministries*, Retrieved from URL 20 December 2019.